The Space Between Us

The Space Between Us brings the connection between geography, psychology, and politics to life. By going into the neighborhoods of real cities, Enos shows how our perceptions of racial, ethnic, and religious groups are intuitively shaped by where these groups live and interact daily. Through the lens of numerous examples across the globe and drawing on a compelling combination of research techniques including field and laboratory experiments, big data analysis, and small-scale interactions, this timely book provides a new understanding of how geography shapes politics and how members of groups think about each other. Enos' analysis is punctuated with personal accounts from the field. His rigorous research unfolds in accessible writing that will appeal to specialists and non-specialists alike, illuminating the profound effects of social geography on how we relate to, think about, and politically interact across groups in the fabric of our daily lives.

Ryan D. Enos is Associate Professor of Government at Harvard University, Massachusetts. He is a leading expert on the intersection of geography, psychology, and politics. His research has appeared in various scholarly publications, such as the *Proceedings of the National Academy of Sciences* and the *American Political Science Review*, and in worldwide news outlets, such as *The New York Times*. Prior to earning his PhD, he was a high school teacher on the South Side of Chicago, an urban space which inspired much of his research.

The Space Between Us

Social Geography and Politics

RYAN D. ENOS
Harvard University

CAMBRIDGE
UNIVERSITY PRESS

University Printing House, Cambridge CB2 8BS, United Kingdom

One Liberty Plaza, 20th Floor, New York, NY 10006, USA

477 Williamstown Road, Port Melbourne, VIC 3207, Australia

4843/24, 2nd Floor, Ansari Road, Daryaganj, Delhi – 110002, India

79 Anson Road, #06-04/06, Singapore 079906

Cambridge University Press is part of the University of Cambridge.

It furthers the University's mission by disseminating knowledge in the pursuit of education, learning, and research at the highest international levels of excellence.

www.cambridge.org
Information on this title: www.cambridge.org/9781108420648
DOI: 10.1017/9781108354943

First published 2017
Reprinted 2017

Printed in the United States of America by Sheridan Books, Inc.

A catalogue record for this publication is available from the British Library.

ISBN 978-1-108-42064-8 Hardback

In memory of Zim.

Contents

Appendices and replication material for this book are deposited in the Harvard Dataverse (https://dataverse.harvard.edu/).

Figures

Preface

The scenes that illustrate this book are all about us. For illustrations, please look closely at real cities. While you are looking, you might as well also listen, linger and think about what you see.

– Jane Jacobs[1]

Among the reasons that the scientific study of society is both difficult and exciting is that society never stops changing.

This book is about what happens when different groups of people live close together – sharing small towns, large cities, states, and countries – yet remain separated in geographic space and, as a result, separated in psychological, social, and political space as well. In ways that have not previously been made clear, this property of being close, yet far, penetrates our psychology and affects our thoughts, behaviors, and collective well-being. It paradoxically repels us from the groups to which we are already close. These repelling forces have shaped behavior, as far as scholars can tell, for all of human history. Yet increasingly, especially in the West, people from different groups that were once widely separated are moving into closer and closer contact, changing the context in which many of us live. This makes those repelling forces more important.

Moreover, these forces influence our democratic institutions. They affect whom we vote for and whether we will share our resources with groups other than our own. Recent events remind us of why this is important.

I finished this book on October 20, 2016. On November 8, Donald Trump was elected President. Although not my primary focus, in revising the manuscript for publication, I added analysis showing that Trump's election appears to have been aided by the very prejudices I explore in this book. My contention in this book is that people living in certain places were affected, probably much more than they realize, by specific aspects of the social geography in which they live. That is, their attitudes and behaviors (such as voting for Trump versus voting for Hillary Clinton) were affected by the size of another group (in this case, Latinos), by the nearness of that group to where they themselves live, and by the extent to which the two groups live in segregation. Thus, in areas where the Latino population had recently grown, previously Democratic non-Latino voters shifted their support to Trump, a candidate who centered his campaign around anti-immigrant demagoguery.

Time and reflection will tell how significant Trump's election was in the course of American history, but there is little doubt that it is significant to many people now. Partisan and ideological concerns aside, the millions of people demonstrating in the streets indicate that people feel that something important is going on. As a social scientist, I too have a sense that we are in a potentially consequential moment. Trump's rise and the success of populist politicians in Europe are a testament to the continued relevance of the ancient prejudices I explore. His election also reminds us that the tentacles of these prejudices extend beyond the domains in which they have an immediate effect. Propelled into office partly by voters' distaste for immigrants, Trump is now attempting to change America's course on healthcare, climate policy, defense, trade, and taxes. Some of these changes, if implemented, will ripple across the globe.

In this book, I try to show the continuity of the influence of social geography across time and space, so that we can understand why the cases of African Americans in Chicago and ultra-Orthodox Jews in Jerusalem have so much to tell us about why Latino immigration seemed to have such sway over Anglo voters in Pennsylvania and other Rust Belt states in 2016; or why Arab and African immigration to Europe is affecting voters there.

The influence of social geography can also be seen, I believe, in how the increasing geographic divide between Democrats and Republicans is widening the already yawning partisan gulf in social and political preferences; this, too, was reflected in the last election. In Chapter 1, I will ask you to consider how attitudes and behaviors of Chicago residents would be different if all the same people lived in Chicago but the South Side were not almost entirely Black and the North Side white. Extending this thinking, I believe, helps us to answer what our behavior would be like if Massachusetts were not blue and Oklahoma were not red. I think it can help to answer why "us versus them" seems increasingly to coincide with "here versus there."

To me, these connections are obvious, but I've spent a lot of time with the evidence. My hope is that by laying out that evidence to others, such connections will enter the conversation as we continue to deal with the wonderful complexities of diversity in a democracy. As data become available, we can look at the trends from 2016 and other recent elections and test, update, and modify the understanding I have offered in this book. So far, some of my findings seem to hold up quite well and seem to help us understand what is currently going on. Most likely, others will eventually have to be reexamined. But that is the nature of the scientific investigation of the social world. The world keeps turning and the lives of the people in it keep churning and it is beautifully complicated to study.

Cambridge, Massachusetts
February 2017

Acknowledgments

The seeds of this book were in the dissertation I completed at UCLA in 2010.[1] Of course, as is normal with science, much of the theory and evidence has been updated, revised, or discarded since then.

It took me a long time to get to the point of filing that paper dissertation at Young Library on a, as always, beautiful spring day in Los Angeles. It took me an even longer time to get to the point of putting the final touches on this book on a cold winter day in Cambridge. I never would have been in a position to do either without many people and it is my sincere hope that they understand how much I appreciate them, even if I cannot adequately express it.

Colleagues in the academy who continue to challenge and guide me and who have spent valuable resources to bring me places, advise me, and nurture my scholarship. Many of you read sections of this work and a few of you read the entire manuscript (even more than once) and it is so much better for what you did. All errors are my own.

At Harvard, my colleagues who have continued to teach me how to be a scholar and teacher and to support my growth. My graduate students who have taught me so much and put their faith in me. You really are the best part of the job. My research assistants without whom much of this book would not have been written. My undergraduate students who inspire and intimidate me.

At UCLA, my teachers who taught me to be a scholar. My graduate student colleagues, who I still hold up as a model for how graduate school should be.

My advisers who became my friends and supported and mentored me and continue to do so. They also taught me how to be an adviser. I can never live up to all they did for me.

Administrators and colleagues at Harvard and UCLA who funded my research.

The teachers at Cal who opened my eyes to social science and the wonders of urban space.

xiv

My friends with whom I've explored many things, including the cities I write about in this book.

My colleagues at Paul Robeson High School. Still the best job I've ever had. The children at Robeson, now older than I was when I was their teacher, who taught me so much and whose influence is in this book.

My family.

My two best friends: my amazing, capable, intelligent, and beautiful daughters.

In October 2004, I met a girl at Liquid Kitty on Pico Boulevard in West Los Angeles. In May 2010, from Boston, she was doing rush corrections on my dissertation as I prepared to submit it. In 2017, I have a family and have been unbelievably fortunate. I no longer need her to proof-read my writing, but that girl at Liquid Kitty made it all possible and continues to make it all possible – and wonderful.

I

The Red Line

The city consequently tends to resemble a mosaic of social worlds in which the transition from one to the other is abrupt.

– Louis Wirth[1]

Though we are generally free to go where we choose, there are still certain places we are unlikely to go. We have boundaries that we are unlikely to cross, the result of prejudices, routines, and networks of other people that create these boundaries and put both physical and psychological space between ourselves and others.

Trains, on the other hand, will cross boundaries that people typically will not. The Red Line of Chicago's elevated train, known as the "L," travels a straight line from north to south. Unlike other lines, it doesn't eventually bend to the west and it doesn't split and offer you a choice of branches. Nor does it circle around, like the trains in the downtown Loop, sending you back where you came from. If a Red Line train starts on the north side of the city, there is nowhere to go but south. Coming from the south side, there is nowhere to go but north. Either way, the train crosses a boundary that its riders typically do not.

In Chicago, the boundary between north and south is the boundary between white and Black. It is not a sharp boundary like an international border; there are complexities, such as the racially integrated Hyde Park neighborhood and an Irish-Catholic neighborhood, Mount Greenwood, on the South Side. But everyone in Chicago knows the boundary is there and most accept that the other side is a place you shouldn't go. For a white person in Chicago, the South Side is a void, populated only by stereotypes. When a tourist – usually white – unfolds a map of Chicago, the South Side isn't even shown.

Chicagoans don't travel from north to south or south to north because there is not only a physical distance between these two parts of the city, but also – and much more importantly – a psychological distance. To people on one side of the city, the people on the other side are simply not like them. That sense of difference puts a space between them. This book is about how and why this space affects thought and behavior.[2]

For a period of my life, I frequently crossed this boundary. On weekday mornings, I would board a Red Line train in my North Side neighborhood to go to work as a high school teacher. On the bitterly cold winter mornings in Chicago, before 6 AM, when the wind would blow off the lake, the train platform on Belmont Avenue was almost deserted. The few people waiting for the train would huddle for warmth under the heat lamps on the elevated platform. The empty train would travel south toward the Loop, eventually abandoning its elevation and going underground, where it would stop under office skyscrapers and a handful of ambitious passengers in suits and ties would get off, ready to be the first to work. Around Washington Street, the train would start to fill up again, but now with people going home from work, and the demographics would change. In Chicago, people whose workday ends at 6 AM are generally not white; they are largely Black and Hispanic. After a while, I was the only white passenger on the train.

As a teacher, I got to work before many people were even awake and I worked until the school building was ready to close at 6 PM. Waiting at 69th and Dan Ryan for my train home, all the tired people waiting with me were Black, heading north to start the workday cleaning and polishing the buildings of the Loop for the white workers from the North Side.

On this evening journey north, somewhere under the Loop, two worlds would briefly meet. South Side Blacks would shoulder out of the train, ready to go to work, and North Side whites would board the train, ready to go home. These two worlds, normally not occupying the same place at the same time, would cross paths as one took the other's place.

At those brief stops, when these groups of people – normally segregated into their different sides of the city – came together, there was a palpable tension. It seemed to me that, somewhere in the back of their minds, these white and Black passengers were thinking about what they might find if they were to stay on the train all the way north or all the way south.

In the downtown Loop there was a mixing of people. On the far South or North sides, there was stark segregation. Over time, I came to believe that Chicagoans kept this image of the distinctly segregated sides of the city in their heads and that it served to organize their world: where they should go and where they shouldn't; how close they felt to different types of people; even whether or not they supported a particular politician.

This book is about how politics is shaped by experiences like those of the "L" riders in Chicago. How the passengers' thoughts and behaviors were structured by the space between their groups – Blacks and whites – and, more generally, how the space between us, wherever we live, affects the way we think and behave every day and affects the way we make consequential decisions, such as whom to trust, with whom to share, and for whom to vote.

I will make the case that for the passengers on the elevated train, one of the most important forces shaping their political and social outlook was the presence of people who were *the other*: for whites, it was Blacks and for Blacks, it was whites. I will argue that their attitudes about the other group were crucially shaped by the geographic location of that group. And I will show that Chicago's "L" riders are just one example of a phenomenon which affects people all over the United States and across the world.

This geographical shaping of attitudes about groups is important because it affects our individual and collective decision-making and, in a democratic society, we must and do make important decisions together, whatever our physical and psychological distance from each other. Black and white Chicagoans, like Blacks and whites in other parts of the United States and like other ethnic and racial groups elsewhere, live largely separate lives: working, shopping, worshiping, socializing, and taking their leisure separately. Most grocery stores, restaurants, and even beaches in Chicago, for example, are either largely white or largely Black. Most people have few, if any, friends from the other group. Despite living separately, we share the same institutions and resources in the public sphere: electing representatives and making decisions on taxing, spending, and matters of law. We use the same roads, water, electricity, and other goods and must decide how these are allocated. The public sphere – government – is like the station under the Chicago Loop where groups come together.

I will try to convince you that socio-geographic space – that is, the distribution of groups on the Earth's surface – has a direct effect on relations between groups and that these effects have political consequences. In broad strokes, the theory I will offer says that the geographic space between groups leads to a psychological space between groups, which, in turn, leads to a political space between them.

There are many examples of this psychological space affecting behavior in the spaces where groups must come together and interact. In New York City, for example, complaints to the police about neighbors making too much noise or blocking a driveway are most common in areas where white and Black neighborhoods come together.[3]

Similarly, but perhaps more significantly, the waves of racialized crime between whites and Blacks in Boston in the 1970s and '80s, including assaults and property damage, occurred along certain streets where traditionally white neighborhoods met expanding Black neighborhoods.[4]

In Northern Ireland, the centuries-old sectarian violence between Catholics and Protestants has a distinct spatial pattern: arson, riots, and interpersonal attacks are most common where segregated Catholic and Protestant neighborhoods border each other.[5]

When the geographic and psychological space between groups is large, we can see its effects across entire societies, shaping how effectively these societies function: Israelis of different religious groups are less likely to cooperate in cities where their groups are residentially segregated than in integrated cities.[6]

And in the United States, white voters in racially segregated counties were less likely to vote for Barack Obama in 2008 than those living in more integrated counties.[7] On a larger scale, countries such as the United States, in which various religions, races, and ethnicities all live but are segregated into different parts of the country, simply don't function as well as less diverse and less segregated countries. They are less likely to solve the collective action problems that need to be solved for a decent quality of life, such as building roads, providing schooling, and helping the needy.[8]

In this book, I explore these and other relationships that demonstrate the powerful impact of social geography on our individual behavior and on the well-being of society. And I ask why? Why does social geography have this effect? My answer is that geography penetrates our psychology – it affects the very way we perceive other groups – and with these changes in perception, it affects our behavior.

WHEN GROUPS OCCUPY THE SAME PLACE

Another way to describe the subject of this book is to say I want to understand what happens when people of different social groups occupy the same location. When two groups – say two religious groups, racial groups, or nationalities – live in the same city or neighborhood, how does this affect the behavior of the individuals making up those two groups? Will they behave differently toward each other than they would have under other circumstances? Will their politics be different?

It's not hard to see how much this matters. As I write this in 2017, liberal democracies in Europe are grappling with immigration from the Muslim world. In the United States, mainstream politics now includes a level of blatant xenophobia that hasn't been seen for some time and elements of that xenophobia hold the reins of power. A contribution of this book is to understand why this xenophobia takes hold.

Today's questions of diversity are, perhaps, unique in their urgency because technological, economic, and political forces are diversifying parts of the world at an accelerating pace, but the problem is of course much older and broader. And, because I will focus on the universality of the way humans react to humans of other groups in the same place, it is worthwhile to emphasize the prominence of the theme of conflict and place throughout human history. Herodotus, a contemporary of Socrates and often considered the founder of the Western study of history, devoted much of his *Histories* to ethnographic accounts of the people of India, China, and northeast Africa, who came into contact with Greeks via their common connection with the Persian Empire. For the most part, what he recounts is conflict. He begins his treatise with a telling sentence about geography and dispute: "The Persian learned men say that the Phoenicians were the cause of the dispute. These (they say) came to our seas from the sea which is called Red, and having settled in the country which they still occupy..."[9] Much of the Old Testament also concerns the occupation of the same land by two or more groups. Later in this book, I will discuss how this psychological impact of space and social groups appears to be a basic building block of the modern human mind, having evolved in our distant past.

Scholars will recognize that the subject of groups and place has a rich tradition in the social sciences. In the United States, modern social science arose contemporaneously with the great waves of domestic and international migration in the mid-twentieth century and the aftermath of World War II. The new disciplines found it natural to examine the social consequences of different groups, usually Blacks and whites, sharing space in America's great cities. Some very influential social science was developed to examine these changes. The social psychologist Gordon Allport, who will feature prominently in this book, focused much of his 1954 book, *The Nature of Prejudice*,[10] on how the coming together of Blacks and whites in American cities affected their prejudices. A little over 50 years later, when Robert Putnam was honored with an international award for contributions to political science, he started his now famous acceptance speech by saying:

One of the most important challenges facing modern societies, and at the same time one of our most significant opportunities, is the increase in ethnic and social heterogeneity in virtually all advanced countries. The most certain prediction that we can make about almost any modern society is that it will be more diverse a generation from now than it is today. This is true from Sweden to the United States and from New Zealand to Ireland.[11]

Of course, social diversity, which has concerned so many scholars, can take many different forms. A proper study of diversity involves not only the demographics of who lives in a particular place, but also the study of space; that is, the distribution of groups across the Earth's surface. Are they integrated with or segregated from each other? If they are segregated, are these separate groups near to or far from each other? Chicago, for example, was about 33 percent Black in 2014. But as is obvious while riding the "L," this 33 percent is not distributed evenly across the city. Blacks and whites are starkly segregated. But what if they weren't? Or what if these two populations, instead of living in different parts of the same city – not all that many miles apart – instead lived in two different cities? Obviously, space will shape the experience of diversity.

The central argument of this book is that geographic space structures social cognition – that is, how people think about other people – and this, in turn, structures our politics. In other words, we use space to psychologically organize our social world and this affects our political behavior. In addition to this central premise, I will make two other contributions. First, I will work to convince you that the effect of social geography is large and consequential – that it affects fundamental aspects of our behavior and institutions. Second, I will demonstrate why social geography has this effect on our behavior – that the effect is direct, working through our perceptions, and not just a result, as most scholarship would have us believe, of interpersonal contact across groups.

Here is an illustration of the theory. Imagine two cities that are identical except that in one city, two groups of people, say Christians and Muslims, live side by side in their neighborhoods, while in the other city, the neighborhoods are strictly segregated, so that Christians and Muslims always live in different neighborhoods. Christians in the segregated city, relative to those in the integrated city, would think that they have less in common with Muslims. They would therefore be less likely than Christians in the integrated city to, say, vote for a mayoral candidate whom they saw as representing Muslims and would make more of an effort to turn out and vote against that candidate.

My theory offers another prediction: say that in one city, Muslims are a small population compared to Christians, while in the other city, Muslims are much more numerous than Christians. Christians in the city with the large Muslim population, relative to those in the city with the smaller Muslim population, would think that they have less in common with Muslims and this, too, would affect their behavior.

Moreover, if this group of Christians live in closer proximity to Muslims in the first city than in the second city, this too will cause Christians in the first city to believe they have less in common with Muslims than do Christians in the second city.

At first glance, this may seem contradictory: how could a group being more numerous or proximate have the same effect as that group being more segregated? But when I go into the psychology behind these three phenomena – the segregation, size, and proximity of a group affecting behavior – I will explain that they spring from the same place in human psychology.

I am claiming that the difference in geography between these two hypothetical cities is *causing* the difference in perception and behavior. Later in the book, I will give a more detailed explanation of what I mean by "causing," but in a nutshell, taking segregation as an example, I am saying that I can show that if you took two groups of people and flipped a coin to determine that some members of each group would live in segregation and others would live in integration, those living in segregation would have different attitudes toward the other group than those living in integration. This ability to demonstrate that a contextual factor, such as segregation, is causally related to behavior has largely eluded social scientists. They have long wished to conduct experiments to establish such effects, but had no way to manipulate city dwellers the way they could manipulate rats or undergraduate students in laboratory studies. The problem is indeed difficult, but not unsolvable. I will later describe research in which I, essentially, flipped a coin to assign segregation. That coin flip – that is, the resulting segregation – changed behavior.

Why does space have this impact? First, geographic space is a very important part of how humans understand the world. We make many judgments about people and things based on where they live or where they are. Just consider names like Harlem, Bel Air, or the South Side of Chicago and try not to think of any stereotypes about the people who live there. Second, people use this geographic space when considering the differences between groups. Why this happens is somewhat complex, but a simple way to think about it is that people use space as a "mental shortcut" – in psychological terminology, a heuristic – to help them organize the world and decide what they think about other groups.

As a simple example of the psychology underlying this impact, imagine two Anglo American women living in two different cities, but identical to each other in all other respects, including that neither has any Latino friends or close Latino colleagues. One lives in a city in which Latinos and Anglos are segregated, the other in a city in which they are integrated. Imagine, too, that everything else about these cities is identical. The Anglo woman in the integrated city might think – consciously or unconsciously – that she and the Latino people in her neighborhood are much like each other. She might assume that they have similar incomes, shop in the same places, and know some of the same people. However, the woman in the segregated city might think – consciously or unconsciously – that the Latinos in her city are quite different from her. She might assume that they make less money, shop in different places, and don't know anyone she knows. And, importantly, I will show that these perceptions become *distorted by geography* – that the woman in the segregated city will assume Latinos are more different from her than Latinos actually are.[12]

A perception of similarity has consequences: it allows you to coordinate with the other group because you believe you share preferences on how to do things like build roads and teach children. A sense of similarity makes you more likely to trust somebody; for example, to trust that they will do their part to pay to build that road. For the same reasons, a sense of similarity makes you more inclined to vote for a candidate from another group, trusting that she is likely to agree with you about how and why to build roads and teach children. This ability to agree and to trust has ripple effects across societies, affecting the comparative fate of nations, making them rich or poor, harmonious or discordant.

WHAT IF THE SOUTH SIDE WEREN'T BLACK?

A useful exercise for understanding the argument of this book and for understanding much of the evidence I will present is to imagine an alternative journey on the "L" train through the geographic space of Chicago. This exercise also helps us to see why the findings in this book are important, not just to academics, but also to people thinking about how cities should be built and other questions of public policy and to people with an interest in an inclusive society.

What if, on a journey on the "L" train, the southbound Red Line passengers were not white and the northbound passengers were not Black? What if a white person boarded on the North Side and rode south into neighborhoods that just had more white people? Or what if the southbound and northbound trains both had a mix of Black and white, so that no matter where she got on or off, she would find herself amongst both Black *and* white people?

It is difficult to imagine that the tension that is so palpable at the Loop stations when northbound and southbound passengers come together would still exist in a world in which the color of a passenger's skin wasn't so tightly connected to where she was likely to be found – to parts of the city in which she was seen to belong or not belong. I contend that social tension would be considerably reduced. Specifically, I contend that if Chicagoans were no longer able to use this geographical distinction between north and south and Black and white to psychologically organize their social and political worlds, their attitudes toward the other group would change. Not only that, they would change for the better – less hostile, less suspicious, less uncooperative. There would still be social and political conflict, of course, but it would be different and, I will argue, less severe.

In Chicago, the counterfactual of a world in which a person could take the Red Line from north to south and not see Black people was once a reality, so while it may be difficult to imagine today, we can actually read about it in historical accounts. In the early and mid-twentieth century, Chicago was a much more white city. Famously Black neighborhoods, such as Englewood and Auburn Gresham, were almost entirely white then. But within a very short time, they became almost entirely Black, due to the great waves of Black migration from the South.

What if these Black Southerners had not moved north, displacing white residents on the South Side of Chicago? Or what if there had been a wave of *white* Southerners coming north? What would Chicago politics look like? Would Chicago be as segregated as it is now? If it were not so segregated, how would things be different?

Even without a deep historical examination, we can be fairly confident that things would be different – that the attitudes associated with the geography of Chicago would not be the same. It is doubtful that uttering the words "South Side of Chicago" to a white audience would be packed with meaning the way it is now, conjuring up stereotypes of crime, poverty, and cultural difference. These stereotypes, in turn, are likely to influence the opinions of whites and Blacks when thinking about politics.

Consider the maps in Figures 1.1 and 1.2. The first is a map of Chicago with neighborhoods colored by their percent Black. Here the familiar racial pattern of starkly Black clusters is striking. This is segregation laid bare. It is these Black swaths of the city that are associated with stereotypes and perceptions of difference for non-Blacks. The rider on the "L" train, moving through space, is crossing a neatly defined boundary from one social group to the next.

With the second map, I have done something simple: I had a computer randomly rearrange the population of the city.[13] The difference is as striking as the segregation itself. Your mind no longer has the easy mental congruence of groups and space and, therefore, the group is perceived as less cohesive. In this non-segregated Chicago, the geographic division of Black and White into South and North is gone. The "L" rider never crosses a boundary that creates a physical and psychological space between groups. Rather, she keeps moving through a continuously changing mix of people. Race and place would be difficult to align in her mind; the physical and psychological space between groups would be diminished. And so we might imagine that, in this counterfactual world, politics, too, might be different. (In Chapter 4, I will show that people actually have social maps like in Figure 1.1 in their minds.)

As it happens, we do not have to rely on counterfactual reasoning to see what the difference might be. As recently as 2004, certain neighborhoods in Chicago underwent a dramatic demographic transformation when government action brought an end to a large portion of the infamous Chicago public housing system, changing scores of blocks that were once almost exclusively Black and poor to white and upper-class. In some areas of Chicago, this dramatically changed local segregation (public housing, circa 2000, is displayed in Figures 1.1 and 1.2).

The demolition of public housing in Chicago in the 2000s is an excellent example of a government dramatically changing the way people live. It is a particularly useful example because, of course, it was the government that, with the best intentions of mid-century urban renewal, built those housing projects in the first place, helping to shape the city's racial dynamics for decades. My evidence shows that by creating a particular geographic space, Chicago's mid-century urban planners were affecting the psychology of intergroup relations. Subsequent inaction helped perpetuate this psychology. But what would have happened if, instead, Chicago had had the political will to integrate public housing, as Boston did in the 1970s, when Blacks were allowed, under police protection, to move into all-white public housing?[14] (In Chapter 5, we will talk to some of the police who oversaw this integration.) This sort of action by the government means that my counterfactuals are less fanciful: because we know about the intentional actions that led to segregation, we also know that, given different intentional actions, a counterfactual world in which cities are less segregated could have or could yet become reality.

In later chapters, we will examine other examples of purposeful action by governments and individuals to reinforce the spatial separation of groups: actions taken by African Americans in Los Angeles concerned about the growing Latino presence in their neighborhood, by the Israeli government building segregated housing blocks that are off-limits to ethnic and religious minorities, and by authorities in Phoenix, where city planning and zoning separates people by ethnicity and income. All of these examples remind us that there is a connection between intentional action – often in the form of public policy – and the way space separates us. It reminds us that we often create

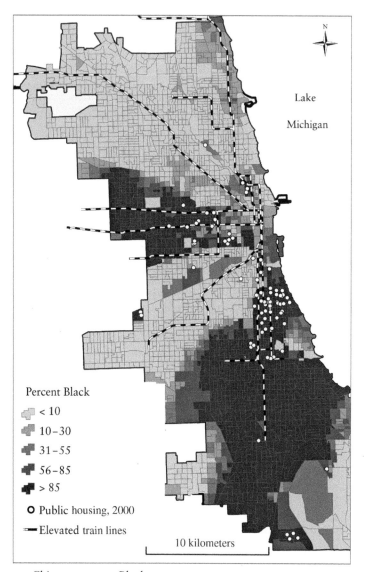

FIGURE I.I. Chicago, percent Black, 2014.

Units depicted are Census Block Groups. Note that the non-Black population is not all Anglo white – much of the population, especially on the west side of the city, is Hispanic.

All maps in this book, with the exception of Figures 1.4 and 1.5 were created by Jeff Blossom and Devika Kakkar, Center for Geographic Analysis, Harvard University.

our own distance between groups and that understanding this phenomenon is therefore no mere academic exercise, but one that should speak clearly to public policy and to shaping the world as we wish it to be.

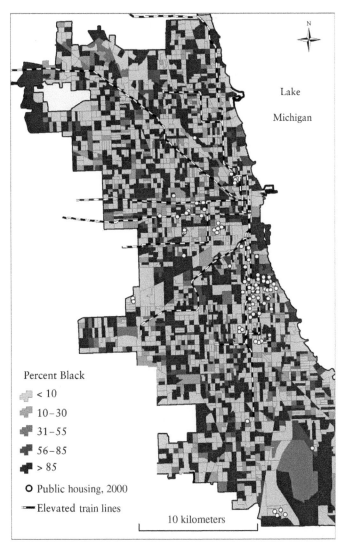

FIGURE 1.2. Counterfactual distribution of Black population in Chicago, 2014.
Counterfactual distribution created by the random reordering of populations across Census Block Groups.

THE ARGUMENT AND FOCUS OF THIS BOOK

I offer a theory of *social-geographic impact*. This theory can be summarized by five points:

1. Human attitudes and behaviors are deeply affected by group identities – the important group categories by which a person will describe herself.

2. Certain conditions, including geography, increase the *salience* of group categories.
3. Among the geographic conditions that increase salience are a group's size, proximity, and degree of segregation.
4. The more salient a category, the more likely it is that one's attitudes and behavior toward it will have group-based bias.
5. These group-based biases have political consequences.

The salience of a category is a way of describing its psychological prominence: When you see another person, what is the first category that you apply to her? Do you see her as Black or white? Christian or Muslim? Old or young? Or do you describe her by a more individual category, for example, as a friend or neighbor? This salience – the emphasis of one category over another – affects how much we perceive that we have in common with another person. Do we see another person as a member of a different religious group, for example, or as just another individual with whom we might share a common identity, such as a nationality?

Salience also affects behavior because our minds are a well of stereotypes – generalities we attach to groups – and salience helps determine which of several possible stereotypes we might retrieve from this well and apply to a particular person. If you encountered an elderly woman, for example, which of her various possible identity categories would strike you most: that she is elderly or that she is a woman? This could affect the stereotyped characteristics you attribute to her: That she is wise. Or patient. Or hot-tempered. When social geography increases the salience of a particular category, then particular stereotypes may come into play and affect people's social, political, and economic actions.

Psychological, Social, and Political Distance

Space and distance are central concepts in this book. There are different types of space: not only geographic space – the location of objects on the Earth's surface or elsewhere in the physical world – but also psychological, social, and political spaces. These spaces intertwine in our minds, affecting how we see ourselves and other people in each.

Social and psychological space does not refer to space on the Earth's surface but rather to space in the social realm and in our perceptions. Distance refers to the closeness of any two groups on these dimensions. *Psychological distance* is the feeling of similarity between members of two groups. For example, does a person perceive that people from another group look and behave like members of her group? *Social distance* is a measure of separateness in social space or the amount of social interaction across groups – do members of different groups shop in the same stores, attend the same schools, worship in the same churches? A central point of this book is that geographic, social, and psychological distance are linked so that each is affected by the other. These will also affect *political distance*, which is simply the amount of agreement between people on political questions: Do people agree on how money should be spent? On which candidate should win? On what policy should be implemented?

Describing the social and political worlds in spatial terms is quite common in our everyday language: you feel that you are "close" to somebody or that a politician is ideologically on the "left" or "right." Across many disciplines, scholars have developed methods to quantify dimensions of space, finding the distance between friends in social networks or the ideological distance between members of Congress.[15] In such research, as we might guess, your location in these spaces – whether you are left or right, close or far away from other groups – affects behavior, including, for example, voting. Geographic space, I argue, affects where you perceive yourself and other groups to be in these other spaces.

It is clear that these spaces are tangled like the roots of a tree, each affecting the other, so that while geographic distance affects psychological distance, psychological distance can also affect geographic distance, compelling people to want to live further away from those they believe are dissimilar to them. And political space, of course, affects geographic space, when those in power can impose segregation between groups by force of law or custom. However, my focus will be in one direction: establishing the previously unexplored effect of geographic space on psychological and, subsequently, social and political space. Figure 1.3 offers a schematic of this process, displaying the dynamic in which positions in geographic space distort positions in psychological space and, thus, affect real and perceived positions in social and political space. The A's and B's in the figure are there to stand in for any meaningful groups in society, such as races, nationalities, political parties, and religions. As these distances in social and political space widen, societies struggle to function: sharing is unlikely to take place across groups who never interact in the social space of businesses, clubs, and public streets. When one group is to the political left and one to the political right, it is difficult to make compromises across this gap and politics grinds in gridlock. This is the space between us and other groups.

Interactions, Social-geographic Impact, and Contact

In demonstrating the effects of space, I will examine *social interactions*. By "interactions," I refer to somebody doing something – directly or indirectly – with one or more members of another group. The interactions of Black and white passengers on the "L" were fleeting and probably, in themselves, inconsequential – but many interactions between groups have much at stake. Ultimately, we care most about political interactions – those in which people come together to make decisions about common resources – but we also care about the attitudes and behaviors that precede those political interactions. One example is the attitudes that a member of one group has about the other group. Does she believe that members of the other group are, say, trustworthy

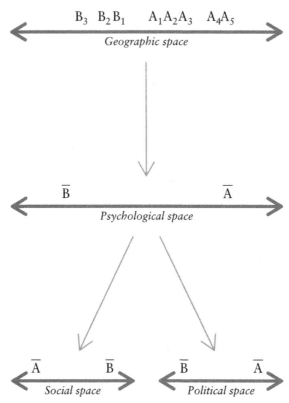

FIGURE 1.3. Four types of space.
Stylized relationship between people in types of space. Individuals (subscripted by numbers) from two social groups are arranged in geographic space. The clustering of individuals in geographic space distorts perceptions of closeness in psychological space, causing members of group A or B to accentuate their perceptions of the differences between groups A and B. This, in turn, structures social and political space, causing political disagreement and a lack of social interaction across the groups.

or intelligent? Sometimes, interactions will be measured using variables that seem abstract, such as the results of games played in a laboratory, but I will describe why these are good representations of the real-world interactions we care about, such as sharing land and providing welfare.

"Interactions" is an imperfect word because it has the connotation of interpersonal interactions, such as two people working on an office project together or having a conversation on the bus. But interpersonal interactions are only a small part of how people can interact. More often, interactions are only institutional, with people from different groups coming together without any direct contact. When people vote, for example, they are interacting with other voters to determine a common outcome, although there is no direct contact.

My argument is that the character of these interactions is shaped by social geography. Social geography can be characterized by at least three dimensions, which I will define in more detail below: the *size*, *proximity*, and *segregation* of groups. In turn, these can influence behavior in at least two ways: perceptually, by directly affecting our cognition, and experientially, through interpersonal contact. The first of these – the perceptual effect – is novel and, I argue, potentially more powerful than experience, so most of my theoretical discussion will be devoted to the cognitive effect of social geography on perception. I call this cognitive effect *social-geographic impact*.

The second mechanism – interpersonal contact – has been thoroughly studied, but with a focus on a particular type of contact. Interpersonal contact across groups can be *brief* – the type that may happen by chance when groups occupy the same place, such as passing another person on the street or seeing her on the train. Jane Jacobs called these "little public sidewalk contacts."[16] Interpersonal contact can also be *extended*, such as having friends, classmates, or coworkers of a different race or ethnicity. To the extent that this book is concerned with interpersonal contact, its primary concern is brief – rather than extended – interpersonal contact across groups.

Extended interpersonal interactions generally fall under the area of psychology loosely known as "Contact Theory." But it is not only psychologists who have focused on extended interpersonal contact. Political scientists, economists, and sociologists often speak of "context" and what they have in mind is a container that can be filled with groups that then somehow interact – perhaps as friends or as competitors. Such an approach is primarily the study of relationships, not of context.[17] In such research, it is the relationships that are important. In fact, the relationships could be removed from the container and studied elsewhere – in a laboratory, for example – as long as the same relationships exist. I am concerned with social geography – the shape of the container itself – that is, whether the groups are segregated or integrated, close to or far from each other, large or small in comparison to each other. To be sure, the study of relationships is fascinating and consequential, but before these relationships can even occur, the shape of the container itself – social geography – already affects our behavior.

It is important to notice that in the previous example (on page 7) of the two Anglo women living in integrated or segregated cities, neither had any close Latino friends or colleagues. In the domain of Contact Theory, attitudes toward the outgroup are determined by extended interpersonal experience, so these two women, given their identical (lack of) interpersonal contact with Latinos, should have identical attitudes toward them. However, in this book, I am arguing that they will have different attitudes, *independent of extended interpersonal contact*, due to the effect of geographic space on their behavior. Social geography creates a space between us in our heads before it creates a space between us in our social relationships.

It is also important to emphasize that the experience of these two hypothetical Anglo women is not uncommon. In many societies, including the United States, extended interpersonal contact across many social divisions, including race and ethnicity, is quite rare. Most people have relatives, friends, and coworkers who are overwhelmingly like themselves. For example, in research I will describe in Chapter 7, we asked Jewish Israelis how often they talk with Arabs. Despite the fact that Arabs make up 20 percent of the population of Israel, *56 percent* of the people we surveyed said that they *never* do. Their interactions with Arabs are thus overwhelmingly the brief interactions, such as passing somebody on the street, that occur when groups share the same space. For most Jewish Israelis then, like people in many societies, their behavior and attitudes cannot be shaped by extended relationships with members of another group, because such relationships simply do not exist.

Although interpersonal contact is not the focus of this book and will intentionally be explored less systematically than social geography, it certainly matters, and its effects must be accounted for in the study of context. Interpersonal contact moderates the effects of social geography on interactions. It does this by breaking down the perceived cohesiveness – or "groupishness" – of groups. This decreases the psychological space between groups. Quite simply, if positive intergroup contact – whether the positive fleeting interactions with people from other groups on the street or in a store or, especially, in a long-term relationship as equals in school, at a job, or on a team – has improved your attitudes about the other group, then the effects of social geography on your attitudes and behavior toward that group will be considerably reduced. In places with higher intergroup contact, perhaps even if this contact is fleeting, social geography will have less impact.

Interpersonal contact can break down the space between groups, but institutions and culture can increase this space. Institutions can reify groups by causing the boundaries of geography, groups, and culture to converge. For example, commercial advertising can be focused on a particular group, thereby causing cultural separation between groups. Politicians can exploit intergroup differences, thereby causing partisan or ideological differences between groups. Such separating institutions may operate more strongly when aided by a social geography that segregates: advertisers and politicians can better target their messages to certain groups and social networks can spread these messages across geographic clusters.

Because contact and institutions can moderate and reify, I must account for their effects as I search for the effect of social geography. If I am arguing that space affects intergroup interactions through a direct effect on psychology – independently of interpersonal contact or institutions – then I must somehow hold the effects of contact and institutions constant. Many of the empirical exercises in this book are designed to do just that – to identify the effects of space, independent of interpersonal contact and institutions.[18]

Finally, this book is not about how social geography came to have its current form or, more specifically, how groups come to be concentrated in certain areas or come to be segregated. For example, much social science and history scholarship treats segregation as a dependent variable and asks why it exists. In this way of looking at things, it is thought that people hold prejudicial attitudes about a group and therefore drive away members of that group or move away from that group themselves. But unpacking the causes of segregation is not the aim of this book. Rather, I am treating segregation as an independent variable and am asking: given that segregation exists, what does it do? I want to show that segregation is not just a result of attitudes and behaviors – it can be a cause of attitudes and behaviors. Once people segregate – possibly but not necessarily because of prejudicial attitudes[19] – their segregation creates or contributes to further attitudes and behaviors.

A common narrative in the urban history of the United States is that, in the mid- to late twentieth century, whites – spurred by forces including their own racism – abandoned the inner cities. The result was (and still is) largely Black inner cities and largely white suburbs. This, of course, did happen, but what I want to suggest is that it's not where the story ends. Attitudes do not remain static. After this sorting occurred, it was the very fact of being segregated that made these intergroup attitudes – driven partly by the psychological forces I will explore in this book – become even more negative and their political consequences even more severe. Prejudice may have helped cause segregation, but then the segregation helped cause even more prejudice.

But of course, from a research perspective, this is problematic because the sequence I just described indicates that segregation is *endogenous* to attitudes; that is, either one can cause the other. In fact, we *know* that either one can cause the other: for example, religious riots in Kaduna, Nigeria in 2000 were caused by tensions between Christians and Muslims and researchers say that the residential segregation resulting from the riots made the tensions even worse.[20] Sorting through such tangled, but important, relationships is one of the contributions of this book.

Moreover, as we'll see, it is not only the preexisting prejudices of a group that cause the group to flee when another group arrives – thereby causing segregation – and it is not only the resulting segregation that causes prejudice. The initial meeting of groups, when groups first come together in space, can also cause prejudice. This, as we will see, happened in the mid-twentieth century when Blacks moved to northern US cities and it also is happening in 2017 as Latinos have crossed over the boundaries of segregation from Latin America and the American Southwest and arrived in largely Anglo communities in places like Ohio and Pennsylvania. In those communities, where Latinos and Anglos came together, the Anglos largely voted in 2016 for the anti-Latino demagogue Donald Trump.

THE LITTLE BEACH AT LAKE YOSEMITE

The beauty of social science is that it is always around us. The supremely complex – yet still understandable – interaction of human beings and their institutions unfolds before us every second of our lives. Our minds are finely tuned to perceive it and social science gives us the ability to find structure and meaning in it. Lake Yosemite is a man-made reservoir about five miles east of Merced, California, a farming community in California's San Joaquin Valley. Merced is where I grew up and, as a child, I would visit this lake on summer weekends. Merced is a remarkably diverse place today, especially for a small city.[21] This diversity was just starting to blossom when I was growing up there – with rapidly growing immigrant populations from Latin America and a major influx of Hmong people from Laos, refugees from the wars in Southeast Asia. I didn't know it at the time, but the city of my childhood was grappling with how these different groups would share the same space and interact in our social and political institutions, much as in any other city where people from different social groups occupy the same place.

Lake Yosemite is not nearly as grand as the name may make it sound, but in the valley, we were far from the ocean beaches commonly associated with California, so on blazing hot summer days we would make use of the one little beach at the lake to splash in the water and play in the sand. This beach and other public places in Merced were my first exposure to diversity. Now, when I think back to that little beach, I see a social science experiment unfolding. It is the only beach on the lake and it is small, just a few hundred feet long, so it is easy to see everyone there. When groups come together in relatively well-defined spaces, such as a small beach or a park, their spatial relationships are readily apparent – we know what groups are present, in what numbers, and how far they are from each other.

I can imagine going to the beach and conducting a study on the clustering of people in that small area. If this example isn't meaningful to you, just substitute somewhere else where different groups congregate in a relatively confined area, such as a shopping mall, a school cafeteria, or a university quad. You can also substitute other groups than those I use here – any groups with identifiable group membership will do: fans of sports teams, immigrants and natives, labor and management, and so on.

People come to the beach in groups. Almost nobody is there alone. Most often, the groups have a common demographic background: Anglo, African American, Latino, Hmong. The backgrounds are apparent by linguistic and physical differences and sometimes the members of a group accentuate their membership by wearing matching shirts or culturally distinctive dress. These groups, with their different sizes and concentrations, are a reminder of how the arrangement of groups in geographic space can affect our attitudes and behaviors.

Thinking about these groups – together in the same place but separated into distinct clusters and often with different physical features, styles, and languages – I play out a hypothetical study in my mind: my research assistants go around with clipboards and survey people. They ask the beachgoers about their willingness to endorse stereotypes about groups. A good place to start might be stereotypes about Latinos. My hypothesis is that the attitudes of non-Latinos about Latinos would vary with the spatial arrangement of Latinos on the beach at that moment.

Imagine you are at the beach with your family and you are not Latino. A group of Latino teenagers arrives, tightly clustered together. Were you thinking of Latinos before? Are you now aware of all the ways they are different from you? Surveying people at random, before and after the arrival of the Latino teenagers, my research assistants might note that the willingness of survey respondents to endorse stereotypes about Latino people increases after that group turns up. The salience of certain identities has increased and perhaps – without knowing it – you have reached into your well of stereotypes and pulled out the Latino ones. These will be revealed when you are questioned by my research team. How big is that group? Is it only two or three people? If so, you probably don't take much notice because you are too busy watching your children in the water. Is it 10 people? Now you notice. How close is the group? Are they far away? Subjects surveyed when the group is far away will have a smaller increase in their willingness to endorse stereotypes about Latinos.

A large family of Hmong people arrives – dressed very differently than the Black family next to them. Are the Black people thinking about Hmong people now, calling up stereotypes about Hmong? A few minutes earlier, when the groups were separated, they almost certainly were not thinking of these stereotypes. If there had only been a single Hmong person, would the Black people even have noticed? A little later, a group of Anglo senior citizens on a social outing arrives. Do members of the Black family now turn their attention to Anglos? If our survey asked about stereotypes about Anglos, the endorsement of these stereotypes should increase.

I've never executed this study at the little beach. It just plays through my imagination when I think about how to research groups occupying the same place. But I have executed analogous studies, not in discrete locations like beaches, but in the real-world laboratories of cities. When a different group is a permanent feature of a particular neighborhood, when interactions with this group are an important part of your daily life, and when that group is politically relevant, will stereotypes about that group be salient to you when making decisions? Will those stereotypes affect your decisions? Will that group come to mind when you are asked about politics?

SOME TERMINOLOGY

In this book, I will repeatedly use certain terminology.

First, by *space* or *social geography*, I mean the location – sometimes relative – of social groups on the Earth's surface. When I speak about social geography, I am talking about the size and location of groups, not interpersonal contact. When I do speak about interpersonal contact, unless otherwise noted, I mean brief interpersonal contact that happens every day, not deep extended contact, such as friendship. *Context* includes both social geography and interpersonal contact.

Local Environment   When studying what happens when groups occupy the same place, a researcher must define "place." If, for example, I want to know how the size of the Latino population in a place is related to the attitudes of Blacks toward Latinos in that place, I must decide what geographic area defines place. Is place a city? A town? A neighborhood? Within those questions, there is another question about how to define the chosen unit. For example, is a city just a single city defined by municipal boundaries, like San Francisco, or is it a collection of cities – a metropolitan area – like the San Francisco Bay Area?

In the study of context, the "right" geographic unit of analysis – the right *areal unit* – is a topic of much discussion and, for readers familiar with this topic, it is surely a question they will ask when reading this book. It raises familiar methodological challenges that I will address in detail in later chapters.

For my purposes, though, there is no single "right" unit, but rather the psychologically salient *local environment* of each individual. The relevant local environment will vary across individuals and within individuals across time and place. Whenever I am describing a dimension of space, such as segregation, it is measured, unless otherwise noted, in the local environment. For example, imagine a non-Latino person who is thinking, if only momentarily, about Latinos. That is, they are salient to her. If, at that moment, I could peer into her "mind's eye," what area would I see? Her immediate neighborhood? The whole city? Something else? In social science, we often do this. We carefully design survey questions to peer into a person's mind and extract a *latent* concept, such as her ideology or prejudices – dimensions that may have no physical representation. We could also hypothetically do this for the latent concept of local environment – carefully crafting survey questions to ask each person what geographic area matters for the research question at hand – something that answers "when you think about Latinos, what area matters?" Scholars have attempted this on small scales[22] but have not yet developed effective tools for measuring the local environment of individuals in large-scale research.

Since we cannot measure the local environment for each individual in a study, a researcher must pick geographic units that best approximate, on average, the different local environments that different individuals have in their minds. This could be a city or a county or a state or any other unit – whatever unit, on average, minimizes the deviation from what a researcher would see if she could look into subjects' minds and see what they are really thinking. In this sense, a researcher is not picking the "right" unit, but rather the *best* unit.[23] This is no different than the operationalization of any latent concept: a researcher measuring intelligence by IQ is hoping to approximate the invisible underlying concept of intelligence. Because people are diverse, an IQ test does not perfectly capture intelligence for each person – for some it might do so poorly – but the researcher designs an IQ test that she hopes, on average, best measures intelligence.

Of course, the local environment may change depending on the question at hand. When thinking about politics, an entire state may be salient or, as I discuss in Chapter 9, an entire nation. And it goes without saying that the local environment may not be captured by administrative or political boundaries, such as ZIP codes or counties. If it is a psychological phenomenon that links geography and behavior – such as psychological salience, which plays a key role in my story – such administrative boundaries may be unimportant. Psychology, while potentially affected by administrative boundaries, is certainly not fully constrained by them: if you are concerned with a person nearby – if she is salient in your mind – you do not stop being concerned because she happened to be across the border in another county. This may mean a researcher will want to construct new units of analysis, not bounded by preexisting borders. Technology has made it increasingly possible to do research without using pre-defined units and I will do this at some points in this book. But, of course, sometimes a researcher must use what's available and must therefore pick the pre-defined unit that best approximates the local environment. (It is important to emphasize that a researcher is never free to make purely arbitrary choices about units or to change the unit of analysis in search of a certain result. That would be bad science and a researcher must work to show she has not done so.)

In the American context, I think the metropolitan area – geographically connected clusters of cities – is often a good choice of unit to represent the local environment. Much of the analysis in this book will use this unit because it is likely salient when people are thinking about racial and ethnic groups: for most people, their metropolitan area contains diverse social groups but is small enough so that people have a general sense of where those groups are and may even occasionally interact with them. In Chapter 4, I will validate this, showing that people seem to have a good sense of where groups can be found in their city. But intuitively, we can also see that people have images of these areas in their heads, knowing where groups can be found, which accounts for the stigma attached to certain neighborhoods and certain sides of the city – as it was for the "L" train passengers in Chicago. Metropolitan areas are, by definition, connected internally by social and economic networks, so that a person can experience – or at least imagine – interacting with individuals from around the area, including members of other groups. (Importantly, a metropolitan area includes much more than the large core city – it can extend into suburbs and even into the more rural areas surrounding cities and the people in these outlying areas can be concerned by groups elsewhere in the metropolitan area. In fact, I will demonstrate this in Chapter 5.)

Even so, the unit of analysis that best captures the local environment will vary across research questions. In some cases, for example, the relevant local environment might be very local – just a certain part of a city. Say that, again, I wanted to understand how the percent Latino in the local environment affected Black attitudes about Latinos. I could measure percent Latino at the city level and compare attitudes across cities. This might effectively capture the local environment, on average, for the people in my study. On the other hand, say I could look into a single city and see the smaller local environments of the Black residents – measuring which residents have Latino neighbors right next door and which do not. It might be that having an immediate Latino neighbor is important – not that the larger city doesn't matter, but that attitudes could also be affected by one's immediate neighbor. I would probably want to measure that if I could – to count who has those neighbors and who does not – and construct local environments on the neighborhood level.

In this book, I will examine situations in which very small areas do seem to be the salient local environment. We will see this in Chicago, where some white voters lived immediately adjacent to a group of segregated Black voters, and in Los Angeles, where some Black residents live immediately adjacent to Latinos, segregated by blocks rather than by entire neighborhoods. In examining these groups, I will focus on this very local segregation. This is not to say that larger patterns of segregation in Chicago or Los Angeles do not affect behavior, but rather that local patterns also may affect behavior. Neither can be ignored if we want to understand what's going on. In one instance in this book, we will see a clear example of the malleability of local environments and how even hyper-local environments can shape behavior. I created social geography by arranging groups of 20 people – segregated or integrated – in a laboratory and saw that even with everything else that could be influencing my subjects kept constant, the social geography of this 20-person local environment had its own power to shape behavior.

Segregation   Segregation is one of three key dimensions of geographic space that make up the social geography of a local environment. A useful definition of segregation, borrowed from other scholars, is "the extent to which individuals of different groups occupy or experience different social environments."[24] This general term reflects the fact that segregation can extend to more than just geographic space. For example, people can be segregated across political parties or by where they work. Although it is possible that all types of segregation affect our psychology in similar ways, increasing the perceived cohesiveness of a segregated group, I do not test the effects of other forms of segregation in this book.

Spatial segregation can be characterized by whether groups are clustered in space, rather than being more evenly dispersed.[25] Clustering increases the cohesion of a group in space, which, I claim, will affect how much psychological space we perceive between groups. Look back at Figure 1.2, in which the clustering of both Blacks and non-Blacks has been decreased in comparison to Figure 1.1.

Clustering can be usefully – though not perfectly – captured by measures of spatial segregation commonly used by social scientists, such as the Dissimilarity Index, which I will use throughout the book. If two groups occupy a larger geographic space, such as a city, the Dissimilarity Index measures the extent to which they both occupy smaller units of that space, such as neighborhoods, blocks, or apartment buildings. If we take the population of a city as the baseline, the Dissimilarity Index measures how evenly spread out the groups are within the city. In places where each neighborhood looks like the broader city, segregation is low. In places where neighborhoods differ markedly in their demographics from the city, segregation is high. You can average the degree to which each smaller unit, such as a neighborhood, is occupied by both groups to have a measure of segregation for the entire city.[26]

See Figures 1.4 and 1.5 for images of segregation, as measured by the Dissimilarity Index, between non-Hispanic whites and Blacks and between non-Hispanic whites and Hispanics by metropolitan area in the United States. A way to see the power of segregation to shape behavior is to compare behavior across the metropolitan areas depicted in Figures 1.4 and 1.5, which I will do in the next chapter.

Size I will refer throughout the book to another key dimension of space – *size* – by which I mean the proportion of a group in the population of the local environment. I am trying to measure size as it relates to a group's psychological salience. In general, things do not become salient – do not rise to importance – because we are considering absolute numbers, say 10,000 people or 8,000 people. Rather, we think in relative terms, using benchmarks – 10,000 is bigger than 8,000, this group is bigger than that group, so it is more

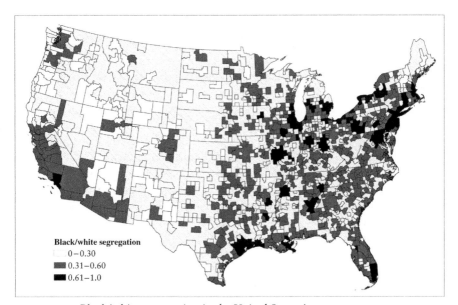

Black/white segregation
0–0.30
0.31–0.60
0.61–1.0

FIGURE 1.4. Black/white segregation in the United States in 2010.

Segregation in CBSA's (see Endnote 21) is measured by the Dissimilarity Index. Classifications of "Low," "Moderate," and "High" are based on Massey and Denton (1993). This figure, and Figures 1.5, 1.6, 1.7, 4.4, 8.2, and N1.1, were created by Riley K. Carney.

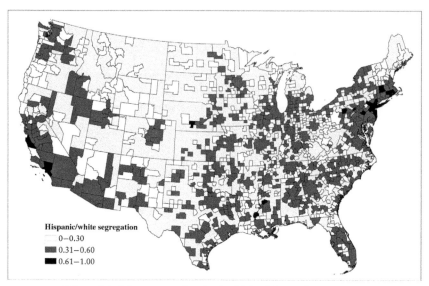

FIGURE 1.5. Hispanic/white segregation in the United States in 2010.

important.[27] This suggests that the size of a group in a local environment should be "benchmarked" against that of another group and, thus, a group's "size" – always relative to another group – should be the proportion or ratio of the numerical sizes of the two groups of interest in the local environment. In other words, if I am asking how the attitudes of a Black person toward Latinos are related to the presence of Latino people in her local environment, the groups of interest would be Blacks and Latinos. If there are 100 Black people and 50 Latino people, the *size* of the Latino group is 0.50. From the perspective of the Latino person, the size of the Black group is 2.00.[28]

Comparing Dimensions of Geographic Space   With definitions of segregation and size in hand, it is important to note how these dimensions of space, in addition to proximity, represent different arrangements of people. To describe the social geography of a place, a researcher can ask distinct questions about these dimensions: Is the population of the areal unit integrated or segregated? Is it diverse or homogeneous? Are groups close together or far apart? Each of these questions addresses a different dimension of space. A group can be high in numbers but also be segregated; or not segregated, but low in numbers; or segregated, but not proximate; and so on.

"Segregated" does not necessarily mean "far away." Two groups can be highly segregated while also being right next to each other; this often happens in dense urban areas. In Boston, the predominately white neighborhood of South Boston ("Southie") abuts the largely Black sections of Dorchester. In London, a Bangladeshi population in Tower Hamlets, just east of the original "City" of London, borders an Anglo community in Greenwich to the southeast and a Black African and Caribbean population in Newham to the northeast. In central Los Angeles, Latinos and Blacks live close to each other, but each in separate blocks (see Figure 8.5 on page 217). All of these groups are segregated by my definition.

A large minority group also can make an area, such as a city, "diverse" but still segregated. Many US cities with large Black populations, such as Chicago and Detroit, are diverse but still very segregated, with Blacks and non-Blacks living in very different parts of the city. This can apply at any geographic level; for example, two groups can live in the same neighborhood, but still be segregated into different parts of that neighborhood.

You can see examples of this in Figure 1.6, where you can imagine that each square is a different city and the different colored dots represent different groups. In the top left-hand city and the left city in the third row, the population proportions of gray and white dots are the same, but segregation is lower in the latter. In the right-hand column, the cities in the second and third rows are similar in segregation and size, but differ in proximity. The prediction of my theory, by the way, is that for the white dots, group bias should be highest in the top left city, where segregation, size, and proximity are all high, and lowest in the bottom right, where all three dimensions are lowest. The other squares should fall somewhere in between. (The difference between the first and third rows of the left column is also approximately the difference between the actual and counterfactual segregation in Chicago depicted in Figures 1.1 and 1.2.)

Social identity groups, ingroups, and outgroups   *Groups* are a central part of this book. When discussing groups, I mean *social identity groups*. A person can be categorized in any number of ways, but some groups are central to her self-concept; that is, how a person categorizes herself. Ask a person to describe herself and she will, almost always, reply by mostly listing categorical memberships: "woman, student, African American," and so on. These groups are part of her self-concept and, thus, are social identity groups. If somebody shares a social identity with you, she is a member of your *ingroup*. If not, she is a member of the *outgroup*.

Group-based bias   Throughout the book, I will examine relationships between space and certain attitudes and behaviors. The attitudes or behaviors of interest to me are those that, on average, are different depending on whether the person with whom one is interacting is or is not a member of one's ingroup. I will call such attitudes and behaviors *group-based bias*, or simply *group bias*. As we will see shortly, there are many attitudes and behaviors that we would expect to differ based on their target. Some are obviously group-based, like holding negative attitudes about a particular group, but some are less obviously group-based, like turning out to vote in an election rather than staying home.

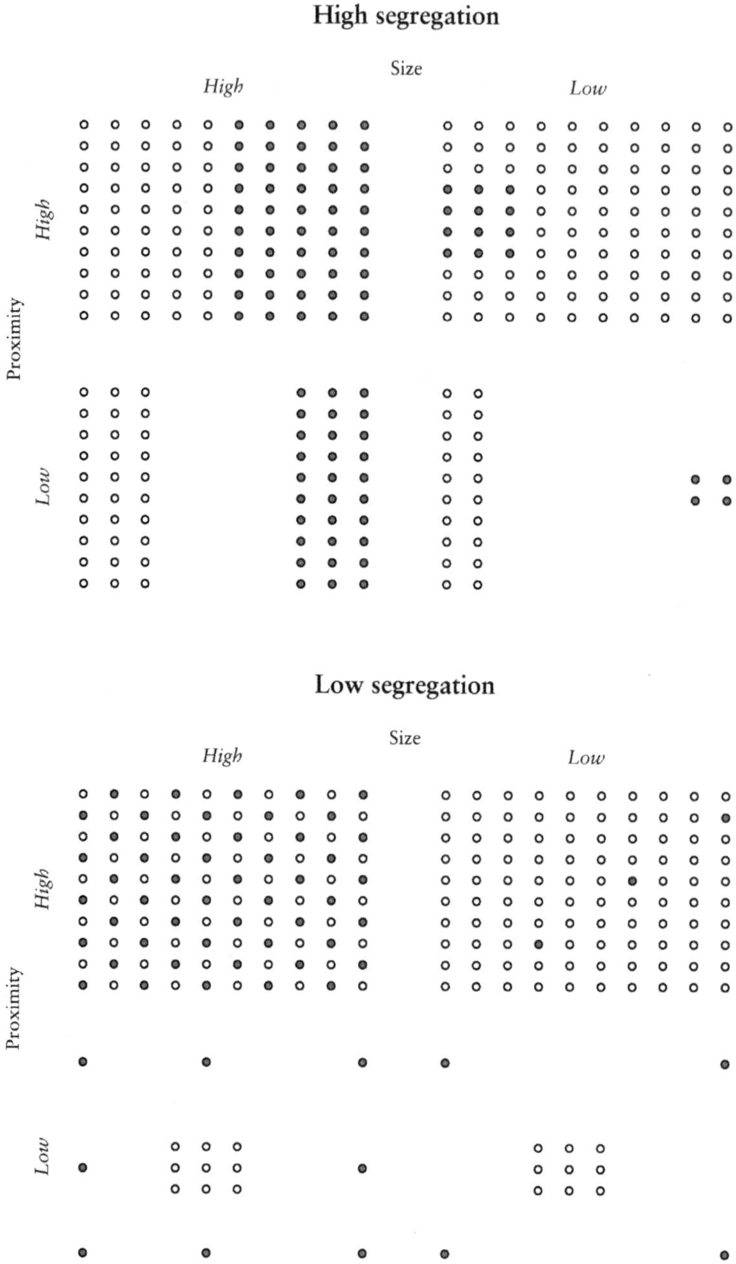

High segregation

Low segregation

FIGURE I.6. Groups with varying segregation, size, and proximity.
Levels of size are from the perspective of the white dots.

One form of group bias is valence ranking; that is, taking members of an ingroup to be superior to members of an outgroup on some particular quality – smarter, harder-working, more honest, better-looking. Much research has shown that such attitudes can manifest in consequential ingroup-favoring behaviors – behaviors that are directly discriminatory. In a laboratory experiment, it may look like this: Give a person $10 and simply ask her to share it with two people. If one of those people is from an ingroup and the other is from an outgroup – and even if those two people don't differ in any other significant way – she will share more with the ingroup member.

Such laboratory studies are analogs to real-world bias, which has been well documented in social science research. A white manager, given two identically qualified job applicants, one white and one black, will more often hire the white one.[29] The same behavior has been found amongst straight managers given the opportunity to hire a gay or straight applicant.[30] In Sweden, a landlord with an option to show an apartment to a native Swede or to an Arab immigrant will more often show it to the Swede.[31] In Israeli criminal courts, Arab judges are less likely than Jewish judges to incarcerate Arab defendants.[32] A county clerk in the United States – the elected official who administers voting and elections – is less likely to respond to an email from a constituent with a Hispanic name asking about how to register to vote than to the same emailed question from a constituent with an Anglo name.[33] All these findings, whether observed in the lab or in the real world, show group-based bias.[34]

On a more extreme level, group bias can become actual violence. We need only think of the race-based violence and property crime that plagued Boston in the 1970s and '80s, the organized lynching of Blacks in the twentieth-century American South, or the genocides in Ottoman Turkey, Nazi-occupied Europe, and Rwanda that spanned the twentieth-century. As I write, concerns about the possible disproportionate shooting of Black men by white police officers is, again, in the news.

We can think of group bias as a continuum: between the extremes of private attitudes and actual violence, we will find varieties such as expressed attitudes, ethnic slurs, subtle acts of prejudice such as not taking an available seat next to an outgroup member on the bus, and harmful, though not physically violent, acts such as discrimination in hiring.

Is it possible that simple geography can cause a behavior as profound as ethnic violence? Yes, but it is important to be clear about what I mean by this. Although, as I argue, social geography is causal, it is *not deterministic*. Geography, like nearly all inputs to social processes, simply changes the probability of a particular outcome – it does not guarantee that outcome. When the outcome in question is something rare, like ethnic violence, geography may cause it to be more likely, though still rare. What this means is that when violence does occur, especially when it is widespread, something *in addition* to geography is likely contributing, such as incitement by politicians – what political science calls *elites*. The 1994 Rwandan genocide, for example, was rooted in ethnic distinctions but is also thought to have been catalyzed by radio programming that explicitly encouraged hatred and violence.[35] This will, of course, also be true of less dramatic behaviors. Ethnically motivated voting, for example, can be caused by geography, but the political ideologies, party structures, and other elements that shape voting along ethnic lines may also be the result of choices made by elites.[36]

Having chosen to examine attitudes and behaviors motivated by one's own and others' identities, we are led to ask what identities are important enough to lead to group bias? After all, there is a functionally limitless number of ways that humans could be divided: by hair color, skin color, religion, alma mater. Why do some matter more than others? Why might a person vote or kill based on their religion but not based on their alma mater?

Of course, there are identifiable – and often predictable – reasons that some group distinctions become important, regardless of geography. For example, politicians can – and often do – exploit distinctions between people for political gain. Using the terminology of this book, elites manage to make certain distinctions salient. They may also emphasize distinctions that have already been made salient by geography. For example, white elites in the postbellum American South chose to stoke the fear of Blacks and did so particularly among whites who lived in areas with a high proportion of Blacks,[37] presumably – at least partially – because the geographic proximity made this fear-mongering more effective. Of course, a society's economic structure can make some distinctions important, as in the antebellum South, where slavery was a crucial economic institution for white elites.[38]

Because these identities can be exploited, their importance or salience can change across time and place. For example, in the United States, many of us care deeply about a particular racial dichotomy: white and Black. In other countries, salient groups are formed around caste or religion. But the salience of these divisions can change. For example, although it may seem odd to many of us, historians have pointed out that, during the Middle Ages, Muslim and Christian soldiers frequently fought on the same side against the Christian emperors of Europe.[39] Similarly, historians have also noted that in Spain, during the Inquisition, the treatment of Jews and Muslims by the Catholic authorities varied intensely across regions based on their local economic position and relationship with local officials.[40]

If we understand that the importance of distinctions varies with time and place, there is a more basic question: Why are identities, of any type, important to human beings at all? Why do we look at other people and categorize them into groups in the first place? Before politicians can emphasize differences between people, these differences must first be recognized by those people. Why do we do this? The entire answer is beyond the scope of this book, but some aspects are well understood. First, it appears to be a universal social tendency: all human societies form groups. These categorizations take different forms in different societies, but it appears that there has never been any society, across time or space, that did not have social groups. Second, the tendency to categorize people into groups appears to be a basic human cognitive process, arising from the role categorization plays in survival and, therefore, reproductive success among our evolutionary ancestors. This basic psychological process of categorization will be a crucial part of the story of why geography so dramatically affects our interactions across groups.

EXPLORING SPACE

To measure the effect of context, context must be allowed to change. This can happen in two ways: by moving across space and by moving across time. To explore why the arrangement of groups in space shapes social and political conflict, we will travel across many spaces. We will look at data from every state in the United States and from other countries. We will look in depth at Boston, Chicago, Los Angeles, Phoenix, and Jerusalem. In these cities we will also see context change with time by looking back at the history of population flows and, in some cases, by changing context through experiments.

In each of the five cities, we can see that geography, demographics, and politics are different in important ways and so each allows me to establish the scope of my argument. Each varies from the others in five ways that are relevant to the subject of this book. Each has a different (a) cultural and institutional context, (b) set of social groups, (c) group-based bias of interest (the dependent variable), (d) level of interpersonal contact, and (e) level of social-geographic impact.

For example, Jerusalem and Boston obviously have very different political institutions and very different cultural norms for intergroup relations. Examining both allows us to understand how sensitive my results are to this variation. And, of course, different pairs of social groups are interacting in my studies of these different cities: Blacks and whites in Chicago, Blacks and Hispanics in Los Angeles, Anglos and Hispanics in both Boston and Phoenix, and ultra-Orthodox and secular Jews in Jerusalem. This range of groups, in addition to the interactions in other cities I will explore, doesn't account for all the different groups interacting in these cities, but it helps to demonstrate the breadth of my argument and its applicability to very different situations. The biases I will explore also vary across the cities, from voter turnout and vote choice in Chicago and Los Angeles to policy attitudes in Boston and Los Angeles to cooperation in Jerusalem and Phoenix. All of these outcomes, I claim, are tied together by the common mechanism I explore in Chapter 3.

Across cities, we will see different amounts of interpersonal contact, helping us understand how that contact, by replacing geography-driven stereotypes with individual experiences, moderates the impact of social geography, ultimately making it less important. However, as I've emphasized, this book is not about interpersonal contact. I therefore try to hold it constant, either by experimentally controlling it or, when that is not possible, by trying to assess the level and nature of interpersonal contact so that I can understand its effect on intergroup interactions. In some cases, like my study of the neighborhoods around public housing in Chicago, this assessment is straightforward; there was so much social, political, spatial, and psychological division between the groups inside and outside the public housing that contact was near zero. In other cases, like in the Black and Latino neighborhoods of Los Angeles, intergroup contact is pretty frequent and understanding its influence is more complex.

Figure 1.7 shows the stylized relationship between interpersonal contact, social-geographic impact, and group-based bias. Together, the variation in these dimensions forms a *plane of context*. The plane is shaded to represent the expected levels of group-based bias. As the shading becomes darker, this indicates greater group-based bias. Notice that it gets darker more quickly

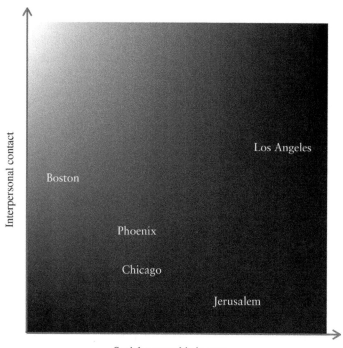

Social geographic impact

FIGURE 1.7. A plane of context: The effects of interpersonal contact and social geography on group-based bias.

The stylized relationship between interpersonal contact, social geography, and group-based bias. The darker the plane, the higher the expected group-based bias. Cities are positioned horizontally based on the logged product of group size and segregation for the group whose group-based bias I measure. Vertical positions are based on my subjective assessments. Each position is specific to the interactions of interest: Anglo/Latino in Boston, white/Black in Chicago, secular/ultra-Orthodox Jews in Jerusalem, Black/Latino in Los Angeles, and Anglo/Latino in Phoenix.

as you move from left to right – that is, by increasing social-geographic impact – than as you move from top to bottom – that is, by reducing interpersonal contact. That is because the evidence in this book suggests that the effect of social geography on bias may be stronger than the effect of interpersonal contact, at least the type that scholars can measure.

Social-geographic impact in Figure 1.7 based on the product of outgroup size and segregation (see Chapter 3 for why this a multiplicative function) for the groups of interest. The placement of interpersonal contact is subjective, based on my understanding of the particular context.[41] Social geography and interpersonal contact are endogenous: a city with high segregation will likely have limited interpersonal contact. This presents a conceptual and methodological challenge that I will attempt to sort out. But also note that these two variables can vary independently; for example, interpersonal contact can vary as a function of institutions and culture, independent of social geography. In Israel, for example, we will see examples of cultural restrictions on interpersonal contact.[42]

Moving across locations on the plane of context will allow us to understand how varying social geography and interpersonal contact affects group-based bias. The positions of cities in Figure 1.7 are specific to the interactions I am studying; for example, Los Angeles is placed where I think it would be for Black/Latino interactions in Los Angeles. That placement does not represent the interactions of, say, Anglos and Blacks in the same city. Chicago and – especially – Jerusalem are toward the lower right because there is very little interpersonal contact between whites and Blacks in Chicago and between ultra-Orthodox and secular Jews in Jerusalem, while at the same time there is high social-geographic impact, since the populations of each group in both cities are large, highly segregated, and in close proximity. Los Angeles is positioned closer to the top because Blacks and Latinos have more interpersonal contact there (often sharing schools, for example), but, from the perspective of Blacks, Latinos are a large portion of the population and, therefore, have a high social-geographic impact.

In each city, one of the populations I explore will be, in certain respects, immigrants – either international or domestic. For example, in Boston and Phoenix, I will look at the impact of immigrants from Latin America, while in Chicago, large-scale interactions between whites and Blacks started with the migration of Blacks from the South. The nature of these interactions and of group-based bias will change over time. A casual student of history can probably recognize that, while there are exceptions, immigration tends to proceed on an *arc of intergroup interactions* from an initial clash to indifference and assimilation of the immigrant group. For example, the Irish immigration to Boston and other cities in the 1840s was met with fierce opposition by natives of those cities. Similarly, the swelling population of Blacks in Chicago in the 1950s provided for virulent bias from whites living on the South Side. The Irish immigrants, of course, eventually became as American as apple pie and, in Chicago, the initial clash softened over time, in significant part because whites moved away from Blacks. Movement along this arc, I will argue, is shaped in large part by social geography and interpersonal contact. One way to characterize each of the cities I will visit is by its place on this arc. Of course, it goes without saying that movement along this arc is not inevitable; while the experience of the Irish is characterized by assimilation, the experience of Blacks is still characterized by exclusion. In the final chapter, drawing on the lessons of this book and focusing on Phoenix as a test case and with special attention to Latino immigration, I will ask what is the likely future of intergroup interactions in the United States.

In the chapters of this book, I am covering the who, what, when, where, why, and if of what happens when groups are in the same place. Starting with the "what" in Chapter 2, I demonstrate the power of social geography by comparing across hundreds of cities, using many different group-based biases. Chapters 3 and 4 cover the "why"; I describe the mechanism by which space exercises this power and demonstrate it in a laboratory. Then, I will cover the "who, when, and where" by visiting the cities mentioned above, showing how social geography affects behavior across different groups, cultures, and institutions. Each chapter is also an opportunity to highlight a particular methodology and a particular challenge in the study of context. I will try to convey why studying context is, perhaps, an acutely difficult enterprise in the study of human behavior. Taking on these challenges will require a host of methodologies, each with advantages and disadvantages. Throughout the book, I will deal with the "if" by showing that geography has a causal effect on our behavior.

A WORD ON CONTRIBUTIONS

Theories of political behavior are often constructed to apply to specific situations or groups. For example, theories often separate the effects of context on majority and minority groups[43] or, even more specifically, the effects of context on one of a pair of groups such as the effect of African Americans on white Americans' attitudes.[44] There is good reason for doing this: specificity can make a theory more concrete and more likely to be correct. Nevertheless, these more narrow formulations can sometimes miss the common underpinnings of behavior, such as the structure of the human mind. The advantage of recognizing such common underpinnings is that it allows us to more readily draw lessons from across time and space because certain features, like the human mind, do not change with the comings and goings of history. In this book, I am striving for a general argument. I want to explain the effect of space on the salience of social groups and I want to show how this affects behavior. So, although it will inform us about socially relevant topics, such as US immigration and even the outcome of a recent US election, my theory should not be specific to any particular social group or to any particular place in a social hierarchy.

The limits of the group- or context-specific models typical of political science are becoming increasingly obvious. Most obviously, the increasing diversity of the United States makes white reactions to Blacks less central – although certainly not unimportant – to understanding the political landscape. And, of course, white reactions to minority groups are not all that shapes politics: interaction between groups in increasingly diversifying urban areas often does not involve whites. Rather, it is a story of interactions between minority groups. Theories constructed around whites reacting to Blacks may even be losing some of their applicability in, for example, a place like Chicago, where much of the local political rhetoric involves the reaction of Blacks to a growing Latino population.

Think back to my opening example of Chicago's Red Line. The psychological salience of that journey and the splitting of "us" and "them" at the Loop in the middle of the city would exist if, instead of Blacks and whites, Chicago were a city of Blacks on the North Side and Latinos on the South Side. In such a counterfactual world, I argue, there would be similar tension and it would animate political behavior. In fact, that situation does exist. If we cross Chicago from south to west, we move generally from a Black area to a Latino area and there is, indeed, a similar tension there.

Finally, leaving recent trends aside, I think my broad theory has an intuitive appeal because it is concerned with easily recognizable aspects of our own behavior. I think we all agree that we are animated by a sense of the world that includes the locations of groups. We can see the location of groups affecting our attitudes about certain places, such as Southie, Harlem, and the others I have already mentioned. What I am dealing with here, I believe, is something – to be blunt – *big*. I am talking about the position of humans on the Earth's surface. And not just a few humans, but masses of humans, divided into groups and arranged in ways that affect our psychology. In a certain respect, our geographic location is one of the most fundamental factors of our existence. It has shaped the evolution and definition of nations. Control over land has animated much of the greatest political thought, from Rousseau to Marx. It is arguable that our geographic distribution is at the core of every major conflict we have experienced. And what I am arguing throughout this book is that our geographic distribution – our social geography – also shapes our individual psychology. It is intertwined with our most basic cognitive architecture. It deeply affects how we perceive other people. Connecting all of this to certain behaviors – especially political behaviors – is less obvious, but that is what I set out to do.

2

The Demagogue of Space

Segregation markedly enhances the visibility of a group; it makes it seem larger and more menacing than it is.

– Gordon Allport[1]

In 2008, the first time that every American voter had a chance to vote for a Black man for President, there was a striking pattern. In some counties, white voters cast far fewer votes for Barack Obama than they had for previous Democratic candidates. For example, in Floyd County, in eastern Kentucky, white voters cast only about 49 percent of their votes for Obama, while, only four years earlier, they had cast 63 percent of their votes for John Kerry. This shift away from voting Democrat was seen in many counties across the United States.[2] In fact, in many counties, Obama received a smaller share of votes than had any of the previous four Democratic candidates.

Of course, there are many reasons this could have happened. But given that the troubled presidency of George W. Bush and the 2008 economic crisis meant it was a favorable election year for Democrats,[3] it seems likely that race may have played a role – that white people were driven away from their traditional party loyalties by a Black man on the ballot. We might imagine that if we had gone to these counties during the 2008 election, we would have found petty demagogues using race to stir up fear by implanting negative stereotypes of Blacks and of a Black president into the minds of white voters.

Some of these demagogues did exist, but in this book, we are searching for something more systematic, something that will affect voters' attitudes and behavior regardless of the actions of any particular politician. Indeed, if we zoom out and look for patterns in the data, we see that in 2008, the demagogue was not any local politician, but rather geographic space itself. Looking across the country, we see that white voters in the most-segregated counties were between five and six percentage points less likely to vote for Obama than white voters in the least-segregated counties. There is a strong reason to suspect that this relationship between segregation and voting was due to Obama's race. Had a white candidate run, segregation would have had no such effect on these voters. The clearest evidence for this is that when a white Democrat was running a mere four years earlier – in fact, every time a white Democrat had run going back to 1992 – segregation had had no such effect on the vote.[4]

In 2008, this was a massive effect of segregation: the gap between the most- and least-segregated counties was almost equivalent to the gap between men and women in voting for Obama.[5] In this chapter, we will see that this was no isolated pattern and that the influence of this demagogue – geographic space – can be seen at many times and in many places. A demagogue that whispers in our ear, playing on our most fundamental psychological tendencies and profoundly affecting the way we think and behave. That includes changing our politics to pit group against group. As I will show in later chapters, it will keep us from standing next to strangers we meet on a train platform and from sharing with our countrymen. It can motivate us to flood the polls but also to vote against our own best interests. And I will establish that this demagogue is indeed *causing* these changes in our behavior. In the next (Chapter 3), I will ask why, exactly, can social geography do this to us? Why is geographic space able to put this psychological space between groups? And I will delve into the human mind to discover the answer.

First, though, I will try to demonstrate the power of this demagogue and show the impressive scope and depth of its influence. I will present a wide range of findings to support this point; we will see the demagogue irrationally changing our behavior toward groups. I will show that the white voters in certain communities who changed their behavior so dramatically when a Black man ran for President were part of a larger pattern of social geography and politics – a pattern that we can see going back in time and still holds sway today. This is the pattern we will see, in different forms, throughout the book. At the end of the chapter, I will show how my original analysis based on recent data relates to a large body of literature, extending to different parts of the world and using different outcomes than those I cover myself and how this pattern fits with what existing social science theory tells us will happen when groups come together in the same place.

It might seem striking that geography has such an effect on our behavior when the prevalence of mass communication and mass culture, and the declining relevance of local community have moved some to proclaim "the death of distance"[6] or that the "world is flat."[7] It seems that the relevance of what is near has vanished from our lives because virtually everything – commerce, politics, violence, some forms of sex – can be manipulated remotely and culture, current events, and politics are increasingly consumed in a mass, non-localized manner. Over 15 years ago, before any of us had smartphones, Robert Putnam described the death of community in the United States in his best-selling book.[8] For Putnam, community was anchored in activities such as fraternal societies, bridge clubs, and – famously – bowling leagues. By gathering people to the same location, these activities bridged the physical and social distance between individuals. The death of these organizations, according to Putnam, came, in large part, with the rise of television and its power as an all-consuming leisure activity. Arguably, this decline has accelerated in the two decades since Putnam wrote this. Telecommunication has entered a new era, in which we not only sit and stare at our television in our living room, but also stare at screens of various sizes almost anywhere we go. Activities such as bridge and fraternal meetings are now encased in computers in our pockets. Local culture seems all but gone. From the death of small-town newspapers – and many big-city newspapers as well – to the globalization of American brands – produced in China and sold all over the world – to the global reach of ideological extremism via the Internet, we seem to be seeing the declining relevance of things local, including politics.[9]

I will try to convince you that, despite the death of distance in the Information Age, the space between groups has a powerful impact on our politics – that there is the primacy of space in our behavior.

THE POWER OF SOCIAL GEOGRAPHY

I will demonstrate the power of social geography by comparing localities across the United States to see how differences in group size, proximity, and segregation are related to a variety of group-based biases. In the several examples below, the analysis is entirely original, having not appeared elsewhere in published articles. For details of these and other original analysis in this book, please see the appendices. I will intentionally focus on recent data, drawn from behavior recorded in the last decade, after an explosion in mobile communication and social networks which might make us suspect that geography is less relevant to our understanding of the world than it once was.

A common form of group bias is negative attitudes toward the other group. There is sometimes controversy concerning what constitutes a negative attitude, but some attitudes are unambiguously negative because they fail the "Golden Rule" test of group attitudes: if you said something about an outgroup, but you'd be offended if somebody said the same thing about your group, then that expresses an unambiguously negative attitude. The very offensive word *nigger* belongs in this category.

One way to look for the use of that word is to see if people search for it on Google. The advantage of using Google searches is that it avoids the problem of "social desirability bias" that is common in surveys, whereby researchers suspect they are not getting the truth from subjects who are unwilling to reveal socially undesirable attitudes when asked. A socially undesirable attitude would be something like anti-Black racism. If people are unwilling to say something that might make them look racist, then attitudes like anti-Black racism will be underreported in surveys. Searching on the Internet, however, is something most people probably consider a private act – or, at least, something less shameful than admitting racism to a survey interviewer – and, therefore, as we probably all know, people will search for all kinds of things on Google that they would never talk about in public.

So, to look for the effect of social geography, I start with data on Google searches for "nigger" because it is unambiguous group bias, unfiltered by social desirability bias. Prior research has shown that these searches are difficult to explain, other than as racial animus: the searching is unlikely to have been done by Blacks; the most commonly searched phrases including this word are "nigger jokes" and "I hate niggers"; and searches for the word were negatively correlated with voting for Obama, but not for voting for previous Democrats.[10]

I looked to see if, across the United States, there was a statistical relationship between searches for this word in a local area and segregation between whites and Blacks. I found a strong and positive relationship. In the United States, as the segregation in an area increases, the tendency for people to use Google to search for "nigger" also increases. There is also a statistical relationship between such Google searches and the size of the local Black population: the more Blacks in an area, the more people search for derogatory terms about Blacks.[11] If we assume that these searches are performed by non-Blacks, then this indicates that non-Black people in more segregated areas and areas where Blacks make up a higher proportion of the population are holding quite derogatory attitudes about Blacks – attitudes so derogatory that most of us would not dare express them in public, but would only search for them under the anonymity of the Internet.

Figure 2.1 shows the relationship between segregation and group-based bias (on the left) and between outgroup size and group-based bias (on the right). We will see this same basic pattern repeatedly – in this chapter and chapters to come. Across groups and locations and different types of biases, this pattern repeats itself: as segregation and outgroup size increase, so does group-based bias. (As I will discuss below, at a certain point, the impact of outgroup size on bias diminishes and flattens.) On these figures, I highlight the cities that I will examine closely in later chapters. The number of searches is measured at the level of a Designated Market Area (DMA). A DMA is, essentially, a television broadcast area, comprised of adjacent counties, so that people in different DMAs see different programming and commercials. Looking across these DMAs, we start to appreciate the power of segregation. To understand the relationship between segregation and group bias, we can compare the extreme cases of a typical non-Black person in the least-segregated media market in the United States (Helena, Montana) and a typical person in the most-segregated media market (Milwaukee). The statistical model tells us that the person in Milwaukee is expected to search for the word "nigger" more than twice as often as a person in Helena, all else equal. Thus racism, as measured by this particular variable, has increased dramatically.[12] A more modest – but also important – effect would be observed going from a place like San Diego to Philadelphia; that is, from the first to the third quartile of segregation. In this case, the typical person would be about 30 percent more likely to

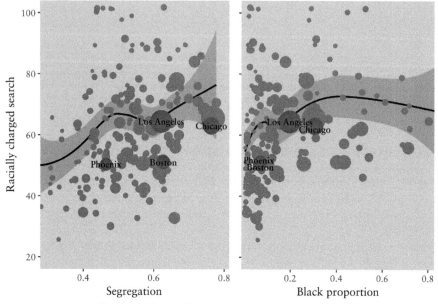

FIGURE 2.1. Racially charged Google searches by segregation and Black proportion.

Relationship between segregation (left) and Black proportion (right) and racially-charged Google searches by Direct Marketing Area in the United States. Point size is proportional to DMA population. DMA population is different than the population of a metropolitan area, thus, for example, Boston's DMA has lower proportion Black than the Boston metropolitan area. Fitted curve is a local polynomial regression with 95 percent confidence intervals.

search for the racist term. A similar exercise of comparing the typical person from the DMA with the smallest Black proportion (near zero in Missoula, Montana) to a person from a DMA with the largest (outside the South, this is Chicago), while holding segregation constant, results in a 40 percent increase in searches.

Of course, as I tell my undergraduate students on their first day of class, "social science is hard." We often don't have tools capable of precisely capturing the relationships found in the complex social world. So while the anonymity of Google searches helps counteract social desirability bias, we might worry about the *ecological inference problem* – the problem of trying to understand individual behaviors based on aggregate data. After all, I can only observe the total number of searches in an area. I don't know who is doing those Google searches or why.[13] For example, it is unlikely, but in these segregated areas the people searching for offensive words for Blacks, despite attempts to control for it, might be other Blacks. This would mean these Google searches represent something other than group-based bias and the evidence would not support my claim that there is a relationship between segregation and anti-Black racism. There are almost never unambiguous relationships in social science, which is why a researcher has to attack a problem in many different ways, and I'll do this by showing that other group-based biases have a similar relationship with geography.

One way to avoid the ecological inference problem is to use surveys to look at what individuals actually say, rather than just aggregate totals. A common survey question asks whether most members of a group are "lazy" or "hardworking" and also whether they are "unintelligent" or "intelligent." Lazy and unintelligent are starkly negative things to say about a group, definitely passing the Golden Rule test of attitudes and qualify as group-based bias.[14]

However, because there is no perfect way to approach a question, here we trade one problem for another and must confront the social desirability problem: people might not be willing to say that members of another group are lazy, even if they believe it. Keeping this in mind, is there a statistical relationship between survey respondents calling a group lazy and unintelligent and the social geography of their metropolitan area? Yes, there is. Controlling for other individual factors, the greater the segregation between Blacks and whites and the larger the size of the Black population in a metropolitan area, the more likely non-Hispanic white people were to describe Blacks as lazy and unintelligent.[15]

It is somewhat hard to grasp how "big" an effect is when it is based on survey responses, but by looking at what the average person says and how much this changes with segregation, we can get a sense of the power of social geography to shape attitudes. These survey questions were measured on seven-point scales from "Lazy" to "Hardworking" and from "Unintelligent" to "Intelligent." Higher numbers mean more hardworking or more intelligent. Among white Americans, the average response about the intelligence of Blacks is 4.7, meaning that your typical white American responds, when asked, that Blacks are more intelligent than not. However, to put this in perspective, when asked about fellow whites, the average response is 5.4. So, on average, whites are willing to tell a surveyor that whites are more intelligent than Blacks by a little more than half a point on a seven-point scale.[16] In a thought experiment in which white attitudes about Black intelligence are affected *only* by where a person lives, if I took a white person from living in a city with the highest level of segregation in the United States (equivalent to Milwaukee)[17] and moved her to a city with the lowest level of segregation in the United States (equivalent to Kappa, Hawaii or Grants Pass, Oregon), this would close the difference between her perception of white and Black intelligence by more than 40 percent. A similar thought experiment of moving a white person from a place with the largest Black population to the smallest would lead to a similarly sized increase in perceptions of Black intelligence.

This pattern of social geography and group bias goes beyond just white and Black Americans. Using the same survey data, I can see the same relationship for the stereotypes Latinos hold about Blacks. Here, too, group bias on the part of Latinos increases with the amount of segregation between them and Blacks and with the size of the Black population.

Are these racist attitudes consequential? Do they reveal anything about what life is like for a Black person in these areas? About how people behave toward one another? Certainly, from the perspective of norms in the United States, these attitudes are distinctly illiberal; calling outgroups, especially a traditionally marginalized group, lazy and unintelligent is not conducive to an inclusive society. Moreover, psychologists have shown that discrimination in beliefs and emotions, while certainly not perfectly, can predict discrimination in actions,[18] so calling people "stupid" may mean you are more likely to treat them as stupid and to treat them poorly in other ways. Indeed, people may well understand how they are perceived by others, even others who don't openly express such attitudes. There is also some evidence that privately held attitudes, like those revealed in Google searches, are related to very consequential behaviors. For example, when Seth Stephens-Davidowitz, the economist who pioneered the method of using Google data to look for racism, used the same method to look for anti-Muslim Google searches across DMAs, he found that a high level of anti-Muslim searches in an area was an indicator of anti-Muslim hate crimes and, fitting a now familiar pattern, that such searches were most frequent in areas with a high Muslim population.[19]

It's worthwhile to pause before moving on and discuss this idea of comparing, as I have done, behavior in a place like Grants Pass to behavior in a place like Milwaukee or Chicago. I will use such thought experiments repeatedly in this book and I understand that a reader might be skeptical. After all, the white people in big cities like Chicago these days are politically liberal and racially tolerant. How can it be that these people, who seem comfortable with diversity, are searching for racist material on the Internet or holding such negative stereotypes about other groups? Of course, not everyone in a place like Chicago is doing this. Statements produced from the type of statistical analysis I use in this book are necessarily about an average, not universal descriptions. Some people in an area are racist and some are not. In these cities, then, even if the average resident is liberal, not every resident is.

It's also important to consider geography. While some of these large cities, such as Chicago and New York, are those in which you might stereotypically expect an embrace of diversity, others are not. Among the most segregated metropolitan areas in the United States are places like St. Louis, Youngstown, Ohio, and Muskegon, Michigan. These cities are also contributing to the national relationship between segregation and group-based bias. And, even in a place like Chicago or New York, the metropolitan area consists of much more than the diverse big city we might picture at first; for example, the Chicago metropolitan area, as it is commonly defined, covers eight counties, stretching far into suburban and rural Illinois.[20] We might have a very different image of the Chicago area if we focused on a white person in, say, Grundy County, Illinois, about 50 miles from Chicago, which is almost 94 percent Anglo white and voted for Donald Trump by a wide margin in 2016. A white person there – living in a local environment of strict segregation – may, as she thinks about politics, be influenced by the large, segregated group of

Black people closer to central Chicago. Finally, and perhaps most importantly, we also shouldn't assume that these liberal big-city dwellers are incapable of group-based bias. As I will show repeatedly in this book – in places such as Chicago and Boston – under the right conditions, they most certainly are.

Another area where we can see the power of social geography to shape interactions is voting in elections – the space where, in a diverse democracy, different social groups must come together to make decisions.

For example, I already briefly looked at the effect of social geography on willingness to vote for Obama, but because this is such an important claim and every approach to investigating it will be imperfect, I should examine it in more detail. As I noted above, there is a negative correlation on the county level between segregation and voting for Obama. The county is a good level at which to start, but using data that has only recently become available, I can examine the entire United States at an even more detailed level – the precinct, the basic voting administrative unit. On average, each precinct contains about 1,700 people. I looked at almost every precinct in the United States – 124,034 of them – to see if I could detect a relationship between the social geography of where the precinct is located and voting in that precinct.

I want to see, in particular, how white people reacted to the presence of a Black outgroup. However, these are aggregate data, rather than surveys, so I cannot directly observe for whom members of different racial groups voted. This means I had to rely on statistical techniques to create "ecological" estimates of the percent of white people in each precinct who voted for Obama. Looking at the relationship between white voting at the precinct level and social geography at the metropolitan-area level in 2008 yields the same striking pattern we have been seeing all along: as segregation and the size of the Black population increase, white voting for Obama decreases.[21]

I can also turn to individual-level survey data to see if the same relationship can be found. This gives me less data to work with, but allows me to see for certain if it is the white, rather than non-white, voters who are reacting to social geography and – if so – to see, among these white voters, who it is who is reacting. For example, is it all voters or just non-partisan voters? The results are more uncertain than using aggregate data, but the same pattern emerges: looking at individual white voters in 2008, when they were asked directly on a survey whom they voted for, I find that the more segregated their metropolitan area, the less likely they were to say they voted for Obama.[22] This finding controls for individual income and education and is, notably, limited to self-described "Independents," which makes sense because partisanship so powerfully determines vote choice in the United States that even social geography has little room for influence (but see Chapter 6).[23]

With these results, we can see the dramatic influence of social geography. For example, once again moving between the extremes of low and high segregation, a white voter in the least-segregated metropolitan area was 10 percentage points more likely to vote for Obama than a white voter in the most-segregated area.

This is a tremendous amount, almost a one-quarter reduction in the overall probability of whites voting for Obama in 2008.

I can take this further because social geography affects not only a person's decision to vote for one candidate or another, but whether that person votes at all. (In the next chapter, I will discuss why voter turnout can be considered a product of group-based bias.) The claim that groups sharing a particular space is related to voter turnout is classic in the political science literature, dating at least as far back as V. O. Key's research in the American South during the 1930s, which argued that white voters were motivated to vote by the presence of proximate Blacks.[24]

While Key's study and other studies had to be limited to certain geographic locations, new – and large – sources of data allow us to see this pattern nationwide. The new data is important because it allows me to avoid the social desirability problem that comes with asking people on a survey whether or not they voted. Many people are ashamed that they didn't vote, so, while we all know that many people don't vote, we also know that many people will lie about it.[25] Fortunately, voter turnout is one of the rare behaviors for which social scientists have an accurate official record. In almost every state, whether or not a person voted – but not for whom he or she voted – is kept on record, often open to the public, as a matter of law. In many states, these voter lists also include other information, such as the voter's address, age, gender, party affiliation, and even race and ethnicity. In the last decade or so, for-profit companies have used modern computing power and storage capabilities to collect and bundle together these records for the entire nation. In recent years, political scientists have also realized that such data would be useful so that we wouldn't have to rely on problematic survey or ecological data to figure out whether or not people voted.

I used this same "big data" to examine the effect of social geography on voter turnout. This means that when I examined voting, I included every person eligible to vote in the United States in 2012. The relationship I found should be predictable by now: looking at over 100 million Anglo white voters in 2012, their voter turnout increased the more segregated the area and the higher the proportion of its population that was Black. In fact, the same pattern can be seen in 2010, 2008, 2006, and 2004. And, as I've emphasized, this isn't just a story about whites reacting to Blacks because the inverse is also true: for the almost 30 million Black voters, we see the same pattern of more segregation meaning higher turnout between 2004 and 2012. The effects on voter turnout are strikingly large; for example, in 2012, moving from the least- to most-segregated area, turnout among Blacks increased by 16 percentage points. And for Latinos too – higher segregation and outgroup size also meant higher turnout during these years.[26]

A Brief Discussion of Causality

I have demonstrated that in the last decade, social geography affects group-based biases across a number of attitudes and behaviors. One of the contributions I hope to make in this book is to demonstrate that context has a causal effect on behavior, something which has largely eluded scholars.[27] I will discuss the challenges of identifying the causal effect of context in more detail in Chapter 4, but because I have presented a good deal of evidence already, it is worth a brief discussion here why I don't think these findings are spurious. That is, when it comes to voter turnout, for example, why do I consider it likely that it really is segregation that is causing voters to vote against Obama and not something else? Couldn't it be, for example, that political campaigns just work extra hard in segregated areas, perhaps because these are where elections are the closest?

Of course, campaign activity probably does contribute to the voting in segregated areas; for example, campaign targeting might be more efficient in these areas because campaigns can more easily guess whom they are targeting. That is okay. I am not making an absolutist argument that social geography is all that contributes to voting and other behaviors; obviously, many other things affect how people vote. But I do argue that social geography has an independent effect on voting and other behaviors. I have some confidence in this because I am able to see the relationship while controlling for a number of other variables and in some cases while comparing local environments within the same state. In this way, I don't have to worry that all the segregated places also happen to be in so-called battleground states where more intensive campaigning tends to change voter behavior. Even within a single state, I find that people in more-segregated places vote more than those in less-segregated places.

In studying segregation, some scholars have also used *instrumental variables* to tackle the problem of identifying its causal effect. Briefly, an instrumental variable is an independent variable that can only affect the outcome variable by first affecting the explanatory variable of interest. For reasons well explored in the econometric literature, this allows us to isolate the causal effect of the explanatory variable.[28] In my case, a valid instrument is a variable that can only affect voting (or the other outcomes I study) through its effect on segregation; it cannot affect voting directly. The economist Elizabeth Ananat discovered that the arrangement of railroad tracks in the nineteenth century could be an instrumental variable for segregation because railroad tracks physically subdivided a city, bounding neighborhoods and concentrating ethnic ghettos.[29] The more railroad tracks cut a metropolitan area into physically bounded areas in the nineteenth century, the more likely the city was to become racially segregated in the twentieth century during the Great Migration of Blacks out of the South. To see an instance of this, look at the map of the Black population of Boston in 1970 in Figure 5.5 on page 137. Notice that the Black population is strongly bounded on three sides by railroad lines. Because these tracks were laid long before the migration happened, railroad tracks are argued to be a valid instrument. A similar approach has been adopted by economists and political scientists in using waterways as an instrument.[30]

Indeed, I can use Ananat's instrumental variable technique for some of the analysis above and with this technique I can recover statistically significant estimates for the effect of segregation on voting for Obama.[31] However, this certainly does not close the case on causality. With these instruments, one might, for example, worry that railroad tracks will affect outcomes like intergroup attitudes by concentrating low-income workers in the same geographic area and thereby creating the type of economic competition that has been shown to be correlated with group animosity.[32] This raises concerns about violations of the *exclusion restriction* assumption that is necessary for a valid instrument.[33] Additionally, for my purposes, segregation is only one dimension of social geography and instruments for the other two dimensions – proximity and group size – are not available for this type of analysis. So even if we have found an instrument for this one dimension of space, we would still be left with questions about the causal effects of the other two.

More generally, there are inherent limits to the ability of such econometric techniques to solve problems of causal identification. A randomized controlled trial (RCT) is the only way to definitively establish the effects of social geography. That is why I conduct RCTs, both in the laboratory (Chapter 4) and in the "field" (Chapters 5 and 8). These RCT's shape my interpretation of the relationship between social geography and group bias: I will demonstrate that survey attitudes and voter behavior will change when social geography is assigned in an RCT, mirroring the results I've shown above, and making me more confident that the relationships I show here are evidence of the causal effect of social geography.

The Broad Power of Social Geography and the Liberal Dilemma

I have intentionally focused on recent social-geographic impact in the United States in order to show its ongoing and broad relevance to our behavior: the arrangement of groups in space – their size, proximity, and spatial segregation – is strongly correlated with group-based bias. But to stop here would mean that I have not conveyed the true impact of social geography. Many social scientists have written about social geography: economists, political scientists, psychologists, sociologists, and others have all, at different times, found that outgroup size, segregation, or proximity is correlated with group bias, although few, if any, of these researchers have recognized that these different effects may be part of the same phenomenon.[34]

Scholars have shown that local outgroup size is related to individual negative attitudes about groups and redistribution,[35] to vote choices,[36] to increases in political participation, including voter turnout,[37] and even to violence.[38] If you were to go to the endnotes and examine the 37 citations from the previous sentence, which is far from a complete treatment of this subject, several things might stand out. First, the scholarship on this topic examines many different social groups, extending far beyond the attitudes of white Americans toward

Blacks – Gay (2006), for example, looks at Black attitudes toward Latinos – and even beyond the divisions of race and ethnicity – for example, Balcells et al. (2015) study religious conflict, Green et al. (1998) study attitudes toward gays, and Charnysh (2015) studies anti-Semitism. And, of course, this phenomenon stretches across societies, from the United States to Northern Ireland, Poland, and elsewhere. Putnam (2007), in fact, argues that the phenomenon is universal. Second, it is remarkable to note the timespan of this scholarship. Just the studies I cite, which leaves a good deal off the table, collectively span almost 70 years. The time-period studied goes back even further, including evidence that violence toward Muslims and Jews in Medieval Europe was a function of the size of local populations.[39]

Other scholars have taken a slightly different approach than those I just covered and have noted that proximity between groups is related to group bias, including both non-violent[40] and violent conflict.[41] In Chapter 8, I will show that proximity between Latinos and Blacks affects ethnocentric voting.

The research I just discussed focused on the effect of group size and proximity on individuals.[42] But, of course, if enough individuals behave in a certain way, that can affect an entire society. If enough people have negative attitudes about other people, so that they are unlikely to trust or cooperate with each other, this might affect their country's overall economic, political, and social well-being. This is because many problems cannot be tackled – at least not effectively – without cooperation and trust. For example, if people cannot cooperate, how will they solve problems like building infrastructure or providing for common defense and welfare?

By looking across countries, we can see how social diversity – that is, having one or more large outgroup populations – affects how well countries function. Scholars who study the variation between countries have found that homogeneous countries function better than diverse ones. Diverse countries and diverse areas within countries are characterized by poor governance,[43] low economic development,[44] inefficient resource distribution,[45] a lack of democratic consensus,[46] and violent conflict.[47] In research which Noam Gidron and I conducted to capture the many ways that diverse countries function more poorly than homogeneous countries, we refer to all these negatives collectively as "socially inefficient outcomes."[48] It is easy to conclude from the list above that the quality of life is generally worse in diverse nations than in homogeneous ones. Indeed, this may match your intuition, because largely homogeneous countries, such as Sweden and Norway, have some of the highest quality of life by many indicators.

This also tells us that the impact of social geography on individual behavior is not a mere behavioral curiosity – it has dramatic consequences. Not only is it powerful enough to affect individuals, but it is important enough to help explain some (though certainly not all) of the remarkable differences between countries: rich versus poor, violent versus peaceful, stable versus unstable. There are, of course, difficulties with making causal claims, but the negative effects of diversity may be responsible for some of the profound differences between places such as Denmark and Zambia or Singapore and India. Noting that these four countries are all democracies,[49] we see the consequences of voters – normally separated by geographic, social, and psychological space – coming together to govern and having to make decisions and allocate resources. It appears that when people are faced with these decisions in a diverse democracy, rather than a homogeneous one, they often choose not to do the things that "make democracy work,"[50] failing to bridge the space between groups by cooperating to share resources and provide for the common welfare.

This reminds us why diversity is such a vexing problem. We are taught in liberal democracies to welcome it; indeed, it is often considered one of our strengths and liberal individuals usually favor diversity as a matter of ideology and public policy. We often support diversity out of a genuine ideological commitment and because we rightly perceive that diversity can improve the performance of many organizations, such as universities and businesses.[51] But looking across the world and even across states and cities within the United States, most of us would rather not live with some of the social, economic, and political consequences of diversity. Various scholars have referred to this tension between a commitment to diversity and the social ills associated with diversity as the *liberal dilemma*.

When faced with these unfortunate facts about diversity, an obvious impulse is toward segregation: if social efficiency diminishes when people must work across the boundaries of race, ethnicity, and religion, then why not avoid this problem by segregating groups? Of course, as we saw earlier in the chapter, this is not the solution because segregation affects individual behavior much as outgroup size does, causing negative attitudes, lack of trust, and an inability to cooperate. Similar patterns can be found elsewhere in the academic literature: segregation is correlated with negative attitudes toward the outgroup[52] and with ethnocentric voting.[53] And these individual behaviors, when added up, can be very consequential, leading to systemwide socially inefficient outcomes. On an aggregate level, we see that segregation is correlated with low-capacity states and civil societies,[54] bad economies,[55] and violent conflict.[56]

WHY DOES SOCIAL GEOGRAPHY HAVE THESE EFFECTS?

Why does social geography have these effects on behavior and attitudes? How can geography shape so many behaviors, across very different times and places, even as technology works to make distance and space irrelevant? The next chapter will take this matter up in detail as I explore the human mind – but, before getting there, it is important to square my findings with the literature on the topic and ask how what I found fits with what we already know.

Reflecting on my original findings and those from the literature I have reported connecting social geography to group-based bias, it should become clear why one of my goals in this book is to specify the mechanism; that is, to understand exactly why these statistical relationships exist. After all, these relationships between social geography and group-based bias seem widespread and robust – they are found across broad ranges of time and place and are powerfully related to a wide range of behaviors. I have also noted that these findings point to a dilemma because diverse societies, something many of us believe are valuable and maybe inevitable, given current population trends, are associated with social inefficiencies arising from group-based bias. But even if we are willing to set diversity aside in the name of improved social efficiency, we have seen that eliminating diversity through segregation increases group-based bias and would lead to the same inefficiency.

So, we want to understand why geography has this effect, not only for scientific value, but because it may inform us about this liberal dilemma. Why would both outgroup size and segregation affect group bias? In thinking about this question, you may have already noted apparent contradictions in these statistical patterns: How can outgroup size and outgroup segregation both be positively correlated with group bias? Furthermore, how can proximity and segregation both be positively correlated with group bias? It seems as if I am saying that having an outgroup close by causes bias but having it far away also causes bias.

In considering this apparent contradiction, it is important, of course to be clear on the differences between these dimensions of space. Look back at Figure 1.6 on page 26 and consider the differences in the social geographies. Not all diverse places are segregated and in this chapter, I've shown that whether a place is segregated will dramatically impact group-based bias.[57] Nevertheless, the scholarly literature and popular discussion of context usually focuses on size, but ignores segregation and proximity. Intuitively, it seems obvious that all these dimensions are important: an outgroup can be big or small, but this has little meaning except in the context of a particular spatial arrangement. If the outgroup is big, but far away, it might not matter at all. If it is big and integrated, that is a much different situation than if it is big and segregated.

Why, then, despite our intuition telling us otherwise, do scholars often ignore the actual spatial relationship of groups when trying to understand how context affects group bias? A primary reason might be that when social scientists consider a mechanism – that is, when they try to explain why context is related to group bias – they are almost always influenced by *Contact Theory*.

Contact Theory and Social Geography

Contact Theory, despite its tremendous influence, is also tremendously misunderstood. When it is properly understood, we can see that it is actually consistent with what I have shown in this chapter. The common caricature of the theory is that as groups of people share a location – say, a neighborhood or a city – so that there is interpersonal contact across groups, prejudice will be reduced. In this caricature, as the size of a local outgroup grows, all else equal, interpersonal contact will increase across groups, so bias should diminish. Conversely, as segregation increases, interpersonal contact decreases and bias increases.

Allport, the psychologist often credited with Contact Theory, was a giant of twentieth-century social science. In *The Nature of Prejudice*, Allport explored the nuances of the relationship between geographic context, human contact, the human mind, and prejudice. His shadow still looms over the field of intergroup relations and I often think that, compared to what he taught us, we have learned relatively little about prejudice since his contributions over 60 years ago. Indeed, many of the statistical relationships I described in this chapter were predicted by Allport.

For political scientists, Allport's argument is often paired with that of Key, another giant of mid-century social science. Key, in a sweeping argument about conservative politics in the American South, argued that racism flourished where cotton cultivation had concentrated large numbers of Blacks. Key and Allport are often treated as being on opposite sides of a debate about what happens when groups share the same place, with Key predicting that local outgroups increase prejudice and Allport predicting that local outgroups reduce prejudice. Put another way, we have Key expecting contact to promote conflict (or racial threat, as it was subsequently called) and Allport expecting it to promote harmony.

Like Key, Allport reviewed mountains of evidence, much of it secondary, and examined patterns of contact between whites and Blacks in residential, occupational, and other settings, which was increasing in northern cities after World War II. Allport described a nuanced relationship between prejudice and groups of people living in the same place. His argument was actually the opposite of the common caricature of "contact" that I described above. Allport asserted that under certain conditions, including economic equality and social integration, residential contact would reduce intergroup prejudice. But he also made a very clear argument about what to expect in the absence of these necessary conditions. When writing about white Christian Americans living in cities with large numbers of Blacks and Jews, he said, "such evidence as we have clearly indicates that such contact does not dispel prejudice; it seems more likely to increase it."[58] Thus, Allport's argument about the relationship between group size and group-based bias is the opposite of that which is usually attributed to him:

Only about 1,000 Hindus live in the United States, but about 13,000,000 Negroes. The former group is overlooked...But were the number of Hindus to rise into the tens of hundreds of thousands there is no doubt that a definite and articulate anti-Hindu prejudice would arise.[59]

He then goes on to speculate that if this conjecture is correct, "we should find evidence that anti-Negro feeling is most intense where Negro density is greatest."[60]

When we see what Allport actually said, we can see that, despite the treatment in the literature, the arguments of Key and Allport are actually broadly aligned. In fact, Allport even supports his argument about contact by citing evidence very close to Key's; namely, that in 1948, white voters in South Carolina were more likely to support the segregationist Strom Thurmond where the "Negro population was densest."[61]

However, somewhere along the line, Allport's actual argument was largely lost to many scholars and many social scientists now cite him to support arguments exactly the opposite of those that he once made. Putnam for example, in his tremendously influential article on diversity and social capital, writes that "the 'contact hypothesis,' argues that diversity fosters interethnic tolerance."[62] Other well-cited political science research has made similar arguments, and many scholars use an empirical approach that looks at the correlation between diversity and group bias in a local area and claim to be testing Allport's argument that certain types of contact reduce prejudice when, in fact, Allport predicted the exact opposite relationship between diversity and prejudice.

When we consider Allport's argument in its proper breadth – that inter-personal contact diminishes group-based bias but that, in the absence of interpersonal contact, the presence of an outgroup increases group-based bias – we can more easily reconcile the seeming contradiction that a large, proximate, and segregated group can cause greater group-based bias. In part, it is simply because, with segregation, there is a large, nearby group but little or no interpersonal contact between oneself and members of that group. But, while segregation and a lack of contact may be observationally equivalent in much scholarship, they are not the same thing. Context, as I mentioned in the opening of this book, is not just a container in which behaviors, such as contact, occur. Rather social geography can influence behavior directly. As I will explore later, they affect behavior through different psychological mechanisms and, as such, policies that increase contact, while leaving segregation in place, may be ineffective in reducing prejudice.

Contact and the Curvilinear Nature of Outgroup Size

None of this is to say that contact cannot have any positive effects, even outside of ideal conditions. In the findings I have presented we can already see the likely effects of contact on behavior and how it competes with social geography for influence. If you look at the details of the original analysis that I have presented in this chapter, you will see a common pattern. The relationship between the proportion of an outgroup in an area and group-based bias is curvilinear (you can see this too in Figure 2.1 on page 38): it becomes greater as outgroup proportion increases until reaching a tipping point and then starting to decrease.[63] This means that when a group makes up a large portion of a place – for concreteness, say 40 percent – each additional person above 40 percent actually *decreases* group-based bias.

If interpersonal contact ameliorates the effects of social geography, then when a group becomes large enough and interpersonal contact becomes frequent enough, group-based bias should decrease. But up until a certain point, increasing group size is still associated with *increasing* group-based bias – indicating that some other force other than contact is contributing to this bias. This, I argue, is the influence of social geography on how we perceive groups. These competing forces may be why previous scholars have also noted the curvilinear relationship between group-size and group-based bias[64] and in later chapters we will see a similar pattern.[65]

But, of course, there is another explanation of this curvilinear relationship and this explanation demonstrates the difficulty in measuring the effect of interpersonal contact on bias. We can guess that people who are willing to remain in an area when the outgroup proportion is large – who do not select to move away – are different from those who will choose to leave rather than be a minority. Those who stay may simply be more positive about the outgroup and less prone to group-based bias. As I will therefore emphasize repeatedly in this book, understanding the influences of outgroup size on group-based bias is difficult – it represents a *selection problem*. It could be that a very large outgroup diminishes group-based bias because of increased contact, but it could also be that people who don't like the outgroup select away. The only way to understand the influence of interpersonal contact then is to somehow isolate it, to measure its effects while holding everything else constant. Some of the research in this book will attempt to do this.

And, of course, outgroup size and contact are also not the same thing. Group size, like segregation, separate from contact and even holding selection constant, will have an independent influence on behavior. We can now turn to understanding why.

3

The Demagogue's Mechanism: Groups, Space, and the Mind

> These cognitive underpinnings of prejudice do not depend on individual differences, for everyone must categorize, in order to function. "Orderly living depends on it" (Allport, 1954). Categorization thus must vary, if it varies, according to context.
>
> – Susan Fiske[1]

Why does social geography affect our behavior? Why can it lead to group-based bias? Why is it so powerful that it can overcome the forces of the modern world that work to close the spaces between us?

In this chapter, I will answer these questions. It is the centrality of both groups and space in the mind that helps to explain why group-based biases – taking forms as disparate as voter turnout and violent conflict – are affected by social geography. Groups are a central part of the way our minds organize the world. Space is, too. Within our minds, space acts as a demagogue, shaping our mental images of groups.

Not long ago, I boarded a flight from Boston to Washington, DC. Across the aisle was a light-skinned Arab woman in a hijab, the Muslim headscarf, and her Black Muslim husband. Despite all my best intentions as a liberal – one married to a Muslim woman, no less – that simple blue scarf turned my mind to every negative stereotype about the danger of Muslims on planes.

When our own prejudices are laid bare, we realize how easily negative stereotypes can be brought to the surface. This is an awful, awful way to react to somebody. I have in-laws who detest flying because they are aware of the prejudices their fellow travelers have about them.

Near the end of the short flight, I looked over and saw the woman unwrapping her headscarf and thought to myself, "She must not be very religious if she will adjust her scarf in public." But rather, it turned out, as far as I know, that she wasn't Muslim or Arab at all. She was just a non-Muslim woman with a scarf around her head, tucked in a certain way that made it look like a hijab. This event stuck in my memory because it was remarkable to feel the accessibility of my stereotypes change so quickly, away from those associated with a Muslim woman and toward those associated with a non-Muslim, "American" woman married to a Black man.[2]

Psychologists tell us that the salience of social categories is a function of accessibility and fit.[3] For me, a headscarf made that woman *fit* the category of a Muslim, which had perhaps been made more *accessible* by her proximity to me and by the context of being on a plane. In a nutshell, social geography is that headscarf. The accessibility of a category is increased by the size and proximity of someone who is – or seems to be – in that category; a person's fit for a category is increased by segregation. That is, a category becomes prominent to you when members of that category are numerous and close and a person becomes a better fit for a category if they cluster around other people from that category.

Why, though, do our minds work this way? Why does geographic space have this effect on the way we see groups? And why does the way we see groups affect our behaviors, such as voting? To understand the influence of this demagogue, I will focus on unpacking two phenomena that are foundations of social-geographic impact:

1. Attitudes and behavior, including group-based biases, are affected by variation in how social groups are represented in our minds.
2. Social geography affects two interrelated variables that help to determine how a social group is represented in our minds: its *accessibility* and its *comparative fit*. Increases in these two variables lead to what is called the increased *salience* of a category and, thus, to increased group-based bias.

The representation of groups in our minds is well understood in the study of cognitive psychology – it is the shaping of this representation by social geography that allows for social geographic impact. After unpacking these mechanisms, I will discuss their implications for the study of context.

To understand this connection between groups, space, and behavior, we have to understand some basic features of human psychology and how it is shaped. Before describing the nature of the variation in the way social groups are represented in our minds and how geography contributes to that variation, I will briefly review three important pieces of background from evolutionary and cognitive psychology.

Categorization, Natural Selection, and Heuristics

The association of attributes with objects through categorization is a basic cognitive process that aids survival. I will eventually talk about categorizing people, but to understand why categorization is important for survival, let's step back and consider categorization more generally. Categorization is how we understand the world. In the language of cognitive psychology, our minds are organized into schema – the networks of associations that come with each category. These schema are how we know what attributes go with an object. So we understand that certain objects – say, elongated yellow objects and heart-shaped red objects – are categorized as bananas and apples, respectively, and that these can both be categorized as fruit. Because we can attach attributes to the schema *fruit*, we understand that these objects – bananas and apples – are likely to be edible and sweet. The association of attributes with objects allows for important distinctions and gives us information about what to do with any particular object: a banana is edible but a piece of metal is not. A knife is sharp and dangerous, but a spoon is not. Without the ability to make these attributions to objects effortlessly and without deliberate thinking, we probably could not survive. We'd either spend all our time trying to figure out whether or not to eat metal or we would make a mistake and eat the metal. You'd find some way to kill yourself before you ever made it out of the house. Because categorization confers such a survival advantage, it is probably a psychological trait on which our ancestors were selected.

Natural selection is the fundamental building block of evolution and is the primary reason that any trait – limbs, gait, cognition, vision, and everything else – can be found in any organism. The foundation of natural selection is simple: (1) individuals vary in ways that are heritable, meaning that offspring will share traits with their parents; (2) not all individuals are equally likely to reproduce; and (3) individuals with certain traits are more likely to reproduce and thus pass those traits to their offspring. In this way, over generations, certain traits that make individuals more likely to reproduce are selected for and spread in a population, while other traits disappear from that population.

When considering natural selection, we often think about physiological traits, such as bipedal locomotion or the opposable thumb, and we are less used to thinking about psychological traits, such as the tendency to categorize. But psychological traits are, of course, important for reproductive success and therefore they, too, will evolve by selective pressures. The ability to make good, quick decisions – for example, deciding when to take flight or when to fight and recognizing dangers or recognizing friends – could certainly have made a person more likely to survive and reproduce in the evolutionary past. Such decisions are aided by a process of categorization; categorizing objects as friend or foe, or as safe or dangerous, or as edible or inedible has obvious advantages. Human ancestors who were better at categorizing were probably also more likely to reproduce and therefore, over the long arc of evolutionary time, the ability to categorize became more and more refined. Now categorization is an effortless part of our cognition; we do it all day, rarely give it a thought, and couldn't do much of anything without it.

We can characterize categorization, whereby we associate attributes with objects automatically by category membership, rather than stopping and consciously thinking about it, as a heuristic or "information shortcut." We use heuristics because our minds have limited processing power.

A struggle for survival with finite mental processing power is one of the core pressures that shaped human psychological architecture. The human mind, through our sensory organs, must take in a functionally infinite amount of information and process it for the purposes of making both conscious and unconscious decisions. To appreciate how much information confronts one's mind moment to moment, consider a computer file that stores information – something like an .AVI or .MP4 containing visual and auditory information. Your personal computer would slow down drastically or freeze if it tried to play thousands of such files at the same time. Now, consider how many sights and sounds enter your sensory organs just walking down a city street. A single moment of this flood of input through your sensory organs is more bytes of information than thousands of .MP4 files; it would overwhelm any machine. Our minds have immense information-processing power, yet this input would overwhelm them, too, if we had not adopted simple rules or shortcuts to efficiently process and react to this information. Because of the limitations on our processing power, much of our cognition consists of adaptive traits designed to make decisions quickly and conserve processing power or to ration processing to concentrate on what is immediately important – heuristics are one of these adaptive traits.

Will we make mistakes using heuristics? Of course. But given that our minds have limited processing power, we can appreciate how these heuristics were an advantage to our ancestors and are still necessary today. From crossing the street, to choosing what to eat, to doing just about anything else, heuristics allow us to overcome our limited processing power. We use one of these heuristics, categorization, to make our decisions quickly by knowing what attributes – color, danger, sweetness, and so on – are associated with the objects – people, animals, plants, vehicles, and everything else – that we encounter as we go about our business.

Categorizing People

When we encounter people, whether in person or indirectly through media, attributes such as trustworthiness, peacefulness, or excitability come effortlessly to mind as a function of the categories into which we mentally place these people. We do this by immediately placing people in social groups. Are members of that group intelligent? Dangerous? Friendly? In the distant evolutionary past, this would perhaps have informed us about what action we should take. Was cooperation likely? Or fighting? Or mating? We may be, and often are, wrong about these attribute associations, but even if individuals often turn out not to behave as our categorization of them led us to expect, we still apply those categories.

In Chicago, as soon as I stepped onto the train, I began grouping people into categories: Black, white, professional, working class, and so on. The other passengers were surely doing the same thing. Today, whenever I walk through the diverse throngs of Harvard Yard, I categorize the people I see as students, custodial workers, foreign tourists, and so on. When I am categorizing, I am also stereotyping. You may be a bit surprised that I will so readily admit to stereotyping because it is a term that, for good reason, has an overwhelmingly negative connotation. But you do it too – constantly and effortlessly. We all stereotype because it is just another way of describing the mental process I have laid out above: the attachment of attributes to objects in a category. An orange is fruit, so it is sweet. A knife is sharp, so it is dangerous. A person is part of an enemy group, so she is dangerous. A person is part of a friendly group, so she might help me.[4] Often, of course, the stereotypes we attach to a category – for example, the tendency of white Americans to attach undeservedness to Blacks[5] – are constructed by elites in politics and the media[6] and, especially when we lack interpersonal interaction with members of a social group, these are the stereotypes we draw from our mental wells.

Stereotypes, like other functions of our mind, are there for a reason. We use them as heuristics for making efficient decisions. I think stereotypes may be described as one of the great contradictions of humanity because to individuals, stereotypes are incredibly useful – indispensable, in fact – but from the perspective of society as a whole, they are associated with many evils, such as the group-based biases covered in this book. Social science is full of such contradictions. The central focus of political science, in particular, is the study of individuals making collective decisions. What makes these decisions interesting and particularly worthy of study is that often what is best for the individual is at odds with what is best for society. There are abundant examples of such "tragedy of the commons,"[7] but what can make the contradiction between the individual and social benefit of stereotypes seem particularly tragic is that stereotypes are a central feature of our cognition – built into the core architecture of our minds because we can't survive without them. Our psychology operates in such a way that in dealing with other humans, we inevitably use stereotypes, yet they are associated with tremendous social problems. And social geography – the subject of this book – shapes these stereotypes and makes them accessible by changing the way groups are represented in our minds.

Variation in the Salience of Categories

What category we apply when encountering a particular person, and thus what attributes and stereotypes we apply to that person, can vary. This variation can be quite important to our subsequent behavior and attitudes.

Choosing – almost always unconsciously – one category over another has profound consequences for how we view another person. From the perspective

FIGURE 3.1. Female.

of the perceiver encountering another person, think of that person – before he or she is categorized – as a blank slate. For example, look at the person in Figure 3.1 and imagine meeting her for the first time. What attributes do you associate with her face? Is she similar to you? Different? Now, look at Figure 3.2 on page 58. Here I have applied an additional category to her, but changed nothing else. You might not be able to help associating different attributes with her. Depending on who you are, she became more or less similar to you, because of the category label I applied. But imagine I had applied a different label, as in Figure 3.3 on page 60. Is she more or less similar to you now that the category is different?[8]

The category we choose at any given moment is called the *salient* category. (With the photos in Figures 3.1, 3.2 and 3.3, I chose the category for you – that is, I made it salient to you – by applying a label.) When seeing a person – like the first, unlabeled face – a "low-level" category, such as the person's name, may be salient. When we apply a group-based label, a "high-level" category – a social group – is salient. This salience of a group identity over an individual identity is consequential. As we will see below, not only does the application of a certain category – woman, Black, and so on – affect the attributes we apply to a person, it affects the very way we perceive and behave toward that person.

A category's salience is influenced by its accessibility and its comparative fit. These determinants of salience are found in the influential social psychology approach known as Self-Categorization Theory, which was developed to understand what causes people to see a collection of individuals – possibly including oneself – as a group rather than as a collection of individuals.[9] Accessibility – how easily something comes to mind – is the availability of a category in an individual's mind based on her particular characteristics and present context; that is, if I have multiple categories available to me, as in Figure 3.2, which one more easily comes to mind for me?

The accessibility of categories will vary across individuals. If, for example, I had been taught as a child that race was very important in judging an individual, then racial categories might be accessible to me when I see people. And, of course, the accessibility of categories will vary, not just across individuals, but across time and place. Categories that once seemed very important in parts of the Western world, such as Christian denominations, no longer have such relevance.[10] Because of this, for people like me living in a, now, largely secular New England, Christian denominational categories are inaccessible. When I see people, I rarely feel inclined to label them with a religion. But this can vary: put somebody in a church and religious identity suddenly becomes quite important. If one social category is constantly privileged over others – that is, more likely to be chosen – it is said to be *chronically accessible*. Chronic accessibility can result from social context increasing the importance of a category. In New England, during its Puritan days for example, when religion was infused into everyday life, religion was likely often a salient category. Also, the fraught history of race in the United States means that, even today, racial categories are often privileged over other identities. Accessibility thus varies across individuals, depending on their personal characteristics, and across context, depending on the cultural, social, historical, and – I argue – social-geographic nature of that context.

A category's comparative fit (or just *fit*) is also important for its salience. Psychologists say fit is a function of the "meta-contrast principle," meaning that our minds become more likely to apply a label the larger the perceived ratio of the difference between groups to the difference within groups.[11]

Imagine coming across a group of four white women with nobody else around. Given that there is no contrast here between women and men, you might not categorize them primarily as women; rather, you might categorize them by lower-level personal characteristics such as their age or even their names. This is because, if there are no men present, the within-group difference (the difference between one of those women and another) is much higher than the between-group difference, which is zero at that point because there is no one there who isn't a woman. On the other hand, if the group included, say, two white men, then the contrast provided would cause you to categorize the women not as young or old but as women, because the between-group difference – between women and men – would be much higher than the within-group difference between one woman and another. If, however, two Black women, rather than two white men, were inserted into the group, then you might categorize by race because the between-group difference between Blacks and whites might seem higher than the within-group difference for one Black woman to another Black woman or one white woman to another white woman. If both Black women and white men were inserted into the original group of white women, it is less clear whether there is more contrast between gender or race, so which category became salient would probably be a function of the accessibility of those categories at that moment.

Another way to think about comparative fit is the degree to which the group is cohesive; in other words, when I see this group, do I think of it as a collection of individuals or as a group? Do they have an attribute that signals

FIGURE 3.2. African American female.

they belong together rather than with another group?[12] This is the *groupishness* of a group. Your immediate nuclear family, for example, is more cohesive than your extended family of aunts and uncles, cousins and second cousins, and so on.

It's easy to think of ways to boost cohesion: uniforms, for example, are a common method. Walking around some cities on a weekday, you often encounter groups of schoolchildren out to visit playgrounds. You might loosely categorize them as students and might recognize individuality within the group. But if the children were all wearing uniforms, you would almost surely consider them a more cohesive unit – more of a group – and the individuals would fade into the background.[13] A consequence of this increased cohesiveness is that, as a non-student, the difference between you and the students is actually more apparent, the boundary between groups is more defined. You are not a student, you are not wearing a uniform, you are a grown-up, a worker. What we will see below is that space, like uniforms, also affects the comparative fit of groups, thus affecting how we see the boundaries between ingroups and outgroups.

Accessibility and comparative fit work in tandem – in statistical terms, interactively – so that for a category to be applied, it must have both fit and accessibility. In other words, each is a necessary condition.[14] Using the example above, when Black women enter the group of white women, then the comparative fit of the category "white" may increase, but this only affects that category's salience if racial categories are accessible – that is, something readily available in your mind to use. If it seems obvious that race will be accessible to you – as may be the case if you live in the United States – think of the group of women including Protestants and Catholics, rather than Blacks and whites. While these religious categories are hugely important to some, they may be completely inaccessible to you in this situation and you would not apply them and the women will not be labeled as Protestants or Catholics.

Category Salience and Group-based Bias

I have gone into detail about how and why we categorize people because categorization is profoundly consequential for our behavior. It affects what we think of other people and how we behave toward them;[15] it affects our interactions when groups come together.

I already noted that because categories are associated with attributes, when a category is applied to a person, certain attributes – often culturally based stereotypes – will be applied to him or her. Different levels of categories, low-level ("Gordon") and high-level ("man"), can also be called levels of construal. We attach stereotypes to these higher levels of construal because they are culturally available – there are stereotypes about men, but not about Gordons. Psychologists also tell us that we apply these stereotypes more readily to high-level categories, such as man or Black, because higher levels of construal are presented as abstractions in our minds, rather than the concrete representations of low-level construal.[16]

So, for example, in the United States, when a person is labeled as the high-level category Black, the attribute of "lazy" will often be applied.[17] This in itself is group-based bias. But even apart from such negative stereotypes, increasing the salience of a category increases group-based bias in other ways.

In addition to making attributes accessible, a key consequence of this variation in the salience of categories is that it affects our perceptions of individuals within those categories. When the salience of a category increases, members within the same groups are perceived to be more similar to each other and to share attributes,[18] while members of different groups are perceived to be more different from each other. This process of psychologically collapsing the differences within a group and expanding the differences between groups is known as *accentuation*[19] and, in the terminology of this book, is increasing the psychological distance between groups. (For an illustration, look back at Figure 1.3 on page 14.)

We may do this because our limited ability to process information – our need for shortcuts – means that we use group membership as a heuristic for the similarity within a group: when we associate a person with a category, we use a shortcut and assume they are more similar to others who share the category than to those outside the category. Rich people become more like other rich people and poor people more like other poor people. Because members of each group become more similar to each other – in psychological terminology, more like a "prototype" – the perceived differences between groups grow. Every rich person becomes the top-hatted tycoon in the Monopoly logo and every poor person becomes a hobo. The difference between hobos becomes small, but the difference between – the space between – Mr. Monopoly and a hobo is great.

One of the first demonstrations of how the application of categories makes members within a group more similar and the differences between groups larger

FIGURE 3.3. Caucasian female.

was made by Henri Tajfel.[20] He designed a simple yet elegant experiment in which he showed subjects lines on a page and asked them to estimate the lengths of the lines. In one experimental condition, he put letters, like "A" and "B," next to the lines. This was a process of categorization – saying this line is part of the "A" category or "B" category. By applying a label, Tajfel had artificially created categories and made them salient. In the other condition, the lines were unlabeled and, therefore, uncategorized. Tajfel found that his subjects were more likely to estimate that the lines in one category, like the A's, were more similar in length to each other than to lines in different categories, like B's, with this simple categorization than without it. People sometimes use the term "labeling" when talking about categorizing people; for example, "you labeled him a trouble-maker." Tajfel showed how appropriate the term "labeling" is when describing categorization because when he literally labeled objects, he showed that it led to categorization and that this categorization affected people's perceptions of the objects.

Variation in the salience of categories not only changes perceptions of difference within and between groups, but also leads to group-based biases.[21] This relationship between category salience and group biases is a key to understanding why social geography is so important to our behavior. As far as I can tell, the assertion that category salience leads to bias is undisputed in psychological research.[22] Negative attitudes and behaviors are more likely to be directed toward a person categorized as a member of an outgroup than toward a member of the ingroup. The more salient the difference in group membership, the more intense the biases.[23]

The most powerful demonstration of this phenomenon is the behavior that results when categories are created out of thin air. Categories were created out of thin air in the experiment, just described, when lines were labeled with "A" and "B." In that case, the salience of a category membership increased with the labeling because, given that the category didn't previously exist, its accessibility and fit were both zero. When categories are created out of thin air and applied to people, we can plainly see the power of these categories to cause group-based bias.

Would you believe that simply telling a person that "you belong to category A" and some other person belongs to category B is enough to induce bias? This was demonstrated in the famous "minimal groups" paradigm, also introduced by Tajfel. The basic framework of this type of experiment, now a workhorse of social psychology research,[24] is that subjects are assigned to a meaningless group at random, say the "A" group and the "B" group or the "Red" group and the "Blue" group. The subjects are then given an opportunity to do something like allocate money between the groups or, using a survey, to assign characteristics to members of the groups. Inevitably, even though the accessibility and comparative fit of these categories was zero just minutes earlier, subjects' decisions will now be biased in favor of their ingroup.[25] This bias can include assigning negative attributes to the outgroup, such as calling them "stupid,"[26] or giving more money to members of one's ingroup than to members of the outgroup.[27]

What's more, in these minimal group situations, subjects not only show bias toward the ingroup but actually try to maximize the difference between the groups; that is, to make the groups as distinct as possible. Tajfel showed this in his original experiments.[28] Say you are given two options for allocating money between the ingroup and outgroup:

- Option A: $8 for the ingroup and $6 for the outgroup
- Option B: $6 for the ingroup and $1 for the outgroup

In experiments, most people choose Option B; that is, they are willing to accept less for their own ingroup – and less altogether for both groups – if it means that the difference between the ingroup and the outgroup is maximized. Psychologists and behavioral economists would say that people gain *utility* from their ingroup being relatively better off than the outgroup. This demonstrates the powerful tendency of categorization to increase perceptions of difference between groups: we are *motivated* to maximize the differences between our own group and the other group and in a way that makes *us* better off than *them*.

This motivation to maximize differences between groups has consequences for how we assign attributes that are clearly good or bad – what social scientists call *valence attributes* – such as intelligence, appearance, and work ethic. Everybody would rather be smart than stupid, good-looking rather than unattractive, and hard working rather than lazy. If you are motivated to increase the difference between groups, your group will always become smart and the other group stupid, your group attractive and other group ugly, your group hard working and the other group lazy.[29] Thus, as could be seen in the survey evidence I introduced in the last chapter, people assign negative valence attributes more readily to the outgroup than the ingroup.

The random assignment of category membership can change behavior in other laboratory settings that are less fleeting. In Muzafer Sherif's famous "Robbers Cave" experiments, in which schoolboys were experimentally assigned to groups at a summer camp, behavior between the "Eagles" and "Rattlers" (names they chose for themselves) quickly descended into competition and derogation, going so far as the Eagles burning the Rattlers' flag and the Rattlers ransacking the Eagles' cabin.[30] Philip Zimbardo's "Stanford Prison Experiment," while remembered more for what it taught us about authority, also showed how the simple assignment of category membership could dramatically change behavior.[31]

These demonstrations show us that the mere act of categorization changes our behavior, even when those categories are ephemeral. Consider then, how significantly categories can shape our behavior when, rather than being arbitrary and inherently meaningless, they are based on something more socially meaningful, such as race or religion. Studies have shown that bias can be induced by changing the salience of these meaningful, real-world groups. For example, among university students, priming the outgroup identity of a rival university actually makes students think that students from the outgroup smell worse than the ingroup.[32] And, with a more consequential behavior, raising the salience of competing professional soccer teams makes fans of one team less likely to lend aid to an injured fan of the other team.[33] Moving to more consequential identities than soccer team affiliation, it has been found that reminding white Americans about African Americans – that is, simply using a word that reminds them about African Americans – increases their use of negative racial stereotypes[34] and that reminding Israeli Jews that they are Jewish increases their willingness to discriminate against Palestinians.[35]

These are examples of researchers artificially increasing the salience of an identity in a laboratory, but events that change the salience of identities can change behavior in real life, too. For many of us, with some reflection, we can see examples in our attitudes and behavior when certain identities are made salient. How do you feel about a rival sports team or its fans when a big game approaches? During an election, do you eagerly consume news that diminishes the character, wisdom, or intelligence of voters for the other party?

We can see a very consequential example of this phenomenon on a mass scale in how Obama's presidency changed attitudes among some white voters by priming the salience of racial identity. The idea is that Obama's election made racial identity so salient for white Americans that their policy attitudes were changed to come into line with their racial attitudes. The presidency being such a prominent position and the event of a Black man holding that position being unprecedented, Obama's presidency has been a nearly constant reminder for Americans about race. Every time white Americans open the newspaper or turn on the television, they are primed with the Black outgroup, making race chronically accessible when thinking about policy and politics. Michael Tesler showed that this caused many people, based on their racial attitudes, to change their policy positions to oppose Obama on issues from healthcare to their preferences for certain types of dog.[36]

SPACE IN THE HUMAN MIND

Space, like social groups, is central to the way we think about the world and, for the purposes of this book, it is important because it fundamentally shapes the way we see groups. In short, in our categorizing minds, space acts as the demagogue. It increases the salience of a group – reminding you of the presence of that group, reminding you of the negative things associated with that group, and telling you that members of that group are all the same – all contributing to changing your behavior.

One day, I was playing pickup basketball outdoors in Lincoln Park, in Chicago. The park being on the North Side, the players were mostly white. Another player's pregnant girlfriend or wife was watching. At some point, a group of African American children, maybe four or five of them – none more than eight years old – gathered around this woman and shyly asked her questions, as children do, presumably about her pregnancy. When there was a stop in the play, her husband or boyfriend turned to these children and told them to stay away from her. I witnessed enough racism in my time in Chicago to write a book just about that, but this incident stuck in my memory, perhaps because of its absurdity. What did he think these little kids might do to her? As a scholar, as I've learned more about groups and space, this event has come to make more sense to me – not as a justifiable thing to do, but as behavior with roots I can understand. Surely this man would have taken less notice if a single six-year-old had approached his partner, but here was a group, tightly clustered around her. This group was, of course, still completely harmless, but – perhaps subconsciously – it became, by virtue of being a group, something different than just some children. Its accessibility and comparative fit increased, it conjured up the stereotypes of Black people as dangerous and aggressive and thus became something more than the sum of its young and harmless parts. This was the psychological impact of social geography at work: a group had become more salient because of its size and proximity. This is the same important, long-lasting, and very consequential phenomenon we see across our cities.

In the era of GPS and maps available with a few keystrokes, we may lose sight of how important space is to the way we think about the world. Not only, as I will describe below, is our spatial memory – that is knowing where things can be found – used continuously and effortlessly as we go about our daily lives, but spatial metaphors infuse our language so that non-spatial relationships are structured using the same spatial logic: friends and allies are judged as "close" or not; political ideologies are aligned "left" to "right;" our feelings and attentions can be "distant."[37] In this book, I describe a relationship between geographic space and certain non-geographic spaces: psychological, social, and political. My metaphorical description of social relationships in terms of distance – near or far – probably sounds perfectly natural to you because we so effortlessly use space to structure our thoughts.

Evolutionary psychologists tell us that the ability to associate objects with the attribute of geographic space – that is, to remember what can be found where – was fundamental to the evolution of the human mind. This makes sense. For a human ancestor in a struggle for survival, the ability to know what is found in certain places would be crucial: water can be found in this location, food can be found in this location, but this location has dangerous enemies. The ability to remember such places would have been selected for, so that those individuals with more advanced spatial cognition would be likely to pass this ability on to future generations.[38] Although humans never developed the advanced navigational sense of some animals, like certain types of birds, our ability to navigate space is nevertheless an impressive trait. In fact, this ability is so central to our minds that we have specialized brain cells – *place cells*, as they are sometimes called – for navigation.[39]

For humans today, this means that space – where things are located – deeply shapes what we think about those things. In the language of cognitive psychology, the geographic location of an object is a salient attribute for evaluating and categorizing an object. Which is to say, when we want to make a judgment about what something is – friend or foe, clean or dirty, safe or dangerous – and what we should do once we know the answer, our mind uses space to make these judgments. Put another way, *we use space as a heuristic.*

An extreme example of the way in which space is tied to our mental representations of objects can be found in "memory champions." These are people who compete to see who can best remember incredibly long lists (for example, digits of π). Their method for remembering such things is to imagine each element of the list to be in a different spatial location in a structure such as a large house – a "memory palace." When recalling the digits, they imagine themselves walking from room to room in the palace, each room containing a digit.[40] So, they are using the attribute of space – as opposed to associating each digit with some other attribute, such as a color – to structure this challenging mental task. The rest of us non-memory champions don't use space for these extreme mental challenges, but we still use it nearly every waking moment of our lives.

Academics sometimes discuss the "curse of knowledge,"[41] which means that once we know something, it is very difficult to understand what it is like not to know it. You once did not know how to add numbers; can you remember now what that was like? I think the curse of knowledge is especially applicable to appreciating how central space is to our cognition and our daily lives. We use it so effortlessly in our moment-to-moment existence that we simply cannot understand what it would be like not to use it.

Still, one way to appreciate the centrality of space is to at least try to imagine that we couldn't use it. As I've noted, in our mental schema, every object has associated attributes. These could include its name, taste, color, smell, and so on, but one of them is usually its spatial location. Now, imagine you had to use some object, but in doing so, you had to forgo using one of its attributes. What attribute could you not live without? Let's say I asked you to use the pen lying on your desk. Some of its many attributes will automatically become activated in your mind – its hardness, its color, other writing instruments you might use instead, and so on. Yet you could use a pen without knowing any of these. Even if you were not allowed to know what a pen was called, I could use other attributes to describe it to you. But imagine if the attribute of location were stripped from objects, so that every time you wanted to use something, you had to find it, even if it were just where you left it seconds ago. How would you function when I asked you to use that pen? You would have to search until you found it. Then you would have to search for the paper to use it on. If you wanted a drink of water, imagine having to comb the entire house for a glass and then for a faucet, rather than just remembering where they were. It is no wonder that space is one of the most accessible attributes of any object – one that comes to mind automatically and is strongly associated with the object in our mind. Things are virtually useless to us without the attribute of space. Space is not the only thing your mind uses in making judgments, but it is a big player and one that our minds have evolved to use a lot.

Spatial Cognition and Outgroups

Bringing the two focuses of this chapter together – space and groups – tells us why space is related to group-based bias. Not only is spatial memory deeply interwoven into our cognition, but when it comes to remembering locations, we are particularly good at remembering the location of people.[42] This, too, is probably an adaptive trait – important to the success of our evolutionary ancestors – because the location of friendly and unfriendly groups could be a matter of life and death. In fact, the intertwining of groups and space in our evolutionary past might be why the specialized brain cells for navigation, mentioned above, are also used for our social cognition.[43] When we think about other people, we literally use the same part of the brain we use to think about space.

In addition to remembering the location of people, we are also particularly good at remembering the location of negative stimuli – things we don't like.[44] It's easy to see how this, too, could have been an adaptive trait: avoiding danger by remembering the location of a snake's lair, a patch of poison oak, or a slippery stretch of ground alongside a precipice. For many of us, our clearest memories of a location are where something traumatic happened.

The combination of these two traits – remembering the location of negative stimuli and the location of people – means that groups and space may be especially intertwined in our minds for groups we don't like. Psychologists call the automatic feeling that you don't like something "negative affect." Of course, as has been shown by countless studies, we often have negative affective associations with certain groups, meaning that when that group category becomes salient, negative stereotypes are the first to be retrieved from your mind's well of available stereotypes.[45] People automatically associate certain groups with negative words, such as "unpleasant" or "bad."[46] And groups can also be stereotypically associated with danger, as with the stereotype connecting Blacks to criminality.[47]

Consulting our intuition, we can see how groups that are stereotypically viewed negatively are strongly tied to spatial locations in our minds. This is how ghettos – South Chicago, South Central Los Angeles, the South Bronx – become both a place and an evocative symbol of danger for outsiders. Our cities speak to this general phenomenon – they are full of examples of the centrality of groups to place. There is a reason that the proverbial "other side of the tracks" seems to exist in every town: people are drawing on mental maps of their cities to attach negatively stereotyped outgroups to locations. In short, the link in our minds between space and groups, especially certain outgroups, is strong. We use space to judge groups and groups to judge space.

Using Space to Judge Groups

We have evolved to use space to organize our world and make judgments, especially about groups of people. And, because we use space this way, variation in social geography will cause variation in our judgments about people.

I believe this intuition flows fairly easily. Imagine yourself on a street somewhere. Now consider an outgroup; for example, immigrants – a nationality outgroup. (This won't work for everybody. If you are an immigrant, for example, then nationality may be chronically accessible to you and will not vary in the following example.) Walking down the street, you may not even think about your nationality until you see an immigrant, but once you do see her, the salience of group identity increases. If there is a large group of immigrants, the salience will increase even more. You will be acutely aware of your own nationality and the foreignness of the other group, the more so the closer they get. This salience opens the reservoir of stereotypes, making you feel different than the outgroup. If we were to measure your group bias, once, when the group was far away and, again, when it was closer, it would have intensified. Next time you are on a street with a diversity of people, see if you can detect this psychology in yourself – the salience of the group is changing because its spatial location is changing.

Extending this same psychology over neighborhoods, cities, and other geographies – we can understand why so much research has shown that social geography is tied to our behavior and attitudes. Changing the geographic space between us changes the accessibility and comparative fit of social categorizations – the psychological space between us. Changing the psychological space between us, which affects our behaviors and attitudes, can in turn change the social and political space between us.

Size and Proximity

Why are large groups more salient than smaller groups? This part is simple: as things become larger, they become more accessible in our mind. What catches your attention more readily? A small building or a large building? A small person or a large person? Similarly, a large group is more salient than a small group. Size and closeness lead to accessibility. Accessibility, when coupled with fit, leads to salience and group-based bias.

This is a simple, parsimonious explanation for the relationship between group size and group bias – an explanation that, incidentally, has nothing to do with contact. Is research necessary to prove that large things are more salient than small things? Isn't it obvious? Maybe so, but in making scientific claims, we shouldn't rely entirely on our intuitions. Fortunately, there is also research precisely on the relationship between size and salience. About 40 years ago, the influential psychologist Bibb Latané set out to show that large things have a greater influence on our psychology than small things. Latané built a general theory of social influence: how do people influence other people? He called his principle "social impact" and demonstrated that the impact of people on other people was moderated by social features, including the "strength, immediacy, and number of other people."[48] In a series of studies, Latané varied the size and proximity of groups of people and measured their influence on subjects' behavior, demonstrating the influence of these two attributes.[49]

On the one hand, this all seems very intuitive. We can only pay attention to so many things at once, so what will be more important to you, something close or something far? Big or small? But like many socio-psychological phenomena, it also reveals one of the oddly paradoxical ways in which the human mind works. Earlier I told you that as group categorizations become more salient, we tend to collapse the differences between people within a group; that is, the perceived coherence – the groupishness – of a group increases. And I have just proposed that the larger the group, the more salient it is and, therefore, the more cohesive. The trick this may play on our minds is that if there is any heterogeneity in a population, larger groups will, on average, be more diverse than smaller groups. But because our minds use shortcuts, we think of large groups as more cohesive than small groups. When confronted with two people, you see the differences between them, but when confronted with 100, they all start to look the same.

And there is, perhaps, an even more profound paradox at work here: because proximity increases the salience of categorizations and this increased salience increases the perceived difference between groups, as groups become closer in geographic space, the perceived difference – the psychological space between us – becomes larger.

This paradox can have profound effects – in Chapter 6, I will describe the great social and political distance – even fear – between Black and white residents of Chicago who lived right next to each other and how this fear diminished as residential distance increased between the groups. We will see this almost everywhere we look: Los Angeles, Boston, and Jerusalem too. Springing from the same psychological roots, this paradox can shape our politics on a much broader scale. James Carroll writes about Cold War-era Air Force generals who, in order to use fear to convince Congress of the need to allocate money for their strategic bombers to fight the Soviet Union, would go to Congressional hearings armed with map projections. They would first show a traditional Mercator projection, with the United States on the left and the Soviet Union on the right. But then, playing on the Congressmen's psychology, switch to polar projection – the top down view – bringing the US and USSR into close proximity and showing a "hulking Soviet Union all set to gobble Alaska, and then the rest of the forty-eight states, from across the narrowest of straits."[50]

Segregation

Drawing on established psychology and aided by introspection, I think we can easily understand why larger and more proximate groups are more salient to us. Knowing also that increased salience makes groups the target of group-based bias, which is also well-established in psychology, we can understand why – as was apparent from the many statistical relationships I've discussed – places with large outgroups also have a high prevalence of group bias. This brings us to the other statistical relationship that was apparent, repeatedly, in data from across the country: segregation is related to bias.

Why does segregation increase group bias? Because, just like size and proximity, segregation increases the salience of group-based categorizations, not by increasing accessibility, but rather by increasing the other ingredient of salience – comparative fit. There are likely a number of related psychological channels through which this happens. The first may simply be perceptual cohesion: when individuals are grouped together, they seem more cohesive and the perceived within-group difference is reduced. Thus, the comparative fit increases: if a group is scattered about, it can hardly be called a group at all. Also, if another group is intermixed, then each group might seem less like a group. You might assume, given two intermixed groups, that there is as much in common between those groups as within each group – comparative fit has decreased, making the groups seem less distinct.

We can also consider boundaries. Cohesion increases with the continuity or "closed boundaries" of a group.[51] Closed boundaries are the difference between organized and pickup basketball. When I was a high school teacher, I played organized basketball in a night recreational league on a team of other teachers. We weren't very good, but we had closed boundaries and strong continuity – we were the same team every game. This probably allowed our opponents to attach attributes to our team: "Oh, we're playing the teachers again. They can't shoot, but they're scrappy." We had high cohesion and thus high comparative fit – any one of us was strongly associated with the team. On the other hand, when I moved to Los Angeles and lived in Venice Beach, I would often go to the famous beachside courts and play pickup games with whomever else was there. I knew individual players, but teams had no continuity. A team would consist of different players from game to game – there were no closed boundaries. This meant that I couldn't attach attributes to teams: no team could be identified as "scrappy" or "soft" or "quick"; rather, the team's players would be assessed as individuals. Any given team had low comparative fit.

This difference in continuity between pickup and organized basketball was continuity across time. Continuity across space can also affect cohesion. Imagining again people of different nationalities on the street (and if you yourself are not an immigrant) – if they are scattered about, would you notice them and think of them as a group? Would the category of "immigrant" or "foreigner" be salient to you? But if that group came together in a segregated mass, clearly separated from other people on the street, its comparative fit would increase. As the individuals (low-level categories) faded into the background, you would start to see an undifferentiated mass of immigrants, more similar to each other and more different from you.

Another way to think about this is that the opposite of having closed boundaries is to have overlapping boundaries. With overlapping boundaries, people from one group overlap into another – members of one basketball team also play for another team in the same league. Psychologists have also approached cohesion from this angle and told us that when the boundaries between groups, rather than overlap, *converge*, the cohesion of a group increases.[52] Convergence means that two people divided by one category are also divided by another category. For example, if people from a certain racial group also are mostly poor, this means that the boundaries of race converge with the boundaries of income. (This may help explain why in many countries – perhaps most poignantly, the United States – race is such a socially prominent categorization: it converges so strongly with class-based categorizations. It is also, perhaps, an example of how segregation, generally, not just geographic segregation, contributes to group salience and group-based bias.)

Look back at Figure 1.1 on page 10 and notice that spatial boundaries can also converge with social boundaries in a city like Chicago (but not in the counterfactual Chicago in Figure 1.2 on page 11, in which segregation is reduced). Social group boundaries converge with spatial boundaries when groups are segregated: Blacks all live on one side of town and whites on another. Because we have such a strong tendency to use space in our cognition, this convergence of spatial and social boundaries is important to us; it increases the comparative fit of groups. In our minds, whites become more similar to each other, as do Blacks, and the two group become more different from each other. When we choose from our mental menu of categories for a group, race – a high-level category, rather than a lower-level category – is an easy choice because space has made these racial groups seem so distinct. The fit of a category has increased. Once that category is applied, with it come the attributes – stereotypes drawn from our well of stereotypes – which we effortlessly apply to members of that group.[53]

Interactive Nature of Size, Proximity, and Segregation

There is an important nuance to the relationship between space and the salience of groups: size and segregation are interactive.[54] This follows from, as discussed above, comparative fit and accessibility being necessary conditions of salience.

In statistical terms, this means that these variables should be a multiplicative function and, indeed, in most – but not all – of the examples I gave in Chapter 2, size and segregation appear to be related interactively.[55] Because proximity also affects accessibility, measures of size and segregation should also, ideally, be weighted by proximity, so that closer individuals or groups are weighted more heavily – this is known as a *distance decay* function.[56] In practice, such weighting is very difficult to do, which is why scholars measure context in a pre-defined local environment. In fact, much previous scholarship on context has implicitly made an assumption of distance decay because they measure a group locally – say, in a county rather than in a state or some larger area. A group doesn't matter much if it is way off on the other side of a large state.

Substantively, this means that as size increases, the effect of segregation increases, and vice versa – so that in a place with a large outgroup, segregation will lead to more group-bias than it would in a place with a small outgroup. With a little reflection, I think we can also see that these variables must behave this way. Consider the situation in which there is a large and proximate outgroup. (You can consult the examples in Figure 1.6 on page 26 if it helps with thinking about this.) That group will be salient. But if that large group were very far away – say, in a different state – its salience would be reduced to nearly zero; the group would be far from the top of your mind. Similarly, if a group is segregated, but not large – say there are only two members of the entire outgroup in your local area and they live right next to each other (high segregation) – the category's comparative fit may be high, but its accessibility will be low; the group is just unimportant to you. But if that segregated group's size increases, it will have more impact on your mind.

When Allport wrote about groups, he noted this interactive effect – the manner in which the perception of a large group would change with different levels of segregation:

Segregation markedly enhances the visibility of a group; it makes it seem larger and more menacing than it is. Negroes in Harlem comprise the largest, most solid Negro city in the world – and yet they are less than 10 percent of the total population of metropolitan New York. If they were randomly distributed throughout the city their presence could not be viewed as a dangerous expanding "black belt."[57]

We can consult our discussion above to understand the psychological under-pinnings of Allport's claim: Harlem made Blacks more menacing because the spatial continuity of Blacks in Harlem and the large size of the Black population there increased the group's comparative fit and accessibility, making it seem more different than other groups and making it easier to attach negative stereotypes; for example, that they are more dangerous.

IMPLICATIONS OF SOCIAL GEOGRAPHIC IMPACT

Having established why it is – through what mechanism – social geography can so powerfully affect our behavior and attitudes, the remainder of this chapter will discuss implications of this approach to the study of context.

The Impact of Social Geography, Rationality, and Political Decisions

We use space as a heuristic. How does this affect our ability to make good decisions?

The accessibility of proximate and large groups is attributable to our minds using a shortcut in deciding what is important. Larger things being more accessible than smaller things and the immediate being more accessible than the distal is probably a result of psychological traits adapted in light of our own limited cognitive power. As I discussed earlier, because of this limited power, our minds continually try to ration our cognitive energy. The salience of immediate and large objects might be a shortcut developed by our minds to preserve energy by focusing on what is likely to be most important – things near and large, rather than things small and far off. Similarly, our minds probably use segregation as a heuristic for fit because it makes sense in the light of our limited cognitive ability; more often than not, things that are close together are more similar than things that are further apart. In fact, so powerful is this tendency that geographers describe it as a "law."[58]

Both of these cognitive processes may seem like they will lead to reasonable inferences. Say you are a Black person and you meet a white person living in your city. How do you think about how similar this white person is to other white people? How different from Black people? Do white people live near you or do nearly all white people live across town in another neighborhood? If the city is segregated – social (race) and spatial boundaries have converged, making these questions easy to answer. Of course, when somebody lives on the other side of town, that person might, in fact, be more different from you than a person who lives close by. After all, attributes like income and lifestyle are not randomly distributed across the city. People in your neighborhood are more likely, for example, to have an income similar to yours than people in a different neighborhood. In a certain respect then, there is something efficient – or rational – about using space to make inferences about other people.

However, once your mind uses this shortcut of space to judge fit with a group – a shortcut it will use quite unconsciously and effortlessly thanks to the centrality of space to our cognition – you will inflate the differences between you and that other person. Not only will you think that he or she has a different income than you, but, because of the process of accentuation, you will also think he or she has a *really* different income than you, inflating perceptions beyond reality.[59] Social impact distorts our "priors."

Will this reliance on social geography as a heuristic lead to mistakes? Will we sometimes be non-rational in our decision making? For example, in using proximity as a heuristic, will we sometimes be more concerned with something trivial right in front of our faces rather than something significant coming down the road? Will we sometimes "miss the forest for the trees?" Of course we will. Evolution, however, does not let the perfect be the enemy of the good. Given that our evolutionary ancestors – like us – had limited information-processing ability, the alternative of not using such heuristics could well have been fatal. What if we didn't immediately know that we should focus on something larger rather than smaller or closer rather than farther? What if, presented with an attack from a mammoth and a mouse at the same time, we had to stop to consider which one was more important? It probably wouldn't take long to figure out, but those split seconds would be crucial to survival.

One of the persistent dilemmas of human society is that decision-making traits from our evolutionary past are still guiding our behavior in the vast, diverse, crowded masses of humanity that are modern cities.[60] An example of this is voters in these cities changing their behavior based, not on reasoned policy considerations, but rather on the size and proximity of an outgroup. In some models of human behavior, politics should be a realm in which the use of heuristics, including those involving space, has little sway over our decisions. After all, politics is important – sometimes a matter of life and death. And it happens over long periods of time. We might think that there would be no need for heuristics when political campaigns, for example, take months and months to unfold and voters have ample opportunity to gather information and weigh their decision. In the language of cognitive psychology, this suggests that politics lends itself to long-term and reasoned, System 2, rather than short-term and heuristics-based, System 1, processing.[61]

But modern politics, involving millions of people and with the actual decision making taking place in representative bodies far from the voter, is what brings into play our ancient psychological traits. After all, modern political and legal systems are supremely complex – to understand them would require more time than any normal person can give – and our single votes, given the millions that are cast, can never be consequential. So, in politics we rely on social identities,[62] "tribal" membership,[63] and we remain "rationally ignorant" about politics.[64] In the fleeting moments when a person goes to the polls or thinks about an issue because she is asked on a survey, a heuristic fills the void of ignorance. Scholarship is full of examples of such heuristics, including those drawn from context.[65] Space informs these heuristics, a demagogue whispering in our ear about what is important and how different Us is from Them. This demagogue – in our mind's eye – drives Us and Them further apart.

Social Geography and Voting Behavior

In the last chapter, I extensively covered voting. Why can voting be considered a group-based bias that is linked to social geography? We are now better positioned to answer this.

To understand this, recall that increases in social-geographic impact – high levels of segregation, outgroup size, and proximity – will cause groups to be perceived as increasingly different. It is this perceived difference that likely translates into certain political behaviors, such as voting. Space can change voters' behavior by affecting perceptions of difference which, in turn, changes the perceived "value" of a vote.[66]

In political science, we are used to thinking about political activity being motivated by the perceptions of distance between groups. In fact, this is the central assumption of any "spatial model" of politics: actors will be influenced by their distance from other actors on some dimension. For example, Downs, in his famous work on American politics, argued that voter turnout is a function of the distance of voters from the parties on an ideological dimension – the ideological space between groups. (This is another type of space, like those in Figure 1.3 on page 14.) Looking at dimensions like the upper one in Figure 3.4, he told us a voter, x_1, would only vote if the distance between each party and the voter made voting worth her time. The farther apart the parties, the more voting is valuable and the more likely the voter is to turnout.[67]

Now, think about Figure 3.4 and imagine Black and white median voters placed on this dimension (as in the lower figure). If Black or white voters share the preferences of their group median, the position of this median will affect the value to her of voting. This could also, of course, affect votes for a candidate seen as representing a particular group, perhaps as we saw with the relationship between the social-geographic impact of Black and whites voting for Obama. (In Chapter 4, I will describe laboratory experiments showing that social geography can affect how ideologically similar a voter thinks other voters are to himself or herself.)

Imagine, for a moment, a stylized electorate of 10 people who are free to decide whether or not to vote on a policy. At the most extreme level, of course, if everyone agrees on the policy, there is no need for anybody but a single person to vote. But the more voters think that other people in that 10-person electorate

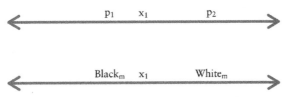

FIGURE 3.4. Perceptual distance on a political dimension with voters and parties (top) and voters and social groups (bottom).

are different from them, including having different policy preferences, the more each should want to vote. Does this apply to the mass politics of modern America, where the electorate consists of hundreds of millions of people? In a formal sense, of course not. Voters cannot rely on such strict rational calculations when casting ballots.[68] But, rather, it is precisely this situation – the complexity and anonymity of modern mass electoral politics – in which heuristics come into play. It is in this situation that a voter, drawing on her local experience, which we know has a primal place in a person's mind, will – perhaps subconsciously – evaluate the value of her vote and be driven to the polls by the sense of the perceived political space between groups.

That the value of a vote can change – it can be worth more or less to you – when your perception of what is at stake changes was the argument of the classic theorist of democratic politics, Schattschneider, who argued that participation will increase as political parties expanded the "scope of conflict."[69] Put another way, participation will increase as political parties become more distinct from each other – when they expand the political space between groups.

This space can affect the perceived value of the vote even when the outgroup has no direct ability to affect election outcomes. Key saw this in how "white power" drove whites to the polls in the 1930s South, not because of anything rational, but because of the symbolic value of their vote was increased by the presence of Blacks:

When applied to politics white supremacy in its most extreme formulation simply means that no Negro should vote. In this sense the phrase is used for its symbolic potency rather than in its literal connotation, for in no state would Negro voting produce "black supremacy."[70]

And, of course, in Key's South, Blacks couldn't vote in any case, so nothing about the presence of Blacks could directly affect a white voter's calculations of how Blacks would affect an election outcome – but the local impact of Blacks still drove whites to the polls. In Chapter 6, I will similarly show white voters in Chicago changing their behavior in response to Black voters, even though there was little chance of election outcomes being affected by their Black neighbors.

How Does Contact Affect Bias? Perception versus Experience

I showed that group bias will be most prevalent with a large outgroup that is *also* segregated and *also* proximate. This seems contradictory if we think contact is all that affects bias. But I have now explained how even without contact – the very arrangement of outgroups in space can change our perception of them. When a group is large, when a group is segregated, or when a group is proximate – holding contact constant – that group becomes more salient. Then, because of the way our mind has evolved to work, our perception of that group – the stereotypes we draw from the well – changes.

Context is not a mere container to be filled with people who may come into contact; rather, the geographic arrangement of these people actively affects our psychology. This is to say that the mechanism by which context affects behavior *is not only experiential, but also perceptual* – the influence of context can be on our perception, rather than just via the experience of interacting with other people. In fact, as we will see in later chapters, situations in which we would expect there to be much intergroup contact – for example, when groups are large and proximate – are correlated with greater group bias, implying that, in some cases, perceptions may be more important than experiences in influencing our behavior. This will also be supported by statistical models where, even when explicitly controlling for interpersonal contact, social geography is still the primary driver of bias (see Chapters 4 and 7).

This is not to say that Contact Theory, when properly understood, is wrong. This thesis has been the subject of great scrutiny and scholars who have examined the evidence from over 50 years of study have said that, on balance, it supports Allport's basic conjecture that contact, under the proper conditions, will improve intergroup relations.[71] Many of us may have experienced it ourselves – my prejudices certainly have changed as life has brought me into more intimate contact with different groups of people. Nevertheless, even if contact does diminish bias, we still must recognize why the occupation of the same place by different groups should be expected, on average, to increase bias, rather than lower it, at least in the short term – as was Allport's prediction and the conclusion most readily drawn from the evidence in this book.

Why would this be? Why might perception overcome experience in the contest for influence over our behavior? I see at least three reasons: First, as I discussed above, space is a preeminent force in our cognition, at the center of our perception formation and decision making. So, for example, even when an outgroup is near enough that we may have contact with them, the spatial arrangement of that group – its size, segregation, and proximity – will still affect our considerations of that group and may, in some respects, outweigh our interpersonal interactions. Given the tendency for proximate groups to quickly segregate after meeting,[72] this means that segregation will often have an opportunity to affect bias, even before contact can take hold.

Second, Allport's conditions for prejudice reduction are seldom fulfilled.[73] One of these conditions was that interpersonal contact would reduce prejudice when members of each group were of equal social standing; his famous example being enlisted soldiers in integrated Army units in World War II. But as social scientists, such as James Sidanius, have pointed out, equality between social groups has never existed in societies with economic surplus.[74] Thus, in any culture other than hunter-gatherer societies, there is group competition for resources and the resources are inevitably shared unequally across groups – often dramatically so. A glance around the world confirms this: although different societies have more or less equality, every society has social groups that are richer and more powerful than others.

Third, not only does equality between groups not exist, but true interpersonal contact across groups seldom takes place, even when groups are proximate. Two groups can live in the same area without having meaningful interpersonal contact of the type that might overpower the force of social-geographic impact. According to a 2013 survey, the average proportion of a white American's friends who were also white was 91.8 percent, a remarkable number given that social desirability pressures might mean that the actual proportion is even higher. Among non-whites, the numbers are still high: the percent of same-race friends is 81 percent among Blacks and 66 percent among Latinos.[75] And, as I noted in the last chapter, in surveys we administered in Israel, over 50 percent of Jews said they never have contact with Arabs.

An implication of this for scholars of intergroup relations is that we should focus more attention on understanding the effects of brief, casual contact that happens in diverse societies, rather than the in-depth contact that happens programmatically in institutions such as the military. If enough of these brief encounters happen and are positive, the encounters may become what is cognitively accessible and a positive example of an outgroup in a person's mind. The effect of these brief, casual encounters may be what induces the curvilinear relationship between group size and group-based bias noted in the previous chapter. If a large enough outgroup is in an area, the bias that was at first increasing with group size begins to wane. In the analysis in that chapter, I did not measure the presence of long-term interpersonal contact with Allport's conditions. However, based on what we know about people's social relationships across racial groups, it is unlikely that such contact was occurring. This suggests that a more casual contact than that suggested by Contact Theory may be reducing group-based bias – not the long-term contact of friends or coworkers, because there is no evidence that is occurring, but simply the casual encounters of frequent interactions with the outgroup on the street, in the store, or at school. With enough of it, this contact may begin to counter the direct effect of space the way we represent other groups in our minds.

Of course, interpersonal contact can also be rare due to existing prejudices and these prejudices can be a result of segregation. This suggests how segregation can contribute to a vicious cycle: once segregation is in place, it gets in the way of the interpersonal contact that could reduce prejudice and, perhaps, lead to the dismantling of segregation. Instead, segregation may lead to more prejudice, which may lead to more segregation. This underscores the endogenous nature of attitudes and segregation; we cannot assume, as scholars, that segregation arises from attitudes rather than contributing to them.

There is also an important takeaway for scholars of context about the measurement of context: regardless of the source of segregation, segregation must be considered. As I discussed above, Allport himself argued that segregation causes prejudice, stating, for example, that "zonal residential contact makes for increased tension."[76] But this point has somehow been lost to most subsequent scholarship. As I noted, many scholars simply measure "contact" as the proportion of a group in an area, entirely ignoring the actual spatial distribution of that group. This is one reason why scholars have taken correlations between diversity and group bias as evidence that Allport was wrong [77] and why other scholars have been able to demonstrate that this correlation actually disappears when segregation is taken into account.[78] Not accounting for segregation, of course, means that we are not even taking the most basic of steps to understand if interpersonal contact is actually occurring: nobody would expect much interpersonal contact to occur in a highly segregated area. And if we are not actually measuring contact, we are not actually testing Allport's theory.[79] Furthermore, I have explained here and will show throughout this book that segregation itself causes bias by affecting our perceptions of a group's comparative fit. This means that, even in the *ceteris paribus* world in which contact is held constant, segregation will still increase bias. Scholars are missing this crucial part of the puzzle when segregation is not taken into account.

The Continued Relevance of Context

A goal of the previous chapter was to demonstrate that, even with the so-called death of distance, the impact that groups sharing the same space has on human behavior is alive and well. From that chapter, we learned this phenomenon, often called "racial threat" in the political science literature, is not confined to a time or place when racial norms were largely different.[80] The findings of this chapter also seem to indicate that even though historical legacies of intergroup bias, such as slavery in the American South, are important in shaping current bias,[81] they are by no means necessary to account for it. Rather, as I explained in this chapter, when we think of group bias as arising from basic psychological tendencies, including the impact of space and groups on our cognition, we should expect it to be widespread. We see the impact of a local outgroup on group bias, especially when that outgroup is segregated and large, not only 50 years ago and not only in the American South, but across the US and other countries, dating back centuries and still here today.

I have offered a model of social-geographic impact; that is, of how the arrangement of groups in space affects the way we think about them. Consider for a moment how this can help us explain a phenomenon which is otherwise difficult to explain. In the 70 years since Key's famous finding, for example, scores of scholars have tried to explain it. An incomplete list of proposed mechanisms includes rational responses to material threat,[82] competition over descriptive representation,[83] stimulation of old-fashioned racial stereotypes,[84] manipulation of fear by interested elites,[85] and preservation of "white power."[86] But none of these mechanisms explains how the phenomenon of "racial threat" extended across time and space: how could voters in Key's South, faced with a powerless outgroup, be driven by the same forces that drove the behavior of whites in the 2008 Presidential election? Or, moreover, why would segregation predict voting in the same way that outgroup size does and why would it predict voting for both Blacks and whites?

None of the mechanisms offered by previous scholarship satisfactorily explains all of this. But I think social-geographic impact can help. I am not claiming that it explains all the behavior we see when groups occupy the same place. No theory can do that; it's simply not how human behavior or social science works. But I do believe that social-geographic impact explains an important part of the variation we see in behavior and that it is fundamental – something we should consider as a first-order explanation of why behavior changes when groups occupy the same place.

This means that I have not crafted a theory applicable only to a specific event or in a certain context. Rather, I have turned to first principles: Because of adaptive pressures in our evolutionary past, space and groups – especially the spatial location of groups – have come to occupy central places in our cognition. From these first principles, we can understand that certain arrangements of groups would change their accessibility and fit and that this will change the groups' salience and, therefore, change our behavior toward those groups.

There have been occasional debates in social science about whether we should bother studying context at all. There was even an article provocatively titled "Why Context Should Not Count."[87] Although I am not sympathetic to that idea, I do see the point: why should we study some concept called "context" if context is just a place where stuff happens? If we care about people interacting with each other, why not just study what happens when people interact with each other? However, this is a critique of a theoretical tradition, long dominant in the social sciences, of treating context as a container in which – but not *because* of which – important things happen. I hope I have made a case that this might not be true. Context – or, more precisely, social geography – can directly affect our behavior and is therefore tremendously important.

My job now is to show the consequences of this theory: if this is why social geography affects behavior, why does that matter? We will therefore have to look for the consequences of social geography in a variety of settings. But first, we will travel into the laboratory to actually see space at work in the mind.

4

Laboratories: Assigning Space

And they said, "Come, let us build ourselves a city..."

– Genesis 11:4

I began this book with the "L" train in Chicago, crossing the boundaries between Black and white. The train made a journey that most Chicagoans, because of the social and psychological space between the two groups – reinforced by segregation – would not make. On the "L" train, we see the great divisions in Chicago. This journey could be repeated for other cities, of course. A bird's-eye view of most of the world's cities large enough to be diverse shows social boundaries mapped onto geographic boundaries. Not all such boundaries are as extreme as Chicago's, with its hyper-segregation between Black and white, but the connections between groups and place are still present. And for most of us, these connections between groups and place are how we bring meaning to the cities. In Boston, Southie and the North End are just names until we associate them with Irish and Italian, respectively. Those geographic boundaries, I argue, don't just coincide with the social boundaries – they reinforce them.

In Figures 1.1 and 1.2 on pages 10–11 (see also Figure 5.2 and Figure 5.3 on pages 132–134), I tried to convey the impact of this social geography by treating the city as a giant puzzle which could be rearranged by an experimenter to disrupt the fit between groups and space by altering the spatial continuity of group boundaries. I claimed that this would break the connection between groups and place and reduce the salience of groups, which in turn would reduce group-based bias.[1]

Of course, in real life, we can't add or remove segregation to alter a group's spatial continuity. The only way, so far, we have been able to test the effects of segregation was through thought experiments, as in the maps, and through statistical comparisons across place (*cross-sectional comparisons* in the language of statistics). This runs us headlong into what statisticians call the *Fundamental Problem of Causal Inference*,[2] because the same city cannot be both segregated and unsegregated at the same time. If we compare different cities, there may be something different about those cities or about the people in those cities – something other than social geography – that is causing differences in group bias.

I can try to make the cities similar by using statistical controls or instruments, of the type I used in Chapter 2. But even with these methods, I am not actually changing segregation, so we cannot be absolutely sure if segregation is causing bias. Being absolutely sure is important: if I am claiming that social geography causes fundamental and important changes in our psychology and, by extension, in our society, I should be as certain as possible about my claim. To be certain, we would like the hand of the experimenter to move groups around in space – to actually create this counterfactual map of Chicago – so that our bird's-eye view revealed a checkerboard rather than a plain division into two parts. Then we could see how behavior changes on this new checkerboard. In this chapter, using a series of experiments, this is essentially what I will attempt to do: to move the puzzle pieces of a city around – create or destroy segregation – and see what happens to behavior.

When moving these puzzle pieces, I want to peer into the human mind – to look under the hood of behavior to see why this is happening. So far in this book, I have only been able to study *revealed* behaviors and attitudes; that is, a behavior we can see (say, gathered from a voting booth) or an attitude somebody tells us directly (say, information reported on a survey). I want to see the latent process behind these revealed behaviors. What is the mechanism behind what they report on a survey or punch in a voting booth? I have offered a specific mechanism – social geography changes a group's salience which, in turn, changes perceptions and attitudes – but I have not actually shown these perceptions and attitudes.

These mechanisms are truly important. Governments across the world try to promote intergroup harmony. They integrate schools and public housing, promote quotas in industries, and often quotas for entry to the country itself. NGOs are involved, too, running summer camps, sports leagues, and entertainment programs aimed at improving intergroup relations. To understand, ex ante, if these efforts will work, we must understand the foundations of what actually promotes and hinders harmony. Does space itself, independent of contact, affect our interactions across groups?

To examine the impact of space on our psychology, I conducted three studies, each demonstrating a different key piece of my theory of social geography and cognition: First, I show that people have sophisticated knowledge about the location of groups in geographic space. This is important to establish because, in order to react to groups on the basis of where they are, one must *know* where they are. (Think about the behavior of the white voters in the 2008 election. That their voting behavior changed as a function of the location of African Americans implies that they knew where these African Americans were.) Second, I show that people in more-segregated areas have different low-level perceptions of outgroups than people in less-segregated areas (meaning segregation affects even our basic perceptions of people). Third, I picked up the puzzle pieces of geography and moved them around, showing that segregation directly changes one's perceptions and causes discriminatory behavior between groups.

For these three studies, I went into the laboratory – either over the Internet or on my university campus. Why a laboratory? As I've mentioned, the beauty of social science is that we can see it unfold all around us – riding the train, standing on the beach, or playing basketball. But that the world is our laboratory also reminds us why social science is so difficult: the social processes, such as the impact of space, that we see unfolding before our eyes can be very difficult to detect and isolate because the situations in which we see them operate are complex and multifaceted. A key aspect of scientific inference is separating the signal from the noise. The signal, for me, is the impact of social geography on group-based bias. But, of course, there is so much noise – all the other things, besides social geography, affecting city dwellers at any given time – that this signal can be hard to detect. As I look out my window right now onto a relatively quiet street in mid-Cambridge, I see people walking by, drivers looking for a parking spot, and rain falling. Animals are scurrying in the bushes and there is the noise of construction around the corner. If I think beyond what I can actually see and hear, I know that the flow of traffic further up the street is affecting the flow I see on my street; the efficiency of public transportation and the layout of residential and commercial use is affecting the flow of pedestrians, as is the rain. Casting my thoughts even farther afield, there are bureaucrats and lawmakers in Cambridge City Hall, the Massachusetts State House across the river, Washington, DC, and elsewhere who are making decisions and setting rules that are affecting my life and the lives of the people around me. These are interacting with international networks of trade and violence. All of this is affecting the complexity of the social space in which I am trying to separate the signal from the noise. This inherent noise of a social space calls for methods that reduce complexity, thus isolating the signal. Going into the laboratory allows me to isolate the signal of social geography from the noise of the social world.

MAPS IN OUR HEADS

We have maps in our heads – mental images of the relative geographic locations of people and objects. As I discussed in the last chapter, we have specific psychological traits that evolved for this purpose. These traits were integral to our ancestors' evolutionary success and are an important aspect of social-geographic impact.

These maps in our heads come in two forms: route knowledge, a linear representation characterized by landmarks, and survey knowledge, which represents space in two dimensions and includes direct spatial relationships in the form of distances and directions.[3] We rely on both. The difference between these two representations is like the difference between driving down a street, which would impart or require route knowledge, and flying over an area or looking at a map, which would impart or require survey knowledge. Different types of experience with space likely result in differences in how one remembers that space. If you often travel through a space, then you probably have route knowledge of it, remembering which landmark comes before which – a restaurant on the highway that means you are approximately halfway there or a yellow house at which you turn left. If, on the other hand, you know a space through mass media or maps, you probably have survey knowledge of it – knowing, for example, that Harlem is between Central Park and the narrow northern tip of Manhattan or that the Mississippi forms a crescent in New Orleans. In either case, our minds draw on the connections between people and place, so that the landmarks we use to define the space are often social groups.[4]

As I mentioned in the last chapter, our minds are especially sensitive to the spatial location of negative stimuli,[5] and this often means social groups. We can see this play out in research on the maps in our heads. A group of my undergraduate students, as their final project, surveyed people in Cambridge and Boston outside subway stops. They showed people a map of Boston and asked people to indicate in which neighborhoods they felt unsafe.[6] They had two experimental conditions, one in which they just asked people this question and a second in which they asked people to first report their race, which is a common method in psychology to make race more salient to the subject.[7] They discovered that when they didn't prime race, the neighborhoods in which people indicated they felt unsafe were unrelated to demographics. However, when they first primed race, Black subjects were more likely to say they felt unsafe in predominately white neighborhoods and white subjects were more likely to say they felt unsafe in predominately Black neighborhoods. Raising the salience of social groups changed the way people thought about space and seems to have brought stereotypes to mind. This project, quite clever from these undergraduate scholars, demonstrated the intertwining of groups and space and how we use groups to bring meaning – safe or unsafe, good or bad – to places.

The precision of our knowledge of space and people becomes greater with familiarity, often as a result of proximity. Many Americans from outside Massachusetts could probably identify the broad contours of racial geography in Boston, having heard of well-known, primarily white neighborhoods like Southie. Somebody with a little additional knowledge of Boston – perhaps someone who visited occasionally from the Berkshires of Western Massachusetts – would know that other neighborhoods, such as Roxbury and Mattapan, are largely African American. But for a Bostonian, these broad contours give way to finer strokes and more detailed descriptions. A person living in Cambridge would know that, from where I sit now, traveling less than a mile east, crossing over Prospect Street on Cambridge Street in Inman

Square, will put you among Portuguese speakers – mostly from Brazil. Head the same distance south toward Central Square and the number of African Americans will suddenly increase, but not before first passing through the small Arab community in between these two squares, home to a mosque and several Arab grocers. Think of your city or town: you can probably identify where neighborhoods change from one group to another – somebody from out of town can't do that.

That detail increases as distances shrink is an intuitive, but deeply important, psychological insight. Psychologists have called it *construal abstraction* and it means that when something is further away, it is represented in a person's mind as an abstraction, rather than a concrete example.[8] In Cambridge, I can tell you block to block what type of people live there, but as I move further away, this detail gives way to general description: Mattapan is Black, Roslindale is white, and so on. Construal abstraction is yet another way that the physical space between groups is related to the psychological space.[9]

Some people find my claim that we can recall this sort of geographic detail, especially where groups of people live, to be surprising or even unbelievable. However, it turns out that most of us are pretty good at knowing where different groups of people live – that is, understanding social geography – especially in our own communities where construal abstraction is low. You may now be asking yourself, "If I'm good at this, why do I get lost without my phone or the GPS in my car?" The answer is probably that you've come to rely on your phone or your GPS and this has broken the connection you used to make naturally between landmarks – including groups of people – and locations. However, as we've learned, groups and space are also central to our cognition, a connection developed in our evolutionary past. GPS, although it probably degrades your "route knowledge," has not yet extinguished this psychological trait. This psychological trait is implied in all that I have argued so far in this book – that people have maps in their heads, the survey knowledge of social geography that means they will react to the size, segregation, and proximity of outgroups.

To first investigate this trait, I brought people from the Boston area into a laboratory on campus. This type of research is, of course, limited because the people willing to come to a university laboratory might be very atypical, but starting with a small, well-defined population can be a valuable first step in research. Subjects looked at a map of Cambridge on the computer and clicked where they would go if they wanted to be most likely to find a certain group: "Where would you go if you wanted to find an African American person?" "Where would you go if you wanted to find a white person?" I took all the clicks on the map and checked them against data from the US Census Bureau that told me where in Cambridge a person would actually be most likely to find these different groups of people.

I remember this initial study well because the visual of the results was striking: a "heat map" that glowed where people clicked and the glow of these clicks showed the spatial accuracy of the subjects. One of these heat maps,

showing where subjects clicked when asked to find Blacks, is displayed in
Figure 4.1. It turns out, people were good at this. The map glows hot around
Central Square and indeed, Central Square is surrounded by Census Tracts with
a high percentage of Blacks. The map also glowed in Alewife (in the upper
left-hand corner of Figure 4.1), which has Cambridge's largest public housing
projects, home to a concentrated mass of Black residents. This group was salient
enough in the minds of my subjects that they could locate it accurately on a
map. They could also place Hispanics, Asians, rich, and poor.[10]

Of course, I wanted to be sure this ability to match social groups with locations was not something particular about the people attracted to a university
laboratory. So I had my research team build a computer application which
allowed people to enter their ZIP codes and be presented with a map of that
area. With this tool, I had people from all over the United States do this exercise.

Social science, like all science, advances through a combination of theory
and technological progress. Modern surveys are really a profound scientific
technology. We can reach out across the United States, or even a larger area,
and quickly – perhaps in a couple of days – gather a sample of the attitudes
and behaviors of hundreds of millions of people. This is remarkable. There are

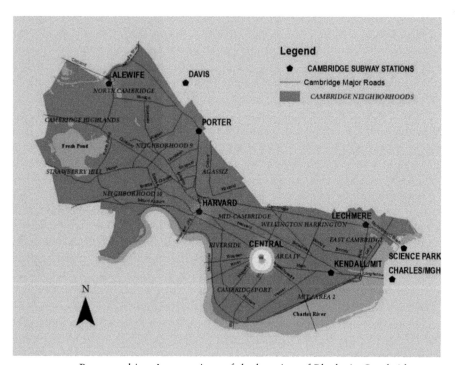

FIGURE 4.1. Boston subjects' perceptions of the location of Blacks in Cambridge.
Screenshot of heatmap overlaid on map presented to the subjects. The light spot near Central
Square indicates the most common answer.

very few things like it in science. I often point this out to my students because the survey has become, like many technologies, so routine that we fail to appreciate what a marvel it is. For the study of context in particular, the modern survey – especially when deployed over the Internet – allows a researcher to effortlessly sample across space to reach almost any geography. This unrestricted movement across space allows for the study of context in a way – such as the comparison of thousands of ZIP codes – that was not possible when context was limited to a single city or to wherever researchers could reach in person.

In my online ZIP-code-based survey, which reached 1,909 people, I again asked, "Where are you most likely to find a Black person?" (and Asians, Hispanics, and whites; see Figure 4.2) and had participants click on the map. Checking their answers against census data, I could again see that people are very good at this, outperforming chance by well over 100 percent (see Figure 4.3).[11] One must appreciate that what these lab and survey participants did is not an easy task. They were looking at a map, which was an abstraction of reality and not necessarily close to their mental image of their local environment, yet they could accurately place groups. So, in fact, these results probably understate the actual accuracy of people's mental maps. The connection of people and place in our minds appears strong.

Moreover, segregation appears to improve this accuracy; where Latinos or Blacks were more segregated from whites, white people were more accurate in finding them on the map. For example, going back to the exercise I used earlier in the book, taking a white person in the least segregated metropolitan area (Grants Pass) and moving her to the most segregated (Milwaukee) would, all else equal, increase her probability of knowing the location of Blacks in their community from about zero to nearly 20 percent. This is just what we would expect if segregation strengthens the psychological connection between groups and space.[12]

Indeed, this is an instantiation of the exercise I presented in Chapter 1 when I asked you to look at Figure 1.1 on page 10. I said that when the segregation of the Black population in Chicago was broken up and groups intermixed, as in Figure 1.2 on page 11, this would reduce our ability to use space as a heuristic for categorization. This implied that we have survey knowledge of the location of groups, the bird's-eye view of where groups live, so that we can use social geography to organize our psychology. This exercise showed that many of us do indeed have this knowledge, and it is facilitated by segregation.

Some social scientists may find this research surprising because many studies have found that Americans are largely innumerate about the demographics of their community.[13] For example, if you ask people, "What percent of your ZIP code is African American," they generally don't know. This is an important insight, but not contradictory to my finding that people know where groups are on a map. People are bad at thinking in percentages or estimating proportions[14]

FIGURE 4.2. Measuring "maps in our heads".

One screenshot from the Web instrument used to measure knowledge of the location of groups. This example is taken from ZIP code 11203, covering the Flatbush section of Brooklyn. Answers shown here are not intended to be accurate.

and people can know that something is concentrated or relatively numerous without having a clue about the actual percentage.

In fact, in my study, people had the same level of demographic inaccuracy as in previous studies – when asked to guess the percent of African Americans, Hispanics, Asians, or whites are in their Zip code, my respondents overestimated non-whites and underestimated whites at rates remarkably similar to what others have found.[15] Nevertheless, my respondents were accurate when asked to place these groups in geographic space. Moreover, these two abilities appear to be unrelated: people in my study who were good at placing groups in the correct location were no better than other respondents at guessing the percentage of that group in their ZIP code.[16]

The question of whether or not people know where a group is located will, even in many modern contexts, be a much more important and practical question than whether people know that group's percentage of the population of a certain area. It is also the type of knowledge that we can imagine as

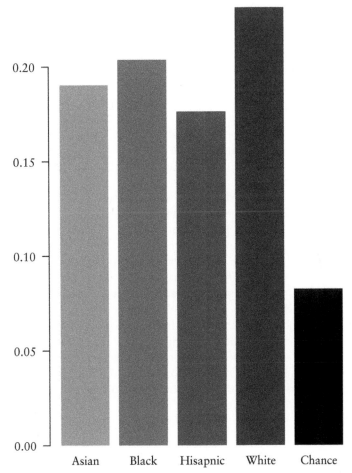

FIGURE 4.3. Correctly locating groups in space.

Percent correctly identifying most-likely location of groups. This is measured by placing the group in the correct Census Tract within the ZIP code. "Chance" is what percent of respondents would be correct by guessing alone, based on the number of Census Tracts displayed to the subjects.

an adaptive evolutionary trait, because the location of groups was important to the survival of our distant ancestors. Furthermore, while understanding the relative size of groups may also have been important to those ancestors, percentages were probably not.[17] By using modern technology to measure our ability to locate groups in space, we can see the long reach of our evolutionary past affecting our cognition in the present, tying neighborhoods to groups and bringing meaning to names like Harlem and Southie. For most of us, this is no longer a matter of survival, but it is still a psychological trait that we find hard to escape and deeply affects our behavior.

MEASURING COMPARATIVE FIT

Showing that we tend to know where groups are located is a first step in establishing the cognitive process underlying the relationship between social geography and group bias. The next step is to actually observe the micro-level changes in psychology – the increase in accessibility and fit – that is driving bias.

To see this mechanism at work, I designed a question to directly measure comparative fit, a necessary component of salience, the driver of group bias. I adapted a test used by psychologists to measure perceptions of similarity within a group.[18] Remember that within-group differences decrease with comparative fit, so perception of similarity is an indication that the comparative fit has increased.

Over the Internet, I showed people a series of 110 faces that were created by morphing white and Black men. The images ranged from 100 percent white to 100 percent Black, with 10 percent intervals in between: 90 percent white, 80 percent white, and so on. With 10 different faces in each interval (see Figure 4.4).[19] I showed each subject every face in random order and asked them to categorize each face they saw as white or Black.

To measure this perceived similarity, researchers look for a "Point of Subject Equality" or *PSE*, which is the point on the continuum of morphed faces where a subject is equally likely to categorize a face as white or Black (see Figure 4.4).[20] If a subject's PSE matched the true racial mixture of the faces, then it should be at 50 because that is when the morphed faces are 50 percent white and 50 percent Black. If the PSE moves down, say to 30, this would mean that the subject categorizes faces that are more than 30 percent Black as Black and a face must be more than 70 percent white and less than 30 percent Black before they say it is white.[21] If non-Black subjects are collapsing differences within the outgroup – increasing the comparative fit – they should increasingly think anybody that looks a little Black is part of the Black outgroup and they should therefore have a lower PSE. Think of this as a measurement of the tendency to lump the outgroup together and exclude people from the ingroup; that is, to think that everyone in an outgroup is the same and thus to increase the space between groups. This is the closing of the boundaries of a group in psychological space and by measuring it, I am directly observing mental categorization of individuals into social groups.

I have said that social geography can increase this lumping – this comparative fit – because segregation increases the perception of cohesion within a group. For my test, this means that in more-segregated places, white survey subjects should have a lower PSE. Across two surveys in the United States, one that was nationally representative, I connected the survey responses of white subjects with their metropolitan area. As social-geographic impact predicts, higher Black/white segregation predicted lower PSE for white subjects. For subjects in more segregated places, the outgroup had greater comparative fit, so those subjects tended to lump a wider range of faces into the Black category.[22]

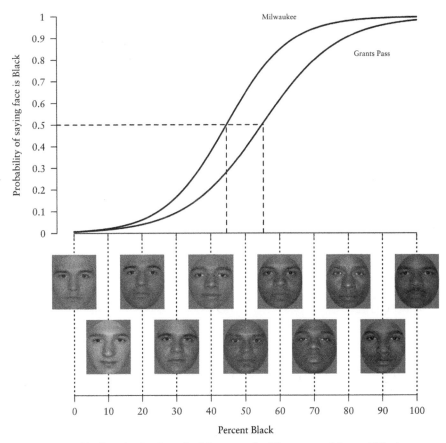

FIGURE 4.4. Finding the "point of subject equality" between white and Black.

The PSE for two hypothetical subjects, one in Milwaukee and one in Grants Pass, Oregon, are represented by dotted lines. The fit represented by the dark lines are purely illustrative. The PSE for each subject corresponds to predictions for white people based on the amount of segregation in Milwaukee (0.45) and Grants Pass (0.55). The faces at each interval are examples from Krosch et al. (2013) and were created by morphing different proportions of white and Black faces, from 0 percent Black to 100 percent Black.

In these abstract psychology experiments, it can be difficult to understand the substantive size of a statistical relationship. Scholars sometimes use "standardized coefficients" to interpret the size of the effect. By these measures, segregation has a large effect on our perception: between one-half and one standard deviation of PSE.[23] Perhaps more meaningfully, this effect means – repeating our thought experiment from Chapter 2 – that moving from the least-segregated to the most-segregated metropolitan area would move PSE by about 11 percentage points. Roughly, what that means is that, if these survey results reflect real-world classifications, the average white person in the most-segregated area would classify about 22 percent more racially ambiguous people as Black than a person in the least-segregated metropolitan area would; conversely, the size of the group classified as white would decrease by 18 percent.[24] Segregation is reifying these racial groups, making the ingroup more exclusive and growing the space between them.

An advantage to conducting my own survey, rather than relying on a study already conducted by other scholars, is that I can add questions to help to understand if social geography is really directly changing our perceptions as my theory of social-geographic impact predicts or rather if, as is usually assumed in the academic literature, segregation simply means that we have less interpersonal contact between groups, which changes our perceptions and attitudes. This is important because, as I've mentioned, in many cases, these two mechanisms are observationally equivalent. Segregation has both effects: it creates less interpersonal contact and also has a direct effects on our perception of groups. But scholars have focused on the former, while neglecting the latter.

To check this, I included in this same survey questions to measure contact by borrowing a well-known measure of interpersonal contact from the psychology literature that asks people how often they have contact with Blacks at work, at school, as neighbors, or as close friends. When this measure of contact is put in a statistical model with segregation and group size to measure its effect on PSE, the effect of contact is zero, indicating that the effects of segregation on perception operate independently of contact.[25] What this means – as I have mentioned before – is that social geography seems to create a space between us in our heads before it creates a space between us in our social relationships.

EXPERIMENTS ON SEGREGATION

In Chapter 3, I described my reaction on an airplane to a woman wearing what I thought was a hijab – how easily negative and damaging stereotypes came to my mind and how these were erased when I realized she probably was not a Muslim. My claim is that, for me, the scarf increased the *fit* of this woman in the social category of Muslim made *accessible* to me by her proximity and the setting of an airplane and, therefore, made that category more salient to me. I have argued that social geography can do the same – and I showed evidence for this in the study I just presented: as segregation increased, so did the fit of faces into the category Black.

After that flight, I consulted the academic literature to see if anybody had ever tested for prejudice, like that which I had so blatantly felt, caused by head scarves. Yes, psychologists had randomly assigned people to view photos of women wearing or not wearing hijabs and discovered that wearing the hijab increases negative attitudes and leads to discrimination.[26]

In these experiments the hijab had increased the salience of the Muslim category and the result was group bias. Since I have proposed a similar mechanism for why social geography affects group bias, I'd like to be able to do a similar experiment: to assign social geography and see if bias increases where the greatest social-geographic impact has been assigned. A key principle of understanding cause and effect is: "to find out what happens when you change something, it is necessary to change it."[27] But social geography, of course, cannot be manipulated, moved, and changed like an article of clothing. The pieces are not so easily removed as a scarf. This, of course, is one of the reasons it has such a tremendous impact – why we see the behavior of individuals and the success of nations affected by their geography. Because it is so hard to manipulate means that it is hard to escape, our public policy choices are constrained by it, and policy intended to change social geography will be difficult to carry out. The persistent racial segregation of the United States is testament to this. This "stickiness" of social geography also presents an inferential challenge: how do I know it is causing changes in group bias if I cannot change it to see what happens?

Despite the challenge of changing social geography, to do so is crucially important to my claims. To understand why, we can revisit the contribution of Key, who was in many ways the father of the study of context in political science. Remember that Key found that, in the 1930s American South, group-based bias among whites was systematically related to the presence of Blacks. The evidence I reviewed in Chapter 2 makes it seem like Key's insight is relevant for understanding modern American politics, too. Moreover, his contribution is still relevant to the scholarly study of context because his method, in its basic features, has been adopted by almost every other scholar studying context in the 60-plus years since he wrote. Key used aggregate data, looking at the vote totals across counties, and with some – by modern standards, rudimentary – statistics, determined that white voter participation and voting for conservative politicians were correlated with the size of the local Black population. Modern researchers tend to use individual survey data, rather than aggregate data, sometimes use a smaller level of aggregation, such as a Census Tract, and may employ more complex statistical techniques, such as "multi-level" models. But the general framework remains: look for variation in a dependent variable, like voting, as a consequence of existing variation in an independent variable, like percent Black, at some level of aggregation, like a county.

But of course, Key's method, like that of most other researchers who have studied this problem, suffers from a fundamental problem with causal identification. Key couldn't really be sure if it was the presence of Blacks that was causing a change in the behavior of whites. This problem is so fundamental to the study of context and to scientific inference more generally that it is worth reviewing before we move on. It is this problem that led me to design and conduct experiments on context.

The Study of Context and the Fundamental Problem of Causal Inference

At first blush, the idea that something caused something else is fairly simple: if X had not happened, then Y would not have happened. If I had not pressed the "T" key on my keyboard, then this letter would not have been written. Pressing the "T" key caused the letter to be written. If I had not stepped on the brake, then the car would not have slowed down. Stepping on the brake caused the car to slow down. But these are trivial examples in which there is no variation: Every time one hits the brake, the car slows; every time one hits the "T" key, the letter "T" appears. Nor are other causes possible: no other letters were pressed before the letter "T" appeared, no other pedal was used before the car slowed. These examples are therefore much simpler than the complex social world in which many variables change at once or in which there are variables that can't be measured.

Social scientists and statisticians have developed specialized languages to describe what exactly it means to *cause* something. One of these is the potential outcomes framework.[28] Here, you say that there are two potential states of a unit (like a person), one that occurs when a particular event precedes it and another that occurs when a different event proceeds it. What, for example, is the effect of aspirin on headaches? A person can have two potential outcomes, one in which she takes an aspirin and one in which she does not. The difference in the state of her headache between these two potential outcomes is the *treatment effect* of aspirin. What is the effect of segregation on attitudes? We can imagine that a person has two potential outcomes: an attitude if her local environment is segregated and an attitude if her local environment is not segregated. The difference in these attitudes is the treatment effect of segregation.

Simple, right? But there is one big complication (not to mention many small ones): we can't have the same person both take the aspirin and not take the aspirin or the same area be segregated and not segregated. This problem is the Fundamental Problem of Causal Inference: we can't know whether the aspirin caused the reduction in headaches or whether segregation caused group bias because we can only observe one of two possible *potential outcomes* (the outcome with aspirin or with no aspirin, the outcome with segregation or with no segregation) at a time. Thinking about Key's evidence in the South, where he argued the "presence of the Negro" was causing bias among whites, the fundamental problem is that, in order to actually know if this causal claim is true, we would need to observe the same whites in two different places at the same time, one with Blacks nearby and one without. This is impossible. In fact, for perfect control, we'd actually need to observe the same whites in the same place at the same time, with and without proximate Blacks. This becomes difficult to even think about.

In the social sciences, the problem of causal inference is particularly severe because we cannot even force subjects to be the same through laboratory control, as can often be done in the natural sciences. For example, when testing the effect of exposing a liquid to a charged particle,[29] a physicist can experiment in a vacuum to ensure that there is no difference between the sample of liquid exposed to the particle and another sample that is not. The physicist would still not be observing the same liquid receiving both treatments at the same time, but would at least be observing two samples of liquid that the vacuum ensures would be identical, so her experiment would be as if she were applying the same treatment to the same liquid. In the social sciences, however, such perfectly controlled experiments are not possible. There are no identical people and even the same person is not identical at different times.

Social scientists traditionally conduct *observational research*, so called because we simply observe what happens in the world, rather than inducing something to happen in the world, such as inducing people to take aspirin in order to measure its effect. For example, in observational research, we could find people – some who take aspirin and some who do not – and see if there is a difference in the prevalence of headaches. Of course, the familiar problem is that people who choose to take aspirin might be different, on average, then people who don't take aspirin. They might be more health-conscious and therefore might exercise more and eat better, so if we see them having fewer headaches, we wouldn't know if it was because of the aspirin, the exercise, or the diet. In this case, we might say that the measured effect of aspirin is potentially spurious and measuring the effect of aspirin might introduce bias in our inferences.

This is a problem of *selection*: people with certain exercise habits choosing to take aspirin is equivalent to people with certain attitudes selecting to live in segregated or non-segregated areas. These selection issues are just a particular case of the Fundamental Problem of Causal Inference that keeps us from knowing cause and effect.[30]

Going back to the example of Key's evidence, we might worry that whites with particular behaviors – a tendency to vote in higher numbers and to vote for political conservatives – also selected to live in locations with many Blacks. If this were true, it wouldn't be the presence of Blacks that was causing bias; it would simply be that, for some reason, people with these behaviors tend to select to live around Blacks. Key himself recognized this. When discussing the high levels of voting among whites in heavily Black counties in Alabama, he wrote:

Whether the high level of electoral zeal of the whites in this area is attributable entirely to the presence of Negroes in large numbers is open to doubt. The whites of the black belt are better educated and better off economically than the rural whites of other regions and these differentials are usually accompanied by differentials in electoral interest.[31]

All studies using a research design similar to Key's have potentially suffered from similar problems of selection and scholars have directly documented the bias that such selection problems can induce in estimating the effects of context.[32] My own research related in Chapter 2, in which I connected social geography to group-based bias, was observational. It used a research design similar to Key's and may also have suffered from problems of selection, although I tried to correct that using instrumental variables and other strategies. But such strategies cannot guarantee that selection is not biasing results – a researcher still must ultimately *assume* that it is true.

Is there anything that can be done to establish cause and effect in the social world? Yes, we can conduct an experiment, or – more formally and exactly – a randomized controlled trial (RCT). Somewhat underappreciated given their enormous contribution to science, RCTs are the fundamental building block of much important knowledge that has been accumulated in the last 100 years, especially in fields like medicine and the social sciences. The beauty of an RCT is that it overcomes the Fundamental Problem of Causal Inference. By allowing us to approximate the same person receiving the same treatment at the same time, it overcomes the problem of selection.

An RCT gets around selection problems by not allowing people to *select* to take the treatment; rather, they are *assigned*. For example, some people would be assigned to a treatment group that takes aspirin and some to a control group that does not take aspirin. The crucial element is that this assignment to treatment or control is made randomly – by the proverbial (or literal) "flip of the coin." Given a large enough group of people, random assignment assures us that the people in the treatment group are, on average, the same as those in the control group. This property of random assignment is mechanically true: assigning things randomly will, on average, ensure that groups are the same. For our purposes, taking people with positive or negative attitudes about Blacks and flipping a coin before assigning them to the treatment or control group would, given enough people, produce groups with equal proportions of people with positive and negative attitudes. If your treatment is a certain type of city, you will have approximated what we set out to do in this chapter: allow the experimenter to move the puzzle pieces of the city, not by moving pieces of the cities, but by randomly assigning people to live in them. If we had a large number of cities and could randomly assign some to be segregated and some not, we could ensure that the cities in the treatment and control conditions were otherwise equal and that the differences (if any) in attitudes we measured in those cities would have to be caused by segregation.

Given the problem of selection and the known solution of an RCT, why have scholars relied on observational research, such as that of Key, to study the effects of context? Probably for the very simple and good reason is that it is really difficult to use an RCT to study context: how can you randomly assign people to a location? This is not the same as assigning somebody to take aspirin or to assign somebody to remove a headscarf. Scholars have occasionally found ways around this problem. My own study in Chicago, which we will discuss in Chapter 6, was a "natural experiment" in which the federal government served as the experimenter, assigning buildings to be demolished in a way that mimicked an RCT. But such opportunities are rare and, ultimately, cannot replace an RCT. The only way to be certain about cause and effect is if the experimenter, rather than the government or somebody else, introduces the cause. Although scholars have made great progress in studying the psychology of geographic space[33] and have randomized interpersonal contact in institutional settings, the experiments I am about to describe and others in this book were, to my knowledge, the first political science experiments to randomize social geography.[34]

For social scientists then, selection bias has remained a fundamental problem for understanding the effects of context. On this subject, sociologist Robert Sampson, said, "the specter of 'selection bias' has been raised to cast doubt on almost all observational research."[35] Much of the research in this book, including the studies in this chapter, are attempts to subdue this specter.

Length

I have claimed that segregation changes the salience of groups by facilitating comparative fit. To first put this to the test experimentally, I took inspiration from Tajfel's experiments, described in Chapter 3.[36] Tajfel categorized lines by putting letters on them and showed that this simple category label caused people to collapse the differences between categorized lines, as we would expect if the salience of the category had been increased. This is the collapsing of difference within group – the distortion of difference so that members of any particular group all start to look the same and the difference between different groups becomes large.

My claims, of course, are about social groups, not geometric lines. But if this tendency really is a basic psychological process, based on our tendency to categorize – if the need to categorize extends to every piece of information that our minds process – then we should see this effect even on inanimate objects. I therefore decided to experiment on lines before experimenting on people. I wanted to know if segregation can facilitate this categorization and subsequent distortion of difference by allowing space to do what Tajfel's letters did. If I could see segregation affecting perceptions of even these basic objects, it suggests that this mechanism is something basic and fundamental – a feature of human cognition – not tied to a particular time or place.

Over the Internet, I exposed subjects to sets of red and blue lines. The lines were of varying length, but the sets of lines, blue and red, were identical other than in color. Using the letter "A," I marked either the longest or shortest line in one of the sets. The experiment was this: in some cases, the blue and red lines were integrated across the computer screen – so red and blue lines were intermixed, one after another – and in some cases, the lines were segregated – all the reds on one side and all the blues on the other. These two cases are the treatment in the experiment, the lines were either integrated or segregated by color. Everything else remained the same. I asked subjects to tell me the length of the line labeled with the "A." See Figure 4.5 for an example of this. (This figure represents segregation as survey knowledge – understanding space from

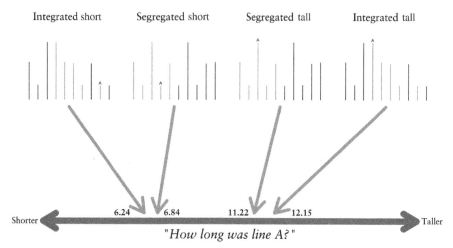

FIGURE 4.5. Measuring the effect of segregation with lines.

Four different stimuli from my experiment to see how segregation affected perceptions of similarity in length. In the actual experiment, the lines were red and blue. I compared the perceptions of the differences in length of the two integrated stimuli to differences between the two segregated stimuli. Responses were in centimeters. On average, the segregated stimuli were perceived as more similar to each other than the two integrated stimuli. The integrated lines also became more different than reality and the segregated lines became more similar than reality. Ratio of long to short lines in reality (averaged across five trials of experiment) was 1.73. As perceived in the integrated condition, the ratio was 1.95 and as perceived in the segregated condition, it was 1.64.

a bird's-eye perspective, one of the two ways we represent space in our memory (See discussion on page 81.) The next two experiments will do the same.)

I wanted to see whether the simple act of segregating these otherwise identical lines by color would affect people's perceptions. If segregation really increases comparative fit, this will cause us to perceive smaller differences within groups in the same way that a headscarf changes the salience of a category and allows the stereotypes to rush into our mental processing. To test for this, I compared the difference in estimates of length of the long line and short line – the two lines that had been labeled – in the segregated condition to the same difference in the integrated condition. Was the difference smaller in the segregated condition?

I showed these lines to over 1,000 people, displaying each set of lines for five seconds so that subjects would not have time to try to precisely measure the lines, but rather would have to rely on their heuristic judgments, just as we so often do in the fleeting social interactions that make up the bulk of intergroup relations. Each subject saw 10 different sets, each set consisting of a segregated and an integrated stimulus, and I averaged the results across these 10 sets.

I repeated this experiment five times, just to be sure that the results were not a fluke. With each iteration, I could see segregation doing its work on people's perceptions: on average, in the segregated condition, people thought the difference between the long and short lines was smaller than they thought the same difference was in the integrated condition (see Figure 4.5) In fact, by comparing the average estimated difference between the long and short lines in the segregated and integrated conditions to the actual difference between the long and short lines, we can see that people behaved exactly as we would expect if segregation-induced categorization is distorting reality: segregated objects became more similar than they really are and integrated objects became more different than they really are.[37] Keep in mind that, because this was an experiment, everything else about the conditions was identical – including the actual difference in the lengths of the lines – and people were randomized into conditions, so there is no doubt that segregation was causing the changes in perception that I observed. It seemed, then, that segregation itself, with no other interference, could change our perceptions. This was the pure impact of space.

Here, I am beginning to rearrange the puzzle pieces of geography, mimicking the results I could see in the surveys I conducted earlier, compelling the demagogue to whisper by using the hand of the experimenter to rearrange social space – to remove the headscarf, if you will. But I have drastically simplified this space by using inanimate objects. This sort of simple experiment, of which I will show one more, allowed me to test my basic premise before advancing to the more complex case of moving humans around.

Color

I am claiming that segregation acts as a shortcut, causing us to collapse within-group difference. Our minds will always turn to these shortcuts first, using them to judge and make decisions, unless our more careful and slower mental processes slow us down. Because our minds must preserve resources, this intervention by our more careful processing does not usually happen.[38] Instead, heuristics reign supreme in the way we perceive the world. It follows that if social geography is one of these heuristics, our minds should not pick and choose where to apply it, but rather will apply it to nearly everything we see. Generally, we will use geography to judge any dimension or characteristic with which we are presented: when people are segregated rather than integrated, we will see their incomes as more similar, their politics as more similar, their appearance as more similar, and so on.

I can show this by demonstrating that geography affects our perceptions across more than one dimension of difference. To do this, I rebooted my experiment: rather than varying the length of objects, I varied the color. I showed my subjects – again over 1,000 of them – red and blue squares on a page. Again there were two conditions, randomly displayed, one with the squares segregated by color and one with the squares integrated by color. I varied the shades of squares so that some were dark and some were light and I marked one of these squares. Using a 100-point scale displayed on a slider, I asked subjects to tell me how dark or light the marked square was (Figure 4.6), from lightest blue or red to darkest blue or red.

I again displayed sets of squares for five seconds and showed each subject 10 sets. I wanted to see if segregation would cause the differences on this 100-point scale to collapse so that the various shades of the squares were seen as more similar. Once again, I repeated the experiment five times to make sure it was no fluke. Once again, segregation changed perception so that objects in the same category became more similar: when the squares were segregated, light objects became darker and dark objects became lighter. Looking at the bottom of Figure 4.6, you can see the subtle, but real effect.[39]

We now are seeing the power of segregation spill over into our perceptions across multiple dimensions. Changing of the length of lines was not just a visual trick, it tapped into something deeper about how our minds use space to organize our perceptions. But, of course, we want to know how far this effect really goes. Does space affect the way we see people, too?

Faces

In my online survey with the morphed faces, I showed that a person's social geography was related to how she categorized people; specifically, whether

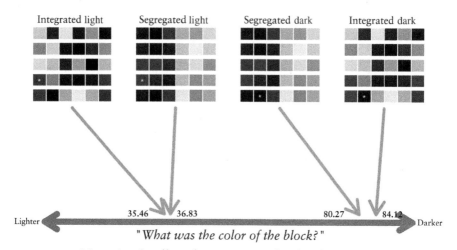

FIGURE 4.6. Measuring the effect of segregation with colored squares.

Four different stimuli from my experiment to see how segregation affected perceptions of similarity in color. In the actual experiment, the squares were shades of red and blue. I compared the perceptions of the differences in color of the two integrated stimuli to differences between the two segregated stimuli. Colors were represented by 100-point slider corresponding to color bar. On average, the segregated stimuli were perceived as more similar to each other than the two integrated stimuli.

she saw a face as white or Black. White people in more-segregated cities were more likely to see faces as Black and I argue that this is because segregation changed the way they categorize people, causing them to lump more into the Black category. The problem, of course, is that even though I had an instrument designed by psychologists to precisely measure this tendency to categorize – to peer under the hood of these behaviors and see the perceptions underlying them – I had not *assigned* the subjects' social geography, so I could not observe the same white person in both a segregated and an integrated city. The Fundamental Problem of Causal Inference means that I can't be sure social geography was the cause of the effect. Something besides social geography could have been driving these results.

The only way to overcome this problem is to randomly assign segregation, just as I did with the lines and colored squares. So I designed another test, this one using photographs of actual people – some white and some Black, and some again morphed to be ambiguous, to see if segregation would change the way people categorized the ambiguous faces. I arranged these faces on a page, sometime integrated by racial group and sometimes segregated. Each page also included one ambiguous face created by morphing together a Black and white face. This face was marked by a red border. When the faces were segregated, this ambiguous face was sometimes grouped with Black faces and sometimes with white faces. I asked subjects to choose a description of the racial appearance of the marked ambiguous face from a seven-point scale ranging from "Very Caucasian" to "Very African American" (see Figure 4.7). Would segregation drive perception causing subjects to lump faces into a category? Would the morphed face become more Black when it was grouped with Black faces and more white when grouped with white faces?

I again showed these faces for five seconds so that people would rely on their heuristic judgments. I showed this to over 1,100 subjects across five different trials. Again, segregation affected judgments. Compared to integrated faces in the control group, subjects thought the ambiguous face was more "Caucasian" when the face was segregated with white faces and more "African American" when the face was segregated with Black faces.[40]

Keep in mind this is the exact same person becoming more white when spatially grouped with whites and more Black when spatially grouped with Blacks. In other words, comparative fit has increased. When psychologists have written about comparative fit, this is exactly the thought experiment they had in mind; namely, that the salience of a category – the label we put on a person – would change if we could pick that person up and move her from one context to another.[41]

Consider the real-life consequences of this. Psychologists tell us that when a person is associated with a category, we tend to represent her in our minds as a *prototype* of that category; that is, as having the attributes we consider typical of that category.[42] These attributes are the stereotypes we associate with groups and we know that the stereotypes that accompany being categorized as

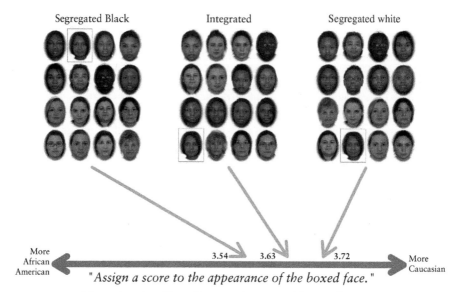

FIGURE 4.7. Measuring the effect of segregation on ambiguous faces.

Three different stimuli from my experiment to see how segregation affected the categorization of faces. I compared the ambiguous face segregated with white faces (right) or Black faces (left) to when it was integrated with both white and Black faces (center). Responses were recorded on a 7-point Likert Scale, with 7 being more Caucasian. The face became more "Caucasian" when segregated with whites and more "African American" when segregated with Blacks.

white or Black will differ: from the perspective of a white person, compared to whites, Blacks might become less hard working and whites more, Blacks less intelligent and whites more. Here I showed that segregation drives us to perceive prototypes: a white person was perceived as more white and a Black person as more Black. Thus, the very fact of segregation can by itself encourage the use of such stereotypes, encouraging us to reach into our mind's well and retrieve the attributes associated with the segregated group.

CREATING A NEIGHBORHOOD

Are the experiments I've shown you enough to prove my point? Have I convinced you that segregation causally affects the salience of group identities, thereby creating the conditions for group-based bias? Perhaps, but I know that segregating lines or squares or even photos of people is a long way from segregating actual people. I wanted to know what happens when people actually experience segregation, not just when they see it presented to them on a screen. How does the experience of segregation affect behavior? When a Black woman looks across Chicago and knows that the group on the other side of the city is different from her, how does that change her perception of that group? How does it change her behavior? When a white man, living in a Boston suburb and rarely coming into contact with Latinos, sees a Latino in his home town, how does the fact that Boston is so segregated affect his reaction? To answer such questions, I wanted to manipulate the puzzle pieces of a city, to create segregation with actual people. The solution – the way to actually experimentally manipulate segregation – was not to pick people up from their own neighborhoods and move them around but rather to create my own "neighborhoods" and invite them in.

To do this, I again went into the laboratory, but rather than doing experiments on the Web, I had to go into a real old-fashioned brick-and-mortar laboratory – literally, in this case, because I used a nineteenth-century brick classroom building at Harvard. I enlisted the help of a creative graduate student, Christopher Celaya, and together we designed and conducted an experiment to create "neighborhoods" – spatial arrangements of segregated or unsegregated people in the laboratory – and see how these neighborhoods affected group bias.

Our design was to bring subjects into the laboratory and assign them to a "minimal group." In Chapter 3, I discussed the minimal groups with which Tajfel and his colleagues had demonstrated that simply randomly assigning people to made-up categories – say, "A" and "B" – would induce group bias. Our own twist was to then assign social geography: to create neighborhoods in which these minimal groups were either segregated or integrated. If my theory of social-geographic impact is correct, then these minimal groups – created out of thin air with no preexisting prejudices – should cause more group-based bias when the groups are segregated than when integrated.

As I will show below, this hyper-local environment, the segregated space that was made salient at the moment of the experiment, consequentially altered the behavior of these subjects – inducing bias in attitudes and costly behaviors.

This was a complex experiment. Much of the experimental research in social science, such as my experiments so far in this chapter, is now conducted over the Internet. When experiments are conducted in person, they often consist of simply bringing subjects into a computer lab to answer questions or to interact with other subjects over locally networked computers. But we were actually moving people around in space and this required a special type of setup, so we needed a particular kind of laboratory – one with over 20 rooms. Thus we took over an entire classroom building to execute this experiment.

A further complication of this experiment was that we wanted our subjects to be what we called "real people" rather than the college students who populate a very large number of psychology studies. Concerns about the number of psychology studies based on American college students have been raised repeatedly, often with general concerns that relying on this sample gives a narrow view of human nature.[43] Our concern was more specific: that these students, because they so often take part in experiments and because they learn about famous psychology experiments in class, would not react to the minimal groups assignment.[44] We also did not want subjects who already knew each other because our dependent variables for group bias might be affected if subjects were part of an existing group. Students from the same university are pretty likely to know each other. With these considerations in mind, we recruited subjects from Craigslist. Our advertisement didn't say anything about segregation or groups, so when subjects came to the experiment, they didn't know what the study was about. Our research assistants also didn't know the purpose of the study, so in that respect, this study had the "gold standard" feature of an experiment: it was double-blind.

We brought groups of up to 20 subjects together in a lecture hall and our research assistants showed them a PowerPoint presentation of images and asked them to choose adjectives describing those images from a list, which they recorded on a sheet of paper.[45]

We deceived the subjects, claiming that their reactions to these images revealed a "perceptual type," but this perceptual type had actually already been randomly assigned by us prior to the beginning of the experiment. We called these perceptual types "Type H" and "Type Y" and those were our minimal groups. Our intention was that the subjects would see the perceptual type to which they were assigned as their ingroup and the other as the outgroup.[46] Of course, we never told them these distinctions were important. Rather, we just let the power of categorization take over to affect behavior. We then manipulated spatial geography so that the distorting power of groups was amplified.

After we had administered the test of perceptual type, the research assistants brought all the subjects to a "waiting room," telling them that the lecture hall had to be prepared for the next experiment (see Figure 4.8). It was in this waiting room that we created our neighborhood – segregated or integrated – and thus the experimental treatment of segregation was administered.

In one condition, randomly assigned, the subjects would be segregated, with members of each "perceptual type" on different sides of the room. In the other condition, they would be integrated, randomly with respect to perceptual type, across the room.[47] The room had rows of chairs, so it really did look like a waiting room you might see at the dentist's office or at the Department of Motor Vehicles. On the desks, we placed folders with further instructions. Each folder was assigned to one of the participants, which allowed us to unobtrusively arrange for them to sit in certain locations. The folders came in two colors, representing the two perceptual types, so the participants could see whether all the Type H's sat on one side of the room and all the Type Y's on the other or whether they were integrated. The different seating configurations while waiting – segregated or integrated – were the treatments. In this experiment, the subjects in the segregated condition were *moving through* segregated space as they entered the room and found their seats, acquiring route knowledge of that space. Thus, between this experiment and the three experiments (lines, squares, and faces) above, which represented space using survey knowledge, I had now covered both of the ways that space is stored in our memory.

The subjects were asked to wait there for five minutes, without speaking or using their phones. After five minutes, we sent each subject to a separate

Photograph of neighborhood or "waiting room"

H Y H H Y H Y H Y Y	H H H H H H H H H H
Y Y Y H H Y H H H Y	H H H H H H H H H H
Y Y H H Y Y H H H Y	Y Y Y Y Y Y Y Y Y Y
Y H H H Y Y H Y Y H	Y Y Y Y Y Y Y Y Y Y
Integrated waiting room	**Segregated waiting room**

FIGURE 4.8. The "neighborhood" we created in a laboratory.

We created a "neighborhood" in the waiting room in our classroom laboratory (top), with orange (Type H) and purple (Type Y) folders arranged on the desks to indicate where the subjects should sit. The neighborhood could be either integrated (bottom left) or segregated (bottom right). In the segregated neighborhood, Type H's and Type Y's were on different sides of the room, in integrated on the same side of the room.

room for data collection. The separate rooms were important because we wanted to ensure that the subjects answered our questions in private so as not to be biased by social desirability. In the rooms, they answered two sets of questions on the laptop we provided: (a) their perceptions of directly observable, physical attributes of the two groups and (b) their perceptions of social attributes of the two groups. They were asked to give their best guesses about the levels of these attributes. The physical attributes were height, weight, and age. The social attributes were income and politics – how liberal or conservative was the average member of each group. Participants also answered the more subjective social and physical questions of whether they had "things in common" with each group and whether the "appearance" of each group was similar to their own.

When people signed up for the experiment online, at least several days before actually taking part, we asked them similar questions about their own personal characteristics: height, weight, age, political ideology, and income. These allowed us to have a baseline to see how much segregation changed perceptions of these physical and social characteristics[48] – would segregation actually affect how tall or heavy or conservative they thought people were, relative to their own height, weight, and ideology? Our prediction was that, relative to the ingroup, a person would find the outgroup increasingly different from himself or herself as segregation increased.

After the participants reported their answers, the experiment was over. We repeated this entire process until we had tested over two hundred subjects in total.[49]

The results of this unusual experiment? After only five minutes of sitting in a certain spatial arrangement with groups that were completely fabricated, our subjects thought that the heights, weights, and ages of people in their ingroup were more similar to their own than the heights, weights, and ages of people in their outgroup were to their own. They also thought that people in their ingroup were more socially similar to them, in terms of politics and income, than people in the outgroup were. As other researchers had found, the simple act of categorizing had collapsed the difference within groups and increased the difference across groups. But here is the key: *this perceived difference between the outgroup and ingroup was even larger when the groups were segregated than it was when they were integrated.*[50]

Think of it: five minutes of segregation was enough to change people's perceptions about other human beings. Consider why these changing perceptions are important. For example, consider our participants' perceptions ˈof political ideology: segregation was causing people to perceive a greater ideological distance between themselves (and their ingroup) and the outgroup when the groups were segregated than they perceived when the groups were integrated. Liberal subjects thought people in their ingroup were more liberal and people in the outgroup more conservative when the groups were segregated than they did when the groups were integrated. Vice versa for conservative subjects. In Chapter 3, I suggested that the reason a behavior such as voter turnout was related to segregation was that segregation was causing voters to see other voters as more or less similar to them, thus changing the value of their vote. The more similar other voters are to you, the less worthwhile the act of voting. The less similar other voters are to you, the more worthwhile the act of voting. This laboratory experiment showed that segregation can indeed have this effect on perceptions of similarity – that the separation of groups in geographic space will cause the separation of people in psychological space and, ultimately, political space.

We might go on to wonder if the distortion of perceptions of social and physical differences, like those I saw in this experiment, affects other group-bias behaviors, such as racial discrimination in hiring.[51] This could happen if people use these distorted perceived differences as heuristics for differences in other dimensions. For example, say a white manager is looking for an employee. She wants to hire the most competent person. But competence is a hard attribute to judge, which makes it just the type of decision for which a person is likely to substitute an "easy" attribute – a heuristic – for the hard one in order to conserve cognitive resources.[52] That easier attribute could be a physical attribute, such as height or weight; after all, she can see these with our own eyes, making them easily accessible to us. If group membership and social geography have distorted the manager's view of height and weight, making her think Blacks are systematically more different from herself than whites, and if these attributes are used as a heuristic substitute for competence, this could cause the manager to think that Black people also have systematically different competence. This would affect the hiring decision because the manager assumes, as most of us do, that she herself is competent and, therefore, that people different from her are less so. This could be extended to other forms of systematic bias, as in criminal sentencing, where perceptions of difference in one social or physical attribute are used as a heuristic for perceptions of guilt.[53]

Changes in Behavior

In this same experiment, we also actually measured whether biased behavior, analogous to discrimination in hiring, was caused by segregation. Every outcome I've described so far in this chapter has been what might be called "cheap talk," meaning that when a person responds to an anonymous survey, there are no consequences for what they say. Such responses might not actually translate into real behavior. We wanted to find out if segregation affects actual costly behavior, the type that matters in the real world and that may be hard to change because, given that it is costly, people will stop and think carefully about what they are doing. If social geography affects costly behavior, then the impact of social geography seems especially strong. The easiest way to make something costly is to involve money, so we gave some subjects $10 in one-dollar bills and asked them to play a "Dictator Game," which economists often use to measure generosity and fairness. This game is simple: you give somebody – the Dictator – $10 and ask him or her to share as much as he or she wants with another person. Then you take note of how much the Dictator shares and how much she keeps. (Not much of a game, actually.) We used a variant of the game in which the Dictator shares with two or more people, which allows you to measure how willing she is to share with different types of people. For example, will the Dictator share more with people in the ingroup than with those in an outgroup? The difference between ingroup sharing and outgroup sharing is a group-based bias.

In our experiment, the game was played in private. The subjects were given an envelope with ten $1 bills and three other enveloped marked "You," "Type H," and "Type Y." They were told to divide up the ten dollars however they wanted and to take the You envelope with them and leave the Type H and Type Y; and the money in those envelopes would be mailed to a randomly chosen subject from that group. In this way, the subject simply put the envelope in her pocket and none of the other subjects knew how she played. After recording the results, we mailed the money as promised.

We wanted to know if the difference between ingroup sharing and outgroup sharing would be greater with segregation. The answer is yes. The amount of difference, about $0.40, was large relative to the usual differences in these games.[54] Keep in mind, these Dictators were dealing with people they had never met before and would likely never see again and they didn't have to give them any money in person – it was completely anonymous. Yet the simple act of segregating them for five minutes caused our Dictators to show more bias in favor of the ingroup than they did when integrated. In my opinion, this is a remarkable result – this was real money being affected by just a few minutes of segregation from entirely made-up groups.[55]

We will see this game again in Chapter 7, where I will discuss going to people's homes in Israel to see how segregation affected sharing across religious groups. Despite its simplicity, this game is a very powerful demonstration – it is pure bias: giving to one person over another, a person you will never see again, simply because they share your identity. This problem, when scaled up across entire societies, we are told, contributes to the civic and economic troubles of diverse societies.[56] In Chapter 2, I argued that social geography contributed to these troubles: that segregation and group size contributed to group-based bias that resulted in social inefficiency. Here we see direct evidence for this: as I segregated this local environment – moving the puzzle pieces around to create segregation – the direct effect was costly bias. Multiply that segregated local environment across entire societies, with socially meaningful groups, such as race or religion, and this inability to share resources – to come together in the public sphere – makes it very difficult for societies to get things done.

In these experiments online and in the laboratory, the noise is neatly trimmed away from the signal. Having created our "neighborhoods" from scratch, we could be confident that the only thing left that could be different about segregated and integrated neighborhoods was our induced segregation, so it has to have been the cause of the changes in perceptions and costly behavior. In these experiments, I moved my subjects horizontally across social geography on the Plane of Context (see Figure 1.7 on page 30) while holding all else constant:

there was no difference in history, culture, or politics – only segregation. Here the demagogue stands in plain sight.

One element of noise that was removed was interpersonal contact. Outside of the laboratory, contact does, of course, affect group bias, thus the difficulty in understanding why segregation affects our behavior. Segregation simultaneously limits contact and affects our perceptions. In these experiments, contact was removed from the equation because it was held constant between treatment and control. We can therefore see plainly that segregation can affect our behavior through a purely perceptual mechanism, even while the experiential mechanism of contact is held in check.

The next question, of course, is: do these experiments tell us anything about behavior in the real world? We will look at a real-world experiment on social geography in the next chapter, but first consider what Celaya and I wrote in our article about these experiments:

Extrapolating from the laboratory to real-world segregation gives a sense of how the outcomes we observe will likely be magnified outside the laboratory, where segregation can be large-scale and long-standing. If segregation can influence attitudes and even induce discriminatory behavior when applied to small, arbitrary groups for mere minutes, then consider its power to shape attitudes and behaviors when it is a persistent feature of an environment and is correlated with meaningful social divisions, such as class, ethnicity, and religion.[57]

And, of course, we have evidence for what segregation can do to attitudes and behaviors when it is persistent and the groups are meaningful because this is what we can see all over the United States and the world. Now, however, we can say confidently that it was segregation and not something else causing this bias – we have proven it in the laboratory with an RCT.

We have now covered a considerable distance – geographically, conceptually, and methodologically – in this book. The purpose of this chapter was to examine the micro-processes of social-geographic impact. In a laboratory and in nationwide surveys, I tried to peer inside the minds of subjects. I manipulated space and, thus, directly saw the impact of space on behavior. We even saw it change costly behavior: social-geography actually changed people's willingness to allocate money to different groups.

Now that we've gone from the macro to the micro and shown in the laboratory that group bias is operating through the mechanism that I claim, I will return to the field to demonstrate that social geography is so powerful that even outside the confines of the laboratory – even when the noise of the real world is allowed to interfere in the experiment – we can still see the power of space to shape our behavior.

5

Boston: Trains, Immigrants, and the Arizona Question

> Geography alone is not gonna change it. If I like to sit and whittle sticks, the fact that you move me somewhere else, I'm gonna still sit and whittle sticks, because that's what I know.
>
> – Chicago Alderman Leslie A. Hairston, 2014[1]

Rafael and Jose were awake every day before 4 AM to make their way across Boston to South Station, the city's main train station. There they would catch an outbound train to the wealthy suburbs to the west of the city, arriving in the village of Grafton before 6 AM. Then they would wait on the platform. When the next inbound train arrived, they would head back to Boston.[2]

According to hundreds of people to whom I showed their photographs, Rafael and Jose looked handsome, intelligent, and friendly. In my personal interactions with them, I found them so. But other rail passengers at Grafton station were uncomfortable and seemed not to want them there.

How do I know this? Because I surveyed these other passengers and their responses were unambiguous. Why were they uncomfortable with these handsome, intelligent, and friendly-looking young men? Because they were speaking Spanish.

Rafael and Jose were at this train station because they were part of an experiment I conducted in the summer of 2012. My goal was to make people think that their neighborhood was experiencing demographic change due to immigration; that is, I wanted to change the social geography of their community. My research team placed pairs of people working for me – "confederates," in the language of experimental research – at train stations to wait for the same train at the same time each morning during rush hour. These confederates were native Spanish speakers. A train time had been paired with another train time at the same station and, randomly – by the proverbial "flip of a coin" (actually by a pseudo-random number generator on my computer) –

one time was assigned to treatment and one to control. The train time assigned to treatment was visited by the confederates; the other was not.[3]

Rafael and Jose were not asked to behave any differently than one might normally behave when waiting for a train. Nor were they told the purpose of the study; they did not know we would ask the other passengers their opinions of them. As such, the experiment was double-blind so that neither the confederates nor the subjects (the people at the train stations) knew what I was looking for or even that they were in an experiment.

The two Spanish speakers looked handsome, intelligent, and friendly, but also looked "foreign" and like "immigrants," according to people who saw their photos.[4] I wanted to know whether being exposed to them would provoke a backlash against immigration from Mexico. I chose the communities visited by Rafael and Jose with a particular feature in mind: they were overwhelmingly Anglo white.[5] In such places, I could simulate demographic change from immigration – the experience of foreign-looking and foreign-sounding people entering a community. Would this experience change people's attitudes about immigration policies? Would they want the law to keep more immigrants out or let more immigrants in? Because some communities were randomly assigned to have the number of Latino immigrants increased and some were not,[6] I was, in effect, controlling the forces of social geography – assigning communities to experience demographic change.

We often think of demographic change, from immigration or other sources, in terms of the cultural or economic impact. Will current residents experience a change in the language they hear every day? Will they feel competition for jobs? But, of course, demographic change also changes a group's social-geographic impact. Because of the existing segregation, one component of the social-geographic impact of Latinos on Anglos in the Boston area was already high and I was, on a small scale, increasing it even further by locally increasing the size and proximity, thus the cognitive accessibility, of one of these two groups. The number of Latinos introduced was tiny, but because these were homogeneously Anglo communities, the relative increase was very large.

By introducing Rafael and Jose into Anglo communities, I was creating the situation that animates this book: different groups of people occupying the same place. I was increasing the social-geographic impact of Latinos and thus their salience to the Anglo commuters. In this experiment, the commuter train platforms in suburban Boston replaced the subway lines in Chicago as the point of contact, where the groups come together across the social and psychological space dividing them. And just so you don't think I only concern myself with trains, let me repeat that we come together in many public places, some spatial – such as on the beach or simply on a city street – and some institutional – such as our local, state, and national governments. Our relationships in these geographic and institutional spaces are intertwined.

Immigrants and natives must share these spaces. Immigration – the arrival of an outgroup – means social-geographic impact is increasing while interpersonal contact across groups is low. When immigrants arrive – speaking a different language, importing their own cultural institutions, and often working in different employment sectors – the native and immigrant populations will have little opportunity for interaction. Of course, interpersonal contact often increases with time, but in these initial stages of immigration – the beginning stages of the arc of intergroup interactions, the type I was introducing in the Boston suburbs – this contact has not yet happened. Looking back at the plane of context (Figure 1.7 on page 30), we see that this situation of high social-geographic impact and low interpersonal contact is the situation in which group-based bias should be highest. Into this situation, I came as the experimenter, altering both space and contact. By increasing social-geographic impact, I moved Boston to the right on the horizontal axis of the plane of context. By randomly changing contact, I also moved Boston ever so slightly up on the vertical axis. My theory predicts that these two forces should move against each other, one increasing group bias and the other decreasing it. What actually happened?

THE "TRAINS" EXPERIMENT

This experiment garnered some attention in the media because it touched on the hot issues of immigration and diversity – issues that have certainly become no less relevant since I executed the experiment. But to academics, it was notable, not because it was a study on diversity – there are countless such studies – but because it was an *experiment on diversity*. Actual experiments on this type of diversity – changing the context of a person's neighborhood – had never been attempted. This experiment addressed whether geography alone can change behavior. Chicago Alderman Leslie A. Hairston claimed it could not in the quote at the beginning of this chapter, when I asked her if the movement of people due to the transformation of public housing in Chicago would change behavior. To her, if a person likes "whittling sticks," she will whittle sticks, wherever you put her. For our purposes, this claim would mean that if a person holds group-based bias, this bias will be found regardless of the social geography in which that person is embedded, perhaps because the bias is a feature of personality or upbringing. As my experiment in Boston and my study of the actual housing projects in Chicago, covered in the next chapter, show, Alderman Hairston was wrong about this.

I am occasionally asked why I did this experiment in Boston. Aside from the fact that I was living and working in that area at the time, it was the right type of area for this experiment because it did not have a large Latino population.[7] It would, of course, be difficult to noticeably increase the Latino population in places like Los Angeles that already have large Latino populations. The impact of Latinos there is already large.

But why, within the Boston area, did I target homogeneously Anglo communities? Wouldn't the residents of these communities already have biases against Latinos? In fact, the residents were not particularly biased against

Latinos; actually, quite the opposite. But even if they had been, communities with very few Latinos are exactly where we want to study the effect of Latino immigration. Studying the effects of immigration in a place with a lot of immigrants is pointless; it is like studying the effects of adding water to a swimming pool. We want to know what happens when a place's demography actually changes in a way that people living there can notice; that is, when immigrants arrive anew.

Thus, the suburbs in this study represented the many similar places in the United States. Sometimes it is surprising to those of us who live in diverse communities to realize that, because minority populations tend to be distributed unevenly, most places in the United States actually look like these Anglo white suburbs. Even though Latinos make up about 17 percent of the US population in 2017, they are mostly concentrated in a few areas, so that in most places, the proportion of Latinos is only a few percent. Thus, in many parts of the United States – in fact in what may be described as the "typical" community – the arrival of Spanish speakers *is* likely to be noticed. Moreover, to the extent that the people in these Boston suburbs were atypical, it is that they were overwhelmingly racially and politically liberal, making these locations *a hard test of the power of demographic change* because these were people who, we might think, would be unlikely to change their attitudes in the face of immigration.

In order to appear that they were local residents, my confederates were visiting the stations in the morning, boarding the trains inbound to Boston. Visitors or domestic workers who would more likely be heading outbound from Boston. Prior to my confederates visiting these nine suburban stations around the Boston area, my research team surveyed people waiting at these stations about their attitudes about politics, including what they thought about immigration policies.[8] They were given a website's URL and asked to anonymously complete the survey at some point during the day. Our assumption was that these commuters would go to work and, after a while, decide they would rather take our survey than actually work. We were right. Hundreds of commuters completed our survey.

With the first round of our survey completed, we now had the opinions of hundreds of commuters on issues of immigration. After waiting a few days, we were ready to cause a change in social geography and see if group-based bias increased. Rafael and Jose were joined by other confederates with similar characteristics – all were Mexicans in the United States on visas – and we assigned pairs of them to the stations. My confederates were crucially important to the success of this project – they had to wake up well before dawn every day and follow the route they had been assigned. Over the course of two weeks, they faithfully followed their assignments, thereby exposing these villages in the Boston area to a small uptick in immigration.[9]

In addition to the commuters' attitudes about immigration before my experiment, we also needed their attitudes about immigration after they were exposed to my Spanish-speaking confederates, this would allow us to see how their opinions changed after being "treated" by immigration.[10] To get these post-treatment opinions, we collected email addresses from our survey respondents and emailed them three days later to invite them back to take our survey again at a later time. In this way, we were able to see how opinion on immigration would become more exclusionary. These opinions were a form of group-based bias because they were targeted at a certain group – immigrants from Mexico – and would presumably be different if targeted at a different group. How would this bias change before and after experiencing immigration on the train platform (keep in mind, the treatment was on the platform, not the train)?

After these early mornings by the confederates and my research team, what did we find?

WHAT HAPPENS WHEN TWO "IMMIGRANTS" VISIT A TRAIN PLATFORM?

After a few days, Rafael and Jose and the other confederates mostly just reported that they were bored, as you might be too if you had to ride the train for no apparent purpose everyday.[11] As might be expected, when they were bored, they talked to pass the time and, as native Spanish speakers, they did so in Spanish. This was a crucial – and planned – element of my study: it introduced Spanish into these communities where it was otherwise rarely spoken. It is also the way in which many people experience immigration: in fleeting moments, but repeatedly;[12] perhaps hearing Spanish in a public place or calling a business and hearing, "Para español, oprima el dos." Thus I was realistically simulating this change in immigration – this slight uptick in social-geographic impact. After three days of – perhaps – hearing a little bit of Spanish on their way to work, we emailed some of our survey participants to see if this small dose of Spanish had caused bias.

The summer I conducted this experiment was my eighth year in academia, so for eight years I had been studying the backlash created when groups occupied the same geographic space – and I'd been thinking about it for much longer. But even I was shocked at what we learned when we examined the data from this experiment. Keep in mind that the commuters were exposed to just two people – *two* – for just a few minutes a day as they went about their daily lives, boarding the train and being distracted by newspapers, phones, people, and their own thoughts. There was no guarantee that anybody would even notice my confederates at all. However, when the survey data came back, when the salience of the outgroup had been increased by their presence, the commuters had reacted by strongly increasing group-based bias – becoming more exclusionary to this group. They had become significantly more opposed to immigration from Mexico to the United States: They were more likely than before to say that the United States should send the children of undocumented immigrants back to Mexico, that immigration from Mexico should be reduced, and, possibly, that English should be the official language of the United States.[13]

Two people had this effect. Two people showed up at these train stations, among the thousands of people that a commuter will pass on the way to work in downtown Boston, and yet commuters, perhaps subconsciously, extended their discomfort from these two people to policy about an entire class of people: immigrants from Mexico. This demonstrates the power of social groups – and the geographic impact of their size and proximity to us – in shaping our attitudes. With this little change, the demagogue of space had whispered rather loudly in their ears.

Rafael, Jose, and their fellow confederates seemed to have sensed the discomfort they caused. Remember that I never told them that they themselves were the treatment in the experiment. They had no idea that we even cared what people thought about them. Nevertheless, in the reports they filled out daily, they said things such as "because we are chatting in Spanish, they look at us. I don't think it is common to hear people speaking in Spanish [here]." After the experiment, the confederates reported that they felt people noticed them for "not being like them, and being Latino."

What did we learn from this experiment? The people waiting at these train stations were largely upper-class, liberal, and white. The overwhelming majority had voted for Obama and they probably considered themselves to be a proud part of the tradition of liberalism in Massachusetts. But two young Spanish speakers for just a few minutes, or less, for just three days had driven them toward anti-immigration policies associated with their political opponents.[14]

This result may seem surprising – and it was to me, too – but it also makes sense when we consider it in light of what we had already learned. Scholars have told us that the backlash against immigrants arises from either (a) a threat to jobs or economic well-being[15] or (b) a threat to culture.[16] In fact, academic debates about the roots of anti-immigrant attitudes are portrayed as a contest between these two causes.[17] The evidence from my Boston experiment speaks to this debate: the commuters in these suburbs were under little threat of losing their jobs to the stereotypical low-wage immigrant (the average yearly income of my subjects was about $140,000), yet they reacted strongly to the presence of these immigrants in their communities.[18] We might therefore think that the commuters in Boston were reacting to a cultural threat of some sort, although this, too, is surprising given that the commuters were liberals whom we might expect to be comfortable with immigration. But I think viewing this backlash as a contest between the effects of economic and of cultural threats, even if both do have some effect, misses something important: the basic effect that immigration has on our cognition.

Immigration changes the size and, often, the proximity of a local outgroup. This is a change in that group's social-geographic impact. Perhaps immigration is setting off the same basic cognitive mechanisms as the presence of other outgroups set off in other situations – Blacks for whites and whites for Blacks in Chicago or even the minimal groups I created in a laboratory. This could explain why – both in my experiment and in other research – people's reaction to immigration seems so divorced from the actual impact of immigrants on their economic well-being[19] but so dependent on the size of a local immigrant population.[20] It might even explain why some studies demonstrate that immigrants do not face an increased backlash by virtue of being culturally very different from the native population,[21] or even why if you speak to Anglo individuals involved in anti-Mexican immigration politics, as I did in Arizona, they will steadfastly maintain that they believe the cultural influence of Latino immigrants to be good for their communities.[22] Perhaps when social geography, playing on tendencies evolved in our distant ancestors, affects our basic cognition, the influence of culture and economics fades into the background.

The geographic impact of the little bit of manufactured immigration in my experiment also suggests what to expect with actual immigration. The geographic impact of a group increases with its size. Given the effect of these two newcomers for just a few minutes each day, imagine the impact of an increasingly large flow of people, starting as a trickle and growing to a flood, on the salience of that outgroup.

We should also consider the impact of immigration as the nature and amount of the exposure changes as a place moves along the arc of intergroup interactions. My experiment was probably true to the way immigration is usually experienced – for fleeting moments each day as newcomers take roles on the edge of society. This exposure was an instantiation of the fleeting treatments I administered in the laboratory that caused subjects to draw on heuristics when making decisions. But with real immigration, these fleeting moments give way to something more permanent. The good liberal people catching trains in the Boston suburbs became exclusionary after just three days. There is a very important follow-on to this point because I also kept track of what happened to group bias over an even longer period. Those findings suggest the over time ameliorating effect of contact, but I'd like to set that discussion aside for the moment because it will be more informative after considering the motivation for this experiment.

This experiment was a big undertaking, especially by the standards of some fields of political science. Well over 30 people were involved and we spent an entire summer executing it. But the experiment helped to demonstrate a paradox rooted deeply in our psychology: the psychological space between us increases when the geographic space between us decreases. By bringing people closer together, I was actually creating more sociopolitical distance between them. My theory of social-geographic impact explains why. But why did I go to all this trouble with the suburban commuters to demonstrate this? Why did I need to do something so complex to test my theory? I was attacking something I call the *Arizona Question*.

THE ARIZONA QUESTION

The Arizona Question is both a question of scientific inference and a question of public policy. The scientific question is: is there a relationship between immigration – or the presence of any outgroup – and group-based bias? The public policy question is: if there is a relationship, what is the proper public policy to address the bias?

Importantly, just as my research in Boston was not about Boston per se, but about any place experiencing immigration, the Arizona Question is not really about Arizona per se, but about any place that has *already* experienced immigration. After conducting this experiment, I went around to various universities giving lectures about the research. I had not really put much thought into the fact that I called this the Arizona Question versus anything else, until after a talk at Oxford, UK (of all places), where a woman from Arizona told me she was offended that I had singled out Arizona. Point taken. Below, I'll explain why I choose Arizona in particular, but in fact, what my Boston experiment indicates is that there is nothing unusual, in this regard, about the way people in Arizona react to immigration. In fact, the people of Massachusetts, given the opportunity, seem to behave very much like the people of Arizona. One goal of this book is to understand why people in Massachusetts, Arizona, and other places all seem to react in the same way. So, in that sense, the Arizona Question is really just shorthand for the *fundamental inferential challenges related to understanding the effects of diversity on behavior.*

Here is the Arizona Question from the perspective of public policy. If American history is any guide, it is seemingly inevitable that some cities – perhaps most cities – will experience new flows of immigration. We don't know what this does to group-based bias among a city's current residents. Will they welcome the immigrants with open arms? Will they react negatively? Knowing the answer would suggest the proper public policy on immigration and tolerance of immigrants.

This question is relevant nearly everywhere in the United States, including places much different from the big cities we often associate with immigration and diversity. In fact, the relevance of this question and the commonality of native reactions to immigrants is a hint that part of the bias against immigrants springs from our basic cognition.

In Chapter 1, I described Lake Yosemite, outside of Merced, California, the farming community in California's San Joaquin Valley where I grew up. In Merced, a good portion of the Anglo population is descended from people who arrived in a wave of internal immigration from Oklahoma during the Dust Bowl. These white immigrants, too, were excluded and exploited, as famously portrayed in John Steinbeck's *The Grapes of Wrath*, set in nearby Tulare. In a similar manner, white Irish immigrants to Boston and other places faced fierce discrimination from the Anglo-Saxon natives.[23] And the descendants of these Irish immigrants subsequently discriminated against Blacks immigrating from the South.[24] The California natives in Steinbeck's novel told the Anglo migrants from Oklahoma, when threatening to expel them, "Well, you ain't in your country now. You're in California, an' we don't want you goddamn Okies settlin' down." And, in a near-perfect example of the commonality of immigrant exclusion, Steinbeck explained their logic:

In the West there was panic when the migrants multiplied on the highways. Men of property were terrified for their property. Men who had never been hungry saw the eyes of the hungry. Men who had never wanted anything very much saw the flare of want in the eyes of the migrants. And the men of the towns and of the soft suburban country gathered to defend themselves; and they reassured themselves that they were good and the invaders bad, as a man must do before he fights. They said, These goddamned Okies are dirty and ignorant. They're degenerate, sexual maniacs. Those goddamned Okies are thieves. They'll steal anything. They've got no sense of property rights.[25]

That people we now think of as "white" could face an exclusionary backlash, using the stereotypes whites now reserve for others, indicates the psychological underpinnings of discrimination and exclusion. Any group of people can be the target of group bias – perhaps because social-geographic impact has increased and time has not yet allowed for interpersonal contact to soften the impulse of exclusion. It follows, too, that the lines of inclusion and exclusion can shift. Today, Irish seems synonymous with Boston. And these "Okies" did put down roots in the California's Central Valley so that, in many ways, Merced and other such farming communities were – and still are – culturally closer to Oklahoma than they are to places like San Francisco.

And the lines of exclusion and inclusion continue to shift. When I was a child, the schools and social services in Merced grappled with a major influx of Hmong people from Laos, refugees from the wars in Southeast Asia. This population grew to be about 10 percent of the city. Familiar stereotypes were applied to this population: that they spread disease, increased crime, cheated natives out of jobs, or were dishonest in business.[26]

Moreover, it seems odd now, but in my childhood, I think it is fair to say that Latino culture and the Spanish language were considered a novelty for most Anglo people in Merced County. I remember that newspaper articles would explicitly identify a person's Latino nationality, saying something like "Mr. Rodriguez, a Mexican." Within 20 years, Latinos had become a plurality in the area.

The social psychologist James Sidanius uses the term "arbitrary sets" to describe distinctions – racial, religious, nationalistic, and others – that vary in importance across time and place.[27] The term *arbitrary* is useful here, I think, because it demonstrates how easily these distinctions can change in importance. At one time, the distinction between Okie and native Californian or between Anglo-Saxon and Irish were very important, but this has faded. However, it's crucial not to confuse *arbitrary* with *random*. The reaction to these groups and the changes in acceptance vary in predictable ways. But *why* do they vary in this way? This is the Arizona Question from the scientific perspective.

Why Do I Call It the Arizona Question?

Of course, immigration is not the only way to produce demographic change. There is also the intergenerational growth of immigrant populations. In the United States, a long-sleeping giant of demographic change, with roots in Latin America, has awoken with profound implications for the future composition of the country. The population trends are now well understood: persons of Hispanic origin currently make up about 17 percent of the US population, but are projected to make up over 30 percent by 2060.

Arizona is at the vanguard of this population change – and therefore of the increase in the social-geographic impact of Latinos – in the United States. Arizona is *already* 30-percent Hispanic. In 1980, it was about 16-percent Hispanic, so that population has about doubled in three decades, while the proportion of the Anglo majority has been reduced. This means that in the last three decades, Arizona has been an exact microcosm of the change expected in the rest of the United States over the next half century. What will happen as this Latino population grows and spreads beyond its current communities? Will group-based bias increase?

How have Anglos in Arizona reacted to this increased geographic impact of Latinos? Looking at survey data, Arizona Anglos, relative to Anglos in other states, have more negative attitudes about Latinos and about immigration.[28] Arizona has also garnered a negative reputation as a place with overly harsh anti-immigration laws[29] and xenophobic public officials, epitomized by the sheriff of Maricopa County, Joe Arpaio, whose department was reported by federal investigators in 2011 to have "a pervasive culture of discriminatory bias against Latinos."[30] Arpaio is a dramatically polarizing figure, so hated by much of the Latino community in Arizona that an immigrant activist in Phoenix told me that children grow up being afraid of him. "[I]nstead of playing, 'The boogie man's going to get you,' [they play] 'Arpaio's going to get you.'"[31] Yet, he was popular with enough people in Maricopa County, presumably mostly Anglos, that he won election six times, surviving recall efforts in 2007 and 2013, before finally being defeated in 2016 while under federal criminal indictment for contempt of court.

So, an easy summary would be that Anglo Arizonians have reacted negatively to the growth in Latino population. It seems that the social-psychological space between Anglos and Latinos has grown as immigration increased.[32] (Of course, not all people in Arizona have the same attitudes and, as I will discuss in Chapter 9, some differences may be due to the forces of contact I explore in this chapter.) If we extrapolate this conclusion to the rest of the United States, we might predict that Anglos in other states, when demographic change makes their community look more like Arizona – when the social-geographic impact of Latinos increases – will also react negatively. This does not bode well for the country's well-being. As many scholars have shown, when a large segment of the population holds negative attitudes about another large portion – that is, when group bias is rampant – democracy and civic culture suffer,[33] and economic growth is retarded.

If growth in group-based bias is the result of the growth of the Latino population, then this growth of the Latino population has ominous implications for the harmony of American society. But does it have to go that way? To answer this question, we would have to know why bias has increased in Arizona. All I have shown is that there was immigrant growth in Arizona and now there seem to be negative attitudes about immigrants; I have not demonstrated causality. Is the bias actually due to the rise in the Latino population or is it due to something else? The Arizona Question is vexing because answering this is very difficult.

Explanations for Attitudes in Arizona

I have offered a particular theory for why group-based bias is higher in areas where groups occupy the same place. But for the sake of understanding the Arizona Question, let's step away from my theory and consider the more general problem of scientific inference. As I said, we don't understand why Anglos in Arizona have these negative attitudes about Latinos. There could be many reasons:

Culture: One of my favorite cocktail party anecdotes is that Arizona was briefly part of the Confederacy during the Civil War. Perhaps today's group bias is indicative of a cultural legacy of racism in the state. There is certainly evidence that sociopolitical attitudes can be transmitted from generation to generation; in other words, that they are a feature of the "culture."[34] Once upon a time, perhaps, this racism targeted Blacks, but now it spills over onto other non-whites. Indeed, we might expect whites who have negative attitudes about Blacks to also have negative attitudes about Latinos because negative attitudes about outgroups tend to be correlated.[35]

Elites: Most people's political opinions are heavily influenced by the opinions of elites, such as politician and pundits.[36] As I have mentioned, scholars have also argued that this influence extends to attitudes about groups.[37] Perhaps politicians in Arizona have effectively exploited anti-Latino attitudes in order to gain office and the attitudes we see on surveys are the result of this exploitation.

Selection: Arizona is a state of migrants, both international and domestic. Perhaps domestic migration is why there are so many people with negative attitudes about Latinos. For example, it could be that people with anti-Latino attitudes move to Arizona when they retire, perhaps because the cultural legacy of the state as part of the Western frontier appeals to political conservatives who also happen to feel negatively toward Latinos. Or perhaps people who are anti-immigrant also, on average, happen to have lower incomes and when making a decision to retire to a warmer climate, find that Arizona is more affordable than Florida. This would mean that people with anti-Latino attitudes are *selecting* to live in a certain place.

Threat: "Threat" is a general term for the negative psychological impact of an outgroup on behavior and it is often thought to be stimulated by the local presence of an outgroup or by contact with the outgroup.[38] It is a shorthand that many scholars would use to describe what I am studying in this book: the reaction of one group to another group in the same place. Threat covers many different mechanisms, including economic and political competition and, in my case, a basic psychological reaction. In any case, threat predicts that the Anglos in Arizona have negative attitudes about Latinos because the Latinos live in the same place.

These explanations are not mutually exclusive but, if we agree that ethnic harmony is a good thing, sorting between them is important because they imply different policy responses. Thus the public policy of the Arizona Question is wrapped up in the science of the Arizona Question. For example, if the problem is a threat, the solution is to somehow address the source of that threat. One possible way to control threat is by limiting diversity, but we might agree that limiting diversity is not desirable, even if it were possible. We might therefore turn to another intervention that targets the people holding negative attitudes about immigrants, perhaps through education. If threat is the main problem, that also suggests that places like Massachusetts, which currently have lower proportions of Latinos than Arizona, should explore policies to preemptively combat group-based bias; otherwise, attitudes toward Latinos will grow increasingly negative as the Latino population increases there, too.

A cultural explanation has different policy implications because it means that, while Arizona might have a problem on account of specific cultural traits, places like Massachusetts will be able to absorb the coming demographic change with little worry.

If the source of bias is elite influence, the policy solution is less clear because demagoguery is a time-tested tradition for politicians across the world. It probably cannot be eliminated without regulating political speech, which, with good reason, is looked upon skeptically in free societies. If selection is the source of bias, the policy implication is also unclear, because this explanation tells us less about the ultimate cause of bias and more about why people with bias happen to have traveled to a certain location.

Threat and cultural explanations fall under what is often called theories of *contextual effects*, which are theories stating that a behavior or attitude will vary across context – say, different states or cities – because something particular about a particular context causes people to behave differently.[39] My theory of social-geographic impact is a contextual theory. Selection, on the other hand, is a non-contextual theory because it has nothing to do with the location itself, but rather with the people who decided to move there. Their attitudes and behaviors have already been shaped by something about them, perhaps their personality or upbringing, and would be the same even if they had decided to move somewhere else.[40]

In broad strokes, contextual theories imply that in a counterfactual world in which a giant picked people up and moved to them to a new location, their attitudes and behavior would start to resemble those of the people in their new location. Selection theories, on the other hand, imply that moving people to a new location will have no effect on their behavior and, rather, if enough of them are moved, aggregate attitudes in the new location could start to look more like those of the people who were moved. Selection theories and contextual theories are often seen as fundamentally different and, indeed, they are: contextual theories imply something "sticky" about the location, independent of who lives there, while selection implies something "sticky" about people, independent of their location.

These broad-stroke counterfactuals are, of course, overly simple. Of course, nobody really believes that behavior is so context-free that moving a person to a new location would not affect her behavior. And nobody really believes that individual personality or habit is so powerful that a person is completely unaffected by her context. When an immigrant arrives in the United States, of course her behavior and the behavior of her children will, with time, start to look more and more American. But the influences of her original culture will also likely mean that she remains a bit different from somebody born in the United States. These broad-stroke theories are useful, not in absolutely describing the world, but in helping us to understand cause and effect. For example, if we claim that context is affecting a person's behavior, we need to account for the fact that selection *could be* – and probably is – also affecting behavior. Nobody doubts that context can affect behavior and careful studies of "neighborhood effects" have strongly suggested it can.[41] However, the exact nature of contextual effects – how much they really matter – is elusive to researchers because selection and context are impossible to definitively pull apart without randomized controlled trials on context. In short, science is poorly equipped for sorting between theories of context and selection.

This difficulty in sorting between context and selection is what makes the Arizona Question so difficult. If we want to know what happens when groups occupy the same place, we run into the Fundamental Problem of Causal Inference because we cannot observe, say, an Arizona with immigrants and an otherwise identical Arizona without them in order to determine whether context or selection is causing bias among Anglos there.

As I'm sure is apparent by now, much of the research in this book is focused on attempts to overcome this problem. I focus on it because it is fundamental. This is not just an academic or methodological curiosity; it is at the very heart of any study of context and of many socially important problems. Anytime we hear in the news that people in X context have Y happen to them, this fundamental problem will arise. When a person says, for example, that there tends to be more crime where there are more immigrants or that aggregate happiness is inversely correlated with aggregate wealth or anything else tying human behavior to place, the problem of selection will arise. It certainly stands in the way of our understanding what happens when groups occupy the same place and of our knowing how to address it through public policy.

The research of many other scholars who have studied context has been limited by this difficulty of separating the effects of context from selection – the "specter" that casts "doubt on almost all observational research."[42] This specter, when it comes to the study of people and place – separating the stickiness of context from the stickiness of people – seems particularly difficult and it has remained, even in all the decades since Key's study, because it is difficult to randomly assign context. I asked above why I would go through all the trouble to design something so complex as my experiment on the train platforms. We can see how it addressed the problem of separating context from selection – the Anglos did not choose to live in an area with Latinos; rather, Latinos were assigned to their area. When we see the Anglos' attitudes change, we know that context, rather than selection, is the cause.

This was similar to the motivation for my laboratory studies in the last chapter – in those studies, because I created context in the laboratory, I was sure nobody was selecting into that context. Thus, selection was held constant. And in Boston I was going through the trouble of assigning context in real world in order to study complexities of the social world in a way that could not be done in a laboratory. These complexities, including repeat contact, are also at the heart of understanding what happens when groups of people occupy the same place, so I will explore those before returning to the answers to the Arizona Question.

Complexities of the Social World and the Ideal Experiment

I often tell my graduate students that when thinking about their research, they should imagine the ideal study – the study they would conduct if they had unlimited resources. Taking this approach, if we wanted to know what will happen to Anglo attitudes when Latinos move into a new city, we could imagine randomly buying houses in certain neighborhoods and moving Latinos into these houses, then measuring the attitudes of the residents with new Latino neighbors versus the attitudes of those without. This ideal experiment would certainly allow us to overcome the Fundamental Problem of Causal Inference – and to begin to answer the Arizona Question – but is outside both financial and ethical bounds.[43]

The thought experiment is nevertheless worthwhile because it allows us to recognize crucial complexities of the social world that we need in order to effectively study context – to really answer the Arizona Question. It seems that previous studies, including my laboratory experiments, were missing at least two crucial items: (a) assigning context, rather than assigning people, and (b) repeat contact.

Assigning Context, Not People

Notice that in my imaginary perfect experiment, I said I would measure the attitudes of the existing residents after moving Latinos in. I didn't say that I would randomly assign some people to move to new locations with Latinos living nearby and assign others not to. Why do I make this distinction? Because what we care about is changing context, not changing people. That is, we care what happens when an individual's community changes around her, not what happens when an individual moves from one place to another. (That's also an interesting question, but a different one.) Studying the mover is problematic because it confuses the problem of a person's context changing – the thing we care about – with the process of moving itself, which is not what we care about. Say we wanted to know how a person's neighbors affected the person's level of trust,[44] so we randomly assigned certain people to move and measured the levels of trust of those who did and those who did not. We may find that those who moved were less trusting of other people. Is this because of their new neighbors or just because they moved and no longer have their old routines, networks, friends, and other comforts of home? With this experiment, it would be difficult to separate these two possible causes of the decrease in trust.[45]

In fact, there have been some experiments in random assignment of context. In the famous Moving to Opportunity experiments, for example, residents were randomly given the opportunity to move out of Chicago housing projects to less-impoverished neighborhoods. The idea was that scholars would be able to isolate the effect of context – specifically, the context of high poverty – by moving some residents out of that context. Many social scientists were disappointed with the experiment's results, which did not, in the short term, show the positive social benefits that some had hoped would come with the massive change in context. For example, some political scientists expected that these residents would become more politically active, but this did not happen.[46] Should we conclude then that context has no effect, that moving people out of high-poverty neighborhoods is of little value? No, of course not, because as Sampson (2008) has pointed out, the effects of the new context to which people are experimentally assigned are inseparable from the effects of the move itself. Perhaps people don't politically participate more after escaping poverty because this random assignment of the ability to escape also disrupted the social ties that encourage political participation.[47]

My experiment on the train platform overcame this problem by assigning my confederates to go to neighborhoods and thus change the social geography of those neighborhoods, rather than getting subjects to go to different neighborhoods. Thus the neighborhoods were changing around the subjects while everything else remained constant and the effect of context – social geography – was isolated.

Repeat Contact

The other element of my ideal experiment – missing from nearly all other studies, including my laboratory experiments – is repeat contact between members of different groups. In the typical study on intergroup relations, subjects are in contact with another group for a short period, maybe 30 minutes, in a laboratory or online before a researcher records the effect of this contact. The subjects never meet again and so the researcher doesn't know how their behavior would have changed on the second, third, or subsequent contacts. Would group-based bias have been reduced? Intuitively, we think such repeat contact may be important – doesn't your level of comfort with somebody change, the more often you interact with them? And, of course, classic research on the topic, including Allport's famous thesis, tells us these repeat interactions are important.[48]

Social geography and contact are interrelated. When social geography changes, the probability of contact changes, too. If members of a group increasingly migrate to a city, not only does their social-geographic impact change, but, all else equal, a person who is not of that group is also more likely to have contact with someone who is. Of course, the growth of a local outgroup population does not mean that the contact will meet the conditions for improving intergroup relations that were outlined by Allport and other contact theorists[49] and the growth of the outgroup does not even guarantee that repeat contact will happen – segregation can powerfully separate people. But when a group comes to a new city and a new neighborhood, there is a good chance that repeat contact, even if fleeting, will occur across groups. If a newcomer moves into your neighborhood, won't you see them more than once? If you went to a bus or a train stop near your home at the same time every day, might you see the same people there? Over time, would you get used to seeing these people there? Would you begin to nod and smile at them? Would these positive interpersonal experiences become accessible to you when using heuristics in intergroup interactions, thus breaking down the groupishness of that group and replacing it with individuals?

Repeat contact may be the way people often experience diversity, but it has been missing from most experiments on intergroup relations. Exposing subjects to a different group once – say by showing them a photo on a computer or having them play games against another player – teaches us something important to be sure. But it teaches us little about the actual experience of living in a diverse or diversifying environment where exposure may be fleeting but also frequent. The exceptions are studies in certain institutional environments, such as college dorms[50] and summer camps,[51] in which the subjects see people from the outgroup every day. But, of course, cohabitation with an outgroup member is atypical in most societies and cohabitation across racial and ethnic groups is certainly atypical in the United States. It is simply not how most of experience diversity. So for scholars to learn about reactions to the diversity that comes with immigration, it is important to learn about the fleeting intergroup interactions that might occur when new immigrants are likely to be cleaning dishes, tending a lawn, or running a small store. The challenge for me and other people studying context is to incorporate such contact into our studies.

When I tell my students that they should think of the ideal study, I tell them that if that experiment cannot be executed – and it almost never can – they should try to find the best practical alternative. This is what I tried to do with my train study. For the first eight years of my academic career, I was thinking about the ideal experiment for understanding context – that of buying up homes and moving people in – and trying to imagine the best practical alternative. It was thinking about how in cities, even if I don't know people, I still sometimes see them repeatedly, that led me to see the commuter trains in Boston as the practical alternative I had been looking for.

When I was in graduate school at UCLA, I lived on the eastern edge of Hollywood. I would take the bus on the famous Sunset Boulevard, westbound toward UCLA. When I got on at Sunset and Western Avenue, Latino residents from the neighborhoods further east would already be on the bus. I would see the same women, always speaking Spanish, every weekday. They stayed in my memory because we would make the journey together as other people came and went. They were housekeepers – heading toward the mansions of Beverly Hills and Bel Air. In my memory, these women never seemed to pause from their conversations as the bus moved through one neighborhood after another. In Bel Air, the housekeepers, who by then had been riding for well over an hour, would say goodbye to each other and, one by one, get off the bus where a car was waiting to drive them up the hill to a wealthy Anglo's mansion.

Public transportation provided routinization, meaning you had a good chance of seeing the same people in the same place at the same time. This is similar to seeing a neighbor every day – perhaps a new neighbor who has moved into your area. The likelihood that the same people are in the same place every day means you can expose them day after day to a treatment – for example, Spanish-speaking immigrants. It was this quality of public transportation that was the inspiration for using commuter trains. They provided the best practical alternative to the ideal study – the same people caught the train at the same time everyday – so without buying homes in a neighborhood and moving people in, I could change a person's context by introducing some new people and then exposing my subjects to those same people day after day.[52]

What Is the Effect of Repeat Contact?

Routinization allowed me to assign repeat contact, thus coming closer to answering the Arizona Question. But how did I measure the effect of repeat contact? I did this by running more than one RCT in Boston. First, there was the RCT of assigning some train platforms to experience the change in social geography via the introduction of the confederates, while some did not. This allowed me to understand the effect of social geography – the change in the horizontal axis of the plane of context. After three days, the subjects of my experiment became more exclusionary: social geography had increased group bias.

The second RCT is that I had randomized the subjects in the treatment group into being surveyed at two different points in time: either three or ten working days (two weeks) after the treatment began. This second RCT allowed for different doses of repeat contact – the change in the vertical axis of the plane of context.

After three days, attitudes toward people from Mexico became more exclusionary than they had been before the treatment. Those surveyed after ten days still favored more exclusionary policies, but less so than the group that had been surveyed after three days (see Figure 5.1).[53] This shows that the initial urge to keep out a group of people after seeing them might have softened. Not that attitudes were becoming positive – for example, wanting to welcome more immigrants – but they were less exclusionary after ten days of contact than they had been after three days of contact.

In the waning days of the experiment, our confederates themselves reported things that made it sound as if people were coming around to them; for example, "people have started to recognize and smile to us." They mentioned that a passenger who spoke to them said "the longer you see the same person

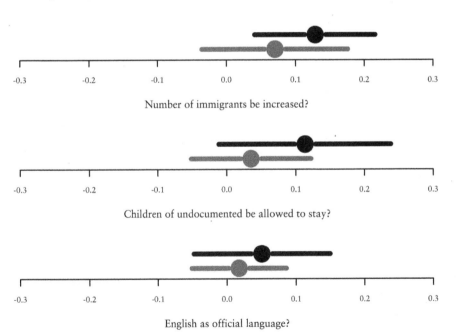

FIGURE 5.1. Effects of the trains experiment, by length of contact.

Effects of the treatment based on three days of repeat contact (black circles) and ten days (gray circles). Lines are 95 percent confidence intervals. Responses were on five-point scales and have been rescaled to 0–1 in this image. This figure is adapted from Enos (2014a).

every day, the more confident you feel to greet and say hi to them." These interactions suggest something about the effects of contact on the group-based bias caused by social geography; namely, that the initial exclusionary reaction had diminished with contact. It's possible that, given enough time, say a month or a year, the aversion would wear off and my confederates would be welcomed into the community. As I address in Chapter 9, perhaps this ameliorating effect of contact is what we have seen in some areas of the United States, such as California, where the virulent anti-immigrant politics of the 1990s gave way to an embrace of immigrants. Perhaps Arizona or Boston, when the time comes, will move along this arc of intergroup interactions from clash to indifference.

Being able to detect this difference between initial and prolonged exposure allowed me to understand the role of repeat contact. The train platforms provided for routinization and this routinization provided for repeat contact of the type that allows people to get to know somebody – perhaps to overcome the psychological space between groups that is caused by social geography. In a sense, then, social geography and interpersonal contact worked against each other.[54]

The fact that group bias changed when the amount of contact with the "immigrant" confederates changed also reminds us of the limitations of observational research on demographic change. Because the effects of contact and social geography are working against each other, it is hard to separate the effects of the presence of one of these mechanisms from the effects of the absence of the other when they have not been experimentally assigned. Without randomly assigning the opportunity for interpersonal contact, as I did by randomly varying the number of days my confederates were on the platform, these two mechanisms are impossible to pull apart and contact and social geography remain muddled, as indeed they are in most research. This muddling is, of course, part of the Arizona Question: unless we can conduct experiments, we are limited in our scientific understanding of the effects of immigration and thus our public policy solutions have little evidence to go on. Is bias just a matter of needing more interpersonal contact? Then perhaps we should turn to schools and other institutions to increase this contact. But, as my experiments have shown, contact is only part of the story; geography, too, is directly affecting our attitudes. And what is the policy solution for geography affecting our attitudes?

What Did We Learn about the Arizona Question?

Because Rafael and Jose's presence at these stations had been randomly assigned in an RCT, I knew that the changes in people's attitudes that we recorded were *because* Rafael and Jose had been there. In other words, I knew that the arrival of immigrants, or people who looked like immigrants, had caused this anti-immigrant backlash. This was a big step toward answering the Arizona Question. I overcame a crucial problem of inference because I used an RCT and thus learned something about the causes of anti-immigrant attitudes in places like Arizona. My experiment showed that it didn't seem to be anything culturally distinct about Arizona, which in turns means that such an anti-immigrant backlash could just as well happen in someplace like Massachusetts. There did not seem to be anything distinct about the people who lived in Arizona, nor did it seem necessary to have demagoguing politicians in the picture – I had controlled for all those factors in my RCT. On average, the only thing that was different between the people who changed their attitudes about immigration policy and those who did not was the experience of demographic change by way of exposure to two Spanish-speaking people on the train platform. Rather than a demagoguing politician, the collapsing of the geographic space between groups had served as the demagogue.

Returning to the question of why I would go through the trouble of designing and executing such an elaborate experiment, I can answer now that it not only made improvements over observational studies that suffer from the problem of selection, but also improved over studies in the laboratory because of the ability to assign repeat contact.

There is not a single piece of social science inquiry that has ever been fully closed based on a single piece of research. The scientific study of society is too difficult to allow for this. Our tools are too blunt: we cannot experiment on humans as we do on subatomic particles or on other animals. It goes without saying that my study in Boston did not close the question of how immigration affects attitudes or the more general question of what happens when groups occupy the same place. But it did, I think, move us considerably along.

The space between groups grew with the insertion, for fleeting moments, of two members of the outgroup. The situations described by Key and other researchers I've described in this book, like the segregation between whites and Blacks in Chicago and like the situation in Arizona, is something more permanent and, obviously, larger in scope. Anglos in Arizona or whites on Chicago's North Side share a place with the outgroup on a permanent basis. In both cases, the outgroup is large. (In Arizona, it is growing.) In both cases, the outgroup animates politics, fueling public policy and demagoguery. Does my experiment say that Boston – in some ways the spiritual capital of American liberalism – could become like this as its own immigration grows?

Trying to answer this question reminds us of the limitations of an experiment such as mine. A single experiment, even a complex one, has only limited meaning when considered in isolation. Often, for the results of a single experiment to have meaning, it has to be part of a larger research agenda, like the ones I have described and those I will describe in the chapters to come. It should also be considered in light of the history, culture, and milieu of a place. By understanding the context of Boston, we can better interpret the results of my experiment and better understand what it can tell us about other places. In the language of experimental methods, we would call this the experiment's "external validity." So, what did we learn? Will other places – including Boston – become like Arizona?

WILL BOSTON – AND THE REST OF THE UNITED
STATES – BECOME LIKE ARIZONA?

When I discuss this experiment, I sometimes hear a response to this effect: "That's not surprising, Boston is a such a racist city." In fact, as I indicated above, the subjects in my study were decidedly to the political left. Most described themselves as "liberal" or "very liberal," over three-quarters had voted for Obama, and most, when asked in the first round of my survey, did not express hostile attitudes toward Latinos or other minority groups.[55] So, we might not suspect that my subjects were the Boston racists I am sometimes asked about. Yet Boston certainly does have a spotty history of race relations and maybe Boston's racism is not captured in my survey questions. If the people of Boston are particularly unwelcoming to outgroups, then maybe this experiment set that off, producing results that would not be found in other cities. If so, this too helps us to understand how well my experiment answered the Arizona Question: perhaps what we find in Boston is not informative for the rest of the United States. The only way to truly address these claims would be to run more experiments in other cities. In the absence of such experiments, we must consult our knowledge about the city and the phenomenon of racism in Boston and assess whether Boston is a good model for what will happen elsewhere in the United States. Doing so also helps us to see the striking continuity of reactions to immigrants across time and place, even within Boston.

Boston's reputation as a particularly racist city is, perhaps, a result of vicious boycotts and riots over attempts to integrate public schools through busing in the 1970s. In Boston's working-class white neighborhoods, such as Southie, angry mobs threw rocks at the windows of buses carrying Black children, a scene so ugly that a former Boston police officer, who specialized in racially motivated crime, said it was " the most hate that [he had] ever seen."[56]

In that respect, Boston was just an example of a phenomenon that played out in the 1960s and '70s in American cities from Los Angeles to New York, as federal courts ordered the integration of schools. However, a longer view of history does make Boston's virulent reaction to integration especially surprising. After all, this is the city that had once been on the forefront of Abolitionism and, by some indications, racial liberalism. It is where Ralph Waldo Emerson traveled from Concord to deliver a speech comparing John Brown – a violent abolitionist, accused traitor, and committed racial liberal – to the crucified Christ, thus fanning the flames of civil war.[57] And where, just a few years later, the first Black Union soldiers paraded through the streets on their way to fight against slavery. A huge relief statue to these soldiers stands prominently in front of the Massachusetts State House in Beacon Hill. Many of the crowded buildings in this neighborhood have plaques marking stops on the Underground Railroad. A block from my office at Harvard stands Memorial Hall, a stunning Gothic edifice dedicated to Harvard's dead from the Civil War. The names of the young men who died in battle is a reminder of how important the cause of Abolition was in Boston and Cambridge. These were not poor young men, drafted to fight for something in which they may or may not have believed, but sons of privilege, volunteering and dying for a cause. The hall was built intentionally to look like a church in a reference to the almost religious reverence with which men of Harvard viewed the cause of ending slavery. Across Harvard Yard sits a statue of Charles Sumner, the radical racial liberal from Massachusetts. Sumner was far ahead of racial mores in the mid-nineteenth century – for example, he opposed anti-miscegenation laws – yet Massachusetts elected him to the Senate and his likeness sits outside the main gate of the state's most famous institution.

Although such generalizations are always risky, it seems safe to say that, qualitatively, something changed in the heart of Boston between the idealistic days of Emerson and Sumner and the 1970s, when Boston's reputation for liberal idealism ran headlong into the reality of racial violence. A longtime Boston resident reminded me during an interview that "we voted for McGovern in '72," but then added, "Yeah, because we have this tremendous belief in the dignity of everybody, and at the same time, we're, you know, beating the shit out of each other."[58] The legendary basketball player Bill Russell was undoubtedly the greatest sports champion Boston has ever seen among its beloved professional teams, winning 11 NBA championships with the Boston Celtics in the 1950s and '60s. Russell, who was Black, called Boston "a flea market of racism." A statue honoring Russell was not constructed until 2013, 44 years after he retired, and long after white Boston sports legends such as Ted Williams had been honored. Many observers attributed this delay to racism among white Bostonians and Russell's often uncomfortable relationship with the Celtics' white fans. This is a legacy that, even today, Boston has never really shaken.

What happened to Boston that changed it so much that its residents had trouble embracing the best player on their beloved team and were willing to throw stones at schoolchildren? We can examine explanations similar to those I offered for Arizona: (1) racism is part of Boston's culture and always was, (2) Boston's racism was caused by opportunistic politicians, (3) Boston became racist when new European immigrants came to the city, or (4) Boston became racist once it had enough Blacks.

We can't observe a Boston with one history and simultaneously observe another Boston with a different history. And it seems unlikely that we can use an RCT to randomly assign any of these treatments, so it is very difficult to know for sure. But thinking a bit about Boston and what we learned from my experiment and the other evidence in this book, we might be able to make an informed guess. This informed guess will tell us if Boston's racism makes it uninformative for thinking about the Arizona Question. We can say, as we just discussed, that Boston has not always had a culture of racism; in fact, quite the opposite, at least by the standards of the time (explanation 1).

When Boston desegregated the schools and housing projects, there were, of course, politicians and other local elites who loudly denounced these policies (explanation 2). In Southie, politicians turned to "pulling a George Wallace" by standing at school doors to block the entrance of Black students.[59] It sounds likely that these politicians fanned the flames of racial violence and Bostonians will tell you that this was their experience. However, the presence of these race-baiting elites is a good example of the inferential difficulties associated with the Arizona Question. We don't know if such race-baiting was a *necessary condition* for the group-based bias that followed; that is, we don't know that grassroots violence wouldn't have sprung up even without racist leaders. Yet, in my experiment there were no local elites, at least not in an immediate sense, fanning the flames of anti-immigrant bias, and there still was an increase in anti-immigrant attitudes. This is, of course, a long way from the violence of the 1970s, but it seems that my RCT tells us that the initial increase in group-based bias does not have to come from politicians.

A popular explanation for Boston's turn to racism is the arrival of Irish immigrants, starting in the 1840s (explanation 3). This is a theory of selection that I have never found persuasive. The theory probably reflects the observation that the neighborhoods of Boston most resistant to Black integration in the 1970s, such as Southie, were largely of Irish stock. But it does not follow that their being Irish is what caused them to be opposed to integration. We could just as easily argue that any working-class group of any ancestry would be threatened by the arrival of an outgroup. And, indeed, there are such examples, such as the working-class Italians and Jews in the Canarsie neighborhood of Brooklyn, who also took to mob violence to block Black children from entering their schools.[60] Furthermore, as my experiment showed, a decidedly non-working-class population, many of whom are not of Irish stock, can be threatened by an outgroup. It therefore seems incorrect to say that people of a certain nationality or income level are particularly prone to bias.

This makes me think we should consider the fourth explanation – the one consistent with my theory of social-geographic impact. Was it threat from an incoming group – an increase in the salience of the group due to changes in social geography – that caused Boston to change its racial culture? In the 1860s, when Sumner was leading the Radical Republicans in Congress to incorporate Blacks into society and Harvard men were dying for the cause of Abolition, Boston was just over one percent Black. In 1940, it was about three percent Black. But by 1970, it was over 16 percent Black. These numbers are telling. The percentage of the local outgroup had changed dramatically, just as the Latino population in Arizona has in recent decades and just as in the suburban Boston communities where I conducted my experiment increasing the local Latino population.

Perhaps, then, the most obvious answer is that Boston became more racist when the outgroup population increased in the local environment. There may therefore be nothing extraordinary about Boston: it is part of a pattern we have seen and will see over and over. It happened in my small hometown of Merced, where the native population was not Irish and the immigrants were Southeast Asian; it happened in the city of Boston where the population is Irish and the immigrants were Black; and it happened in Arizonas, where the natives had come from Ohio and New York and other Rust Belt states and the immigrants had come from Mexico and elsewhere in Latin America.

But this explanation also raises another question. Keep in mind that I said above that the commuters in my study started to feel more at ease with my confederates as time went on. And with Black immigration in the 1950s and '60s, we can see a similar pattern. A new population with low contact arrives and, with this increase in social-geographic impact, group-based bias increases. But if subjects in my experiment started to feel at ease with the Latino immigrants to their community after just a couple weeks, why was racism toward Blacks still so apparent in the 1970s, after the major influx had already occurred? If it is not part of white Bostonians' culture to be racist, shouldn't they have had enough time to get used to their Black neighbors and to overcome their aversion? This question highlights what my experiment also suggested and what other evidence in this book has shown us. First that the size of the group matters – immigration does not usually stop with two people, it grows and sometimes becomes a flood of change. In many cases, like Blacks in Boston, an immigrant population will become a substantial portion of the population, thus consequentially increasing the salience of the outgroup. Second, segregation matters, not only because it limits contact but also because it is an interactive component of social-geographic impact, amplifying the effects of an increase in the size of the local outgroup. As we have seen, the phenomenon of groups living in the same place, but living segregated lives, dramatically affects group bias. The people of Boston were largely segregated by race and still are. The geographic and psychological space between these groups was large and still is.

Thinking in counterfactuals, we might say that Boston's racial history would have been different had people lived in more integrated communities – that is, if an institution or law had funneled newly arrived Blacks into neighborhoods that were and remained diverse. Of course, the history of residential segregation in the United States tells us that this is easier said than done.[61]

The role of segregation may also help us understand why the experiment on the train platforms could increase bias with only two people. Consider the map in Figure 5.2, which is a map of Boston and surrounding communities with Census Tracts colored by percent Hispanic. Notice the clustering of Hispanics in geographic space: within Boston's city limits and in a few of the working-class inner-ring suburbs to the north, such as Everett and Chelsea. There are sharp discontinuities going across borders; for example, moving across the border from Boston to the more affluent town of Dedham to the southwest. Dedham is about 90 percent non-Hispanic white and – perhaps related to its homogeneity – it still governs itself by a modified type of town meeting, as it has since the seventeenth century. One sees another sharp discontinuity moving

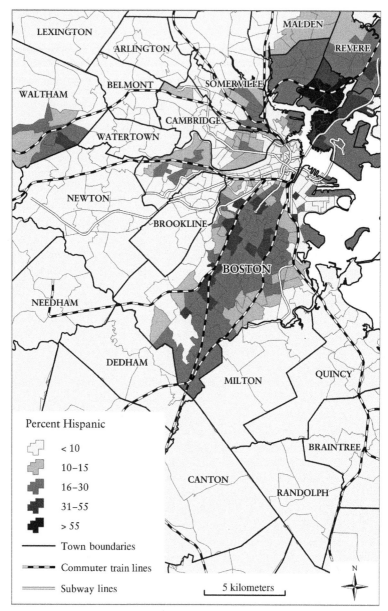

FIGURE 5.2. Boston and neighboring communities, percent Hispanic, 2014.
Units depicted are Census Tracts.

across the border to the west from Boston to Brookline, the leafy community
where many of the Boston area's elite live and home of *The* Country Club, so
named because it was one of the original country clubs in the United States.

These discontinuities are, of course, not accidents. They exist across many borders from larger cities to smaller suburbs where communities used zoning laws to keep the poor out and implicitly to maintain racial homogeneity, thus contributing to the clustering of racial minorities in central cities and older suburbs, such as Chelsea (62 percent Hispanic), where the older and smaller housing stock prevents such zoning.[62]

The subjects in my experiment were traveling from the west to the east, moving through this segregated environment – coming from these homogeneously white suburbs into Boston, with its clusters of Hispanic population. To give some perspective on levels of segregation in Boston: Hispanics in Boston are segregated from whites at almost double the national average of Hispanic/white segregation and at about the same level at which Blacks are segregated from whites in Los Angeles.[63] Based on the studies in the last chapter, we know that many of my subjects probably had accurate maps, such as Figure 5.2, in their mental images of the Boston area. When I raised the accessibility of a group by introducing it into this segregated world, the reaction was strong.

Now look at the counterfactual map in Figure 5.3, where the clustering of Hispanics has been rearranged, randomly, by a computer. Here the two worlds – Anglo and Latino – are not so separate. The space between groups is not so stark. My claim is that this change would also affect the comparative fit of groups and, therefore, the perceived difference. What would be the result of my experiment in this counterfactual world? My guess is that sending Rafael and Jose to the same locations in this counterfactual world would not have produced even a blip in the attitudes of the commuters in my experiments.

These maps point to the power of social geography. They suggest, as I have argued, that segregation itself affects group-based bias. Moreover, they suggest that segregation overpowers some of the ameliorating effects of contact between groups. Surely, these commuters had contact with Latinos in their daily routines at work and when taking part in commerce in downtown Boston; after all, Latinos are nearly one-fifth of Boston's population and work disproportionately in the service industries, serving food and doing other tasks for people like the Anglo commuters on these trains. The introduction of just two extra Latinos could not have made a meaningful change in the total number of Hispanics they see or interact with every day, just in the number they see and interact with near home. It could therefore be that their strong reaction was in part a result of people simply caring more about what happens near to their homes, as opposed to further away – a process psychologists call "territoriality"[64] – so the Latinos in downtown Boston did not stimulate aversion but those turning up in their local communities did. However, drawing on the theory I have offered, the mixing and churning of people in Boston's diverse downtown means that the comparative fit of people in a group there is low: you see two people on a crowded street downtown and you are not sure to what group they belong or even if they belong to the same group at all. In the homogeneous white suburbs, however, the comparative fit of people to a group is high: a white person sees two Latinos together in this Anglo suburb and the

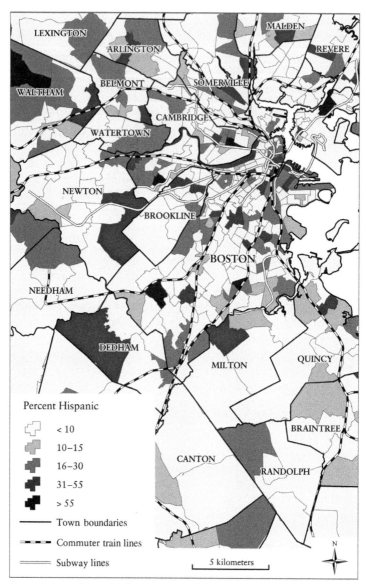

FIGURE 5.3. Counterfactual distribution of Hispanic population in Boston and neighboring communities, 2014.

Counterfactual distribution created by the random reordering of populations across Census Tracts.

Latinos' similarity to each other grows in her mind, while the distance between Latinos and Anglos grows larger. More generally, what this demonstrates, I think, is that the way people form attitudes about other groups involves far more than just contact. It also involves the changes in the salience of groups induced by certain types of exposure in certain contexts – in this case, a highly segregated context.

At the risk of confusing the reader, I have been switching back and forth between Hispanic immigration and Boston's history of anti-Black racism because I believe they are two sides of the same coin. In both cases, the reaction is an example of group-based bias driven partially by social-geographic impact. This is not to say that there are not unique elements to the bigotry applied to any particular group or that bigotry has the same impact on all groups, but only to say that some part of it, wherever it springs up, does spring from the same source. As we saw in the last chapter, the vital ingredients of social-geographic impact are segregation and an increase in the size and proximity of a population; these ingredients are present for both the Hispanics in my experiment and Blacks in Boston in the 1970s.

We can also see these ingredients fueling the violent group bias between whites and Blacks in Boston in the 1970s and '80s. Francis "Mickey" Roache was the Boston Police Commissioner from 1985 to 1993. Before being elevated to commissioner, he was the head of the Boston police department's Community Disorders Unit, which was tasked with policing racially motivated crime. In 2014, I interviewed Roache, by then the Register of Deeds for Suffolk County, Massachusetts. Given that our conversations were about social geography, his office was most appropriately located in what was once Boston's West End, which had been predominantly Jewish and Irish before massive urban renewal forced those populations out. Roache was elderly, headed for retirement, but eager to talk. We sat for hours as he and his former law-enforcement associates recalled the history of racial crime in the city.[65] Roache had lived and worked this history: growing up in Southie and graduating from South Boston High School, the very school he was then assigned to in the early 1970s to protect Black students from white residents throwing rocks at their buses.

The late 1970s were times of serious disorder in Boston. In Roache's words, there were "hundreds of incidents where rocks were flying through windows, Molotov cocktails…an enormous problem with racial violence."[66] This violence followed the court-ordered desegregation not only of the public schools but also of large all-white public housing projects in traditionally white neighborhoods, like Charlestown and Hyde Park. Just as small numbers of Black students entering South Boston High School had provoked violent reactions, single Black families moving into white housing projects also provoked violent reactions that Roache and his officers had to handle.

To me, this is a real-world analogy to my experiment and to the mechanism I propose to explain what happened when Rafael and Jose visited train stations: in a highly segregated environment, a small influx of an outgroup population stimulated group-based bias. I find the parallel between these two situations – separated by time and place – to be tantalizing.

Roache and his colleagues, charged with handling racially motivated crime, had of course thought deeply about the predictors and causes of that form of bias. From my perspective, what was most remarkable about my conversations with them was how much social geography was part of their explanation for crime. Over and over, they pointed to the same cause for violence in Boston: Black and white segregation and the meeting of the segregated populations along neighborhood boundaries.

On the bulletin board in my office hangs a map drawn for me during one of these conversations (shown in Figure 5.4). A rough outline of Boston, it has lines slashing down the page representing certain streets which were the lines of racial division and across which groups met:

We crammed all Black people into the Blue Hill Avenue corridor [and] it began to pop up along the border line...

So we began to see all the racial activity happening was around the borderlands, right? And a big one was where the population of people that was second generation began to push out of the Blue Hill Avenue narrow corridor, began to push east across Washington Street and into the neighborhoods between Washington and Dorchester Avenue. That's how it became a big ... racial battleground.[67]

Compare this map to Figure 5.5, which is a map of Boston and the surrounding communities by percent Black in 1970. The segregation – the Black people "crammed...into the Blue Hill Avenue corridor" – is strikingly

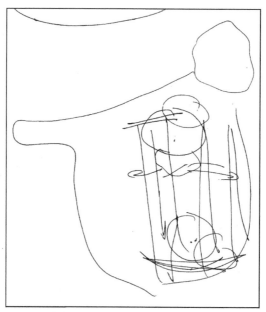

FIGURE 5.4. Boston's racial division and racial crimes, drawn by former police officer. Drawn for the author during interview in January 2014.

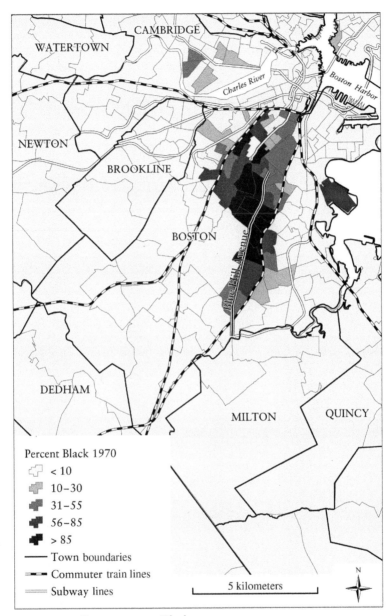

FIGURE 5.5. Boston, percent Black, 1970.
Units depicted are Census Block Groups.

apparent.[68] The slashing lines marking the corridors of conflict can also be plainly seen on this map. (Note, too, the confinement of Blacks between the railroad lines and recall the discussion of railroad lines as a statistical instrument for segregation in Chapter 2.)

Hearing this from these long-time observers of group-based bias was amazing to me. Here was real-world experience, right in line with the academic theory I had developed. To these Boston police officers, streets such as Blue Hill Avenue were the racial "borderlands," the areas where segregated groups came together. In other words, they were the equivalent of the "L" stations I had observed in Chicago, but with outright violence rather than just tension.

The exact elements of social-geographic impact are all there: segregated communities, a growing Black community where "the pressure begins to build,"[69] and the points of geographic proximity between these neighborhoods. In fact, in later discussions, the officers suggested that the reason the integration of public housing in the neighborhood of Charlestown was smoother than that in other parts of the city was that Charlestown, separated from the rest of Boston by Boston Harbor, was further away from a larger Black population – the counterfactual claim being that had this housing project been nearer to that large Black population, whites would have reacted just as violently to the court-ordered integration.

The persistence of this pattern is remarkable. Repeated again in Boston, across different times and groups. As I will discuss in detail later, the same pattern – segregation and an increase in the outgroup population producing an increase in group bias – can be observed in Arizona, Chicago, Los Angeles, and elsewhere. This sort of persistence across time and place should make us wonder what could be so fundamental that it can make the same thing happen in such varying contexts. My answer is the central role that social groups and space play in human psychology.

What does this tell us about the future of Boston? As its Latino proportion continues to rise, will Boston become like Arizona? The conditions seem to be present and the psychological basis of group-based bias suggests that, given those conditions, any place can become like Arizona. Even my brief discussion of Boston's racial history seems to indicate that a cultural legacy has only so much "stickiness." Even with powerful currents of liberalism and cues from elites, attitudes about outgroups can change within a few generations or even within one generation. In the segregated real world, the social and psychological space between Hispanics and Anglos in Boston is already large. And as we saw at the train stations, it only took a very small stimulus to make it even larger.

POSTSCRIPT 2016

On November 9, 2016, a day after the election of Donald Trump and less than a month after I finished this manuscript, an article in the online magazine *Vox* stated: "Enos's commuter train experiment is Trump's electoral strategy in a nutshell."[70] The author, Dylan Matthews, was referring to Trump's demonizing of Mexican immigrants on the campaign trail. In many ways, Trump's campaign, using the symbolic trope of building a wall between Mexico and the United States, was the solidification of a trend we have seen in American politics for some time. Mexican immigrants have increasingly been given the role of the bogeyman of American politics, to such an extreme degree that they may arguably have replaced Blacks in this role. Trump's use of the stereotypes so often applied to outgroups – of Mexican immigrants both as a drain on social welfare and as murdering rapists – demonstrates how elites can raise the salience of an outgroup: conservative politicians have turned to the immigrant as a convenient scapegoat for problems. But as Matthews's reference to my experiment indicates, Trump's rhetoric also shows the powerful influence of social geography.

Trump may or may not have made use of social-geography-induced attitudes knowingly, but he certainly seems to have done so effectively. His most dramatic gains – that is, where a greater percentage of voters voted Republican than had done so in 2012 – were in the places where the Latino population had grown most quickly. Looking at these patterns, in combination with what we learned from my train experiment, provides a relatively clear answer to the Arizona Question. Using county-level data, we can see that where the Latino population had grown most quickly between 2000 and 2014, Trump made the greatest gains over Mitt Romney, the Republican presidential candidate in 2012. We do not see any such relationship with recent demographic change when we compare Romney's voter share in 2012 to that of John McCain, the Republican presidential candidate in 2008 (see Figure 5.6). This was, to use the metaphor of this chapter, the rest of the country becoming like Arizona: states with strong traditions of Democratic voting, such as Pennsylvania, swung dramatically toward Trump. For example, Luzerne County, adjacent to Scranton, Pennsylvania, had experienced an almost 600 percent growth in its Latino population between 2000 and 2014, and, after decades of voting Democrat in presidential elections, gave Trump 12 percentage points more votes than it had given to Romney in 2012.[71]

We can see this pattern on the individual level too. Individual-level data reveals that it was not only Democratic places, like Luzerne County, but that it was registered Democrats in those places, who swung to Trump. Using survey data, I found that Anglo Democrats voted for Trump at the highest numbers in places where the Latino population had grown the most. The effect was large: moving from a county with no change in percent Latino to a county with the median change (a 57 percent increase) raised the probability of a Democrat voting for Trump by five percentage points. In 2012, too, the Hispanic population had been growing, but survey data shows Romney received a substantially smaller boost from it.[72]

This shift does indeed seem to be the electoral equivalent of the forces studied in my Boston experiment. In fact, what I was trying to simulate by assigning Hispanics to train stations had actually played out over the last decade in some parts of America. Towns with very low Hispanic populations – sometimes near zero – saw a sudden increase and white Democrats in those towns – much like

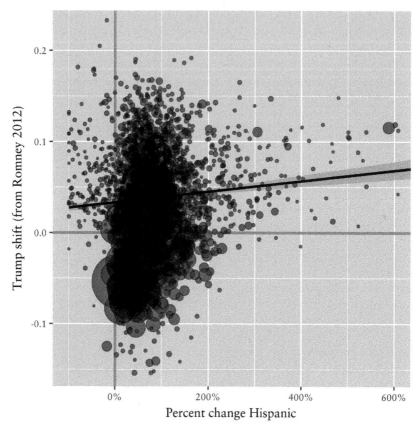

FIGURE 5.6. County change in percent Hispanic, 2000–2014, and Trump vote shift.
Y-axis is county percent for Trump in 2016 minus county percent for Romney in 2012. Diagonal line is OLS regression line. Points are scaled by population in 2014. The figure does not show the entire range of Hispanic growth (−100 to 1,600 percent) or the entire range of shift in Republican vote (−0.367 to 0.233 percentage points).

the white Democrats waiting for their trains in the Boston suburbs – took a dramatic step to the right. That meant voting for the politician who had made the exclusion of their new neighbors a centerpiece of his campaign. Meanwhile, in places like California – where immigrant populations are also still growing but have already been there a long time and where processes of integration and interpersonal contact have brought Anglos and Latinos together and weakened the demagogue of space – Trump, in many ways a flesh-and-blood demagogue, did much more poorly.

In this chapter, I asked if an exploitative politician was a necessary condition to move attitudes and behaviors against an outgroup and, because my Boston commuters had changed their attitudes with no such politician, I speculated that it might not be. In fact, Trump may have taught us that such a politician is, at least, not sufficient. Although in the course of the loud and virulent Presidential campaign, voters in all parts of the country surely heard about Trump's anti-immigrant rhetoric, they did not all respond to it. Rather, it was the voters where the immigrant population had suddenly increased who were influenced by Trump's rhetoric of deportation, exclusion, and vilification.[73]

6

Chicago: Projects and a Shock to Social Geography

Every great city has its bohemias and its hobohemias; its gold coast and little Sicilies; its rooming-house areas and its slums. In Chicago, and on the Lower North Side, they are in close physical proximity to one another. This gives one an interesting illustration of the situation in which the physical distances and the social distances do not coincide; a situation in which people who live side by side are not, and – because of the divergence of their interests and their heritages – cannot, even with the best of good will, become neighbors.

– Harvey Warren Zorbaugh, *The Gold Coast and the Slum*, 1929[1]

When an "L" train on Chicago's Red Line emerges from beneath the Loop heading south, it rumbles above the streets for a distance, then slips between the northbound and southbound lanes of the Dan Ryan Expressway, just south and east of the enclave of Chinatown. For the rest of its journey, the passengers have a view of the mighty expanse of South Chicago on both sides of them. Taking this train on my morning journeys to teach, I would read the *Chicago Tribune*, using the journey to keep up with the news. As we traveled south, around the time we reached US Cellular Field, where the White Sox baseball team plays, I would often put down my paper and marvel at the scenes to the east, across the northbound traffic lanes. Hulking over the expressway were the scarred and burned structures of Stateway Gardens, part of the massive expanse of public housing known as the "State Street Corridor" stretching along State Street from north to south.[2] In the collective American imagination, these projects were the epitome of public housing – decrepit, large, dangerous, Black. They stood right along the expressway so that people traveling to the North Side of the city, where most white people were probably going, could not help but see them. The projects had scars of fire coming out some of the windows, like permanent black eyes. The buildings seemed larger than they actually were – perhaps just because they were so ominous – and seemed closer than they actually were, looming over the freeway, probably reflecting the subtle fear they invoked in those passing by.

Between 2001 and 2004, as I rode the southbound trains, the projects would be especially noteworthy, not only because of their infamy, but because they were now being demolished. The demolition was a remarkable feat of reverse construction, which helped make their death as inglorious as their life. When the famous Pruitt-Igoe Homes in St. Louis, some of the first large-scale public housing the United States, were demolished, it was done with explosives, providing dramatic black-and-white photographs of an institution vanishing in an instant. But when the homes of the State Street Corridor were demolished, backhoes were somehow lifted to the top of these buildings and used to rip them apart, one story at a time, over the course of months. An observer on the Dan Ryan or on the "L" would see a building with its top jaggedly ripped off right next to one that was fire-scarred, yet structurally complete.

It was as if dynamite were not an appropriate end to these buildings; rather, they required a method of demolition that spoke to the despair of those who had lived inside. It seems strangely fitting: those projects were probably the most visible example of the failed program of mid-century public housing in the United States. In the 1950s, the neighborhoods where the projects now stood had been cleared and tremendous reinforced concrete buildings had been constructed in the best spirit of modern scientific functionalism, with the promise of humane and affordable housing. People had been displaced and concrete had risen. Now, once again, people had been displaced, but this time the concrete that had appeared was being made to disappear. These buildings were literally and slowly ripped apart from the inside, paralleling how poverty, crime, and the associated despair had figuratively ripped apart the buildings' communities from the inside.

To white people in Chicago, these projects had housed a large, segregated, and threateningly close outgroup: tens of thousands of Black people in the perfect spatial arrangement to influence the thoughts and behaviors of their white neighbors. After the projects were demolished and the outgroup dispersed, I learned that the presence of this Black population, before it was dispersed, not only caused emotions like fear, but even changed the behavior of white people, including even how they voted.

When considering the experience of whites living near to the housing projects that were eventually demolished, we can see a severe case of social-geographic impact. Here was an outgroup: large, segregated, and extremely proximate. Because many projects were high-rises, the group was stacked vertically, which increased its spatial concentration. In general, Chicago is a city where Blacks and whites are socially, economically, and residentially segregated – they "typically don't live, work or play together."[3] In the areas near the housing projects, this segregation was actually amplified – their place on the plane of context even more extreme than is captured by looking at the entire city. Because interpersonal contact between the two groups was nearly zero, social geography seemed to be nearly the only contextual influence on behavior. And then, despite their close geographic proximity, the social and psychological space between these groups was tremendous. My theory predicts, when the social-geographic impact was lessened by the demolition of the projects – that is, when the whites no longer had this large, segregated Black population so nearby – white behavior changed dramatically.

With this exploration of the fall of the Chicago housing projects, I will demonstrate the impact of social geography on a scale we have not seen yet – a massive dose of a segregated, proximate, and large outgroup. I will also be able to precisely measure the impact of proximity and size on group-based bias. And, we will also be able to see voting clearly change in response to social geography – something I claimed was true earlier in the book, but for which the causal connection to geography was unclear. Finally, because intergroup relations in Chicago is a subject with a rich scholarly history, we can see the continuity of the effects of social geography, even in the same locations in the city, going back almost 100 years and continuing to this day, reminding us of the universality of social-geographic impact – that it is not a phenomenon isolated in a certain time in history, but something that springs from deep within our psychology and can be seen across time, even as culture, technology, and the groups in question change.

ASSIGNING PLACE ON A LARGE SCALE

So far in this book, I have used experiments, both in the laboratory and the real world, to assign people to new places and see how their behavior is changed. By making changes to local environments – by adding two people to a train platform in Boston or arranging twenty people in a university classroom – for example – I observed the causal effect of context on a small scale.

But small-scale change is not what we actually care about. I sent two putative immigrants to train platforms and, although we did see a change in attitudes, we don't believe two immigrants is actually a very big deal. What we care about is the type of disruption to social geography we see in phenomena like the large-scale immigration from Latin America – which has dramatically changed the demographics of many states in the Southwest in recent decades – or like the recent mass immigration from the Middle East to Europe that has become a political high explosive in many countries.

Here, again, we see the challenge in social science research: even when experiments are carefully conducted, there are almost always questions of external validity. To what extent can the findings be extrapolated across different situations? This is one reason, of course, that I study my chosen phenomenon in different locations and with different populations, moving from Boston to Chicago and, in the next chapter, even out of the country. But even then, the complexity of the social world calls into question our ability to extrapolate across scales, from small to big. This might not be so limiting in the natural or physical sciences. Physicists, for example, could use precise mathematical predictions to extrapolate from the original fissions of single atoms to fissions large enough to become self-sustaining to those large enough to unleash nuclear energy and weapons. Thus, these scientific milestones came in a progressive order as the technologies and materials became available; for example, having enough radioactive material.

The achievements of these nuclear scientists were works of genius indeed, but consider how much more direct it is to extrapolate from a single atom to millions of atoms than it is to extrapolate from a small group of immigrants to a flood of immigrants. When looking around the world, we can see large-scale demographic changes – like the recent demographic shifts in some states in the United States – but because of problems of selection, we don't know the effects of these shifts on bias. To overcome selection, we can introduce small-scale changes in a laboratory or in the field, thus causally identifying an effect, but because of the complexity of the social world, we don't know how the effect we observe in our experiment extends to an entire system in the real world. There is no mathematical formula taking us from two immigrants to thousands to millions, nor can we realistically conduct tests on large-scale immigration in laboratories where the signal can be separated from the noise. However, opportunities can arise fortuitously that allow researchers to overcome these limitations. That's exactly what happened in Chicago when the federal government made a decision leading to the demolition of these projects. For once, both aspects – causal identification and large-scale, real-world results – were united in a single phenomenon.

Starting around the year 2000, the federal government decided it was time to end large-scale public housing, such as the projects in Chicago. With this decision came the demolition, during the years between 2000 and 2004, of 13 of Chicago's 87 high-rise projects. This, in turn, meant the relocation of about 25,000 people – in effect, the relocation of a small city – nearly all of them Black.[4] The former residents were dispersed widely, some staying in the same general area and some going to entirely new neighborhoods. This was, of course, a tremendous disruption for those who were moved. But it was also important in a different way to the people who remained behind – those who didn't live in the projects, but lived close by – because their long-time neighbors were rather suddenly gone. This was a dramatic change in social context, as if an experimenter had assigned the neighbors of the housing projects to a new place. It was thus a "natural experiment."

The particular social geography of Chicago, a place with dense and highly segregated neighborhoods, is what made this experiment so informative. This dense segregation meant that near some of these projects were not only Blacks who, when the projects were demolished, saw their Black neighbors disappear, but also a large number of whites who saw a large number – in some cases almost all – of their Black neighbors disappear. In certain neighborhoods, such as the "Gold Coast," a wealthy white neighborhood on the North Side lakefront east of the Cabrini-Green housing project, the demolition of the projects eventually resulted in the removal of nearly all of their Black neighbors – their context became dramatically less Black. (To get a sense of how dramatic this was in some cases, see Figures 6.1 and 6.2.) By the logic of my theory, this should have dramatically reduced the accessibility of the Black outgroup for the remaining white residents and, as such, lowered their group-based bias.

This happened in other neighborhoods, too, if less dramatically. In Bridgeport, the historically Irish working-class neighborhood which houses US Cellular Field and has produced five mayors of Chicago, the Stateway Corridor of housing projects stood immediately across the Dan Ryan, which seemed to serve as a metaphorical – and somewhat literal – moat between the white and Black populations – a space between the groups. The people of Bridgeport saw the projects on the other side of this moat being torn down, as I did from the train. They surely thought about what this meant for the racial composition of their local environment. Largely within four years – and then continuing slowly over the next decade – these concentrated masses of poverty came down and their Black residents – the outgroup – dispersed. How did this affect the behavior of the white residents left behind?

SOCIAL GEOGRAPHY AND THE RACIAL POLITICS OF CHICAGO

The removal of Blacks from certain neighborhoods was the removal of the tension I had noted on the "L" train. But rather than a brief fleeting tension, this was a permanent tension in people's lives – a significant part of the way they organized their world. The projects were places where the other lived, places where white people didn't go – a hulking mass of the outgroup, visible from across the freeway. A group had had a dramatic permanent presence and then suddenly it went away. Could this change – a decrease in the salience of the outgroup – affect the way people behaved and even affect their politics?

In reflecting on Chicago politics, I thought it could, which is why I launched this study. The presence of the outgroup was – and still is – a salient feature of Chicago politics. Blacks, whites, and – increasingly – Latinos come together in political space. They all vote in the same municipal elections for mayor, in the same state elections for senators, and in the same national elections for the president and they are all bound by various national, state, and municipal laws. But the social, psychological, and physical space between groups is apparent everywhere and this separateness shapes what happens in those political interactions.

In 1983, an unprecedented mobilization by Blacks elected Harold Washington, the city's first – and still only – elected Black mayor. Washington defeated Jane Byrne, who was white and the city's first – and still only – woman mayor. She had risen to power in the Daley machine and won office in 1979 after an inter-machine conflict. She then lost to Washington in 1983 and again in 1987. Scholars of urban politics have argued that in the single-party systems that characterize bit cities, where nearly everyone in power is a Democrat, competition often breaks down along racial and ethnic lines.[5] The fight between Byrne and Washington is especially notable for this: contemporary and historical accounts report on the palpable racial tension during these elections, which were largely portrayed as a fight between two racial groups and between the North and South sides of the city.

Byrne, who was notably progressive, campaigned on a strategy that was the political manifestation of social-geographic impact. In interviews for the documentary film *Eyes on the Prize*, Byrne explained how her campaign intentionally announced that she was canceling all campaign visits in white communities in order to campaign in Black areas of the city. Counterintuitively, these visits to Black neighborhoods were designed to appeal to white voters because, when Byrne traveled to the South Side, including to the housing projects, she was met by hecklers and protesters in support of Washington. Byrne hoped these images, broadcast by local news, would galvanize white voters.[6]

When Washington was victorious, as one observer told me, it "kind of leveled the playing field to upset the hell out of everybody."[7] Washington's tenure seems to have increased race-based anxiety among many whites. Some white Democrats even became Republicans in the wake of Washington becoming the city's most prominent Democrat.[8] This anxiety among whites may have changed in form or degree over time, but it was still there in 2000 when the projects came down. And between the racially tinged election and the fact that Blacks lost power so quickly in the city after Washington died in office of a heart attack in 1987,[9] a similar anxiety remained among Black Chicagoans two decades later. A belief I heard many times from Black acquaintances in Chicago was that Washington was assassinated by vengeful whites.[10]

Social geography shapes the fraught racial politics of Chicago. Segregation – Anglos on the North Side, Blacks on the South Side, and Latinos on the West Side – plays a leading role. Would Byrne's strategy have been possible without the spatial separation of Blacks and whites? Consider the counterfactual of a less-segregated Chicago, like that in Figure 1.2 (page 11). Would Byrne have been able to go to a clearly defined Black community, in the hopes of finding a crowd of antagonists? Of course, the fact that each group constitutes a large share of the population contributes to the influence of social geography on politics: in 2014, Chicago was 33 percent Black, 29 percent Latino, and 32 percent Anglo. No group is politically or socially inconsequential. These large outgroups are present in the minds of voters when they go to the polls. If Blacks had been only 10 percent of Chicago's population, would Byrne's strategy have been possible? The significant presence of Blacks – and their place in the imagination of whites – was animating a campaign strategy.

My claim is that social geography contributed to the manifest tension in Chicago. It was the demolition of the housing projects and the relatively sudden alteration of that social geography that allowed me to test whether this was the case. The salience of the local outgroup was suddenly altered – how would this affect behavior of white voters going to the polls?

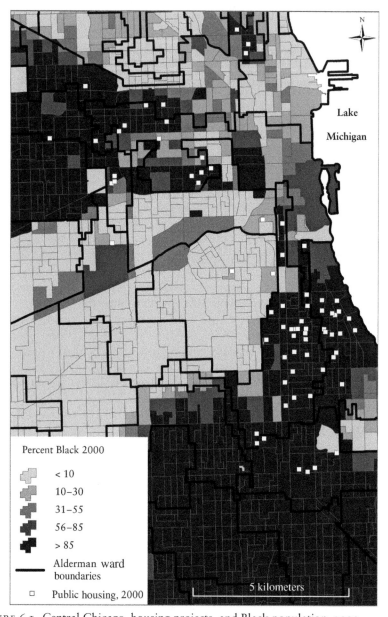

FIGURE 6.1. Central Chicago, housing projects, and Black population, 2000.

Notice how the aldermanic district lines closely follow the boundaries of the former housing projects, thus politically segregating the residents.

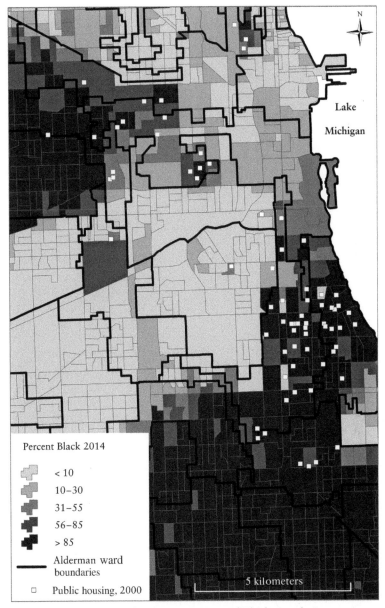

FIGURE 6.2. Central Chicago, housing projects, and Black population, 2014.

Notice the dramatic change in the Black population in some areas, including Cabrini-Green in the northeast and around the ABLA homes southwest of there. (ABLA was a name for the conglomeration of the Jane Addams Homes, Robert Brooks Homes, Loomis Courts, and Grace Abbott Homes.) Aldermanic districts are from 2000.

WHAT HAPPENED WHEN THE PROJECTS WERE DEMOLISHED?

I treat this change in the housing projects as an experiment and thus it involves a treatment and control, just like my experiment in Boston, where the treatment was the change in social geography by the insertion of confederates I had hired. In this case, the treatment is the change in social geography that resulted from the demolition of the housing projects. The treatment group is white voters living near the demolished projects. I can compare this treatment group to three different control groups: white voters living near projects that were not demolished, Black voters living near the demolished projects, and white voters living elsewhere in the city.

Like my experiments in laboratories and on train platforms, this natural experiment overcomes problems of selection. Even though there was no randomization, the demolition had an important feature: neither the residents of the projects nor the residents living near them selected their treatment. Rather, the treatment – a decision made far away in Washington, DC – selected them. I can therefore say that the decision to change who lived in the neighborhood was *exogenous* to the characteristics of the white residents. In a fully randomized experiment, randomization insures that the treatment is exogenous: because it is randomly assigned, it cannot possibly be systematically related to any characteristics of the subjects. In my Boston train experiment, for example, the subjects treated with the presence of my two confederates could not systematically have had more negative attitudes about immigrants than the subjects who were not treated with the presence of my two confederates.[11] In Chicago, there was no randomization – no researcher was in charge. But the projects were targeted for demolition in a way that seems unrelated to the characteristics of the subjects – it was based on an algorithm of size, vacancy, and the cost to rehabilitate – so it was unlikely that there were consequential differences (a) between the white subjects living near the projects that were demolished and those living farther away or (b) between those who were living near the projects that were demolished and those living near projects that were not demolished.[12]

However, even if we think of both my Boston study and my Chicago study as experiments, there is a major difference between the application of the treatment in the two cases. In Boston, the outgroup was introduced; in Chicago, it was taken away. Of course, taking away a treatment can also allow us to measure its effects. If you had a group of people all taking aspirin to prevent heart attacks and you randomly assigned some of them to stop taking aspirin, you could measure the prevalence of heart attacks in the group that stopped taking it and this would tell you the treatment effect of aspirin on heart attacks.

In this case, the indicator of group-based bias in which I was interested was voting behavior. We saw in Chapter 2 that whether a person votes and for whom she votes is strongly related to social geography, and I argued that this was a result of the way geography changes one's perceptions of the local outgroup. Because much of the Chicago project demolition occurred between 2000 and 2004, the presidential elections in 2000 and 2004 provided a measure of voting habits before and after the demolition and, like my experiment on the train platforms, I could measure this change on the same people at both times, before and after the treatment had been applied. Nationwide, I claimed that it was the presence of the outgroup that was causing voters to turnout to vote against certain candidates. When this presence is taken away, like in Chicago, voter turnout should decrease. Black voters near the demolished projects and white voters elsewhere – either near non-demolished projects or in other parts of the city – form control groups because they are people for whom we should see no change in voting behavior if it really was the change in local social geography that was affecting behavior.[13]

After the housing projects were demolished and the social-geographic impact of the local Black population was reduced, white voters living near the projects, relative to white voters elsewhere in Chicago, massively decreased their voter turnout; for the closest white voters, the change was between 10 and 15 percentage points (see Figure 6.3). This means that, out of 100 white voters who were living near these projects and had been voting, 10–15 simply stopped voting after their Black neighbors left. For Blacks, there was no change at all. There was also no change for whites who were still living near housing projects that were not demolished.

To make this comparison of the turnout of Blacks and whites and to compare the turnout of whites living near demolished projects and whites living near non-demolished projects, I found matching samples of voters to construct my treatment and control groups. I matched voters who were of the same gender, age, and political party and who lived in homes of the same value[14] and I matched white voters with their nearest Black geographic neighbor. In this sense, I am making an apples-to-apples comparison, holding everything else constant in an attempt to mimic a randomized controlled trial. A voter in my treatment group and a voter in my control group are of the same age, gender, and party and live very near each other in homes of equal value. Yet, depending on their race and their proximity to the projects, they react completely differently to the change in social geography.

Moreover, I could see that prior to the demolition, all of these groups of voters had *parallel trends*, meaning that the changes in their turnout rates were similar from one election to another. It wasn't until 2004, after the projects came down, that the changes in their turnout rates diverged, with turnout for white voters near the projects decreasing much more dramatically than for white voters in the rest of the city. All of this makes it seem that the changes in behavior I documented were not a matter of demographic differences between white people living near the projects and white people living further away or even differences between Blacks and whites living near the projects, because all these people looked demographically very much the same and even behaved similarly before the projects were demolished. Rather, it seems that

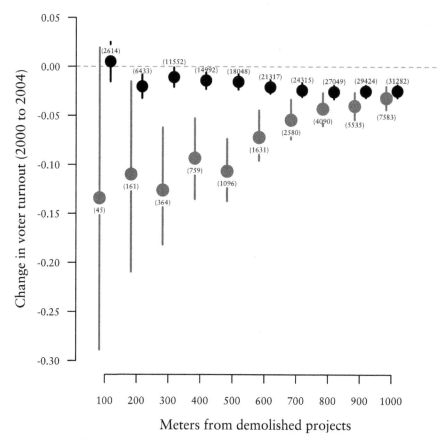

FIGURE 6.3. Changes in voter turnout after the housing projects were demolished.
White voter turnout is represented by the gray dots and Black voter turnout by the black dots. The distance on the horizontal axis is the distance of voters from the housing project (in meters). Each dot represents the change in turnout between 2000 and 2004 for the group of voters living near the housing project, compared to the group of voters living further away. Solid lines are 95 percent confidence intervals. The number of voters living near the demolished projects is indicated in parentheses. This figure is adapted from Enos (2016b).

for white voters near the projects, part of what drove them to vote was the social-geographic impact of their Black neighbors and that the change in social geography caused this impact to vanish.

As we saw by comparing across cities, whites changed not only whether they voted, but for whom they voted. Prior to the demolition, the white voters near the projects were 5 to 10 percentage points more likely to vote Republican than white voters elsewhere in Chicago. But after their Black neighbors were removed, these white voters started to vote Democrat at higher rates, much as we might stereotypically expect residents of a large city to vote. As with voter turnout, there was no similar change in the vote choices of Black residents or of white residents living near projects that were not demolished over this same period, indicating that it was living near Black people that had made these white people vote more Republican. (Since I cannot observe how any individual voted, I used ecological inference techniques, like those described in Chapter 2.)

Is voting Republican a group-based bias? Not always, of course, but for some voters, such biases can contribute to it. People holding more conservative views about race, as measured on surveys, are more likely to vote Republican.[15] More generally, it should at least be clear that political parties have differing appeals when it comes to race. In fact, there is a remarkable consistency across the world: in most countries, a particular party represents the dominant ethnic group and people who value social hierarchy favor that party.[16] This is why, in a different era of American politics, Democrats in the South appealed to white voters with more racist attitudes and why those voters abandoned the Democratic Party in favor of Republicans when Democrats became the more liberal party and Blacks joined the Democrats.[17] And, of course, when Democrats were the racially conservative party, Key found that whites were driven to vote for them due to the presence of a salient local Black population, presumably as an expression of group-based bias – in my study in Chicago, the party label has flipped, but the pattern is quite similar.

There is more evidence that whites living near the housing projects were voting in a way that reflected group-based bias: when these white voters had a chance to vote for a Black man, this too was affected by the presence of their Black neighbors in the housing projects. Before Barack Obama became President, he ran in four elections in which his name appeared on ballots all across Chicago: the 2004 US Senate primary (against another Democrat) and general election (against a Republican), in the 2008 Democratic presidential primary (against Hillary Clinton), and in the 2008 general election (against John McCain).[18]

If the presence of the local Black population was driving group-based bias in the white voters, it may have affected how they voted for Obama. All of the elections in which Obama ran took place after 2004, when the majority of the projects that were to be demolished were already demolished, so I couldn't do the before-and-after comparison that I described above. However, I was able to compare voting by whites living near projects that had been demolished to voting by whites living near projects that had not been demolished. White voters near the projects which were still standing – those who still had a proximate Black outgroup – were far less likely to vote for Obama than whites near the demolished projects – in some cases almost 20 percentage points less likely.

There's more, though. Because Obama once faced off against a Black candidate, we can see if he paid the same penalty among those living near housing projects when facing a Black candidate as he did when facing a white candidate. In 2004, Obama ran for the Illinois senate. After a scandal sidelined the original white Republican nominee, Obama's opponent became Alan Keyes, the inflammatory Black conservative who moved from Maryland for the purpose of running for election in Illinois. This allowed me to compare how voting for Obama went when he ran against another Black man to how it went when he ran against a white man. Would he face the same penalty? If living near Blacks caused white voters to vote against a Black candidate, we shouldn't expect to see this penalty when both candidates were Black.

And indeed, with a Black opponent, Obama's 20-point deficit with white voters near the projects disappeared. The housing projects seemed to have had no influence on that particular election. In my opinion, this is pretty strong evidence that social geography was at work here and that the voting behavior of whites near the housing projects represented a group-based bias: when Obama ran against white opponents, he was disadvantaged among white voters living near Blacks, but when running against a Black opponent, he was not.

With these results on turnout and on voting for Obama and other candidates, I am presenting a causally identified validation of the cross-sectional observational relationship between social geography and voting in 2008 that I explored in Chapter 2. Across cities in the United States, turnout across multiple elections and voting for Obama in 2008 was related to both the segregation and the size of the local Black population. Looking only at these observational results, issues of selection can cast doubt on my claims that social geography was causing the observed voting pattern. But with this natural experiment in Chicago, we see social geography influencing the exact same behaviors in the way that we should expect if it is social geography that is causally shaping voting behavior.

As in the observational studies looking across cities, I don't observe the underlying psychology taking place in the voter's mind. Rather, I see a behavioral manifestation of this psychology in how – or if – the voter votes. In the observational studies and my field experiment, I saw that social geography could change people's attitudes. In my laboratory experiments, I saw the microfoundations of these attitudes and behaviors, as even low-level perceptions were changed. I argued that these changes in perception would lead to changes in behavior. With this accumulation of evidence, I can make assumptions going in the other direction: I assume that the changes in voting behavior in Chicago are a result of changes in attitudes and perceptions. For white residents living near the projects, after social geography changed and the salience of the Black population was reduced, Blacks may have been perceived as less different and stereotypes may have even become less available in their minds. When white voters went to the polls and, like we all do, drew on heuristics to help them vote, they cast their votes with a less distorted view of Blacks in their minds – with the demagogue having less of a say.

These common results from different modes of investigation should give us confidence in these findings. The sun is a gigantic collection of individual self-sustaining nuclear reactions; when physicists brought such nuclear reactions into the laboratory and could see the process unfold before their eyes and on their instruments, they knew the two phenomena were the same and they could transform these reactions into a tool of tremendous power. Here, on a much more modest scale, voting in the United States is a widespread process of individual choices shaped by social geography. When I am able to isolate it in a relatively well-controlled corner of the world, I know that it is the same process shaping voting in Chicago that is shaping voting in these other American cities.

Holding Contact Constant

There is another important reason why I think it is a change in perception, induced by social geography, that is leading to these behavioral changes. As in my laboratory experiments, the other primary suspect – interpersonal contact – was virtually held constant. In Chicago, despite the close proximity of whites to some housing projects, whites typically had almost no close contact with their Black neighbors in the projects. They gathered in different places, patronized different stores, and attended different schools. The housing projects were an extreme case of segregation – one racial group was concentrated and demarcated by signs, fences, and custom into a separate space. Cabrini-Green was within walking distance of Lake Michigan beaches, a popular destination for Chicagoans during the summer heat, where anybody could gather, but even here there was a disconnect – spatial, psychological, and social. This was described to me as, "very much awareness of us and them, Black and white. Like we can go [to the beach] but...I wouldn't say [we] belong. We're not part of the community."[19] In the 1980s, when violence in Cabrini-Green was reaching alarmingly high levels, observers and critics noted that Mayor Byrne's Gold Coast condo was within a few blocks of Cabrini-Green, yet the worlds were so divided, physically and socially, that this violence could rage unabated while the mayor and other Gold Coast residents lived in comfort and security.[20]

For the whites in my study, behavior was dramatically affected by people with whom they had no interpersonal connection, demonstrating the power of social geography as an independent force. This lack of connection also means that after the projects were demolished and the Black population removed, the level of interpersonal contact changed little or not at all. It had been near zero and was still near zero. Thus, the impact of contact on group-based bias was as if it had been controlled in a laboratory – as, in fact, it was in my own laboratory experiments. There was no movement along the vertical axis in the plane of context, but the social geography did change. The changes in behavior, therefore, should be attributed to this change in geography. Once again, we see the mighty force of space – and space alone – affecting behavior.

The Effect of Distance, Size, and Segregation

In this study, rather than looking at a collection of voters in a geographic unit, like a city, I took individual voters from a list of all voters in Chicago and placed them at their exact addresses.[21] An advantage of this design is that I can precisely see the effects of proximity in a way that has not yet been available in this book. When dealing with cross-sectional city comparisons, for example, the variable of proximity is hard to capture and thus an important dimension of space – one that will affect social-geographic impact – is neglected.

Segregation and proximity are, of course, not the same thing (I showed this in Figure 1.6 on page 26). Two groups, say Blacks and Latinos, can be equally segregated in two different cities; for example, in both cities, all Latinos might live in a single neighborhood and all Blacks might live in a single neighborhood. But proximity could still differ; in one city the two neighborhoods might be a mile apart and in the other, 10 miles apart – to either group, the outgroup should much more salient in the former city, than in the latter. Common measures of segregation, including those I have used in this book, do not capture this variation in proximity.[22]

Because I could precisely geocode the location of each individual, I knew the distance of each voter to the nearest housing project and, thus, the outgroup's proximity to her.[23] This allowed me to measure the intense effect of proximity: voters closest to the projects, where the psychological accessibility of the outgroup should be the greatest, dramatically changed their behavior when the projects were demolished and this effect diminished, almost linearly, with distance from the edge of the project. In fact, the effect goes to zero outside of about one kilometer (see Figure 6.3).

This effect of distance demonstrates that the relationship between segregation and group-based bias in our cross-sectional comparison of cities may mask heterogeneous effects within cities because group-based bias may not be evenly distributed across a city. It may be the residents closest to the outgroup – those living on the borders of segregation – who are driving the outgroup bias. In fact, this is what the Boston police officers I interviewed saw in the 1970s: the nearer to the borders between Black and white neighborhoods, the more racially motivated crime there was and it was what was noted by scholars of conflict in places from New York City to Belfast.[24] (Below, we will see another example of this proximity phenomenon from Chicago in the 1950s.)

The effect of distance also reminds us of the contradiction I noted in earlier chapters: that as groups become closer in geographic space, the distance in psychological space actually grows. Of course, geographic proximity can mean more interpersonal contact and this will close psychological distance – but in Chicago, cultural, architectural, and other barriers had prevented contact and the boundaries separating groups had converged. Despite the white and Black residents living so closely in space, there was tremendous psychological distance between the groups. For whites, this distance was enough to change the way they voted.

My theory also predicts that the impact should vary with outgroup size – and it does. The larger the proportion of the local Black population that the demolished project contained, and thus the more psychologically accessible the outgroup, the greater the effect the removal of that population had on behavior. Moving from a situation where the population in the housing projects was only about 10 percent of the local Black population, as defined by the proportion of Blacks living in the housing projects in a one-kilometer radius from the projects (analogous to the Henry Horner Homes on the near West Side), to a situation where the projects were near 100 percent of the local Black population (analogous to Cabrini-Green on the near North Side), the size of the effect increases by around 10 percentage points.

Notably, once again, this change in behavior as a function of size and proximity did not materialize for Black voters. Their voting behavior was consistent, no matter how close to or far from the project they lived and no matter how large the projects had been. This indicates, once again, that the behavior resulting from this change in social geography represents a group-based bias.

The other dimension of space that I theorize affects group bias is segregation. That is harder to capture with this data because segregation is usually defined by comparing units such as cities and here I am only looking within one city. Nevertheless, segregation seems to have also mattered. The largest effect was for voters living near Cabrini-Green, which was not the only project on the North Side, but with was certainly the largest and best known and was also, by virtue of being an outpost of Blacks in a white part of the city, perhaps the most segregated of all the demolished projects – spatially, culturally, and psychologically isolated from its neighbors. Cabrini-Green residents spoke of "the Gold Coast versus the Soul Coast."[25] It was here that, for white voters, the comparative fit of the Black outgroup would have been the highest and we would have expected the largest effects according to my theory. For white voters living near projects on the South and West sides of the city, the local segregation of whites and Blacks was much lower and I would therefore expect, as the data showed, whites near these projects to experience a smaller change in behavior.

The Effects of Race and Class

A natural question arises from this research: which social identity – race or class – was made salient in this natural experiment, thereby causing the change in behavior I observed? I am claiming that social geography made the Black outgroup salient and that this salience changed white behavior. But, of course, the residents of the housing projects were not only Black, but poor. Is it possible that it was poverty, not Blackness, that the housing projects made salient and that poverty, not Blackness, was motiving the non-poor whites living near the projects? Political scientists might think of this as determining whether race or class is the treatment. To put the question in terms of a counterfactual: had the residents of the housing projects been Black people who were not poor, would they have had the same effect on their white neighbors?

It seems that the answer is yes – that race, not class, was the causal effect and, therefore, that a non-poor Black population in these housing projects would have also created bias. From other randomized controlled trials that vary both the race and income of individuals, we can see that the race of a person with whom somebody interacts seems to trump class.[26] In my study, too, we can see the primacy of race over class in the fact that even when income was held constant, Blacks did not respond to the demolition of the housing projects and the removal of their Black neighbors. In this sense, I was looking at Black residents who are just as wealthy as their white neighbors and, yet, are not reacting to the poverty next to them – not changing their voting behavior when the poverty is removed. This is a sign that it is race, rather than class, that is driving behavior.

This distinction is, of course, important. Race in the United States carries legal and cultural significance that class, perhaps, does not. And my counterfactual is, in fact, not always counterfactual. While public housing is an extreme manifestation of racial segregation, segregation has served to concentrate Blacks in the United States across class lines so that even middle-class Black Americans often live in relatively high-poverty neighborhoods.[27] Thus, when non-Black Americans see concentrations of segregated Black Americans and this results in group bias, they are probably responding not to the fact that those others are poor, but to the fact that they are Black. As we have come to understand, the differences between these poor and non-poor Blacks is collapsed in the non-Blacks' minds. That may well be why so few non-Black Americans know of the middle and upper class Black neighborhoods near the ghettos of poor Blacks; for example, in the South Shore neighborhood in South Chicago and in Baldwin Hills near the Crenshaw District of Los Angeles.

This being said, it is important to keep in mind the psychology of this convergence of boundaries. From the perspective of the white neighbor, not only were the residents of the projects different because they were poor, but they were different because they were Black, and the fact that these differences converged in space, psychologists tell us, distorted the differences even further. So it is race, not class, that is causing the change in voting behavior, but class is in there making the effect even stronger than it would be otherwise by making the Blacks seem even more distinct. Of course, wealth and race usually do converge in the United States – white people are, on average, wealthier than Blacks – but in Chicago, because of the geographic concentration of poverty, they converge particularly strongly, increasing the comparative fit of the race category. Moreover, in the case the Cabrini-Green area, where we saw the strongest effects, the wealth of the surrounding white people means that the distinction between groups was even clearer and the salience of the outgroup even greater.

That the convergence of geography with race *and* poverty raised the comparative fit of the population in the projects – making the impact of the local outgroup even greater – is a crucial takeaway from this study, from both a scientific and a public policy perspective. It demonstrates how the alignment of wealth with other social distinctions, as seems to happen nearly universally in human societies,[28] affects the likelihood that certain policies will have their intended effects. The concentration of poverty in public housing will usually mean the concentration of race or ethnicity, too, and we can see how this concentration serves to change the way we view these already disadvantaged groups – making the space between them and higher-status groups even greater. The recent turn in urban planning away from such concentrations of poverty and toward "mixed income" public housing, while often focusing more on variables like social capital as a justification, may also be a tacit recognition of the poisonous psychological impact that homogeneously poor and minority housing has on intergroup relations.

METHODOLOGICAL AND THEORETICAL ADVANCES OF THIS STUDY

As I mentioned in previous chapters, the basic design of studying context is almost always the same: take two variables, such as outgroup size and voting, and see if they are correlated across geographic units, such as counties, cities, or states. This was the basic design I used to compare group-based bias across cities in Chapter 2. My study in Chicago, like my laboratory experiments and my field experiment in Boston, had an advantage over these previous studies in that it overcame problems of selection. But it also had another advantage because scholars using the standard design to measure contextual effects face another problem known as the *Modifiable Areal Unit Problem* or MAUP. This problem bedevils almost any researcher using data that has been aggregated into areal units and it has severely limited much of the previous research on the subject of context.

MAUP is the problem that the chosen boundaries of an areal unit may induce variation in the dependent variable in addition to or even at greater levels than the underlying process of interest. What this means in practice is that the answers a researcher obtains about a question of contextual effects can vary depending on how the lines of geographic units are drawn. This is a general problem, going beyond just research on context: researchers – and all of us in everyday language – often take continuous variables, like "intelligence" or "wealth," and make them into discrete categories like "smart," "stupid," "rich," and "poor." In doing so, we make a decision about how to divide this continuous variable and that decision will affect who is categorized as "poor" and "rich." Such decisions have consequences for research. If we say that being "poor" affects your life outcomes, such as health, it matters whom we label as poor. Similarly, a population – Blacks in the South, for example – are spread out across the Earth's surface in a continuous fashion. But a researcher usually must divide this population into discrete categories – areal units – and her research may then be affected by how these areal units are divided.

Imagine, for example, that you took the Alabama counties that Key studied in the 1930s and looked, as he did, for the correlation between percent Black and white voter turnout. This would be a simple process using a modern computer (it wasn't simple in Key's day) and the resulting correlation coefficient would tell you about the relationship between a local Black population and white turnout. But now imagine you took the same data but used a computer to randomly perturb the location of the borders of these counties so that people, without moving, would have the county in which they lived changed. This means that, without anybody actually moving, the percent of Blacks living in each county and also the percent of white turnout in each county would change.[29] Nobody would have changed their location, but, nevertheless, this would likely mean that the correlation between percent Black in a county and white turnout would change and, with it, our conclusions about the relationship between these two variables. If you stop and think about it, that is a bit odd and disconcerting. If we think it is the location of an outgroup that is causing a behavior, then our estimate of the relationship between that group's location and the behavior of interest should not depend on where lines are drawn on a map. But since we must rely on areal units, defined by these lines drawn on a map, we are subject to this problem.

A related but slightly different problem is the *Problem of Scale*, which has to do, not with how the lines of aggregate units are drawn, but with the choice of aggregate unit itself. If, for example, Key had chosen to measure the relationship between the local Black population at the state level rather than the county level, would he still have found a correlation? Would it have been as strong? Stronger? It is often possible to make an argument for any of several scales being the right one, so questions of scale can often be used to cast doubt on contextual research. It was this problem that led me, in the first chapter of this book, to discuss the need to define place as a *local environment* and for researchers to pick areal units that best fits individual local environments for the question at hand, rather than search for the single best unit.

These two problems of aggregation – MAUP and the Problem of Scale – are known to plague contextual research.[30] A fairly well-known example of this in political science involved the findings by Micheal Giles and Melanie Buckner. In an article entitled "David Duke and Black Threat: An Old Hypothesis Revisited," they researched the 1990 election for one of Louisiana's seats in the US Senate, which involved David Duke. Duke was openly racist – a prominent member of the Ku Klux Klan. Giles and Buckner demonstrated that in counties adjacent to counties with a high proportion of Blacks, white voters were more likely to support Duke. The researchers took this as evidence of the continued relevance of the phenomenon Key described in the 1940s.[31] But Stephen Voss challenged these findings in an article called "Beyond Racial Threat: Failure of an Old Hypothesis in the New South." Voss showed that if one did not "clump" the counties with their adjacent city, as Giles and Buckner had done, the finding went away. In other words, if the counties and cities were not treated as the same areal unit, the findings did not hold. Voss took this as evidence that the South had shed the attitudes that had created " threat" during Key's time.[32] This is a classic example of MAUP. There is definitely an underlying socio-spatial phenomenon – Black proximity and white attitudes – but the relationship one finds between these two variables is dependent on how lines are drawn; in this case, whether the units are "clumped" together.

These two problems – MAUP and the Problem of Scale – are not unique to the study of context, but they may be particularly acute there because the researcher typically has a choice about the unit of analysis. Social science research is often the study of individual processes, such as how a person's personality or income or some other individual characteristic affects behavior. In this type of research, the researcher has no choice of unit – it's always the individual. Some other research topics, even though they don't involve individuals, are focused on well-defined units, such as businesses or federal agencies. These units are also less subject to problems of MAUP or scale. For example, if a researcher wanted to understand the effect of county health services on lifespan, the areal unit is not modifiable because these services are automatically delivered at the county level; there is no continuous process that is being aggregated up.

There are ways to lessen the impact of these aggregation problems on research. For example, in Chapter 2, I showed that the relationship between social geography and group-based bias could be found using different areal units: counties, Designated Market Areas, Metropolitan Areas, and so on. Because the relationship holds across multiple units, I am less concerned that my choice of scale has affected my inferences.[33] However, this is only an indirect way to minimize the problem because all available pre-defined areal units could have similar problems.

My research in Chicago, however, overcame these problems because I did not rely on pre-defined areal units. I knew the exact location of each individual and measured distance continuously from each project. Since I was not turning space into discrete units, I did not have to worry about MAUP. Using individuals, I could construct any number of areal units – to define the local environment in a flexible way – and show that my inferences were not subject to problems of scale as well.

It was partially the ability to harness newer data and technology that allowed me to do this. A reason previous scholars have used aggregate units is that individual-level data were not available to them. When I started this project, voter files, now commonplace in political science research, were a relatively new source of data. Using GIS software, I was able to measure context using the precise location of over one million people, measuring the distance between every one of these million people and each of the 87 housing projects in Chicago, thus creating 87-million continuous measures of distance.

Technology aided in other ways. For this research, I needed to know a voter's race, but this is not reported in the voter file, so I developed an algorithm to make probabilistic estimates of a voter's race based on her name and location. This method was later picked up by other researchers and similar methods were independently developed and used by political campaigns.[34] This allowed me to use race even when I could not directly see it. Later, my research team wrote a computer program to extract the data on home ownership and home values and connect it to a voter file in order to match voters across treatment and control, on whether she was a homeowner and, if so, how much her home was worth.

CHICAGO AND THE POWER AND PERSISTENCE OF SOCIAL GEOGRAPHY

The behavior I saw in Chicago – whites changing their voting dramatically and Blacks not at all – may lead to two quite opposite reactions: first, that it is remarkable that behavior changed in this way and, second, that it is remarkable how predictable this change was. These reactions, which may seem inconsistent, actually contribute to a common point: that the psychology of groups and space can significantly drive human behavior and drive it in a consistent way, across very different times and places.

Power

Here we see the remarkable power of social geography. Between 2000 and 2004, the voters who lived near the projects did not, on average, experience any consequential change in their economic situations, personal characteristics, or political milieu. But their behavior changed significantly because who was living around them changed. Moreover, on observable characteristics, some of these white voters were, other than for race, almost exactly like their Black neighbors who also remained: same income, same age, same home values, same political party, almost the same address – and anything that did change about electoral politics changed for both Black and white. Yet these white voters changed their behavior while their Black neighbors did not. That Black voters, who were identical to white voters in every observable way, did not change the way they voted makes it unlikely that any change in material well-being – such as a change in crime prevalence or home values – was responsible for white voters changing their behavior.

Note also that the voters living inside and voters close by the housing projects were not in the same local voting districts, so white voters also did not change their behavior because the demolition of the projects caused any change in the composition of their local electorate and, thus, a change in competition with their Black neighbors over who was elected. Chicago's electoral lines had been drawn, intentionally or not, to separate whites and Blacks. The lines tightly hugged the housing projects, winding in and out of the white neighborhoods – a case of racial and economic gerrymandering (see Figure 6.1).[35] This gerrymandering, and the fact that votes were being cast in Senate and Presidential elections where each vote is but an unimportant drop in the bucket of millions of votes, remind us of the potential for social geography to shape political behavior even in situations where it seemingly should not – even when votes are not "rationally" related to social geography.

In Key's studies of the 1930s South, white voters were driven to the polls by the presence of Blacks who could not even vote and, as such, had no direct political impact on the white voters. In Chicago, 70 years later, we see white voters again irrationally driven to the polls by the social geography of their Black neighbors who were of little direct political consequence.

In general, voting habits are hard things to move; people don't change them often. Modern campaigns are premised on the fact that, for various social and personality reasons, some people vote in most elections and some people rarely or never do.[36] Causing voters to change their habits more than just a little is very difficult. For example, experiments to increase voting by directly contacting voters and pressuring them to vote usually changes turnout by around one percentage point,[37] not the double-digit change we saw among whites living near the projects.

And that's just changing turnout. Changing for whom people vote – in this case, from Republican to Democrat – may be even more difficult. In fact, recent political campaigns have largely abandoned trying to change for whom people vote, relying instead on turning out their own voters. This is likely because partisanship is a social identity, similar to identities like race and religion. Studies have found that, over time, partisan identification is roughly as stable – meaning it doesn't change – as racial and religious identification.[38] In particular, a person's choice of party doesn't usually change in response to a short-term stimuli. A survey by political scientists in 2000 and 2004 asked voters what issues were most important to them and found that even when candidates of a voter's own party disagreed with her policy positions on 60 percent of these personally important issues, only about 30 percent of the voters would consider voting for the other party's candidate instead.[39] It appears that partisanship powerfully tethers voters to candidates.

Consider now that in running for office, Obama faced a 20-percentage-point penalty among white voters because those white voters lived near Blacks. This is a tremendous margin in an election – much larger than the margin by which most major political campaigns are decided. So, for example, if all Black candidates get 20 percentage points less of the vote than a white candidate among certain white voters, Blacks in the United States will face a large penalty in elections, making it difficult to win.

Social geography – the space between groups – can make a real difference in our politics and can affect voting behavior in magnitudes unrivaled by political campaigns. I argue that the proximity, the segregation, the size, and the extremely low interpersonal contact with an outgroup, and the convergence of racial and income boundaries all add up to the perfect conditions for group-based bias, leading to large effects such as a 20-point swing in how people voted. The size of these effects, even as large as it is, aligns with the other evidence in this book. In Chapter 2, the statistical model I presented on the effects of outgroup size on voting for Obama in 2008 showed about a five percentage-point effect moving across the range of outgroup size. Using this as a baseline, we can see the 20-percentage-point effect in Chicago – perhaps one of the most extreme cases we can imagine in the United States – as remarkable, but plausible.

Persistence

Reflecting on Chicago, such a large effect also feels, not only possible, but perhaps predictable. Any observer of Chicago knows the oversized place those projects had in the minds of residents – the extreme physical manifestation of the convergence of race, class, and geography in the city. You could see it on the "L" train as the white passengers would stop their conversations and stare. You could hear it in everyday conversation and in urban legends such as the tale that US Cellular Field was riddled with holes from bullets fired across the Dan Ryan Expressway from the Stateway Gardens. The projects represented something tremendous and distorted in the sociopolitical imagination. What the unique opportunity of this natural experiment allowed me to do was to quantify this representation. Intuition and the predictions of my theory of social-geographic impact said the effect should be large – and, indeed, it was.

The effect is also predictable when we look across the scholarship on groups in the same place, especially in Chicago, where so much research has occurred. In remarkably different times, places, and political settings, we see the same effects of social geography on political behavior, indicating that the effects of groups and place on our behavior spring from our basic psychology.

Key argued that the wellspring of Southern politics was the "presence of the Negro" and that politics was at its most excited state in the areas with many Blacks. These white Southerners, Key argued, were psychologically agitated by the presence of their Black neighbors, in a way that Southerners in places with fewer Blacks were not. Key was studying a place where the systematic oppression of Blacks had been central to the entire economic and social system. In most of the South, it was necessary to explicitly exploit fears of Blacks in order to gain political power. Keeping in mind the obvious differences, I believe we saw the same basic psychological phenomenon at work in Chicago that Key saw in the 1930s South. In Chicago, of course, despite the campaign tactics of Byrne and other politicians, the explicit racialization of politics is nowhere near its level in the 1930s South, but the psychological presence of the outgroup may be comparable. Indeed, the wellspring of Chicago politics has always seemed to be the presence of the outgroup.

From my personal observations of Chicago, the "presence of the Negro" seemed to be a constant background sociopolitical issue for white residents. I avoided telling white people that I worked in the South Side neighborhood of Englewood because it would inevitably bring a reaction based on stereotypes, usually alluding to my personal safety. To borrow another term from Key – which is simultaneously offensive, evocative, and useful – the white residents of Chicago suffered from "Negrophobia." What my study in Chicago allowed me to do was to quantify this continuity between the politics of the 1930s South and twenty-first-century Chicago.

If you look a little deeper, the continuity between the 1930s South and contemporary Chicago – connected through the common thread of psychology, space, and intergroup relations – becomes even more apparent. In *The Nature of Prejudice*, Allport often cites from the dissertation of Bernard Kramer, written at Harvard in 1950 in what was then the Department of Social Relations.[40]

Kramer never published his dissertation, so in order to read it, you have to retrieve the original typed manuscript from the Harvard archives. Kramer's research sites were Cambridge, Massachusetts and two neighborhoods in Chicago: Greater Grand Crossing and Auburn-Gresham.[41] These two Chicago neighborhoods sit directly east and south of Paul Robeson High School, where I taught, and the social space of these neighborhoods overlapped with Englewood. Greater Grand Crossing is where I would get off the "L" and walk down 69th street to work. When I was there in the early 2000s, outside of fellow teachers and the police, I remember seeing another white person in the neighborhood only once. I was so surprised that seeing him stuck in my memory. Perhaps because the stark segregation of Chicago made the comparative fit of race so high, I immediately categorized the young man as white because social geography made race salient. Had there been other white people around Englewood (it was less than 0.05 percent white in 2010), I likely would have chosen another category. In fact, passing anybody else on the street in Englewood, I never categorized them as Black – they all were – but rather in lower-level categories, such as gender or occupation. I imagine that when the residents of Englewood saw me stepping off the "L," white was the immediately salient category. A decade later, when I conducted my train platform study in the Boston suburbs, the highly segregated environment probably also raised comparative fit. When the white residents of those homogeneous suburbs saw my Latino confederates, ethnicity was probably immediately salient.

But when Kramer was researching in the 1950s, the neighborhood was quite different. The streets were filled with racial tension as a white majority – European immigrants and their descendants – interacted with a rapidly growing Black minority. Kramer surveyed these white residents and found that the most hostile attitudes toward Blacks were found in the streets immediately adjacent to the Black ghetto, in the areas where the populations were adjacent, but not integrated; that is, where the outgroup population was large, most proximate, and segregated. In short, an exact parallel to the pattern I saw in voting when the housing projects were demolished.

It is striking that the population of whites studied by Kramer was entirely gone a mere 50 years later. The old school building immediately next door to the school where I taught was once where the children of working-class whites were educated.[42] I knew elderly white people in suburbs of Chicago, like Schaumburg, who had grown up and gone to school there. Their parents may have been surveyed by Kramer and the "threat" he asked about was likely the grandparents of the Black children I taught.

Kramer extended his study to neighborhoods in central and east Cambridge and he found patterns of behavior between working-class whites and Blacks similar to the patterns he saw in South Chicago – so we have extended this pattern of reaction to a proximate outgroup even further across time and space. But we can go even further back in time. In 1929, Harvey Warren Zorbaugh published *The Gold Coast and the Slum*, a telling quote from which opened this chapter. Considered a classic of urban ethnographic sociology, the book focused on the near North Side of Chicago and the juxtaposition of rich neighborhoods like the Gold Coast and the poor – and now vanished – Little Sicily. (This was, in fact, exactly where the Cabrini-Green housing projects were eventually built, but in Zorbaugh's time, there was no significant Black population in the area.) Zorbaugh was struck by how, despite the physical proximity, there was no sense of community in these areas:

In fact, it is doubtful whether, in any proper sense of the word, the "Lower North Side" can be called a community at all. It is a region; one of the characteristic regions of a metropolitan city, remarkable for the number and kinds of people huddled and crowded together in physical proximity, without the opportunity and, apparently, with very little desire for the intimacies and the mutual understanding and comprehension which ordinarily insure a common view and make collective action possible.[43]

Zorbaugh noted, as I have, that this roadblock to collective action had consequences for a society's ability to govern itself, which he explored in the inability to work together in the Community Councils of the area. Here he found a manifestation of group-based bias in the interactions necessary for effective governance. In the Chicago I studied, that manifestation was the refusal to vote for a Black candidate. (We will see this inability to cooperate across groups, even when it would clearly be beneficial to do so, again in Chapter 7.)

To Zorbaugh, of course, the lack of "mutual understanding" that stymied collective action was notable because it happened despite the proximity of groups. But as we have seen, this lack of mutual understanding may happen *because* of proximity – just as the white voters in Key's south, living close to Blacks, were gripped by "Negrophobia" in a way that whites elsewhere in the South and those in the North were not. Similarly, the whites of the near North Side, who lived near Blacks – many of whom were migrants from Key's South and had replaced the Italians of Zorbaugh's Little Sicily in the newly built Francis Cabrini Homes – had their behavior changed by their proximity to those Blacks. Indeed, the findings of Zorbaugh, Kramer, Key, and myself suggest something counterintuitive: if the same interactions between groups occurred – such as voting in the same elections, sitting on the same Community Councils, and sharing the same resources – but the groups were separated by distance so that the salience of the outgroup was diminished, then shared governance – coming together in political space – might actually improve. But if proximity actually undermines our ability to govern together across groups, this liberal dilemma is a big problem for a liberal democratic society, where diversity is often considered not only inevitable but desirable.

The continuity is striking. Kramer, working in Chicago and Cambridge in the 1950s, found results with hints of Key's South in the 1930s and similarities to what I found in the 2000s. And Zorbaugh had already found the same pattern that I found in one of the exact same locations 80 years earlier when a different set of groups lived there. His evidence, focusing on the relationship between Italians and others, reminds us that this phenomenon extends well beyond Blacks and whites in the United States and, as we have seen and will see, I found similar group bias across other times, groups, and places, including Boston, Los Angeles, and Jerusalem. Chicago, with its severe segregation – manifested most starkly in public housing – was just an extreme example of the same pattern we can see in so many other places.

WHAT WAS LEFT?

Zorbaugh's slum, the overcrowded section of the near North Side known as Little Sicily, was cleared in the 1940s and '50s in an effort to combat the effect of that context on health, delinquency, and social relations. The first residents of the new Frances Cabrini Homes were Italian-Americans, but over time, they were replaced by a uniformly Black population. It was the state that made this massive change to social geography.

More than 50 years later, the state made another massive change to social geography when it demolished Cabrini-Green. So what I am calling a natural experiment did not come from nature at all, but rather from a government. When the state builds in a city – creating roads, parks, housing, or other public works – or when it regulates how others can build by zoning for use and density, it is shaping social geography. States shape social geography in other ways, too, such as regulating immigration and engaging in urban planning.

The role of governments in shaping social geography presents a conundrum and reveals the limitations of urban planning in fixing the problems created by the space between groups, especially in a world in which segregation is already so widespread and has created a tremendous social-political space between groups. The conundrum here is that the state, especially in a democracy, is made up of people who hold prejudices or who were elected by people who hold prejudices – prejudices that are reinforced by social geography. When the space between groups is large – due to railroad tracks, freeways, international borders, and other manifestations of state action – there is a powerful inertia opposing policies that try to dismantle the social geography that has created the space in the first place. Recall the violent reaction, described in the last chapter, to the integration of all-white public housing projects in Boston. This sort of violence spills over into voting behavior – both of them partially springing from a common psychological source – which makes it hard for public officials to act.

This complex mix of bureaucratic, electoral, economic, and geographic forces had brought about both the rise and the fall of Chicago's public housing projects. Separating and measuring these forces, so that we can understand the impact of each, is the job of a social scientist.

A beautiful thing about being a professional researcher is that your job is to create new knowledge. You can become the first person in the world to know something. Most people never experience that. While in graduate school, in the summer of 2007, I begin my study on Chicago and the demolition of the housing projects. It was, more or less, my first experience of the sensation of creating original knowledge. I spent days and nights in my office at UCLA working on it – often not leaving until dawn. I was becoming the first person, as far as I know, ever to know that people in Chicago changed their voting behavior when the projects were demolished. Even years later, that time was in many ways the most gratifying and exciting of my professional life.

My interest in this question – what was keeping me awake until dawn – came from life experience. The first time I visited Cabrini-Green, walking through the "gated fortress"[44] in the late summer of 2001 when the area was still full of residents, I didn't know how much the place would come to influence my research. But I do remember being stuck by graffiti I saw scrawled in large letters across the base of one of the high-rises – so struck that I copied it into my notebook: "What the fuck?"

When you are a social scientist, you tend to carry your theories with you everywhere, seeing the world through the lens of your academic ideas. The last time I visited the South Side sites of the former State Street Corridor projects, in April 2014, the demolition, which I had once watched daily from the train window, had left huge empty spaces in the city. Nearly every occupied building was matched by a vacant building or an empty lot. But the sites of the former projects were qualitatively different from other empty lots. They didn't have the haphazard emptiness of abandonment. They were great symmetrical cuts in the fabric of the city, squared-off areas where it looks like something ought to be but somehow isn't. There was nothing but empty grassy fields – massive lots indicating the size of the buildings that once stood there. A few of these massive cuts contain institutions that were built to serve the people who once lived in the projects: a giant church, a medical building, an elementary school.

Empty streets through empty lots. Surgical scars on the city. Not something that you'd expect in the great metropolis of Chicago. The orderliness of the emptiness reminds you that this change to social geography was intentional. In a few areas, the hulking, ominous high-rises have been replaced with small-scale developments, strangely disconnected from the neighborhood. They are bright and cheery, but sit in the middle of huge empty lots, like a new housing development in a distant suburb.

Traveling to Cabrini-Green on the North Side, I found most of it gone, too. But because Cabrini-Green was in the middle of a rich white neighborhood, the transition away from public housing had unfolded very differently than it had on the South Side. While the South Side projects had left vacant lots – the outposts of projects on the North Side were being swallowed by new construction in this white neighborhood.

The Cabrini-Green high-rises had been demolished and only a small portion of the former public housing row houses remained. Most were surrounded by chain-link fences and had a simple orderliness to them. Windows were boarded up and odd decorations – pieces of Asian-style garden art – dotted the landscape. The management office still had its signage, including a sign indicating its handicap ramp. The place reminded me of an old military base with its boarded-up barracks. All around it though, there were no vast empty lots and eerie empty redevelopments, but a constant movement of the young white people who now lived in the new developments where the projects once stood. For me, at least, there was something disconcerting about this because I knew these were places that used to loom large in the imagination of white Chicagoans, places which they avoided even though some of the finest white neighborhoods were very nearby. At the same time, these places had had a powerful effect on their white neighbors' behavior, including the way they voted.

The Black residents of Cabrini-Green were not all gone. As I walked around the perimeter of the old row houses, I was shocked to see that some were still inhabited. This wasn't illegal squatting; these houses were still maintained by the housing authority. Had I thought carefully about the demolition schedules, I might have expected this, but probably would have been no less shocked because their juxtaposition with the new gentrifying neighborhood was so stark and because this contrast seemed to be a perfect microcosm of everything I had been studying.

Here was about a block and a half of Black people surrounded by looming developments of white people. As I walked down Cambridge Avenue, the street through this last remnant of Cabrini-Green, it was filled with the remaining Black residents, boisterously enjoying being outdoors, just as one would see on a spring evening on the South Side. Just behind them were the new developments, with the balconies on their upper floors looking right down into these last bastions of poverty. The residents of the remaining row houses – residents, you might say, of an abandoned era of urban planning – seemed to me like the last of an indigenous people, with the rest of the world changing around them. Two police cars were parked on Cambridge Avenue: two cars monitoring about a block and a half of people. They were there to keep an eye on the only concentration of poor Black people left in a place that used to be nothing but poor Black people.

I found myself not far from where I had once taken out my notebook and copied down "What the fuck?" One might well ask. What is it like to know that everybody is waiting for you to leave because your poverty is getting in the way of white people's happy and heralded rediscovery of America's cities? The police, like the old cavalry outside the reservation, will watch you to make sure you stay in your place until your inevitable removal. Although this portion of Chicago was a slum even before Cabrini-Green, you can't help but feel that it is being "reclaimed" by whites. Having been away in the suburbs for a while – largely to get away from you – they have now decided they want to live in the city again. They want to walk by the rumbling "L" train and feel that urban vibe. But they don't want to be around Black people and Chicago's finest will therefore keep you in check as this chapter of urban renewal mercifully comes to an end. Soon, luxury condos will rise where the projects once stood and the last of the row houses will be gone. The mistake of concentrating Black poverty on Chicago's North Side will be swallowed up by development. The terror of Cabrini-Green, where white people were warned not to go, will be forgotten, and white people will return. For now, though, white police officers are there to supposedly protect someone like me – the only other white person in that single remaining bit of ghetto.

Take a moment to consider this last remaining sliver of a housing project in Chicago. A group of people, racially distinct and very obviously set apart from their neighbors, were concentrated into a small area. The demarcation between this one block of blight and the glittering city – the separation of Black from white – could not have been sharper. In the extremely unlikely case that anyone of either group was not acutely aware of the line between them, the police were there to make that clear. I am sure that stereotypes about Black people ran rampant in the minds of the white residents. Now consider a counterfactual: what if you took those same residents of the remnants of Cabrini-Green and dispersed them so that the surrounding areas were desegregated? With the Black population dispersed throughout the densely populated area of skyscraping condos and four-story row houses, abutting each other as closely as possible, would rich, white city-dwellers even notice a nearby resident who was Black and poor? If so, how large would this Black person loom in their minds? I believe the evidence is accumulating that under such circumstances, poor Blacks would not be as prominent, not as *salient*, and not as threatening as they had been when they were gathered and segregated in the last, dying, portions of Cabrini-Green.

7

Jerusalem: Walls and the Problem of Cooperation

What makes it possible for cooperation to emerge is the fact that the players might meet again.

– Robert Axelrod[1]

In the summer of 2013, I stared out the window of a fourth-floor apartment in Neve Yaakov, a Jewish neighborhood in Jerusalem. Looking deep into East Jerusalem, in an area much of the world considers occupied Palestinian land, I could see the gray slabs of the snaking concrete wall erected by the Israeli government to separate Israel from the West Bank. At the kitchen table across the room sat an Israeli woman, an immigrant from Kazakhstan, working at a computer while her infant slept close by in a crib.[2]

This particular view of the wall – called the "separation barrier," "security fence," or "apartheid wall," depending on who is speaking – stuck vividly in my memory because it seemed so appropriate, given the reason that I found myself in this woman's home. On the laptop my colleagues and I had provided for her, she was deciding whether or not to share money with an Arab and another Jew, who had also been given money and asked to share it with her. She was playing a "Prisoner's Dilemma" game, the classic game of cooperation designed to measure trust. Scholars argue that it captures the dynamics of trust necessary for the collective action which, in turn, is necessary for societies to function successfully. I had come to Israel to collect data from subjects like this woman in order to understand how social geography, the space between us created by walls and governments, affects our ability to cooperate – to solve the dilemmas of collective action represented by this game.

Out the window, I could see one of the starkest examples of man-made segregation you will find. This was what I had come to Israel to understand: when people segregate themselves, often intentionally, can a society still function well? Can a segregated society reach the levels of cooperation necessary to care for the young, old, and sick and provide for the common welfare? Or does social geography – the mighty demagogue – stop us from doing these things?

I had been to Israel before. In late summer 2011, I found myself on a hilltop in an olive orchard outside the town of Bir Zayt in the Occupied West Bank. This was a beautiful place dotted with olive trees, sand-colored rocks, and views of the surrounding hills. My host, a political scientist at the local university, had decided to put off his meeting with a French diplomatic representative to the Occupied Territories to drive me up to these hills – taking the diplomat with us. As we ate olives directly from the tree and his French guest stood by looking both bored and confused by this unscheduled trip, my host described the hills we could see in the distance. Each was characterized by who lived there – a Palestinian village or Jewish settlement. The settlements, on hills to the North, East, and West, were surrounded by walls and fences – physically, ethnically, culturally, and legally separated from their neighbors. Perhaps more than anywhere I had ever seen, this was the social, political, and physical manifestation of the space between groups.

The physical separations in Israel are striking. Literal or figurative walls are everywhere. In Jerusalem's beautiful Old City, separation takes the form of the names of the quarters: Armenian, Christian, Jewish, and Muslim. It can also be seen in cities and villages, starkly segregated as Arab or Jewish. There are exceptions with more mixed populations, such as Haifa and, of course, Jerusalem itself, but within these cities, the various populations are largely segregated into separate neighborhoods. These separations occur on an even more micro level; for example, there are roads and other public spaces in the West Bank that are legally closed to Palestinians. There are spaces in Israel that are de facto ultra-Orthodox religious communities, demarcated by the controversial practice of string barriers that allow for activities during the Sabbath but also keep out many modern practices, such as driving cars.[3] There are large immigrant communities in which languages other than Hebrew are heard on the street and seen on signs for businesses.

I focus my discussion on Jerusalem – a place near the extremes of high social-geographic impact and low interpersonal contact (see Figure 1.7 on page 30). Not only is the population of Jerusalem, like that of Chicago, split between three dominant groups (37 percent Arab, 27 percent ultra-Orthodox Jews, and the rest mostly non-ultra-Orthodox Jews), but the levels of segregation are also high. Proximity, too, is extreme. In Chicago, I demonstrated the large impact of a very proximate and segregated outgroup on behavior by examining the population of white Americans living near largely Black neighborhoods like Cabrini-Green. Such spatial arrangements are commonplace in Jerusalem, with the force of strongly-held cultural practices – and sometimes the state – maintaining segregation between groups that live in very close proximity. It is striking to see a large group of ultra-Orthodox Jews, with their distinctive black coats and hats, passing through the Damascus Gate of the Old City and through the adjacent Arab Bazaar on their way to segregated neighborhoods surrounded by Arab neighbors. Surely such separations – these obvious spaces between groups that happen even with such close proximity – will affect behavior. Do they affect behavior strongly enough to prevent cooperation – a basic building block of successful societies?

In this book, I theorize and test a basic psychological phenomenon and its effect on politics. This theory, because it is rooted in our basic psychology, is supposed to be applicable anywhere that we can find groups and geography – in other words, everywhere. To give credence to this point, I showed that the theory applied to minimal groups I created in the laboratory, groups that were not specific to any time or place. But so far, I have not tested my theory on real-world groups outside of racial and ethnic groups in the United States. In this chapter, by traveling to Israel and looking at the effect of social geography on Israel's inter-Jewish cleavage between secular and ultra-Orthodox Jews, I am expanding the conditions under which my theory has been tested and bolstering my claim of its universality. I am testing across a very different institutional, political, and cultural context than I have previously done.

In Israel, we collected data in 20 distinct locations in this small country (see Figure 7.2). Each of these locations occupies a different place on the plane of context. By moving a laboratory across these locations, we were able to collect unique data across the plane, while holding the institutional context fairly constant. Some of these locations have large outgroup populations (like Elad, north of Ben Gurion Airport in the center of the country) and some are quite homogeneous (like Modi'in-Maccabim-Re'ut on the border of the West Bank, north of Jerusalem). Some are integrated (like Safed in the far north, above the Sea of Galilee) and some are segregated (like Ashdod on the coast).

The patterns of group-based bias visible in Israel have deep implications related to a point that I raised in Chapter 2 and have hinted at in all of my previous findings: the power of social geography to shape the cooperative interactions that allow a society to be successful. We know that individuals are less likely to cooperate with members of outgroups than ingroups. We also know that more homogeneous countries are more successful – thus places like Denmark tend to be more stable, rich, and democratic than places like Zambia. Here I combine these two sides of the same coin to show that individual-level cooperation varies with social geography – that when groups come together in the same place, that the size and segregation of those groups affects cooperation. With this, we can see the power of social geography to shape the comparative fate of nations.

THE COOPERATIVE CHALLENGE OF PUBLIC GOODS

In Israel, I focused on behaviors that underlie the allocation of public goods; that is, the processes by which we pay some individual cost, like taxes, in order to build things and provide services that people besides or in addition to ourselves use, such as schools and assistance to the poor and elderly. Providing public goods is a central function of most governments.

The willingness to allocate to a public good can be characterized by many behaviors. One is the simple willingness to share even if there is no expectation of getting something in return, as when we volunteer for service or, perhaps, pay taxes even though we know the benefit goes to others. Another is cooperation with an expectation of reciprocity – I contribute because I expect others to cooperate, too – as when we yield on the road because we expect others to yield to us in return.

Choices to contribute to a public good are often made in private and with little consequence for not contributing; you can still drive on a road even if you didn't pay the annual registration fee on a car. Some public goods create nothing tangible; the orderliness of streets and traffic, where we obey the speed limit and other rules of the road, is a public good. Of course, each of us can gain a little by breaching the rules that keep it orderly; for example, by speeding or rolling through stop signs to get to the airport on time. As long as we don't cause an accident, doing so imposes only a minimal cost to the overall welfare – the street traffic is still pretty orderly despite our speeding. Thus, our individual incentive is to speed. But were we all to speed, traffic would become dangerous or inefficient or both. Our individual incentives *not* to contribute to the public good – the orderly traffic – create a Commons Problem.[4]

The decision to contribute or not to public goods by sharing or cooperating, especially in free societies, is often left to individuals. But, of course, the danger of these situations is that cooperation will unravel and nobody will contribute – that because we each can use the road without paying our taxes to support it, pretty soon nobody is paying for it. This unraveling is the *problem of collective action*.[5] Societies therefore sometimes enforce cooperation through laws and other incentives to overcome collective action problems: taxes to take care of the poor or traffic laws to ensure the quality of the Common of roads. These laws are the famous "sovereign" of the philosopher Thomas Hobbes.[6] In Hobbes' day, the sovereign was a monarch. In democratic societies, it is the institutional bodies – the political spaces – where we come together to make laws.

But in the absence of – or sometimes despite – such a sovereign enforcing cooperation, a lack of cooperation can mean insufficient public goods as individuals fail to do their fair share and resources are underfunded or the Commons will be abused. Everyone loses. When we think of social problems, what often comes to mind are failures of collective action: bad roads, schools, and sanitation; vulnerability to lawlessness; and other problems that lower the quality of life.

These problems of collective action – failures to cooperate – are as old as society itself and particularly vexing. But, of course, there is a solution to the problem of cooperation: the "shadow of the future," in Robert Axelrod's poetic words. If we will keep facing the choice to cooperate or not – that is, if we have repeated interactions – it becomes rational for us to cooperate because cooperation, rather than each person for herself, allows us, on average, to gain more resources in the long run.[7] The intuition here is simple: if you know that you will never see somebody again, it makes sense to look out for yourself. But if you have to be together, in the long run, isn't everybody better off through cooperation? In fact, this tendency to cooperate based on the possibility of repeat interaction may have been favored evolutionarily.[8]

Social groups complicate all of this. The space between groups affects our ability to solve the problems of collective action, such as building roads, following rules, or providing welfare. The reason for this is simple: we share or cooperate less with members of the outgroup than with members of the ingroup. As the psychologist Joshua Greene tells us with regard to sharing the Commons, "Humans nearly always put Us ahead of Them."[9] Some scholars have suggested that our ancestors' need to know whom to trust in repeated cooperative interactions is the very reason that group-based distinctions are so important to our psychology. Knowing who else would cooperate was once crucial to survival, so social groups evolved as a mental shortcut for understanding that you will have repeat interactions with people, thus making cooperation the best choice of behavior. Regardless of where this psychological trait came from, we do, in fact, use group categories as a shortcut for knowing whether or not to trust somebody. We associate the attributes that lead to cooperation, such as trustworthiness, with our ingroup more than with an outgroup.

An inability to cooperate with an outgroup means that in diverse societies the cooperation that must occur when groups come together does not happen. Part of this may come from a common belief that the members of outgroups are likely to free-ride – that even if you work hard to pay for the road, members of the outgroup will not.

Moreover, even when free-riding is not a concern, it seems that humans are less likely to share with members of the outgroup than the ingroup, simply because we want "Us" to have more than "Them." This was what Tajfel saw in his famous "minimal groups" experiments[10] and I saw in my laboratory when I assigned individuals to groups that were equally as meaningless: when people were asked to share, they favored the ingroup over the outgroup for no good reason. And we can see this outside the laboratory too: when people know that a public good – a school or a road or a hospital is likely to be used by the outgroup, they are less likely to want to contribute to that public good, even if it has no direct impact on them.[11]

This micro-level psychological trait that characterizes a space between individuals of different groups has implications for diverse societies. Extend the micro-behavior – not cooperating in a "two-person game" – across an entire society and that society will not function efficiently. We have seen the vestiges of this tendency throughout the book. In Chicago in the 1930s, Zorbaugh examined the community councils of the near North Side – institutions in political space designed to facilitate cooperation and regulate the

Commons – and declared that the area's diversity made the community councils ineffective.[12] And decades later, in the same location, the social groups of Blacks and whites were unable to come together in social and political space to solve the social problems of crime, poverty, and despair in the housing projects, even though both groups would have benefited from doing so.

On a larger scale, diverse societies are, indeed, less socially efficient, characterized by large-scale failures of collective action.[13] We can see this in our mental accounting of nations. The "Third World" includes a number of large, heterogeneous societies created in the wake of decolonization in places like Africa. It is because the haphazard creation of states made them heterogeneous, the logic goes, that they are characterized by poor public goods distribution: an inability to build roads, hospitals, schools, and other institutions that require sharing and cooperation. Habyarimana et al. (2007), using methods similar to what I used in Israel, set out to explore the micro-foundations of these problems in Uganda, a society with many failures of collective action, and explicitly connected such failures to an inability of individuals to cooperate across ethnic lines.

In modern, large-scale societies, where interactions are often anonymous and fleeting, group-based heuristics for trust and cooperation have, perhaps, become even more important. We often don't "play" repeatedly with the same people so that we can learn their behavior and base our cooperation with them on what we know about their past cooperation with us. We see people for fleeting moments, perhaps on the train platform or on the street, and have to decide whether to smile at them or whether to let them go ahead of us when we board the train. More importantly, in governance, we communicate with people across great distances and we must make collective decisions with millions of people whom we don't know and with whom we will never have any interpersonal interactions, never mind repeated interactions. In doing so, we must rely on mental shortcuts – guesses about whether we can trust those other people, whoever they are, to do their part. This is where social identity may be even more likely than in the past to guide us.

Because of Axelrod's insights, scholars know that the shadow of the future – repeat interaction – is a hopeful solution to the problem of collective action. An implication of this is that we cannot ignore social geography – after all, social geography shapes how often we have repeat interactions with people. Social geography, of course, also affects our perceptions of similarity between groups. If a particular social geography makes members of a group seem more different from yourself than they do in another context and you think of yourself – as we all do – as trustworthy, this may affect your perceptions of the trustworthiness of the other group and, thus, your decision to cooperate.

What this demands is that I test for cooperation and sharing across locations, to see how it varies with social geography.[14] That is why in Israel, we took our lab from location to location, across the plane of context, to understand how social geography affected behavior in the sort of micro-interactions that, in the aggregate, characterize successful societies. I studied two behaviors: the tendency to cooperate and the tendency to share – if these vary with social geography so that in places with a larger outgroup or a more segregated outgroup, sharing and cooperation are diminished, then we learn more about how social geography contributes to the comparative fate of nations.

THE ISRAELI CONTEXT

To an outsider, the dominant issue in Israel is the conflict between Israeli Jews and Palestinian Arabs. But for the last 10 years or so, if you asked a typical Israeli Jew about the group with which she is most concerned, she would likely speak not of her Palestinian neighbors, but rather of her fellow Jews. Perhaps the most salient intergroup difference for Israeli Jews is between non-religious or moderately religious Jews and the ultra-Orthodox, a distinctive group of socially and religiously conservative Jews. Within each of these populations there is, of course, significant heterogeneity and the non-ultra-Orthodox category includes varying levels of religiosity and cultural practices, including people identifying as secular, traditional, and religious. It is clear, however, that there are political and cultural divisions between these last three groups and the ultra-Orthodox, such that sociopolitical cleavages are often defined in terms of ultra-Orthodox and non-ultra-Orthodox.[15] I therefore focus on the cleavage between ultra-Orthodox and other Jews and, for convenience, I refer to all non-ultra-Orthodox as secular, even though that is only accurate for a portion of this group.

This conflict, between a highly visible minority and a dominant population, manifests itself in attitudes, political behavior, and even occasional violence. In fact, some polls suggest that secular Jews find the ultra-Orthodox to be more of a threat than Arabs.[16] One report on the topic went so far as to say, "the most primal fear of many secular Israelis is that [ultra-Orthodox] are taking over our cities and neighborhoods."[17] There is no doubt that the intensity of such sentiments varies over time, but the point remains that the cleavage between ultra-Orthodox and secular is a central concern in Israeli society and one that has a remarkable spatial component because the distinctive lifestyle of the ultra-Orthodox means they tend to live in clusters, highly concentrated and separate from other groups.

The ultra-Orthodox, called "Haredim" in Hebrew ("those in awe of divine power"), are a population with cultural roots in late eighteenth- and early nineteenth-century Europe. In response to the perceived assimilation of Jews into mainstream European society, this socio-religious movement set out to define a culture that was distinctly Jewish, adopting distinctive dress and other customs which it maintains to this day, including a tendency to speak Yiddish rather than Hebrew, a separate mode of schooling, and close observance of some rabbinical law.[18]

It is this last point that probably creates the greatest overt consternation in their secular neighbors, because it often involves (a) strict separation by gender, even in public spaces such as markets and buses, and (b) self-imposed underemployment by men, stemming from the practice of day-long religious study. The ultra-Orthodox are also characterized by low levels of educational attainment, disproportionate reliance on government services (due to underemployment), and a refusal of military service. Politically, too, they are to the right of the median Israeli Jew.

The cultural differences between ultra-Orthodox and secular Jews often lead to confrontation. When I visited the city of Bet Shemesh, southeast of Jerusalem, it was not long after an incident in which an ultra-Orthodox man had demanded that a woman passenger move to the back of the bus to enforce gender segregation. When the woman refused, angry ultra-Orthodox men smashed the windows of that and two other buses. Posters around the city showed the ultra-Orthodox men in chains with the claim that the chains were analogous to what the government was doing to them in asking them to ride with women (see Figure 7.1). The subsequent mayor's election in Bet Shemesh was portrayed as a contest between ultra-Orthodox and a coalition of non-ultra-Orthodox attempting to stop their takeover of the city. An Israeli host in Jerusalem was once telling me about the practice in ultra-Orthodox communities of sometimes violently enforcing their religious

FIGURE 7.1. Ultra-Orthodox political poster, Bet Shemesh, Israel, 2013.
Photo by the author, August, 2013.

restriction against driving during the Sabbath. During the Second Intifada, she said, when Palestinians had a widespread campaign of sometimes violent civil disobedience, she often had to choose whether to drive through a Palestinian neighborhood and be stoned for being Jewish or through an ultra-Orthodox neighborhood and be stoned for driving at all.

Many observers describe the ultra-Orthodox living situation as *self-segregation*, driven by their differing and strongly enforced religious and occupational practices and, importantly, by their gender roles. The state often plays a role too, building housing exclusively for ultra-Orthodox and having to police customs, such as gender segregation, that cause clashes with their neighbors. There is little desire among the ultra-Orthodox for living in integrated neighborhoods: 58 percent of the sample I collected in Israel said they would prefer to live in an entirely ultra-Orthodox neighborhood and almost 75 percent said they would prefer a neighborhood that is at least 80 percent ultra-Orthodox. These numbers are striking because ultra-Orthodox are usually poorer than other Jews, so they are clearly choosing social identity over economics. These make for important differences that separate the ultra-Orthodox from other minority groups I have examined in this book: after all, the segregation of the ultra-Orthodox involves a level of intentional choice that is certainly not the case for, say, Blacks in the United States.[19] Most African Americans express a desire to live in integrated neighborhoods, but are kept from doing so by social and economic barriers and legacies of past legal restrictions.[20]

Nevertheless, with the ultra-Orthodox population, we can see parallels with minority groups in other countries that are useful to consider. Making comparisons between groups is always a risky business and it is not my intention to say that the political or social situations of the ultra-Orthodox and other minority groups are similar. Rather, it is my intention to show that the reaction to outgroups, across human societies, is often the same and, as I have emphasized repeatedly in this book, that these reactions are shaped by social geography, so that when people see differences across groups, these differences become distorted and amplified.

In 2009, the ultra-Orthodox population was estimated at around 14 percent of the Jewish population of Israel but, much like other immigrant populations in Israel and elsewhere, it is growing rapidly, from both immigration and a high birth rate. Traditionally, ultra-Orthodox preferred living in segregated neighborhoods in Jerusalem or in Bnei-Brak. But population growth and a demand for affordable housing meant that the ultra-Orthodox started to appear in new cities and in new neighborhoods in Jerusalem in recent decades. Reflecting what is probably a popular sentiment among secular Jews about this growth, one of our research subject in the coastal city of Ashdot told us, "Haredim spread like a disease."[21]

These dynamics make for striking intergroup relations. Listening to left-wing Jews talk with pride about organizing to keep the ultra-Orthodox from moving into their communities, I couldn't help but be struck by how this dynamic was the mirror opposite of the historical integration of Blacks in the United States. Liberal Jews would tell me that they were "organizing to keep the Blacks out," by which they meant ultra-Orthodox, with their distinctive black dress. So here we had liberals organizing to keep conservative "blacks" out of their neighborhood, and these political conservatives were strongly dependent on state subsidies, which angered liberals. This demonstrates, of course, that the political relevance of social geography does not at all have to be what it is in the United States, where it is the political conservatives who often feel threatened by some ethnic minority group.

A newspaper article about the growth of the ultra-Orthodox quoted a left-wing Israeli city council member in Jerusalem:

First of all, Israel has to define what is Haredi and what is secular, on a regional basis. I'm in favor of living in the same city, but not intermingled. That's impossible. The idea that Haredi and secular Jews can live in mixed neighborhoods has proved impossible. The Jerusalem municipality has to define in advance what's secular and what's religious. There can't be Haredi schools and Yeshivas [religious schools] in secular neighborhoods because that's how a process of Haredi takeover begins. I don't want to quarrel with the Haredim, but I want to live separately, to get them to let me live as I wish.[22]

Now imagine a right-wing Southern city council member saying those words about Blacks in the 1960s. Of course, the situation in Israel is very different from the situation in the US and the comment in Israel may not convey the same oppressive intentions it would have had in the US. But whether such a comment could be justified in either case is not the point; rather, it is to see how a psychological space between groups makes a physical space between groups hard to close. In a sense, this quote defines the liberal dilemma, even though it is with a very different group than those we often associate with this dilemma. This liberal person in Israel believes in integration and would like to see it, but believes it is impossible in a practical sense. On top of that, these groups must share a political space – as citizens of the same country, they need to cooperate in order to solve collective action problems – but segregation, though it solves the liberal dilemma, makes this cooperation even more difficult.

Here, then, are two groups with a tremendous social, political, and psychological space between them. Of course, a similar situation exists with the Jewish majority and Arab minority, but in thinking about the cooperative challenges that plague diverse societies, there is something even more interesting about ultra-Orthodox/secular relations. Ultra-Orthodox and secular Jews are both part of the Jewish majority in Israel and legitimately powerful in the political system – ultra-Orthodox parties have entered coalitions as the "king-makers" in the Israeli parliament – so it is not a matter of one high-status group clearly imposing its will on a low-status group, as Jews do with Arabs or as whites do with Blacks in the United States, but rather two groups who must cooperate, must arrive at some consensus for the country to operate efficiently.

Jerusalem as a Public Good

In Israel, the largest concentration of ultra-Orthodox is in Jerusalem. This city, of course, is a point of perpetual debate and fascination, not just in Israel, but world wide. For my purposes, it is notable because of its extreme social geography and its examples of the interaction of social geography and public goods allocation. Consider the public good that is Jerusalem itself, somehow trying to be a holy site of the three major Abrahamic religions and the capital of two nations.[23] In a certain respect, Jerusalem is a marvel of successful public goods distribution because all three religions use it successfully. But, of course, there is also great difficulty. Claims to ownership or access to certain public goods are intensified in particular spots. The Church of the Holy Sepulchre – in some Christian traditions the site of Christ's crucifixion and burial – is managed by no fewer than six Christian denominations,[24] which sometimes results in violent clashes over the allocation of space. The Temple Mount is home to the Dome of the Rock and other Muslim holy sites, the location of the destroyed Jewish Temple and, at its base, the current location of the Western Wall of the former Temple. These spaces are often a source of political and violent conflict within the Jewish population and between Jews and Arabs over the rights to use them. The Western Wall abutted an Arab neighborhood[25] and thus was a point of much dispute over access to a public good until that neighborhood was destroyed in 1967. The space around it still creates an issue of how to distribute a public good within the Jewish population, sometimes because different traditions have different rules separating men and women.

The geographic impact of the two primary groups, Jews and Muslims – in close, but segregated, arrangements – on each other is very high. This high geographic impact, in turn, probably affects the groups' ability to cooperate for the allocation of public goods; namely, the religiously significant places I have been describing. Paradoxically, as I mentioned in the last chapter, groups more distant from each other with lower social geographic impact may be better at cooperating; this may contribute to why the relationships between Muslims and Christians and between Jews and Christians often seem much less fraught than the relationship between Muslims and Jews. An interesting question is how much of this is due to the declining geographic impact of Christians in the city as that population dwindles (current estimates put the Christian population of Jerusalem at two percent).[26]

To secular Jews, on the other hand, the ultra-Orthodox have the perfect ingredients for group-based bias. It is large (and growing), proximate (maybe even more so than the Arab population, which tends to be more isolated on the east side of the city), and strictly segregated. And because of the cultural barriers and norms, contact between secular and ultra-Orthodox Jews is near zero. A secular Jewish resident of Jerusalem told me once that he had never talked to an ultra-Orthodox person. I found this claim incredible until I had collected my own survey data on the matter. In my sample, largely representative of Israeli Jews, almost 40 percent of secular Jews said they interacted with ultra-Orthodox only once a month or less and 16 percent said they never did. Incredibly, even in Jerusalem, where ultra-Orthodox make up a substantial part of the population and of the social fabric of the city, over 32 percent of secular Jews interacted with ultra-Orthodox only once a month or less and 10 percent never did.

The impact of this can be seen in everyday conversation. Talk to secular Israelis and they will express their deep concern for the growing ultra-Orthodox population. I experienced this myself before I even got to Israel. There is a large ultra-Orthodox population in New York City. They don't fly during the Sabbath, which starts Friday night, the night of the week I happened to fly from New York to Israel to do this research. The gentleman next to me struck up a conversation and, reluctantly – because research is always hard to explain and can lead to uncomfortable conversations when there isn't time to explain it carefully – I told him about my forthcoming research in Israel. Overhearing, the man behind us, about my age, eagerly showed me what he had just tweeted using his phone: "The best part about flying on Friday night? No Haredim!" Such sentiments can spill out into open conflict, like the bus violence in Bet Shemesh. Of course, much of this has to do with deep cultural divides, like those on gender roles, but we have to wonder whether in a counterfactual world in which Jerusalem occupied a different place on the plane of context, would this tension be less severe?

The extremes of social-geographic impact in Jerusalem can be seen by comparing it to Israel's other large city, Tel Aviv. There is much less intergroup tension in that city, which is largely homogeneous (8.3 percent non-Jewish, compared to 37 percent in Jerusalem, and only 1.1 percent ultra-Orthodox, compared to 27 percent in Jerusalem) and unsegregated (dissimilarity of 0.28, compared to 0.63 in Jerusalem). Being newer, the city is spread out and less dense and thus groups are less proximate, which will also lessen bias. Selection, of course, plays a role in the different characters of the two cities, but, as we have seen repeatedly and will see again in this chapter, once selection has done its work, the force of geography itself seems to shape behavior and attitudes.

TAKING THE LAB INTO THE FIELD

For this project, I was fortunate to be able to team with Noam Gidron, a political scientist with local knowledge of Israel. Together we took a laboratory into the field in Israel. Our main goal was to see if social geography affected individual behaviors, such as cooperation and sharing, that underlie the allocation of public goods. Our expectation was that – just as we had seen with survey data across the United States and in the laboratory on campus, over the Internet, and in different cities – group-based bias, sharing, and cooperating more with the ingroup than the outgroup would increase with segregation and outgroup size.

Laboratories often make it possible to collect precise behavioral measures, such as a willingness to cooperate, that cannot be gathered on a survey. In laboratories, we can also measure costly behaviors, as we will see below, that avoid the problem of "cheap talk" found on surveys. Of course, laboratories are usually rooted in one place, like a university campus, but they don't have to be. Scholars studying outside the United States have been leaders in this regard – often setting up lab-in-the-field studies where a laboratory is set up in a particular neighborhood or village, rather than on a college campus.[27] The idea behind such studies is to take the lab to the population of interest, thereby avoiding the common criticism of a lack of external validity leveled at attempts to understand human behavior by endlessly studying American college sophomores.[28]

When a lab is taken into the field, it is usually only taken to one location. Yet we have seen that social geography dramatically affects our behavior, so this should give us pause, especially when studying cooperation, because we know that the logic of repeat interactions means that variation in social geography can be important. We know then that the results of measuring intergroup behavior from a laboratory in a certain location – say one that is diverse but unsegregated – will vary systematically from behavior measured in a location that is, say, equally diverse but more segregated. Because of this variation, extrapolating results collected in a single location from the micro to the macro can be misleading. Noam and I set out to overcome this problem by taking our laboratory to 20 locations across the plane of context in order to capture the influence of social geography. (This research design, of course, can mean results suffer from selection bias – a problem I have discussed throughout the book. Below, I will discuss how we tackled the problem in this research.)

We took our lab from place to place – to four neighborhoods in Jerusalem and to 16 other cities (see Figure 7.2). Like it often does, technology enabled this research because our lab consisted of lightweight laptops that our research team could carry from house to house, so we actually brought our lab right into people's homes. We wrote a specialized computer program that allowed our subjects to answer questions and play games – then translated it all into Hebrew. We first pre-tested our experiments on Israelis over the Internet, again taking advantage of our ability to reach into people's lives from across the world.

Our team of local workers would travel from community to community with our lab and fan out to various homes, chosen with a randomization system.[29] We spoke to people in English, Hebrew, Yiddish, Russian, and Arabic and ultimately collected over 400 responses from ultra-Orthodox and secular Jews (the survey itself was always in Hebrew).

Allocating Public Goods

We designed our games to study sharing and cooperation and the motivations underlying these behaviors that make public goods possible (they were modeled

FIGURE 7.2. Locations studied with the lab in the field in Israel.

We visited 16 cities and four Jerusalem quarters. The primary neighborhood in the Jerusalem quarter is labeled. Locations were selected to provide variation on the plane of context.

after Habyarimana et al. (2007), with some twists of our own). In each game, our subjects played against members of both the ingroup and the outgroup. If our subject was an ultra-Orthodox, the outgroup "opponent" was a secular Orthodox Jew, and vice versa.[30] These other players had played the games previously and we had recorded their moves and programmed them into the computer.[31] We didn't explicitly identify the other player as ultra-Orthodox or secular, but a participant could see a picture and it was obvious by the person's style of dress (94 percent of our sample correctly identified to which group the other player belonged). See Figure 7.3 for an example of what this looked like. Our subjects were playing for real money, so their behavior was consequential and the effect of social geography would have to be powerful to affect it.

Cooperation

To understand if social geography influenced cooperation, we had our subjects play the classic Prisoner's Dilemma game. They had an opportunity to

FIGURE 7.3. Playing a public goods game with a secular versus an ultra-Orthodox player.

In actual experiment, faces were not blurred.

cooperate by sharing shekels (NIS, the Israeli currency) with another player
or to defect by not sharing. They played against another player who had the
same options and both players made their moves in private without the other
knowing. The key to this game, a workhorse of behavioral economics, is that if
both players cooperate, they both win more than if they both don't cooperate.
However, you can win even more than that if the other player cooperates and
you don't, which gives you an incentive to defect.

This creates a situation where both players, even though they'd be better
off by cooperating, will defect – a Commons problem. As such, in order to
cooperate, a player must trust that the other will do the same. If you cooperate
more with the ingroup than with the outgroup, this is a group-based bias and
one that can be very costly, especially when this micro-behavior is scaled up to
a macro-phenomenon and a whole society finds itself unable to allocate public
goods.

In our study, cooperation was indeed much higher with the ingroup: 70
percent of players cooperated with the ingroup, compared to 54.5 percent
who cooperated with the outgroup.[32] This is a 15.5-percentage-point change
in cooperation and reveals a striking fact: even when participants *knew* they
might benefit by cooperating with an outgroup member, they only did so about
half the time. Imagine if everyone shirked in almost half of their interactions
with other people. How well would your household work if you didn't do your
chores, didn't pay your portion of the rent, or took more than your fair share
of food? How well would your business work if half your workers didn't come
to work? How well would your country work if half its citizens didn't pay their
taxes?

What about the impact of social geography on this tendency to cooperate
more with the ingroup than with the outgroup? Looking across the results
from the range of cities to which we traveled, we could plainly see the
effects of social geography. The more segregated the city or neighborhood
and the greater the size of the outgroup, the less likely players were to
cooperate with the outgroup, relative to the likelihood of their cooperating
with the ingroup. For example, moving from Tel Aviv to Jerusalem, across
these extremes of segregation, our statistical model predicts that the bias in
cooperation displayed by ultra-Orthodox toward secular would increase by
100 percent, so that an ultra-Orthodox person in Jerusalem would show an
almost 40-percentage-point gap between her cooperation with members of her
ingroup and with members of an outgroup.[33]

With these results, we can also observe the striking continuity in the way
social geography affects bias: the same statistical relationship we saw in the
United States, using observational data about attitudes and voting, can also
be seen in Israel when looking at social geography and cooperative behavior,
including the interactive nature of segregation and outgroup size and the
curvilinear nature of the effect of outgroup size, so that when outgroup size
becomes high enough and interpersonal interaction becomes inevitable, bias

starts to decline. (See Figure 7.4, which is the relationship between social geography and sharing, described below. This same pattern holds for all outcomes in this chapter.)

This is especially apparent with the behavior of the ultra-Orthodox: their tendency to cooperate increases as they become a smaller portion of the population. Being only a small minority in many cities, they cannot help but interact with secular Jews. They may therefore have more experience with positive interactions which could challenge the negative perceptions created by space alone.

Remember that when we asked secular people how often they interacted with ultra-Orthodox, over 40 percent said only once a month or less and 16 percent said never. When we asked ultra-Orthodox how often they interacted with secular people, 45 percent said daily and only 5 percent said never. The brief, casual encounters with the outgroup, common among minority group members, seem to be affecting their cooperative behavior.

However, it is important to note that, even in the face of interpersonal contact, the power of social geography is still apparent. In checking the influence of social geography on behavior and attitudes, I added a control for interpersonal contact to the statistical model. With every result in this chapter, in no case did it eliminate or even substantially diminish the influence of social geography.[34]

In our lab, we also looked for other signs of cooperation, including just a willingness to work together. To understand, as a simple matter of fact, whether subjects felt they could work effectively with the outgroup, we presented them with a box of Legos and asked if, given the job of putting it together, they would prefer to work with an ingroup member or an outgroup member.[35] Unsurprisingly, subjects overwhelmingly preferred to work with their ingroup. But this, too, varied with social geography: in locations with higher social-geographic impact, our subjects were even less willing to work with the outgroup – considerably so. If we repeat the thought experiment of moving from the level of segregation in Tel Aviv to the level in Jerusalem, our subjects' bias – the likelihood of choosing to work with the ingroup over the outgroup – increases by over 300 percent. This is true for either group, with both groups approaching an 80-percentage-point pro-ingroup bias in Jerusalem.[36]

Trust

What is the source of this behavior? Why would you choose not to cooperate with an outgroup member, even if it might be mutually beneficial? Part of it, of course, is trust. Do you trust the other player to cooperate? We can see this in the data: when we simply asked subjects how much they trusted the outgroup, 31 percent of ultra-Orthodox said "not at all" or "only a little" and 43 percent of secular said the same. I speculated earlier that a lack of trust may reflect perceptions of difference between oneself and the outgroup. If one thinks the

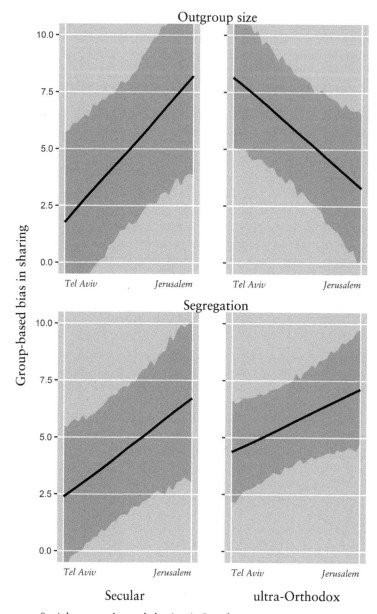

FIGURE 7.4. Social geography and sharing in Israel.

Change in sharing, as measured by distribution of NIS in Dicatator Game, when playing with an ingroup member, rather than outgroup member. Figures represent the change in bias predicted when moving from the outgroup proportion in Tel Aviv to Jerusalem (top row) and level of segregation in Tel Aviv to Jerusalem (bottom row) for secular (left column) and ultra Orthodox (right column).

outgroup is different from oneself and believes oneself to be trustworthy, that certainly creates the possibility that the outgroup is *un*trustworthy. This means that if perceptions of difference are driven by social geography, as they should be if social geography is making an identity salient, then trust should also vary with social geography. And it did: the higher the social-geographic impact, the less our subjects trusted the outgroup.[37]

We can also see very directly the influence of trust on how people play in the Prisoner's Dilemma because we asked our subjects, after they had played, why they chose to cooperate or not. Amongst those who showed group-based bias in their play – that is, who chose to cooperate with the ingroup, but not with the outgroup – trust was the most-cited reason, mentioned by 43 percent of ultra-Orthodox and 34 percent of secular participants.[38]

Sharing

Of course, there may be good reasons why somebody would cooperate with the ingroup and not the outgroup in a Prisoner's Dilemma game. After all, cooperation is a strategy, not just a reflection of prejudice. And trust can be learned from experience, so perhaps a lack of cooperation just reflects the experience of having tried to cooperate with the outgroup before and having been cheated. People learn from this behavior and don't repeat their mistake. We might also expect that, even without prejudice, people will simply prefer to work with an ingroup member when it comes to a task like putting together Legos. Wouldn't you get more done and be more efficient working with somebody with whom you share culture and maybe language?

These mechanisms for behavior would not make the finding that ingroup bias in these behaviors varies with social geography any less important. But the geographic variation does indicate that there is something more than these mechanisms at work – that the willingness to cooperate reflects not only a strategy, learned from past experience, but also something closer to a prejudice coming from the distorting power of social geography. We can see this when we look at other behaviors and attitudes that are not strategies, but merely a willingness to share with the other group – a behavior that is clearly discriminatory because it fails the "Golden Rule" test of group behaviors and attitudes. We found that even the simple willingness to share varies with social geography; that is, with the degree to which space is distorting the way we treat others.

To study this, we had our subjects play a Dictator game against an ingroup member and an outgroup member. This was the same basic game my subjects played in the laboratory at Harvard in Chapter 4. We gave the players an allocation of shekels and allowed them to keep as much as they wanted and anonymously give as much as they wanted to an ingroup member and to an outgroup member.

This captures the simple act of sharing – giving away something you have in order to help another. If you give more to the ingroup than to the outgroup, this shows group-based bias. Social geography powerfully affected bias (see Figure 7.4). Our statistical models tell us that if we picked up a non-ultra-Orthodox Jew and moved her from Tel Aviv to Jerusalem, this bias would increase by almost 350 percent (1.8 NIS to 8.2 NIS).

The commonality of human behavior can be striking. Here was the same behavior I saw in our laboratory in a Harvard classroom. There, I changed costly behavior by moving groups around in a room on the second floor of Sever Hall in Harvard Yard. Here, the contested and meaningful divisions of various Israeli cities were changing the costly behavior as well.

Sharing Neighborhoods and a Nation

A larger question of sharing is whether you will share a particular public good: space. Will you open your neighborhood and your country to other people? This question lies at the heart of the subject of groups occupying the same place. Group-based bias also manifests itself in subjects wishing to keep the outgroup out of their neighborhood and even out of their country. We presented subjects with a "Social Distance Scale," which was designed by the sociologist Emory Boardus in 1926.[39] This scale is designed to elicit willingness for social contact. It asks what is "the closest relationship you would find acceptable" for a group? and gives these options:

1. Close relatives by marriage
2. Close personal friends
3. Neighbors on the same street
4. Co-workers in the same occupation
5. Citizens in your country
6. Visitors to your country
7. Would not accept in your country

Participants are instructed that choosing a low-level relationship, like relative, implies that they are accepting all the higher levels as well. It is an operationalization of the psychological space we have seen operate throughout the book. We asked subjects to use the scale to signal acceptance of different groups. Here again, the answers vary across the ingroup and outgroup and, predictably, vary with social geography. The willingness for contact decreases with segregation and outgroup size (and includes the familiar curvilinear effect of outgroup size).[40]

This mirrors the familiar pattern of response to immigration – as the outgroup grows locally, there is a greater urge to exclude them altogether, even from your country – to construct a wall, perhaps by law, to increase the space between groups. This is what we saw in Boston, where the experimental introduction of a local outgroup led to support for exclusionary public policy among commuters. The demagogue of space works across vastly different places and groups to bring about the same outcome: an unwillingness to share social space.

Identifying the Effect of Social Geography without an Experiment

As I've emphasized many times in this book, a limitation of observational research is the problem of selection. My research in Israel was also observational. Although it included experiments and a laboratory, there was no randomization of context, so the effect of context is unidentified. People with high preexisting levels of group-based bias may select to live in places with high social-geographic impact and thus the results described above may not reflect the causal effect of social geography. This was a trade-off we chose to make: we wanted precise measures of biases in behavior, such as cooperation, across places, so we decided to sacrifice causal identification for the ability to gather this unique data. The advantage of testing a theory across multiple methods and locations is that not every piece of evidence has to stand on its own; rather, it can be part of a larger puzzle. In Israel, despite the potential bias from selection, we found results consistent with my studies in which causal identification was possible, such as my laboratory and field studies in Boston and the natural experiment in Chicago.

But this doesn't mean we ignored issues of selection altogether. Because we were designing our own data collection, rather than relying on data from somebody else, we could design it in a way to minimize problems of selection. For example, a very direct way to investigate whether selection is a problem is just to ask people if they selected where to live based on the variable of interest, such as her feelings about living around the other group.

In our survey, we included a large set of variables that tried to measure whether or not a person had selected to live where she lived based on her intergroup attitudes.[41] We did this first by asking direct questions like, "Do you live where you live because of the religion of your neighbors?" Perhaps even more direct, we just asked them for the location of their previous home and then, using GIS software, found the demographics of where they used to live. Then we looked to see if they had moved into a more homogeneous location. If they had, this suggested that they had selected away from the outgroup. We also took a less direct approach by asking people how free they felt to move to a new home and checking their income to see if they could afford to move. If they felt less free or had less income, we assumed they were less likely to select away from the outgroup.

We also asked people about their ideal neighborhood to see if they wanted to exclude the other group from their neighborhood, we took this as evidence for a preference for segregation and that selection might be a problem. To do this, we gave our subjects a schematic of a neighborhood and asked them to pick the neighbors they would like to have: ultra-Orthodox, secular, or Arab (With the explicit statement that it wouldn't affect their property values.[42] See Figure 7.5 for an example.)

This measure gave us a plain view of how widespread the preference for segregation is in Israel: when subjects were asked to build their hypothetical neighborhood, many chose neighbors exclusively of their own ingroup – over

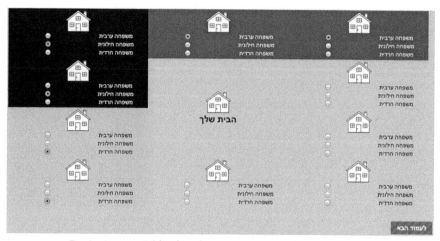

FIGURE 7.5. Designing a neighborhood.

Subjects chose whom, by group, they wanted to live in each of 10 houses around their own house (in the center), designating ultra-Orthodox with yellow, secular with blue, and Arab with green.

half of ultra-Orthodox subjects preferred exclusively ultra-Orthodox and more than 30 percent of secular preferred exclusively secular. Majorities of both groups designed neighborhoods that were close to exclusive, with 80 or 90 percent of the houses filled by their ingroup. (A much larger portion of Jews, 88 percent, excluded all Arabs.) Thus, the bias for one's ingroup was clear. But this measure also allowed us to separate those who desired to select into an exclusive neighborhood from those who didn't.

With these tests and others, we divided people into those who may have selected where to live in a way that would bias our results and those who appeared not to have selected where to live in such a way. We then checked our results on these two different populations. The results were unchanged whether we looked at people who were likely to have selected or those who likely had not, indicating to us that our results, as best as we could tell, were not driven by selection. While nothing can match the power of a fully randomized controlled trial, the threat of selection bias was greatly reduced by our research design.

IMPLICATIONS

In Israel, we conducted a true "out of sample" test: I had built this theory using observations and data mostly from the United States and gone to another country to see if the theory was supported there. With this evidence, we see more of social geography's broad reach across cultures, histories, and groups.

There are other lessons that I think we learn from this study, both for scholars and for those of us thinking about how to use public policy to build better societies.

Lessons for Researchers

There is an important point for scholars studying comparative politics, where claims about an entire country are often made based on data from a single location. In fact, one reason we undertook this research was to address what we saw as the danger in making claims about the underlying causes of social inefficiency based on studies in single locations. To study public opinion in the United States, for example, we would never do a survey in Omaha and say it represents public opinion in the entire United States. In an article Noam and I published on this research, we wrote the following:

When scholars only test a single location, it is difficult to know how representative of the country it is. By establishing an expected relationship between behavior and two variables that could be measured in any locality – segregation and diversity – we offer scholars a tool for benchmarking their findings. For example, was the research conducted in an area with low segregation? If so, the findings probably reflect the low end of intergroup animosity and estimates of levels of discriminatory behavior should be considered as downwardly biased if imputed to the entire country. The opposite would be true of research conducted in highly segregated areas.[43]

Even if we bring the laboratory to the field, we have to consider how our results are affected by where we choose to put that lab. Once we appreciate the power of social geography to shape behavior, the conclusions we draw from a single location should be dependent on the social geography of that location. You can see me following my own advice in this book: when I study a single city, I am careful to fit it into the plane of context because I know that the group-based bias recorded in Jerusalem, for example, is informative, but might be much stronger than we see elsewhere.

It is not that previous scholars using labs in the field made a mistake by choosing the locations that they did. Often these were chosen for a specific purpose; for example, Habyarimana et al. (2007), wanting to know why diversity affects a country's welfare, went to a diverse part of the country to see how people behaved. However, what we tried to contribute in our research – and what I have tried to emphasize throughout this book – is that when we go beyond thinking of an area as a container that can hold this or that mix of people to thinking of the space between these groups as having an independent causal effect on behavior, we can see why choosing a single location can be misleading.

We may be able to see this in the results of Habyarimana et al. (2007), who had their Ugandan subjects play a series of games, including three directly analogous to the games we had our subjects play: a Prisoner's Dilemma game, a Dictator Game, and a cooperation task similar to our Lego task. Only in the Prisoner's Dilemma game did Habyarimana et al. find group-based bias, so they concluded that it is lack of cooperation – a choice of a strategy not to cooperate with the outgroup member – that is solely responsible for social inefficiency in diverse countries. But in Israel we found something different. All the behaviors we collected demonstrated group-based bias, suggesting that social inefficiency in diverse countries is not driven by a single type of strategy, but rather by a general group-based bias that characterizes all the many types of interaction between groups.

Why the difference? It could be that Uganda and Israel are just different places with different groups and what holds in one country does not hold in another. This is, of course, possible. I think, however, that the weight of the evidence in this book suggests we take seriously a different possibility: measuring group-based bias by studying intergroup relations in a single diverse neighborhood – in other words, in a place with low segregation – might lead us to downplay the extent of group-based bias in a country.

However, this is not only a message for those who study in countries other than the United States, although it should give researchers pause when setting up permanent laboratories in other countries. Even more permanent are the psychological and economics laboratories on college campuses. They implicitly assume that the behavior they measure is free of contextual influences. But how can this be? We traveled to 20 locations in Israel and found that, even within the same basic social structure, costly behavior varied dramatically across this relatively small country. Shouldn't we expect dramatically different results from American laboratories in locations with social geographies as different as, say, those of Cambridge, Massachusetts and College Station, Texas?

Our findings also suggest that scholars should strive to measure space more carefully when comparing social efficiency across countries. It is accepted in the literature that social efficiency is negatively correlated with diversity and segregation across countries. It is notable, though, that segregation has never been meaningfully measured cross-nationally. When comparing countries, scholars usually use blunt measures of segregation, such as measuring the average homogeneity of large subnational units. For example, this would be like looking at the United States and comparing whether people who live in New Jersey are generally of a different ethnicity than people who live in New York. There is probably value in this approach, but it also likely masks the power of spatial segregation to shape our micro-behavior and to lead to macro-consequences. What we would really like to see are not only the social-geographic patterns of New York state but also the patterns within New York City, Albany, Rochester, Buffalo, and so on, because we might guess that, like Tel Aviv and Jerusalem, Buffalo and New York City are very different places. This will help to reveal the impact of social geography on group-based bias. In other words, when comparing countries and talking about the effects of diversity on a country, we cannot just treat countries as containers for diversity, but must be sensitive to the variations of social geography within those countries.

Lessons for Public Policy

We see a familiar pattern emerging in which social geography seems to interfere with the ability to mend rifts in society. Israel is a country with deep anxiety about its inter-Jewish cleavages, while its ultra-Orthodox population lives in an increasingly segregated geographic pattern with minimal intergroup contact. As usual, as the space between groups grows larger, it is not clear how the political will can be mustered to reverse this course.

This, of course, can be said for another source of anxiety in Israel: the question of the civil rights of the Arab minority, especially in the Occupied Palestinian Territories. As an extreme case of how geography shapes this issue, consider the settlements of Jews in the Occupied West Bank. If we were to measure group-based bias toward Arabs among the Jewish settlers, we would likely find high levels. From a scientific perspective, of course, we would worry about selection and think that the correlation between living there and their attitudes may not be driven by social geography, but rather by the preexisting attitudes of people who chose to move there. But regardless of their attitudes before they moved, these settlers have selected into living near an outgroup population that is large, proximate, and extremely segregated. This is much like the situation in the United States in the mid-twentieth century, only slightly reversed. Hostile whites moved away from inner-city Blacks and then looked back at this close, yet very segregated population and with this backwards gaze, their hostility toward this group increased. The situation of West Bank settlers is even more extreme: they are a group driven by nationalism or religion to move, not away from, but into a population toward which they may have high preexisting hostility. Then geography, the mighty demagogue, goes to work to increase their hostility. Indeed, this could contribute to the settlers' strong support for right-wing political parties, which are increasingly influential in Israeli politics and reinforce the Israeli government policy of supporting settlements. The attitudes induced by social geography get in the way of fixing problems of social geography.

What is notable about both American whites fleeing to the suburbs and Jewish settlers moving to the West Bank is that these movements are not the result of disconnected individual preferences. Both American suburbanization and Jewish settlement in the West Bank are aided by government policy[44] and these policies, partially due to the space they create between groups, increase group bias. This is the government giving a platform to the demagogue. Israeli law makes such exclusion possible in explicit ways: it is legal for cities to use vague regulations concerning the cultural fit of prospective immigrants to exclude ultra-Orthodox and Arabs. I am not trying to judge the relative morality of suburbanization and settlement policies, but rather to point out, as we have seen before, that once the state helps to shape segregation, it is probably contributing to group bias that will then make it even harder to dismantle the segregation. This was true when the United States created racially segregated housing projects and suburbs and it is probably true as Israel creates exclusive housing for ultra-Orthodox in Israeli cities or for settlers in the occupied territories. The parallel between the United States and Israel can also be seen in that both are, of course, rich and powerful countries, but the strain of intergroup conflict, often aided by policy that creates space between groups, drags on the resources and social captial of each nation. One lesson from this book is that such policies, even ignoring their implications for equality, badly damage intergroup relations.

When we think about the differences across countries, scholars often point out that much of this variation can be attributed to diversity. The grand failure of a society-wide game of Prisoner's Dilemma contributes to the unfortunate negative correlation between diversity and such important outcomes as democracy and economic growth. This is the liberal dilemma. But when we look at the relationship between segregation and group bias, we also understand that this dilemma is not simply a case of diversity leading directly to negative outcomes. Segregation, too, can play an important role – it distorts the space between groups, making us unlikely to want to share our neighborhoods and country with members of a different group and hurting our chances of cooperation. And segregation means we have little chance of repeat interactions, so the anecdote for collective action problems is not present. Countries that cannot solve collective action problems fail not only because they are diverse but because of how that diversity is spatially organized.

We also see that, for many societies, segregation is passively allowed or even actively encouraged. Walls do not rise by chance. Perhaps the leaders of these countries think that the negative outcomes of segregation can be countered in other ways or maybe even ignored if certain groups are removed from the political process, as were Blacks in the American South and as are Arabs in the West Bank. But in a democracy, in which all groups can participate but must still find a way to come together across the social space forged by segregation, the consequences of social geography for human behavior are laid bare.

8

Crenshaw Boulevard, Los Angeles: Contact and Exit

For where does one run to when he's already in the promised land?

– Claude Brown, *Manchild in the Promised Land*, 1965[1]

And then I remember my dad said, "It's going to change" because you could see it. I guess he could, I couldn't, I didn't really understand it.

– Charles, Crenshaw Boulevard, Los Angeles, 2009[2]

I've already written of taking the bus in Los Angeles westbound on Sunset Boulevard from Hollywood to UCLA in Westwood. Continuing in that direction and reaching the terminus at the Pacific Ocean will put you in Pacific Palisades, one of the most homogeneously white locations in Los Angeles County – 89 percent Anglo. But if, instead, you took Sunset Boulevard eastward all the way to the end, you would reach another demographic extreme. As the name on the street signs changes from Sunset Boulevard to Cesar E. Chavez Avenue and then to Avenida César Chávez, you will find yourself in Boyle Heights and East Los Angeles, 97 and 95 percent Latino, respectively. These neighborhoods are by some measures the least diverse places in Los Angeles County – almost entirely Latino and overwhelmingly of Mexican heritage.[3]

A bird's-eye view of the Los Angeles Basin's Latino population shows them in all but the most exclusive sections of the city, but also shows a steady increase in Latino density as you move away from the ocean, culminating in the homogeneous bastion of East Los Angeles. (See Figure 8.1. In this and in the other maps in this chapter, black dots represent the exact location of individual Black voters and gray dots represent the exact location of individual Latino voters (see below for how I do this).)

Visit East LA and Boyle Heights and you will likely hear nothing but Spanish. But look at the street signs and you will see names that seem out of place, such

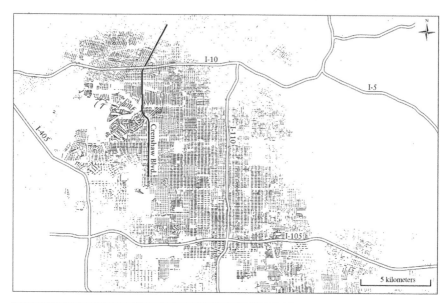

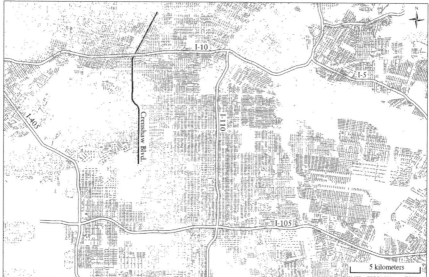

FIGURE 8.1. Black and Hispanic voters in the Los Angeles Basin, 2008.
Locations of individual Black (top) and Hispanic (bottom) voters, as identified from the official voter file in 2008.

as Eagle, Wabash, and McBride. These names are there, of course, because these neighborhoods weren't always Latino. Built up in the first half of the twentieth century, they were primarily Anglo, with a large Jewish population in Boyle Heights.

In some respects, a neighborhood like Boyle Heights represents taking my experiment of introducing a few immigrants on the train platforms of white Boston suburbs to its logical extreme. As immigrants enter a community, even if some natives welcome them, others with a distaste for the new group will leave, which in turn may allow more immigrants to enter, which may cause more natives to leave. Eventually, even those who initially welcomed the newcomers, now feeling out of place, will leave too. Diversity is unstable and, under many conditions, complete homogeneity of one type or another is the only equilibrium.

A neighborhood, of course, does not *have* to move to an extreme – to go from Pacific Palisades to Boyle Heights. This chapter asks about the neighborhoods that don't. What happens to intergroup interactions when a neighborhood doesn't go to a demographic extreme? Rather than a neighborhood becoming all Anglo or all Latino, what if we can observe a point where the neighborhood is mixed? With a mixed neighborhood, rather than the dynamic of social geography playing out across entirely segregated neighborhoods, we see changes in demographics happening block to block.

To investigate this, I will turn to the social geography of Blacks and Latinos in Los Angeles – two groups that have, for some time now, shared neighborhoods. I will use some methods similar to those I have used already, but I will also introduce a new source of data: focus groups. With these I will let people describe, in their own voices, how social geography in these neighborhoods affects their lives.

In addition to these focus groups, I will again turn to experiments and observational data to measure the impact of each group on the other's political behavior. I show that for Blacks and Latinos, voting behavior is changed when the other group is made salient. Furthermore, because of the close intertwining of these groups in this city, I can see proximity vary substantially – a Latino in East Los Angeles is far away from most Blacks, while a Latino in Inglewood is very close. This variation allows me to explicitly test the effects of proximity on voting behavior – I show that the impact of the outgroup is very different for Latinos in these two different parts of the city.

DYNAMICS OF SEGREGATION

The economist Thomas Schelling famously simulated the process of segregation by taking a checkerboard and covering it with dimes and pennies representing two social groups.[4] Schelling showed that, given plausible assumptions about preferences for diversity – say, that people do not want to be an extreme minority in their neighborhood – and the ability to move freely, clusters of groups would form quickly and eventually give way to complete segregation, with the dimes and pennies completely separated – having moved to a new neighborhood or city. (For an example, see Figure 8.2.)

Schelling revealed a serious problem for those who believe diversity is good for a society: even if we assume most people are tolerant, diversity is still

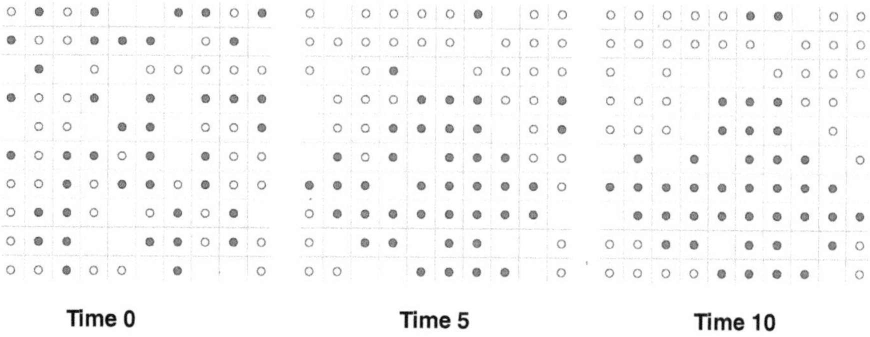

Time 0   **Time 5**   **Time 10**

FIGURE 8.2. Simulation of a dynamic model of segregation.

Sorting at start (Time 0), middle (Time 5), and near the end (Time 10) of Schelling's dynamic model of segregation with subjects wanting neighborhood to be at least 50 percent ingroup members. Gray and white dots each represent different social groups. At each point in time, people who do not have at least 50 percent ingroup members in surrounding squares will move to an open square. Movements continues until everyone is satisfied with their neighbors or cannot improve by moving. See Schelling (1969, 1971).

likely to unravel into segregation. All it takes is for people not to want to be a minority. We can imagine that even well-intentioned, non-bigoted people have good reasons for not wanting to be a minority. It can be difficult because you can't speak the common language or you want your children to grow up not feeling too different from their peers. This is where the theoretical liberal dilemma becomes a personal dilemma, one that people often resolve by exiting.

In Schelling's model, as the least-tolerant people – those who cannot stand to live around anybody of a different group – move away first, the population proportions will shift ever so slightly and then the slightly-more-tolerant will move away and the population proportions shift ever so slightly again and the slightly-more-tolerant move this time. With this, even those who are very tolerant find themselves as minorities where they were once a majority and they, too, will move. Soon a neighborhood or city will become homogeneous.

We can critique how well Schelling's model captures the complete parameters of segregation, but there is little doubt that the process he describes captures the overarching dynamics. On top of the simple mathematical process he described, economic and political forces – including the collapsing of home prices – make neighborhoods more affordable to poor immigrants and the process of transition accelerates.

The urban landscape of the United States is littered with evidence of Schelling's model at work. Some evidence is in the names. Why was a section of Cabrini-Green named after Frances Xavier Cabrini, the canonized Italian-American immigrant? Because the first residents were mostly Italian immigrants from the Little Sicily slum that Zorbaugh wrote about. These residents rapidly departed as Blacks moved in and soon the project was left with only the name to suggest its original occupants. We can also see evidence in structures. North Lawndale on the West Side of Chicago lost around 90 percent of its white population in about a decade. Black ghettos are often characterized by storefront churches – small venues in vacated commercial buildings – but North Lawndale is dotted with Baptist and African Methodist churches in impressive freestanding stone buildings. Why is this? Because these buildings were once synagogues, before the flight of the Jewish community.

This pattern – driven by selection based on attitudes – speaks to the difficulty of identifying the effect of segregation on bias but also raises seemingly intractable public policy problems. To avoid this fate of segregation, something must keep people in place; for example, people may be unable or unwilling to move. But in the United States, with a history largely defined by cheap access to land, the ability to easily find new places to live has meant that moving away from outgroups has generally been a readily available option even for those without great means. Pair this freedom with toxic racial politics and the rise of the automobile and the result is that majority populations have rarely been tied to changing neighborhoods. Thus, the Schelling model plays out over and over again.

In Los Angeles, over the twentieth century, we see the Schelling model play out: Anglos pushed further and further west, moving away from Blacks, Latinos, and Asians and, at first, leaving lower-status white groups, like the Jews of Boyle Heights, behind. But even Jews, as their status increased, pushed further west, creating neighborhoods like the Fairfax District, southeast of Hollywood. The population of the San Fernando Valley, the quintessential suburb, was largely a result of whites leaving diversifying parts of Los Angeles and of East Coast cities.[5]

As the Schelling dynamic unfolds, social geography is also changing. From the perspective of the majority residents, the size and segregation of the outgroup increases and, if my theory is correct, so will group-based bias.

The once entirely white neighborhoods of Boston, such as Dorchester (discussed in Chapter 5), are example of this dynamic. Conflict between whites and Blacks manifested along Blue Hill Avenue and block by block, neighborhoods changed their demographic composition. The process in Dorchester, as in many neighborhoods, was relatively short-lived; in just a few decades, some whites fled to suburbs such as Brookline and Newton and others moved more locally to create the patterns of segregation we see today.[6]

Dynamics of Segregation among Low-Status Groups

In some neighborhoods, however, the Schelling model seems to stall. Look across Los Angeles and you can see neighborhoods that never reached Schelling's equilibrium. In these neighborhoods Blacks and Latinos share space. In the 1950s, some communities in Los Angeles County, such as Compton and Watts, changed almost overnight from entirely white to Black. A textbook example of the Schelling process of segregation. Now, over the last 20 years, these famously Black communities have become majority Latino. But Blacks did not leave entirely; Compton and Watts were still 33 and 37 percent Black, respectively, in 2010. The Schelling process never finished.

Blacks and other low-status groups facing demographic change will not exit as quickly as whites did from Compton and Watts because (a) they often have less wealth with which to do so, (b) they may face discrimination and have less choice of where to move, and (c) they may value the community ties in their current location, especially when faced with the alternative of being an extreme minority elsewhere. In Compton, Watts, and other parts of Los Angeles, we see neighborhoods that look almost frozen in the Schelling dynamic – as if the simulation had stopped part-way through. Having never reached Schelling's equilibrium, these neighborhoods look permanently like Dorchester did in the 1970s, with alternating blocks of social groups – in this case, Black and Latino. Segregation is defined, not city to city or neighborhood to neighborhood, but block to block.

These neighborhoods are stuck in place on the arc of intergroup interactions – not moving toward full assimilation like we have seen with immigrants in some communities, but certainly beyond the early stages of a clash. There is a manifest tension, as my theory suggests will happen when the social geographic impact of a group increases with immigration, but with the sharing of a neighborhood, the ameliorating effect of interpersonal contact pushes back, allowing for a stable, if not problem free, harmony.

In some respects, groups being "stuck in place" with a local conflict is what Key observed in the South 70 years ago, when poor whites shared local environments with Black neighbors – neither group had great means to move and improve their situation. The presence of these Black neighbors animated white politics. However, there is an important difference in Los Angeles because these neighborhoods are occupied by two low-status groups.

By examining two low-status groups, I am making an important departure from what has been the focus of this book; namely, the reactions of high-status groups, such as Anglos, to low-status groups. This is crucial because it tests the limits of my claims about social geography. Much of the study of intergroup relations is concerned about status generally,[7] political and economic power more specifically,[8] or the specific attitudes of whites.[9] Such theories claim that behavior is dependent on one's sociopolitical status. While this may be true, I focus on something more general – a basic cognitive process that should affect any group, regardless of its status or power. Nevertheless, as I have gone through the who and the where of social geography, other than the ultra-Orthodox population in Israel, which is less clearly defined as a low-status group, I have not examined the effect of social geography on low-status groups. If social geography plays on our basic cognitive processes, then the reactions should be similar across groups, but, because low-status groups have less mobility than high-status groups, there are important differences in the reaction to an outgroup: defense of a local environment becomes paramount. The need for defense animates politics. But, at the same time, the inability to exit means that interpersonal contact can do its work. These two forces come together in these racially mixed, low-status neighborhoods.

LOS ANGELES

By focusing on Blacks and Latinos in Los Angeles, I am moving to a new region of the plane of context. For Blacks, social-geographic impact and interpersonal contact is higher here than in any city I have examined so far (see Figure 1.7 on page 30). If this seems counterintuitive, consider that Blacks in Los Angeles are a small minority, decreasing in population share. Furthermore, the existence of Black enclaves such as Baldwin Hills and Latino enclaves such as East Los Angeles means that the level of segregation between these groups is relatively high (Black/Latino dissimilarity was 0.52 and Anglo/Black was 0.65 in 2010). But, in fact, typical measures of segregation probably understate the actual segregation in Los Angeles because much of the separation between Latinos and Blacks happens at a much finer level, alternating from block to block within neighborhoods, and our measures of segregation are not equipped to capture this.

Furthermore, because Blacks are a small minority and segregation occurs on a micro basis, interpersonal contact between Blacks and Latinos can be relatively high. By population percentages alone, we should expect that Blacks will have to have brief interactions with Latinos regularly.[10] But these interactions will happen even more frequently than we might expect if we were dealing with a high-status group because Black residents of Los Angeles do not have the same opportunity that Anglos do to seek exclusive institutions, such as private schools, that will limit contact between groups. This changes the dynamic of context and moves groups into a place on the plane where we should expect less group-based bias than in another city with similar levels of social-geographic impact.

With the Latino population, too, I am doing something which I have not yet done in this book, which is a systematic examination of both sides of demographic change – asking whether we can see the influence of social geography on immigrants to a neighborhood and on the people already living there. The dynamics of contact may also be different; interpersonal contact will be limited for some members of an immigrant group due to language and cultural barriers and because of the large size of their local population, they are less frequently in contact with the Black minority group.

Blacks and Latinos share much of the Los Angeles Basin (see Figure 8.1), with only a few neighborhoods that would be called "Black" – by most observers – in the same way that the South Side of Chicago is "Black." It was, of course, not always this way. The population of Blacks in Los Angeles swelled in the first half of the twentieth century, attracted by jobs, especially in the defense industry that was booming in California. There was also a persistent idea, perhaps a myth, that Los Angeles offered the American ideal of racial tolerance. Many Blacks moving to Los Angeles from the South expected a place where they could find greater racial tolerance and more opportunities than they would find in the South, the Midwest, and Northeast.[11]

This expectation was never fully realized. Some scholars point to the Watts Riot in 1965 as the end of the short-lived dream of a racially harmonious Los Angeles[12] and argue that it hastened the sharp segregation between Blacks and whites. However, it is important to realize that because of these Schelling-type processes, other cities arrived at similar levels of segregation without a catalyzing event like a riot, so it is not clear if the riot really caused the segregation we see in Los Angeles today.

One way or another, what did manifest in the 1960s and after were core Black communities in the southern part of the Los Angeles Basin, in places like Compton, South Central Los Angeles, Watts, and Crenshaw. These communities became centers of Black culture and political power, contributing national figures, such as Maxine Waters, the long-serving member of Congress and Tom Bradley, the only Black mayor of Los Angeles. These communities also supported locally powerful politicians: the white Los Angeles County supervisor Kenneth Hahn and his son, the former mayor James Hahn; and Bernard Parks, the police chief who came to power after the 1992 Rodney King riots and later joined the city council. In Compton, a separate municipality, the city government came to be controlled by Blacks (as it still is today, despite the numerical superiority of Latinos in the city).

However, in recent decades, there has been an enormous change in the population proportions and relative power of Blacks and Latinos in Los Angeles. In 2010, Latinos made up 49 percent of the population of the city, while Blacks made up 10 percent. In 1970, the proportions had been 17 percent and 18 percent, respectively. (For Los Angeles County, the Latino and Black proportions were 47 and 8 percent, respectively, in 2010 and had been 18 and 10 percent in 1970.) Of course, the rise of the Latino population coincided with an opposite change in the proportion of Anglos, which dropped from 61 to 29 percent of the city in that same period.

Differing Responses to Demographic Change

When Schelling wrote about his model, he speculated on whether segregation, so common in American cities, was socially efficient, meaning that people could satisfy their preferences for living with the level of integration they preferred. He speculated it was not, because integrated neighborhoods appeared to be so rare:

A special reason for doubting the social efficiency in aggregate segregation is that the range of choice is often so meager. The demographic map of almost any American metropolitan area suggests that it is easy to find residential areas that are all white or nearly so and areas that are all black or nearly so but hard to find localities in which neither whites nor nonwhites are more than, say, three-quarters of the total. And comparing decennial maps, it is nearly impossible to find an area that if integrated within that range, will remain integrated long enough for a couple to get their house paid for or their children through school.[13]

Schelling was partially right: empirical investigations have shown that in the United States, especially for minorities, a preference for a diverse neighborhood does not mean they can live in one.[14] But with respect to the stability of neighborhoods, Schelling was missing something. For example, Census Tract 2349.02 in Los Angeles County, which Crenshaw Boulevard runs directly through (see Figure 8.1),[15] was 66 percent Black and 34 percent Latino in 1990 and 20 years later was 56 percent Black and still 34 percent Latino. Schelling was wrong, in this respect, because he only considered models of neighborhoods in which both groups had full movement. He may have felt he could make such an assumption at a time when Blacks were displacing whites in America's central cities, so that whites were rapidly leaving and falling real estate prices meant that Blacks could easily move into those homes. This is much different than a situation in which Blacks have nowhere else to go.

The difference in mobility for whites and Blacks in the face of demographic change can be seen in the social geography of Los Angeles County. The growth of the Latino population in neighborhoods like Boyle Heights meant that Anglos moved to new parts of the county. Separate municipalities with the power to zone away poverty created places where low-status groups could not afford to live, such as the coastal communities of Manhattan Beach and Palos Verdes Estates (both around 80 percent Anglo white and about 1 percent Black or less in 2010). Within the City of Los Angles, too, zoning created bastions of wealth, such as Bel Air, that remain homogeneously white.

But Blacks were less able or willing than whites to move. Latinos, like immigrants to other cities before them – including Blacks themselves – moved to areas of cheaper housing, which in Los Angeles often meant Black and Asian communities. I already mentioned Compton and Watts, but the crowding out of the Black community also happened elsewhere in the county, including places like Inglewood and South Central Los Angeles.

While the Latino population of communities rose, some Blacks may have been reluctant to move, thinking back to the hard-fought victories that had allowed them to live there in the first place.[16] Until 1948, when the US Supreme Court effectively abolished restrictive covenants, which barred homeowners from selling to non-whites, Blacks could not buy homes in many of the subdivisions of Los Angeles.[17] In the 1950s, even moving to places like Compton was often met with organized violence from whites.[18] In the 1980s and '90s, when the Latino population started to rapidly increase in these communities, the earlier resistance and restrictions were within the living memory of many Black residents – they felt they had earned the right to live in those neighborhoods. Furthermore, even Blacks who were willing to leave may have been unable to do so due to a lack of affordable housing elsewhere, held back by the fear of being an extreme minority somewhere else, or hampered by transportation needs that made the more far-flung suburbs impractical.

That Blacks respond differently than whites to an influx of immigrants can be seen in simple numbers. Between 1990 and 2010, the Black population of Los Angeles County shrank only 14 percent, from 992,974 to 852,780. During this time period, the Latino population increased by 37 percent, from 3,351,242 to 4,599,258. Some of the stability of the Black population reflects reproduction counterbalancing emigration, but even so, this is a comparatively stable population. In contrast, the county's Anglo population *decreased by 51 percent*, from 5,035,103 to 2,772,785. Some of this change is likely a result of Latino-Anglo intermarriage or changes in ethnic identification on the Census, but much of it reflects white flight in response to the growing Latino and Black communities – nearby Orange County saw its Anglo population *grow* by 7 percent over the same period. And compare the stable Black population of Los Angeles to the white population of places that famously experienced white flight: Suffolk County, Massachusetts, which includes Boston, saw its Anglo population decrease by 45 percent and Wayne County, Michigan, which includes Detroit, saw its Anglo population decrease by 52 percent.[19]

Using lists of voters, I can see even more direct evidence for the residential stability of Blacks in Los Angeles. I looked at Black voters living in the Los Angeles basin in 1992 and then looked to see what proportion of them were still living there in 2008. Of the Black voters in the basin in 1992 who were still alive and living in California, 90 percent were still living in the basin 16 years later, even as the size of the Latino population had dramatically increased.[20]

Low-status Groups and Group-based Bias in Los Angeles

Research on Black/Latino relations in Los Angeles was among my first inquiries into intergroup relations. When I first started conducting this research and presenting the work at conference and other venues, I was surprised by some strong reactions. Many people I talked to did not agree that I was finding group-based bias by Blacks targeted at Latinos (or vice versa, as we will see below). A common objection was that bias was likely to come from a group in power, such as Anglo whites. Such a premise would mean my claim there is a common cause of the behavior of Blacks in Los Angeles and, say, whites in Chicago was unfounded. This objection is rooted in theories of prejudice as a manifestation of a threat to power.[21] But once we think of prejudice as partially a cognitive phenomenon – something affecting all human minds – then group-based bias between low-status groups seems more plausible. It is also notable that the locally powerful group in parts of Los Angeles was not whites but Blacks.

As we have seen, group-based bias often occurs when groups must share public goods. In Los Angeles, Latinos and Blacks do have to bridge the social distance between themselves to share public goods; for example, in 2015, the school of a typical Black student in the Los Angeles Unified School District was over 50 percent Latino. We have already seen how schools and other such public goods suffer in many diverse countries when groups are in close enough proximity that they must share, but the social-psychological space between them prevents them from cooperating.

In 2003, I spent some time working at a Watts middle school, which, like Watts itself, had a mixed population of Blacks and Latinos. The school's staff were constantly concerned about violence between Black and Latino students. The threat was probably exaggerated, but nonetheless made a strong impression on the teachers and on community members. In fact, six years later, not far away in Crenshaw, when I was conducting the focus groups which I will describe in more detail below, a participant volunteered, "There's a strong tension still between the African Americans and the Latinos and it even goes into the schools."[22] Historians recount violence between Black and white students in Compton middle schools during the transition in the 1950s.[23] The tension disappeared when the white students all left Compton, but in Watts and Crenshaw, the Black students never left.[24]

You can also, very plainly, hear this tension when talking to Los Angeles residents. In my focus groups, a longtime African American resident of Los Angeles described how the growing Latino population has translated into tension:

Through the whole time I went to Crenshaw – I got [out] of high school in '76 – I never seen a Latino in the area, none, [except] if they were coming by working or something. And then I remember my dad said, "It's going to change" because you could see it. I guess he could, I couldn't, I didn't really understand it. But then in a 10-year span, it's just like 10 and 12 families on one street. It's like wow....But it's just amazing. I try to get along with everybody but it's always some kind of tension because of something.[25]

Looking at racial politics in Los Angeles, we can also see hints of conflict between Latinos and Blacks. For example, when Antonio Villaraigosa was elected in 2005 – the first modern Latino mayor of Los Angeles[26] – it was a landmark in the rise of Latino demographic and political power there and sent shock waves through the Black community, which had seen its political clout diminish over the years,[27] much as the election of Harold Washington had roiled whites on the North Side of Chicago.

When Villaraigosa ran in 2001 and 2005, Black precincts voted heavily against him, largely choosing to back James Hahn in 2001 and Bernard Parks in 2005.[28] Is this a group-based bias? Think back to my description of the mayoral race in Chicago between Jane Byrne and Harold Washington and how racial identity came to fore in a one-party competition. The politicians were all Democrats, so the decisions were not obviously ideological. Rather, we might think that much of this voting was based on racial identity.

Contrast this with the voting behavior of Anglos, whose voting in these elections seems to have been much less influenced by group-based bias. It was liberal white voters who provided much of Villaraigosa's support and liberal white voters from the same parts of the city who had supported Bradley in 1973.[29] Whites are the population for whom Blacks and Latinos should be least salient. White voters, concentrated on the west side of the city in the mountain and beach areas, are largely removed from Blacks and Latinos deeper in the Los Angeles Basin. Those two groups, on the other hand, are closely proximate and tightly segregated and one is growing in proportion to the other. Thus, they are precisely the groups whose voting behavior we would expect to be strongly influenced by social-geographic impact.

CRENSHAW: EXIT OR VOICE

Crenshaw Boulevard has a poignant place in Los Angeles history, in the psyche of Southern California, and even in wider pop culture. Much of the "low-rider" culture of Los Angeles was based on Crenshaw Boulevard. Black youths used to cruise in custom cars and the area became a center of LA rap culture in the 1980s. The place is much more varied than observers from a distance would know. On the eastern edge of Crenshaw is Leimert Park, a community planned in the 1920s and centered around an Olmstead-designed park. Baldwin Hills overlooks from the west, with beautiful sprawling homes, and is referred to as the "Black Beverly Hills."

Crenshaw is also just west of where Black and Latino populations come together. Look at Figure 8.1. Crenshaw Boulevard is on the west of these maps. Blacks are concentrated to the west and immediately to the east of it. The greatest concentration of Latinos is east of Interstate 110 and the Latino community expands westward, creating increasingly mixed Black and Latino neighborhoods until, at Crenshaw Boulevard, it hits one of the last majority Black neighborhoods in Los Angeles.

In fall 2009, in an elementary school classroom in Crenshaw, I spent days talking to groups of Black Crenshaw residents about social geography. The purpose of these focus groups was to understand, in an unstructured way, its impact on their politics.

Like any research technology, focus groups have their advantages and disadvantages. One disadvantage of qualitative research in general, of course, is that the interpretations are more subjective and harder to quantify. This can also raise concerns about research transparency. However, there is no shortage of quantification in this book, so I can focus on the advantages of this type of research. Interview-style research allows me to seek answers to questions without offering a pre-defined structure that guides subjects to the answers. For example, in previous chapters, I looked at survey data asking people whether they thought certain groups were "lazy" or "unintelligent." The danger in such questions is that subjects might not have an opinion on this matter at all, but feel compelled – or at least willing – to offer one when asked.[30] They might have an opinion but only a weak one and, unless the survey questions try to gauge the strength of such opinions, this nuance will be lost. And, of course, subjects might have other opinions about groups that are not included in the survey questions; for example, maybe they do not think of members of that particular group as "lazy" but do think of them as "dishonest."

Open-ended designs, like focus groups, are less prone to these problems; rather than asking somebody whether she thinks a group is lazy, you can simply ask her what she thinks of that group and record whether or not "lazy" is offered up. As such, opinions are able to come out in a more naturalistic way, as they might in everyday conversation. Of course, group pressures for conformity and other issues arise, but such issues also affect everyday conversation.

The groups I gathered included between 5 and 10 subjects. Seventy-two percent of the participants were women and were all African American, with an average age of 48 (range of 25 to 76). All were registered voters. Subjects were recruited by posting signs around the neighborhood.[31]

Maps in Their Heads and on Paper

Across these focus groups, a pattern emerged that reflects the impact of space on our sociopolitical interactions: when asked about place, the conversation inevitably leads to people, which will then probably lead to politics, which will come down to public goods.

Before we talked about place, I asked participants to draw social geography. Asking people to draw a map of their neighborhood is supremely interesting.[32] I just told them to draw whatever was important to them and, with this prompt, the spatial detail of their mental maps unfolded on paper (see examples in Figure 8.3).[33] With these maps, you learn what is important – what is salient – to people and what defines their local environment. Anything could have gone on that map – why did she choose what she did? You can also see the rich detailed knowledge that people have of their neighborhoods. Streets and buildings were identified and attributes were attached, such as a building's purpose. An area might be labeled safe or dangerous. You can also see the central role of social categories in defining space: for some participants, corners, intersections, and streets were identified as places for "Mexicans," "homeless," "Black gangbangers," and others. Such areas are often defined in terms of valence characteristics – "good" or "bad" – perhaps because they are populated by certain groups. As I discussed in Chapter 3, this is one of the reasons that the spatial distribution of groups might affect our behavior. We know whether places are good or bad and the negative affect tied to certain groups means we are likely to remember where those groups are.

After the maps were drawn, we would talk about what was on them. The accuracy of these mental maps and the ability to associate a group with a place was apparent in the conversation; for example, one participant located Asians

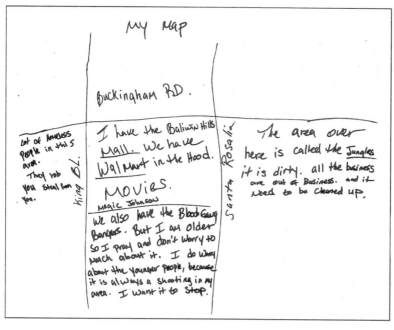

Wendy's map

Contents of Wendy's map:

MY MAP

Buckingham RD.

King BL.

Lot of homeless people in this area. They rob you steal from you.

I have the Baldwin Hills Mall. We have WalMart in the Hood. MOViES. Magic Johnson

We also have the Blood Gang Bangers. But I am older so I pray and don't worry to much about it. I do worry about the younger people, because it is always a shooting in my area. I want it to stop.

Santa Rosalia

The area over here is called the Jungles it is dirty. all the business are out of Business. and it need to be cleaned up.

Kamila's map

Contents of Kamila's map:

5th Ave

Dorsey Village

Good area

Bad area

Elementary Sch

10th Ave

Shopping Center

64th St

65th St

60th

To 3gd

Taco Bell

Donut Shop Laundry Mart Dry Clean

Education School

Slauson

Crenshaw

Hike Pale

59th & 5th

60th

Victoria (Danger Zone)

63rd

Brynhurst (Danger Zone)

WEST BLVD (Danger Zone)

FIGURE 8.3. Maps of Crenshaw, drawn by two residents.
Maps of their neighborhood, drawn by Kamlia and Wendy, during focus group in October 2009. Wendy's map is rotated 90 degrees.

as "right by Crenshaw and King" and another described Latinos as being in "the lower 60s," meaning the area of Crenshaw where the numbered streets start at 60th. Other participants described the presence of Anglos in View Park.[34] These responses are instantiations of the "maps in our heads" that I discussed in Chapter 4 and show how residents connect people to place and, in doing so, allow social groups to affect their behaviors and attitudes.

Defending the Neighborhood

Because my focus groups were conducted with African Americans in Los Angeles and particularly in Crenshaw, hanging over them was the process of neighborhood change that had brought a new social geography and new interpersonal contacts to so many Black residents of Los Angeles. Here is what Jerry, a participant, said:

Years ago, the East Side used to all be Black before we graduated to Avalon. We got across Avalon and came this way...and then we conquered Crenshaw...and View Park. Years ago, all Central Avenue used to be Black and one or two Mexicans...and then eventually when we left out, the Mexicans came in and took over.

Jerry was in his sixties and had lived in the community for decades, so his scope of history was longer than most, but his connection of groups to place was not unusual and neither was the accuracy of his description of population movement. Looking at a map, we can see what Jerry was talking about. The "East Side" was the area around Central Avenue, which was, at one time, the center of the Black community in Los Angeles. Over time, especially after World War II, the Black population of Los Angeles expanded to new areas, mostly south and west, across Avalon Boulevard, to take advantage of the Cold-War-fueled industrial boom in Los Angeles with jobs being created in cities such as Hawthorne, Inglewood, and the areas of Los Angeles built up around the Los Angeles International Airport. As racial covenants ended, making more housing available, Blacks moved to View Park-Windsor Hills, an upper-middle-class neighborhood with beautiful Spanish colonial homes in the hills, and other areas around Crenshaw Boulevard. And now, as we have seen, it is the Latino population of this area that is increasing.

The sense of this demographic change – that Latinos are crowding, if not displacing, Blacks – was palpable in these focus groups. When I asked where one could find Latinos, I would hear answers tinged with resentment: "All over." "They're everywhere." "Astronomically risen."[35] One participant told me, "Pretty much the minority is the new majority." I asked, in order to be sure, "And are we talking about Mexicans in this case?" "Yes."[36]

It is not surprising that with demographic change comes group-based bias in the form of protection and exclusion. My experiment in Boston confirmed the intuition many of us have about this. But there is something different in this case: not only can Blacks not flee as easily as whites did from inner-city neighborhoods, but there is a sense amongst them that a place must be defended. The sociologist Jonathan Rieder spent years observing the Brooklyn neighborhood of Canarsie as it struggled with the integration of Blacks in the 1970s. He noted an attitude similar to the attitude I saw in Crenshaw. In his case, Jewish and Italian immigrants in Brooklyn felt a special connection to a place they had fought to be able to live in and now thought they were losing to Blacks. Rieder quotes a woman saying, "Most of us who live in Canarsie came from ghettos. But once we made it to Canarsie, we finally had a little piece of the country. It was like we had moved to a little shtetl [the Yiddish word for a village]."[37]

Here, in Los Angeles, it might be fair to say that the attitude of Blacks may have been similar and, at least, if not even more, intense. Obviously, history and context are important, including the racial covenants that were in force within living memory and, of course, the longer history of the oppression of Blacks in America. The strong sense of collective political efficacy among Blacks[38] – where the fates of individuals and the entire group are intertwined – may be at work in the defense of these neighborhoods too. Doubtless, the Jews in Canarsie, with connections to the Holocaust, also had the burden of a collective sense of vulnerability, but they also had the option of exit – an option the white residents of Canarsie mostly took (it is now less than 6 percent white). Black residents of a community like Baldwin Hills – who within memory had not even been allowed to live there, who had no collective example of fleeing to a new location, and who saw no clear alternatives for where middle- and upper-class Blacks could live in a majority Black neighborhood – may well have taken a special interest in their neighborhood's defense.

Rosslyn, a 65-year-old woman who had lived in the area for 30 years, told me: "You may see a Hispanic [in Baldwin Hills], you may see an Asian, you may see a white, but predominantly we have *kept it Black* [emphasis added]." She went on to tell me that while other neighborhoods had seen an influx of Latinos, Baldwin Hills and the surrounding neighborhoods were "the only thing that we have left that has not been, you know, taken." When Rosslyn said this, Gigi, a 47-year-old woman, interjected: "That's ours!" "You mean Black?" I asked, to make sure I understood. "Yeah, this is the only thing we have in our community that's still ours."[39] Look at the maps in Figure 8.4 and you can see the bird's-eye view of what Gigi was talking about; Baldwin Hills is still almost entirely Black.

Public Goods

As we have seen, questions of place involve questions of public goods. My subjects, many of whom were poor and reliant on public services, waged the familiar battles over the public good that is schools. This particular clash may be as common as it is in part because it is tangible: you can see the allocation of resources and space in the presence of outgroup children in classrooms. We saw this in South Boston and it was one of the main issues animating the white residents of Canarsie. After the end of Cabrini Green in Chicago meant that two schools were no longer needed in the area, White and Black residents of

FIGURE 8.4. Black and Latino voters of central Los Angeles, 2008.
The location of individual Blacks (block dots) and Latinos (gray dots) voters in central Los Angeles in 2008, drawn from exact locations listed in the voter file.

the area around the former project were at odds over whether two schools, one mostly white and one almost entirely Black, should be merged.[40]

For my focus group participants, the public good was summer school classes, which they saw as unfairly going to Latino students learning English. Participants complained about seeing "pamphlets" only in Spanish, when they used to be printed in Spanish and English, and that "special education for Spanish-speaking" students was being offered in "an African American community."[41]

The public good of roads – a public good with a distinct spatial pattern – also came up, with subjects stating that Villaraigosa filled potholes first in Latino areas of the city. Jeanette, who was 58, said:

I can tell the difference by standing further east from over here...is we don't get our streets paved as much as it is over there. It's more bumpy and rough over here than it is over in the Latino areas.[42]

As we've seen over and over, when voters have to come together in democratic institutions – to cross the political space between groups and make collective decisions – the presence of the outgroup hangs over politics and people hear the demagogue of space whispering in their ear.

Animating Politics: Exit of Voice?

This sense of geographic pressure and a need for defense seemed to animate politics; it was an instantiation of the psychological connection between geographic impact and political participation that I have proposed throughout this book. One participant offered:

I think there's a statistic that the Mexican population is going to triple in America...Let's just face it, politics is about who has the most votes...They're going to be very catered to as a political base because they make votes.[43]

In a different focus group, Janet, 37 years old, said with reference to politics, "You have more Latinos taking over."[44]

The economist Albert O. Hirschman presented a simple model of consumer behavior in the face of the declining quality of a relationship with a firm or organization: they can *exit* or use their *voice* to try to improve the situation.[45] Hirschmann applied this to immigration: citizens subject to a particular government could choose to try to improve their situation (voice) or leave (exit). The implications for the movement of groups in geographic space is obvious. Many of the Black citizens of Los Angeles were migrants or children of migrants from the South[46] who had used the exit option when they had no political voice. The white citizens in the neighborhoods of Los Angeles to which these Blacks moved, such as Compton and Watts, quickly used their own option of exit. A strong political voice for Blacks in Los Angeles was hard-won and initially, when Blacks were still locked out of the power structure, their voice perhaps included the "politics of violence," like the Watts Riot in 1965.[47]

Eventually, the voice of Blacks in Los Angeles became real and powerful, as did the voice of Blacks in other urban areas in the United States, even if their voice in national and state politics continued to be muted and serious inequalities remained.

The Latino population are also immigrants or the descendants of immigrants who used the option of exit – in this case, from Latin America. Now this population is causing Blacks to face a decline in their political clout – essentially, the same situation that Anglo voters had once faced in places like Compton, but without the option of exit that the Anglos had. With exit unavailable or undesirable, I could see the residents of Crenshaw urging the use of voice by voting. A focus group participant made this connection very plainly:

If we aren't cognizant of this fact, we will get re-shifted in that balance very, very easily because – now let's face it – we have in the city, Villaraigosa, who's the mayor, we just have the new Supreme Court judge, [Sonia] Sotomayor, and the list goes on. [Hilda] Solis now has been nominated to be the Labor Secretary and the list goes on. So if you just watch that a little bit, it should make us be more sensitive to the fact that if we don't watch the balance, we will start cutting their grass and cleaning their houses.[48]

The connection between social geography and the need for political voice was illustrated by Sandra, who made a point that I remember vividly, perhaps because the event she referenced was so memorable and captured so perfectly how social geography can affect politics and can create a contest over whose voice is to be heard and who gets what. In talking about how the presence of Latinos activated her politically, she referred to the rallies organized on May 1, 2006 in Los Angeles and other cities, calling for immigration policy reform, especially to ease the plight of the millions of undocumented Latino immigrants.

I was involved in a survey project when these protests took place, so I was there to witness the awesome display of half a million marchers on Wilshire Boulevard in central LA. I remember walking along with the crowd and feeling the energy. There seemed to be an endless flow of people through the steel and glass lining the wide street. I bumped into a friend of mine who was a principal at a middle school near MacArthur Park, just west of downtown LA. It was a weekday, but her school had let the students out and, she claimed, they had been joined by their families. To me, such a display of collective action was inspiring, but then I was a social scientist living in Westwood, not somebody subject to the impact of the growth of an outgroup. Someone like Sandra in my focus group, probably reflected much more accurately the reaction of many people, especially in the Black community, where the social-geographic impact of the Latino population was greatest. Sandra spoke about voting because of the size of the outgroup. (I argued that voting can be a geographically motivated group-based bias in Chapter 2):

When I seen the march...part of May Day...they had two or three of them. When I seen the mass of Latinos, Mexican-Americans, whatever...that's a lot of people.

Let me tell you, this country is made up of illegals. Now whether I like it or not, they're coming…They coming, whether we like it or not. They're sneaking over. They have not decided if they are going to open the gates and let them in. *That's why we vote* [emphasis added].[49]

PROXIMITY AND VOTING IN PERPETUALLY TRANSITIONING NEIGHBORHOODS

Members of my focus groups had said, essentially, that social geography was causing them to vote. If this is true, is there other evidence for it in Los Angeles?

In parts of Los Angeles, where the inability of Blacks to exit probably means that the Schelling checkerboard has not and will not, in the foreseeable future, reach its fully segregated extreme, segregation plays out on a small scale. Blocks have become either entirely Black or entirely Latino as members of these groups, not able to escape the neighborhood entirely, sort themselves within it. If you peered down from the bird's-eye view and looked closely at parts of Los Angeles, you would see an entirely Black street next to an entirely Latino street next to another entirely Black street and so on.

Most maps of racial demographics obscure such patterns. Say you looked at a choropleth map, the type I have used repeatedly in this book, on which average levels of a population in areal units are represented by colors or symbols. Unless the areal units are city blocks, this sort of street-by-street variation cannot be seen.[50] The only way to see this sort of detail is to know where individual people live. This can be done by identifying the location of voters from a voter file, which has the exact addresses. With these exact locations, you can see patterns, such as block-by-block segregation, that are not visible using areal units provided by the government. I made such maps using the 2008 voter file from Los Angeles. As I did with my research in Chicago, I imputed every individual's race using an algorithm I had developed based on name and Census geography (see Chapter 6). Using a person's name to identify him or her as Black or Latino is very accurate, especially in these neighborhoods where essentially only Blacks and Latinos live because Anglos have departed.

To see these maps, look at Figures 8.4 and 8.5. In Figure 8.4, we can only see the broad contours of social geography. Find Crenshaw Boulevard and notice the thick concentration of black dots – Black voters – and then move east. While it is hard to see at first, notice that the gray dots – Latino voters – start to become more visible. Go far enough northeast toward the areas I described at the beginning of the chapter and those areas become almost entirely Latino. But look more closely between the two extremes – for example, in the north center of the map or just east of Interstate 110 in the center of the map – and you'll see blocks, close in proximity, that are almost entirely Black or almost entirely Latino. Look at Figure 8.5, zoomed in to a smaller section of Inglewood, the city to the south of Crenshaw, and you can see this pattern more clearly: one block almost entirely Black and the next almost entirely Latino.

FIGURE 8.5. Black and Hispanic residents of a section of Inglewood, 2008.
The location of Blacks (black dots) and Latinos (gray dots) voters in Inglewood in 2008, drawn from exact locations listed in the voter file. Notice the alternating neighborhoods.

We have learned that proximity and segregation will animate group-based bias. Here we see micro-level segregation within a local environment in conjunction with proximity. The predictions I have made say that an outgroup should be most salient when it is proximate and segregated – among Blacks and Latinos in Los Angeles, this is what we see and, with the proper data, we should be able to see this salience animate behavior.

Proximity and Group-based Voting among Latinos

We have seen more than once that proximity can affect voting. In Chicago, where the effect was causally identified, white voters altered their voting behavior as a function of their distance from the demolished housing projects. In a sense, these changes in white voting behavior happened as certain neighborhoods in Chicago, especially around Cabrini-Green, were transitioning to entirely white, completing the Schelling-style sorting. In Los Angeles, where we seem to be stuck in a perpetual transition, could I see a similar effect on voting? To test for this, I first looked at the behavior of Latinos in response to Blacks.

In 2008, the fact that Obama was on the ballot again provided an opportunity. I investigated the Democratic primary, held in June in California, when Obama was running against Hillary Clinton. I focused on the primary, rather than the general election, because few Latinos in California will cross party lines to vote for Republicans, but given the opportunity to vote against a Black man in a party primary, social geography might come into play. This was the behavior I documented among white voters in Chicago, where the opportunity vote against a Black candidate had clear elements of group-based bias (see Chapter 6).

To study this, I needed to know three things about each voter: location (address), race, and who he or she voted for. The first two came from the voter file and from my imputation of race. The latter is trickier because, obviously, a person's voting choice is private. I could use surveys, but then I generally couldn't know where a given voter lived with sufficient detail. I could apply ecological inference techniques, as I did in previous chapters, but this brings uncertainty and has to rely on assumptions, so I didn't want to use such techniques unless there was no alternative. I therefore turned again to voting precincts, the smallest geographic level at which votes are reported in a defined spatial location. (I made use of precincts nationwide and in my Chicago studies; see Chapters 2 and 6.)

Los Angeles has voting precincts that are small enough that many precincts are almost completely homogeneous. In central Los Angeles, where most residents are Black or Latino, even if a precinct is not completely homogeneous, this wasn't a problem: Anyone who wasn't Latino was most likely Black, so if Blacks nearly universally voted for Obama, then whatever variation in vote choice there was across these precincts should come from Latinos.

I determined voters' race using the technique I discussed in Chapter 6 and I placed these voters in their precincts using GIS and analyzed precincts in Los Angeles County that were at least 90 percent Latino. These are very homogeneous places – the areas in Figure 8.4 with almost nothing but gray dots. I measured the distance of these homogeneously Latinos places to the nearest concentrations of Blacks; namely, precincts that were more than 90 percent Black. These are also very homogeneous places – the places with entirely Black dots on Figure 8.4. Finally, I correlated the distance between these Latino and Black precincts with the percentage in the Latino precincts who voted for Obama. When I looked at the effect of proximity to Blacks on voting for Obama in these heavily Latino precincts, I found that it was strongly negatively correlated; that is, the closer Latinos were to these concentrated groups of Blacks, the less likely they were to vote for Obama in 2008. This effect of proximity was strong indeed. Amongst Latinos living the closest to Blacks – around a kilometer away – fewer than sixteen percent voted for Obama, but this percent ticks up rapidly as distance increases (see Figure 8.6). Latinos less impacted by the proximity of Blacks – those spatially separated into neighborhoods away from Black neighborhoods – were more likely to vote for Obama.[51]

These findings are what we would predict if proximity to a group is changing its salience and invoking group-based bias. Of course, this was not an RCT and we have to worry about the problem of selection. But it is notable that

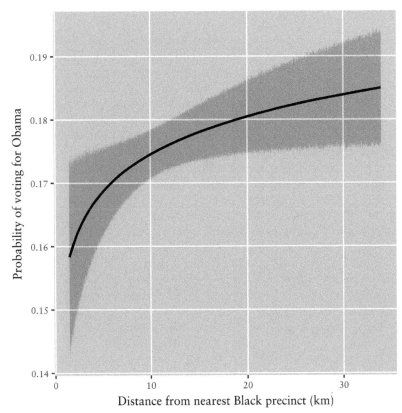

FIGURE 8.6. Proximity of Latinos to Blacks in Los Angeles and probability of voting for Obama in 2008.

Distance between Latino precinct and Black precinct is in kilometers. 95 percent confidence interval is displayed.

these Latino voters behaved just as the white voters in Chicago did in the same election – and that result *was* causally identified. Here, using different data, we see the same pattern emerge that I found using surveys and ecological inference techniques: the Latino voters in Los Angeles are subject to the same impact of social geography. It is not easy to think of plausible alternative explanations for this pattern. Were the Latino voters who lived a mile from Black voters any different from those who lived a half-mile from the same Black voters? Probably not in any meaningful way, other than the salience of their Black neighbors (and other factors were controlled for). These results might also be described as a behavioral manifestation of the social-spatial awareness we have seen throughout this book. If the proximity of Blacks was really causing Latinos to vote this way, then the mental maps of Latinos must have been detailed enough to know where these concentrations of Blacks were.

Priming Social-geographic Impact

Often in social science, there are variables that we believe are causal but that we cannot randomly assign. Social scientists therefore spend much time lamenting that they cannot prove the causal effect of variables that they believe affect sociopolitical behavior. For example, I have had any number of conversations in which somebody said, "If only we could randomize party identification": that is, if only we could randomly assign somebody to be a Democrat or Republican, we could see how belonging to a party affects behavior. Of course, this is (generally) not possible.[52]

To overcome this problem, researchers often rely on cognitive priming; for example, priming party identification[53] in order to make it more cognitively accessible. The idea is that one's behavior – say, answering a survey – is more likely to be affected by a variable – say, one's political party – if that variable has been made cognitively accessible than if it had not been. This allows researchers to measure the variable's effect on that behavior. For example, a researcher may randomly assign half of the subjects to receive a prompt before a survey question that says something like, "Think about the political party to which you belong," followed by a question about whether the subject supports a certain policy. The researcher can then see if the level of support for the policy is different for those who were primed and those who were not. If levels are different, it is presumably because subjects thought about their party in responding and this affected their answers. Thus, although I, as a researcher, can't make you be a Republican as I choose, I can take two Republicans and make one of them temporarily *think* more like a Republican than the other.[54]

Social geography, as we have seen, is also difficult to randomly assign. In the last study, I couldn't assign proximity, but perhaps it, too, can be primed. In the same 2008 election for which I measured the effect of social geography on the vote choice of Latinos, I conducted an experiment to see if I could prime social geography for Black and Latino voters and thereby affect their voter turnout. We have already seen evidence that social geography affects voter turnout and I have argued that this is because the salience of the outgroup changes perceptions of it, making voting seem more important. If this is the case, then I should be able to increase voting by priming social geography – essentially by saying to voters, "Hey, there's an outgroup over there."

My priming experiment relied on people's geographic knowledge – the same geographic knowledge that seemed to be present for the Latinos whose voting was affected by their proximity to Blacks. I looked at the voter lists and found neighborhoods like Crenshaw, Lynwood, and Compton in which Blacks and Latinos lived in close but segregated blocks, like those in Figure 8.5. Here I thought I could prime social geography to stimulate voter turnout. To do so, I sent letters to 4,253 Black and Latino registered voters (see example in Figure 8.7).[55]

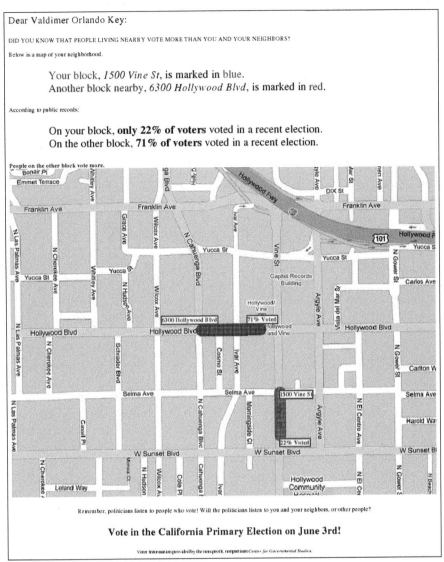

Dear Valdimer Orlando Key:

DID YOU KNOW THAT PEOPLE LIVING NEARBY VOTE MORE THAN YOU AND YOUR NEIGHBORS?

Below is a map of your neighborhood.

Your block, *1500 Vine St*, is marked in blue.
Another block nearby, *6300 Hollywood Blvd*, is marked in red.

According to public records:

On your block, **only 22% of voters** voted in a recent election.
On the other block, **71% of voters** voted in a recent election.

People on the other block vote more.

Remember, politicians listen to people who vote! Will the politicians listen to you and your neighbors, or other people?

Vote in the California Primary Election on June 3rd!

Voter information provided by the non-profit, nonpartisan Center for Governmental Studies.

FIGURE 8.7. Letter sent to voters in Los Angeles.
This letter shows an area in Hollywood, which was not actually part of the experiment.

I was careful to choose voters who lived in certain locations: the letters were sent to Blacks living on city blocks that were, on average, 89 percent Black and to Latinos on blocks that were, on average 90, percent Latino. Each letter contained a map of the voter's neighborhood, which looked like an online map circa 2008, when the experiment was conducted. The map highlighted the voting turnout rate on the voter's block compared to that of another block nearby.

The letter might have said, "On your block, only 22% of the voters voted in a recent election. On the other block, 71% of voters voted in a recent election."

Some of the letters were randomly assigned to point to a block made up of the outgroup (Blacks for Latinos and Latinos for Blacks) and some to blocks made up of the ingroup (Latinos for Latinos and Blacks for Blacks), but the letters never mentioned the race or ethnicity of the voters on the other block. The recipient could only know what group lived on the other block if they already knew their social geography. There was also a control group, living on these same blocks, who received no letter at all.

The key here is showing that voter turnout can be stimulated depending on who is made salient; that is, who on the block was pointed out in the letter. If voter turnout could be increased simply by making a group salient, no matter which group it was, then the effect of sending a letter pointing to the ingroup should be the same as the effect of sending a letter pointing to the outgroup. But if the effect was greater when I pointed to the outgroup, that meant that the salience of the outgroup stimulated political activity, as my theory suggested. I was essentially saying, "Hey, remember there is a different group of people over there and they vote, too."[56]

Months after the election, I checked the effect of my experiment, using the updated voter file to look up the turnout rates amongst those to whom I had sent a letter. In general, Black voters who received the letter were more likely to vote than those in the control group. But, more importantly, among Black voters there was a strong effect of increasing the salience of the outgroup: Black voters who received the letter pointing out the voter turnout in a nearby Latino block were much more likely to vote than Black voters receiving a letter pointing out the voter turnout in a nearby Black block. In fact, the statistical model indicates that for some recipients the letter's effect on turnout was perhaps as large as four percentage points (these results are model dependent).[57] The letter – which, in essence, said, "Hey look, there is a group over there" – had greatly increased turnout, but only when that "group over there" was an outgroup.

However, I also found, as we often do in social science, some mixed evidence for this claim. The results for the Latino recipients were pretty much zero; there was no difference between whether I compared them to the ingroup or to the outgroup and very little difference in the effects on the treatment and control groups. It's not entirely clear to me why this happened, but it could very well be due to differences in the geographic impact of the Black population on Latinos compared to the impact of the Latino population on Blacks – Latinos are simply a much larger group.

CONTACT IN A PERPETUALLY TRANSITIONING NEIGHBORHOOD

In Chapter 6, I discussed Bernard Kramer's study of the Chicago neighborhoods of Greater Grand Crossing and Auburn-Gresham in the 1950s. These neighborhoods were in transition; the white population, overwhelmed by the social-geographic impact of Blacks and with very little interpersonal contact, was gone within a couple decades.

As populations became intermixed in closely segregated blocks, proximity between groups increased. It was in those intertwined neighborhoods that Kramer discovered the most negative attitudes toward the outgroup. It was in blocks with similar geography that I was able to prime social geography to stimulate voting and that Latinos voted overwhelmingly against the Black candidate – a manifestation, I argue, of the same group-based bias Kramer had discovered. Perhaps though, the difference between Kramer's Chicago and my Los Angeles is that in Chicago, the white population moved away too quickly to experience the ameliorating effect of interpersonal contact.

Although proximity increases social-geographic impact, it also provides for interpersonal contact. When groups are positioned block to block, the casual encounters that we saw decrease animosity over time on the train platforms are likely to occur: passing each other on the street, shopping at the same stores, and riding the same buses. Of course, these brief interpersonal interactions are not always positive; in Canarsie, Rieder tells us, the Jews and Italians strongly disliked their street encounters with Blacks.[58] For many of us, this is our sole image of diversifying neighborhoods: a place of conflict. When I would talk to white Chicago suburbanites who had fled the South Side in the 1950s, their memory of a neighborhood in transition was of a place where Blacks and whites fought and victimized each other. I have never lived in such a neighborhood and have never had to make the choices that they did, but the counterfactual that was never realized by these white Chicagoans – because they had the option of exit – was what would have happened had they stayed.

What we saw in Canarsie and in Chicago was, perhaps, the norm for encounters over the short term before one of two things happens: either one group exits or reciprocity becomes the norm (see Chapter 7). The inefficiency of a confrontation every time you walk down the street is too great to sustain – people must either exit to avoid such conflicts or learn not to have them. Although not universally positive by any means, there is successful racial mixing in central Los Angeles – enough that many neighborhoods have lost their former meaning. Crenshaw is only partially Black; Spanish is commonly heard in Koreatown; Thai is heard in Little Armenia. These neighborhoods are not without their problems, but you can walk down the street in complete safety and ease – reciprocity is the norm. For those residents for whom exit was not an option, cooperation is a way to improve their neighborhood; that is, to have their "voice."

Groups without exit must intimately share institutions: they attend the same schools and are represented by the same candidates on the city council. This is a very different situation than when two groups are in a superordinate institution – say, voting for the same school committee or in the same mayoral election – but not in the same local institutions. Yes, Blacks in Los Angeles were concerned about public spending on exclusive goods, like English language classes for Latinos. But this problem is, perhaps, more tractable than the allocation of money across schools that are geographically inaccessible across populations, as is the case in Chicago, where Blacks, Latinos, and Anglos live in different areas, generally go to different schools, and share few elected representatives. When individuals are geographically segregated into schools, allocation across these schools is a zero-sum game: what goes to one school goes to one group and not the other. As a high school teacher in Chicago, for example, a common complaint I heard from my Black colleagues was the perception that politicians allocated money to Latino-dominated schools on the West Side for electoral gain.

Occasionally, the sharing of institutions and geographic space may even provide, not just fleeting contact, but the deep interpersonal contact that Allport studied, especially when geography brings people into close, unsegregated proximity and exit is not an option. As Donald, who was 50 when he took part in one of my focus groups, put it about Latinos, "My neighbors – they're right next door. We barbecue, we drink, we wave at each other. It's very common."[59] Carlo, who was 36 when he took part in a different focus group, made the same point: "I have a lot of Latino friends. They on my street in the neighborhood. We tend to get along, we barbecue together, party together."[60] Later in the conversation, Carlo illustrated just what we'd expect from Allport's research. Under the right circumstances, interpersonal ties can defeat the negative effects of geography:

See, I grew up in the neighborhood and I grew up with a lot of Latino friends. We've been friends for twenty-something years. We still party together. We grew on up together in the neighborhood so we get along.

NEIGHBORHOOD CHANGE AND LONG-TERM DIVERSITY

I started this chapter by moving from Pacific Palisades to Boyle Heights. Pacific Palisades is a neighborhood that, in broad strokes, has never undergone demographic change. On another hill, about 20 miles away, Boyle Heights is a neighborhood that completed the Schelling transition, the process of displacement that characterizes group-based bias in reaction to social-geographic impact. Going there now, you could travel down Breed Street, right off Cesar Chavez Avenue (earlier known as Brooklyn Avenue), and find Breed Street Shul, once the largest Orthodox synagogue west of Chicago and now vacant and surrounded by fences. The Jewish population has entirely exited.

On the other hand, by looking at neighborhoods that remain diverse, we come close to witnessing neighborhoods in transition – the type that fascinated social scientists like Allport in the 1950s. In this sense, we can learn something about what these cities were experiencing in the 1950s and understand that what Allport and others were seeing observationally was probably the same group-based bias that I am demonstrating using different methods. But these Los Angeles neighborhoods are also much different because, here, both groups are low-status with less option to exit.

A lack of exit justifiably has negative connotations; after all, equal access to mobility is important to a just society. At the same time, there is something hopeful about situations, such as that in Crenshaw, where groups have been constrained to live together, especially if we believe that, despite the group-based bias I can detect now, the long-term trend on the arc of intergroup interactions may be toward greater harmony based on increased interpersonal contact. In the United States, Latinos are expanding their geographic reach and often the initial landing place of new immigrants is near the inner-city cores long dominated by Blacks. This may cause initial tension, but as Blacks and Latinos continue to mix in America's urban cores, their relations may improve. As the historian Josh Sides puts it, talking about the Latinization of South Central Los Angeles:

Although it is a frustrating development to many of South Central's longtime African American residents, it will present their children with an opportunity that they themselves never had: the opportunity to grow up in a racially mixed community.[61]

The failure to complete Schelling's dynamic reduces the power of the geographic demagogue.

There is a tension between choice and diversity. The complete freedom to move – highly valued in free societies – is the freedom to segregate. Of course, we have seen that Anglos, often the high-status group with the option of exit, have frequently exercised that option. It is notable that when choice was restricted, the residents of Crenshaw, for example, built a community that is not without hardship but also has weathered the twentieth-century storm of urban decline and seems to be emerging as a stable, vibrant community – one in which diversity is a strength.

The state has a role here. Governments that offer different service levels and restrict the use of land to keep people of certain incomes in or out are affecting the utility and availability of exit for citizens.[62] The beaches of Southern California are a great example. The coastline of Los Angeles County is a string of separate municipalities: Santa Monica, Manhattan Beach, Redondo Beach, Hermosa Beach, and others. Each of these, especially the latter three in the South Bay area, are bastions of Anglo exclusivity. Once characterized by worn cottages, they are now crowded with multimillion-dollar homes, trying to fit as much square-footage as possible into the lots near the beach. South of Santa Monica, however, a tiny sliver of the City of Los Angeles touches the ocean: Venice. This community, built as a vacation resort complete with the canals for which it was named, was annexed by the city in 1926. The canals and amusement piers were paved over and went into decline. For many years, as part of the larger city, Venice did not have its own school district and could not control its zoning, so property values were much lower than they were in the other beach areas. This made it possible for racial minorities to became part of the Venice community, including a large population of Blacks. With this diversity came the vibrancy that made Venice famous for its muscle beaches, pickup basketball, surfing at the Venice breakwater, and tattoo parlors.

Venice was simply more interesting than other beach communities. In recent years, this very diversity has sent home values skyrocketing as the "creative class"[63] have turned to Venice as an attractive place to live. The remaining houses on the canals, once considered dirty and undesirable, are now home to movie stars.

There is a lesson here on the power of the state to shape diversity and, with it, quality of life. While zoning battles raged in Los Angeles and elsewhere, Venice – somewhat by accident – was left alone. Other beach communities, wielding their municipal zoning powers and their exclusive schools, remained homogeneous. Now Venice is thriving.

In closing this book, we will think about the mixing of groups across two different cities, Phoenix and Tucson, and how the different designs and cultures of these two cites – seemingly so close socially and geographically – have greatly affected their trajectories on the arc of intergroup interactions.

9

Phoenix: The Arc of Intergroup Interactions and the Political Future

So the Lord scattered them abroad from there over the face of all the earth, and they ceased building the city.

– Genesis 11:8

In this book, in order to study the influence of context, I have moved across space and time. One way to experience a change in context on a tremendous scale, across both space and time, is to travel south across the United States toward the Mexican border. Start at a city in the Midwest, say Chicago, and as you travel south, with each mile toward the border, the Anglo proportion of the population will decline and the culture and people will become more Latino.[1] Figuratively, you will be moving through time as the cities become not only less Anglo but also generally less dense, with the older, more compact cities of the Northeast and Midwest giving way to the newer, sprawling, car-based cities of the Southwest. In a Midwestern city like Chicago, where so much social science – including parts of this book – has been focused, you are in the urban past. When you reach a city like Phoenix – low-density and only 120 miles from the Mexican border – you are in the urban future.

Chicago and other big cities of the Northeast and Midwest represent not only the urban past but also, with their large Anglo white and African American populations, the demographic past. The populations of these cities were a result of the previous great migration – northward and westward – of African Americans from the South. Now, different currents are flowing: Anglos are moving south and west and Latinos are coming north. The demographic future of the United States is found in the meeting of Anglos and Latinos in these sprawling, fast-growing communities near the Mexican border.[2]

Keep pushing south from Phoenix on Interstate 19 through Tucson and into the emptiness of the beautiful Sonoran Desert and, right before the road terminates, it will bend sharply east and put you on the dusty streets of Nogales,

Arizona, a community straddling the border with Mexico. Here, you will find the extreme conclusion of demographic change. In Nogales, as in East Los Angeles and other communities where the Anglo population has ceded to Latino newcomers, while you will see some English – street names such as "Morely," "Robins," and "Nelson" (see Figure 9.1) – what you hear will probably be entirely Spanish (see Chapter 8). Nogales is about 95 percent Latino: in the 2010 Census, of the 20,837 people in Nogales, 19,793 were Latino and, of these, 18,778 were of Mexican ancestry. The incongruity of street signs and spoken language demonstrates context changing with time. Over the decades, the Anglo population of Nogales has nearly disappeared and the cultures of Mexico and the United States have blended together.[3]

This movement of people from Mexico, up through Nogales, Phoenix, and other cities in Arizona and eventually into more and more other states is the force shaping the future of intergroup relations in the United States. Over time, this population will continue to spread further east and north. Unless there is a dramatic turn in current trends, the United States is on the way to a significant – perhaps unprecedented – demographic change. It is unlikely that the tide of immigration from Latin America or the imbalance in birth rates between Latinos and Anglos will slow before the sizes of the Latino and Anglo populations become much closer to equal. In this final chapter, I ask – drawing

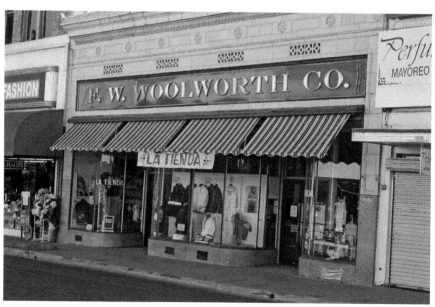

FIGURE 9.1. Central Nogales, Arizona, near the border.

Notice the "La Tienda" store that has replaced the Woolworth's. The US–Mexico border is within sight from this store. Photo by the author, November, 2014.

on the evidence from this book – what will intergroup interactions look like in the face of this demographic change?

Given my emphasis on the continuity of phenomena – on the way social geography affects groups similarly across cultures, time, and space – a reasonable starting point is to suppose that past waves of immigration – from Ireland, Italy, and Germany – provide a model for how natives will respond to the current wave of immigration. But there is nuance here that must also be explored. The cities now absorbing immigrants are much different than the cities that absorbed the immigrants of the past and the nature of immigration is itself arguably different, first, because today's immigrants are perceived as more homogeneous than those of the past and, second, because they arrive overland across an international border. Arguably, then, the role of social geography in the demographic future has no exact precedent and there is some reason to believe that the backlash against the growing Latino population will be more severe than even the backlash against previous immigrant groups. To investigate this, I will examine Phoenix, a city that, by many indications, represents the future of social-geographic growth and change in the United States.

Despite some perceptions of the rebirth of famous old central cities like Brooklyn and Boston, population trends are largely moving in a different direction. Between 2000 and 2015, Brooklyn grew at 5.2 percent, while Phoenix grew at 14.6 percent and Maricopa County, where Phoenix is located, grew at 24.2 percent. Of the 10 largest cities in the United States, the fastest-growing are San Antonio, Houston, Dallas, Phoenix, and San Jose. The eleventh-largest – Austin, Texas – grew 18 percent between 2010 and 2015. Despite social science's fascination with other cities, it is in the fast-growing cities of the Southwest – low-density and car-based – that we see the social geography experienced by an increasingly large portion of Americans. As Americans, both natives and immigrants, move to Phoenix and other such cities and as Latinos spread into more and more of the United States, will the space between us shrink, grow, or remain static?

WHAT WE HAVE LEARNED

In this book, I have conveyed three main points: (1) the important and direct impact of social geography on our behavior; (2) the mechanism behind this impact; and (3) the implications of this mechanism for our study and understanding of context.

Social geography, I have argued, creates a psychological space between groups and this space affects our behavior. I set out to demonstrate the sheer pervasive power of the influence of social geography. It operates across many domains of our behavior, affects many important outcomes, and does so across cultures and positions on the social hierarchy – rich, poor, majority, minority. With statistical analysis, we were able to see social geography operating across the United States, even in an era when space and distance seem to be less powerful constraints on our lives. Using administrative records, surveys, and other data, we saw that segregation, size, and proximity are correlated with political behavior: how we vote, whom we support, what we will say about other groups. In these findings, there are hints that the source of these correlations is deep in our psychology; it even surfaces in private behavior, like searching the Web. Looking deeper, we saw that space affects how we perceive other groups to be similar or different from us and even our willingness to share and cooperate with them. It is widely believed that the willingness to share and cooperate scales up to affect the comparative fates of nations and we might therefore believe that social geography has some role in these fates. Recently, we learned that social geography likely shifted votes toward Donald Trump and that this shift may have had a significant effect on the 2016 election outcome. Regardless of how Trump's presidency is or ultimately will be viewed, this is a weighty demonstration of the influence of social geography. And, of course, there are still many other intergroup behaviors and attitudes that I did not measure in the course of this book, but that are likely affected by social geography.

By traveling across space to different locations on the plane of context, we were able to see how differing levels of interpersonal contact and social-geographic impact shaped intergroup interactions. At one extreme is Jerusalem, where group-based biases are barely or not at all concealed and politics is organized openly around these cleavages. Social-geographic impact is also extreme in Los Angeles, but there, the slow-moving nature of change and, perhaps, fewer cultural and institutional barriers to contact have allowed for less group-based bias between Blacks and Latinos. Boston has levels of interpersonal contact similar to those in Los Angeles, but Latinos are a much smaller group in Boston than in Los Angeles. This may be why the Anglo population in Boston, as my experiment showed, although not immune to bias, finds the presence of that outgroup much less salient. Chicago lies between Boston and Los Angeles. And while the study of no single city allowed for a representative measurement of group-based bias in cities, looking at patterns across the entire United States and in Jerusalem allowed me to examine the entire range of the relationship between social geography and bias and see that these particular cities are part of a larger trend.

I argued that the effect of social geography on our behavior is causal: the very position of groups vis-à-vis other groups will affect our behavior. Establishing a causal effect of social geography has long been difficult for research on context, with selection casting doubt on many findings, but with the accumulated evidence of this book, the causal effect of social geography seems clear: our behavior is affected by the groups that live around us and the precise way in which our own group and those other groups are arranged in space. Nature provided examples of this: when the housing projects were demolished in Chicago, the social geography of white voters changed and their behavior changed with it. We could also see the causal effect of social geography when I, as the experimenter, changed social geography or its psychological importance. In Los Angeles, voters turned out to vote at higher rates when I increased the salience of social geography by reminding them of the presence of the proximate outgroup. In Boston, I actually changed the presence of the outgroup in people's everyday lives and their policy attitudes changed along with it. In the laboratory, I changed the arrangement of groups in space and, because of this, their perceptions and behavior also changed. In Israel, social geography, credibly separated from selection, was directly tied to bias.

By visiting a laboratory, conducting surveys, and making other tests, we also learned *why* social geography has these effects. Of course, as social scientists have argued for over half a century, intergroup interactions are affected by interpersonal contact: interactions improved in the presence of interpersonal contact, like that between Blacks and Latinos in Los Angeles, and were strained in the absence of interpersonal contact, as with whites and their Black neighbors in Chicago. But with this book, we discovered that social geography matters on a more fundamental level. It interacts with cognitive structures from our evolutionary past, shaping our behavior in the present. Social categorization is a basic feature of our cognition – something we do naturally – and it tends to color our social interactions. The geography of groups changes the salience of these group-based categories: the size and proximity of groups affects the cognitive accessibility of categories and the segregation of groups affects the comparative fit of categories. As decades of social science research has taught us, when the salience of a group-based categorization increases, so does group-based bias: attitudes toward the outgroup become more negative, group-based discrimination increases, and, as I showed, perceptions of differences between groups spill into political behavior, such as voter turnout and vote choice. In short, the space on the Earth's surface opens up the space between groups in our minds and this, in turn, opens up political and social space. Conflict ensues because in this social space, groups must share resources: schools, healthcare, sidewalks, caring for the needy, and anything else that we must provide collectively. And conflict ensues in the political space because in a democratic society, we share the institutions, such as representative bodies, that make decisions about sharing these resources.

I also demonstrated the microfoundations of the process of social-geographic impact. Asking subjects about their knowledge of the location of groups in their community, I found that, despite the difficulty of the task, people tended to know where these groups could be found. I also directly measured categorization and saw its link with segregation. And when I showed people objects in the vacuum of a randomized, controlled trial – in which only social geography was varied – this change in social geography caused changes in low-level perceptions, such as estimates of height and weight. Even when contact is held constant, social geography itself seems to shape our social cognition.

In supporting these arguments, I have also offered some guidance for the study of context and behavior. Of course, we have to consider how social geography – context – can be causally identified. But we also have to think about how we define context: it is no longer simply a container for action. Rather, space itself shapes our behavior. We therefore have to study the contours of geography: not only how many members of various groups live in an area, but do they live close to or far from each other? Are they segregated or integrated?

Emphasizing the primal role of space in our psychology reveals the universalness of the influence of social geography. There is a striking continuity between the past and present. Drawing an arc from the studies of Allport to my findings almost 70 years later, with many scholars in between, shows the consistent effect of social geography on behavior. Of course, the behavior of politicians matters. We saw that in Trump's gains with Anglos – beyond that of previous Republican candidates – in places with large groups of Latinos. And of course, the history of an area matters. We will see that in this chapter when I examine the diverging intergroup relations in different places in Arizona. But we also see the limits of these influences, most starkly in the laboratory, where there were no politicians and the groups had no social meaning, yet groups still showed bias, and their bias was shaped by social geography. Therefore, as scholars of intergroup relations, even before we start talking about politics, culture, and economics, we must examine social geography.

THE ARC OF INTERGROUP INTERACTIONS: PHOENIX AND TUCSON

What does the future hold for intergroup relations? An easy prediction is that, over time, the native backlash against Latino immigrants will soften. When we think of the interactions with other immigrant groups – such as the Irish in Boston and the Okies in California – history has arced from clash to indifference and assimilation. Part of this arc, of course, is selection: natives with high levels of intolerance exit – this is the Schelling sorting I discussed last chapter – and, eventually, many immigrants who achieve higher status also exit and assimilate into the native population. We can see this arc across time and space as we travel toward the border of Mexico, from the recent initial clash in places in Ohio and Pennsylvania, where Latinos are new, to an eventual softening in places like Southern California, where the Latino population has been growing for decades and residents have experienced contact for generations.

In California, as I was growing up, politicians tried to exploit the space between groups and were often successful. Pete Wilson won the governorship in 1994 with ominous television commercials about immigrants "who keep coming…" and schools and communities were riled over bans on social services, including language instruction, to immigrants. Looking at California in 2017, such anti-immigrant politics is almost unimaginable. California moved quickly along the arc: it turns out that Wilson was a last gasp of mainstream anti-immigrant bias and California became a bastion of liberalism. (As I discussed in the last chapter, Anglo selection away from parts of California in the last 30 years can be seen, so part of this turn to liberalism may come from out migration and, as we saw with residents of Crenshaw, this is not to say anxiety about immigration doesn't exist.)

A hopeful view of where America finds itself now is that Donald Trump – seemingly propelled into the White House partially by anti-immigrant sentiment, fueled by the social geography we saw in Chapter 5 – is another Pete Wilson, representing the death-throes of anti-immigrant bias. Perhaps demographic replacement and intergroup contact will move the communities that shifted toward Trump, in Pennsylvania and elsewhere, toward greater acceptance and they too will become relative bastions of tolerance, as Los Angeles and other formerly anti-immigrant communities in California did.

We can see this arc, not only by comparing a state with itself across time, but also by moving across space within states. Arizona is, as I discussed in Chapter 5, in many ways the vanguard of demographic change because its demographics resemble what those of the United States as a whole are expected to be in coming decades. In my little experiment in Boston, we saw a change in attitudes over a short time after the initial meeting of two groups in an area. Anglo attitudes immediately became sharply anti-immigrant and then, over time, appear to have softened. My experiment, representing the very beginning of the arc of intergroup interactions, was trying to capture the dynamic of intergroup contact in Arizona. The early stages of these interactions manifest in the clashes over immigration politics and the nativist demagoguery used by some politicians in that state. But look within Arizona and nuance appears. In two different places within the same state – that is, holding political and many cultural aspects constant – we see two different points along the arc of intergroup interactions.

The first stages of the arc can be seen in Phoenix. In 1950, the population of the Phoenix metropolitan area was 374,961. (The city of Phoenix had only 106,818, while Philadelphia, today the largest city in the United States *after* Phoenix, then had over two million.) But since then, four million people have poured into the Valley of the Sun, most of them Anglos – from places like New York, Pennsylvania, and Ohio – with little previous contact with Latinos. To meet these Anglos came Latinos, migrating north from Mexico and elsewhere to work in the booming construction industry and other service jobs. Thus you have an explosive combination in Phoenix and other desert boom towns: a native population rushing to fill a place that is largely empty and meeting an immigrant population rushing to fill the jobs that this new native population creates.

It is as if an experimenter had thrown these groups together in the test tube of context to watch how they would react. When I was visiting Arizona, a man I had arranged to interview googled me before we met. Having read the media reports about my study in Boston, he mused about the situation in Phoenix:

It's interesting, about putting the Hispanics in the train stations and how that affects [attitudes]. Well, now [with] Hispanics coming through here, you're...setting up the same study [here in Arizona] that you did [in Boston].[4]

In the last 40 years, the Latino population of Phoenix has grown by over 700 percent. This is tremendous growth – a flood of immigrants, the grand culmination of the small process simulated by my little two-person experiment in Boston. I speculated that if we could see attitudes turn sharply negative after the size of the outgroup was raised by just two – a seemingly minute change in social geography – we would see them become much more negative with the addition of one million members of the outgroup, as was the case with Phoenix's Latino population between 1970 and 2010.

The predictable result of this meeting of Anglos and Latinos in the desert – in particular, Anglos with little previous contact with Latinos – is a backlash. In this case, the backlash took the form of anti-immigrant politics. Much of that was personified in figures like Joe Arpaio, the long-time sheriff of Maricopa County. More generally, immigration animates politics in Arizona. When I spoke with the long-time Maricopa County Supervisor, Mary Rose Wilcox, a Democrat, she said of the politics of the area, "We live, eat, and breathe [immigration]."[5] Immigration is *the* issue for political conservatives in Arizona: every single conservative politician I talked to when I visited Arizona named "securing the border" as the most important issue. And it is an issue that creates a milieu tinged with tension and conflict. A state representative from a Phoenix suburb told me that people see the issue of immigration as "us against them" and that she sees "Anglos defending their race...It's almost at a fever pitch."[6]

Over time, however, these attitudes will soften. This is the other end of the arc of intergroup interactions. Start at the border in Nogales and move north and the first sizable city you will reach is Tucson, a city that is considerably further along on the arc of intergroup interactions than Phoenix. Contact between Anglos and Latinos in Tucson has been taking place for over a century.

Talk to residents of Arizona and they will often refer to the boundary of the Gila River. This river is approximately the boundary followed by the Gadsden Purchase of 1854 that brought the area south of the river into the United States (see Figure 9.2). South of the river, where Tucson is located, is an area originally settled under the Spanish and Mexican governments, while north of the river, including Phoenix, is an area that, except for American Indians, was largely unsettled at the time it became part of the United States after the US-Mexico War. For Arizona residents, the Gila River is the mental dividing line between northern and southern Arizona. The demographics of these areas, at least in terms of percent Latino, are largely similar, but the interactions between groups across space and time are very different.

Comparing the parts of Arizona north and south of the Gila River is informative because they are in a single state and therefore the culture and politics are largely held constant; only the variables on the plane of context

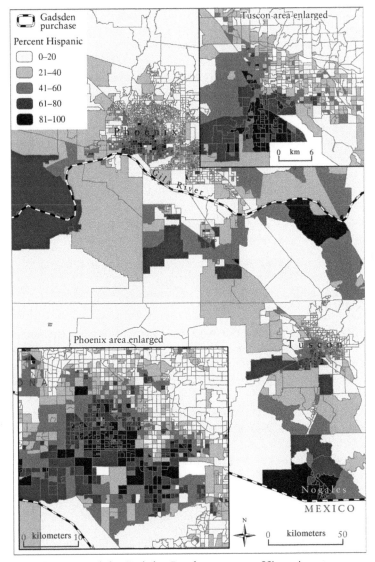

FIGURE 9.2. Arizona and the Gadsden Purchase, percent Hispanic, 2014.
Units depicted are Census Block Groups.

differ. North of the Gila, where two groups met and continue to meet in an area sparsely settled only 50 years ago, the experience with contact is very low. South of the river, intergroup contact has a much different history. In 1854, when Mexico sold the narrow strip of land on its northern reaches to the United States, this brought Mexicans, including those of Anglo-Saxon,

Spanish, and Indian heritage, into the United States.[7] With this came an area in which generations under Mexican rule had created a circumstance of cultural mixing – one that still influences the region today.

Especially before strong border enforcement became the norm in the area – with the change in immigration laws, guest worker programs,[8] and the shifting of the geography of overland undocumented border crossings due to the enforcement of the border around San Diego, California – the populations of border communities in Arizona and Mexico, like those of other border communities, were fluid. The communities had been this way for generations, with families, occupations, and culture spread out across both sides of the border. Tucson and other cities close to the border reflect this.

In contrast with Phoenix, where the populations meet with little previous experience across groups, the culture of Tucson is shaped by a tradition of interpersonal contact and, in many cases, it is the type of deep interpersonal contact that Allport suggested was important. I was told:

[T]he border towns had this huge multicultural, intertwining camaraderie, intermarriage, interlocking of all the customs…They go back and forth to Mexico… Really, we have whites and Mexicans intermarrying, intercultural church groups, people that actually work together and live together.[9]

This difference in experience with contact manifests in the sociopolitical divide between these two regions. If you ask Arizonians about immigration politics, they will point to the north/south divide with little or no prompting. This divide, they will tell you, is characterized by different interactions – from the interpersonal to the political – between Latinos and Anglos. When I spoke with Jonathan Rothschild, the Democratic mayor of Tucson, the wall of his office was adorned with a map of Mexico, something hard to imagine in Phoenix. He summarized the difference across the regions simply: "It's just a different vibe…I don't understand north of the Gila. I don't understand it at all."[10] A high-ranking police officer in Tucson put it more bluntly:

If you go and look at the Gila River, it's the dividing line in clearly the politics and the views…We don't hate Mexicans in Southern Arizona. But they sure do in Northern Arizona.[11]

This divide is also sometimes discussed in the popular press,[12] but we don't have to rely entirely on anecdote or impression: to the extent that the difference in group-based bias between the north and south is reflected in voting and political ideology, the divide can be quantified. In this book – for example, with voters in Chicago – I presented evidence that group-based bias can manifest in politically conservative voting and ideology. Between Tucson and Phoenix, with different levels of contact resulting in different group-based bias, we see this play out again. Tucson and the border counties of Arizona, in contrast to other counties in Arizona and the American Southwest more generally, are shifted to the left in national voting, more often favoring Democrats than

Republicans.[13] We can see the sociopolitical divide in ideology, too. Scholars have devised methods to estimate average political ideology on a dimension of Left to Right (see Figure 3.4 on page 73) for the citizens of small geographic areas; say, the average ideology for a city or county. These numbers have no absolute meaning, but can inform us about the relative position of units such as individuals, cities, and states. With higher scores being more conservative, Tucson and Pima County come in at −0.22 and −0.07, while Phoenix and Maricopa County are 0.04 and 0.11. To put this in perspective, that means that Tucson is ideologically close to Rhode Island (−0.23) while Phoenix is close to Nevada (0.07).[14]

To be clear, I don't have a Pollyannaish view of intergroup relations in Tucson. Talk to people there, especially members of the immigrant community, and they will recount many examples of systematic group-based bias. Nevertheless, the contrast with Phoenix is also clear. Moving across the Gila River, from one culture of contact to another, creates differences in the space between groups.

Thus, even within a single state, we can see intergroup interactions changing as different communities have had different amounts of time to move along the arc: an instantiation of the common claim that when contact is allowed to take place, interactions will arc toward harmony. However, most of the United States has not had centuries of intercultural mixing between Latinos and non-Latinos. The period along the arc that precedes the position of Tucson – the early stages of contact between Latinos and non-Latinos – is where most of the United States is now and it is a period ripe for group-based bias. The question is, where will the arc of intergroup interactions go from here? As the generations go by, will Phoenix and other places become more like Tucson?

In answering this question, it is crucial to acknowledge that this arc from backlash to harmony has not materialized for all immigrant groups. The most obvious example in the United States is the fate of Black immigrants from the South. When groups meet in an urban space, there is bias between the newly proximate groups and then segregation quickly takes over – often within just a few years – which, as we have learned in this book, causes *even more* group-based bias. When the great social science of the mid-twentieth century was written by scholars like Allport, the North was in this initial portion of the arc of intergroup interactions. African Americans from the South had rushed north to take jobs during and after the wars of the first half of the century. In the mid-twentieth century, the great metropolises of the North saw wrenching tension and bias as whites and Blacks lived block to block in the same neighborhood, which was recorded in the social science surveys of the time, such as Kramer's work in Chicago's Greater Grand Crossing. Then there was a great reshuffling of space – the Schelling dynamic – leaving the tremendous segregation apparent in the first maps I showed in this book (Figure 1.1 on page 10). More group-based bias filled the new geographic space between the groups. Law and order candidates, such as Richard Nixon, effectively filled this space by exploiting white fears of Blacks.

We see the parallels with Latinos from Latin America rushing northward to take jobs, first to places like Phoenix and then elsewhere, further and further north and east into the United States. In places like Los Angeles, after an initial clash, the space between Anglos and Latinos seems to have considerably closed. But the closure of space between whites and Blacks has been much more modest. While aspects of life certainly improved for many Blacks once the dust had settled after the mid-century internal migration,[15] the post-1970s social, political, and psychological space between Blacks and other groups, especially whites, remains large. As the evidence in this book has shown, the social-geographic impact of Blacks still drives white group-based bias. Why is this? Perhaps because the geographic and social segregation of these groups has remained large. The cultural stigma against Blacks is so strong in white America that segregation remains shockingly high and interpersonal contact, through friendship and marriage, remains low. In the United States in 2010, the typical white child attended a school that was just over eight percent Black, a number that is similar to the percent Black in a typical white American's neighborhood.[16] Even in relatively diverse institutions, such as some schools, the actual daily experience of contact may be limited by clusters of racial homogeneity.[17]

We may say that this still-yawning gap between white and Black America is an exception in an otherwise inevitable arc of intergroup interactions – perhaps stalled by the unique combination of the legacy of slavery and the phenotypical differences between whites and Blacks that allow whites to more easily enforce social exclusion. But this would be misguided. There are certainly groups who, despite their phenotypical and cultural similarities to the majority group, have experienced centuries of group-based bias. Jews in Europe are, perhaps, the most poignant example. Arguably, the only thing that diminished this bias was the incredible destructive event of World War II and the Holocaust, which not only decimated the European Jewish population but also destructively reshaped the culture of Germany and other nations and greatly reduced the social-geographic impact of Jews. Roma in Europe have also remained a permanent, segregated underclass. One has to ignore much of history to consider integration and improvement in relations inevitable, even with the forces of contact working in their favor. Therefore, to understand the future of intergroup interactions in the United States, not only for Latino immigrants and Anglos but also for Blacks and other groups, we have to consider the particulars of each situation. Knowing what we do about social-geographic impact, contact, and changes to the urban environment in the United States, where will intergroup relations go from here?

IMMIGRATION AND THE FUTURE OF SOCIAL GEOGRAPHY

Any discussion about the future of intergroup relations in the United States should first recognize that the character of current immigration is arguably different than that of past immigration. Arguments about the changing nature of immigration, including arguments about assimilation, often enter into debates about the merits of immigration policy, especially for immigration from Latin America.[18] It is not my intention to contribute to such debates, but rather to point out that the nature of immigration to the United States, as it has many times in the past, is changing. With this change, based on what we know about the psychology of intergroup relations, the impact of immigration on the native population will likely also change.

First, in 2017, immigrants as a share of the population are near an all-time high. That in itself is meaningful, but the impact of the immigrant population may also be changing because the size of the Latin American immigrant population, over half of whom are Mexican, means that immigration to the US has never been so homogeneous. Group Latin Americans together – as indeed many non-Latinos do, seeing the various subgroups as phenotypically and linguistically indistinguishable – immigrants from this region make up the largest single group ever to come to the United States. No other international immigrant group – not the Irish, not the Italians – was so monolithic.[19]

From the perspective of Anglos and other native populations, the monolithic nature of the immigrant population likely changes its salience, leading to the bias I've explored in this book. Because of its size, the accessibility of the group is greater and its comparative fit increases with its increased cohesion. The term "immigrant" thus becomes synonymous with Latino or Mexican. When an immigrant group is homogeneous, it more easily becomes "us" versus "them."

Furthermore, the continued salience of the outgroup of Mexican immigrants is aided by Mexico's proximity to the United States. Immigration from Mexico is, all else equal, much easier than from other countries and it will likely continue, barring dramatic changes in laws or, perhaps even more important, a change in the economic disparity between Mexico and the United States. Mexico's nearness also means that, even if the children of immigrants assimilate into Anglo culture, the immigrant population will be refreshed, maintaining what for Anglos is a culturally and linguistically distinct outgroup. Arguably, assimilation of immigrants may also be slower because immigrant enclaves can be refreshed constantly with newly arrived immigrants, thus providing other immigrants a connection to their home country.[20] This lack of assimilation for the population as a whole – even if successive generations do assimilate – may mean that Mexican immigrants will remain a differentiated outgroup, more analogous to Blacks as a permanent underclass than to other immigrant groups that successfully assimilated and shed their underclass status.

Increased immigration, of course, can also change the cohesion of ingroup identities – for some natives increasing the association between American and

Anglo or white. For example, studies have found that increasing the proximity of groups in a laboratory will increase the influence of ingroup identities on social attitudes. And recently, Anglo identity has been shown to be increasing in strength in the United States, perhaps in response to Latinos becoming more numerous and proximate.[21] The recent rise of right-wing nativist parties in Europe and the embrace of anti-immigrant rhetoric and policy by many Republicans in the United States may be evidence for this and, of course, the political rhetoric of these parties can itself contribute to group-based bias.

A shared international border – a factor that didn't exist for groups coming from overseas or for African Americans migrating from the South – may also change native reactions to immigration. Drawing on the evidence I have presented, we might believe that, for natives, this border changes the psychological impact of the immigrant group.   An enforced international border makes groups supremely segregated. Often, as is the case with Mexico from the perspective of Anglo Americans, the outgroup on the other side of the border is also quite large. For many Americans, such as those in Arizona, this outgroup is also proximate. Large, proximate, and segregated – we know by now what those ingredients add up to.

A border is not only a physical barrier but also a process by which the state puts its authority behind the convergence of identities.[22] The border itself creates a perception of difference. In fact, countries that are more homogeneous tend to have stronger and better-defended borders.[23] This correlation between homogeneity and border strength is what we would expect if a border serves to create psychological space between groups and the native population then demands that this border be defended. Think back to the experiment I discussed in Chapter 4, in which I showed people racially ambiguous faces and measured the point at which subjects drew a line between Black and white (the point of subject equality). When white people live in a segregated place, the line they draw between white and Black becomes sharper – they keep more people *out* of their ingroup. In a homogeneous country, a defended border might be thought of as a policy manifestation of this psychological phenomenon.

The irony, however, of the prominence of the Mexican border in US politics is that the border many people imagine – the sharp barrier between Mexico and the United States along which some people say we should build a wall – doesn't really exist. You can see this, of course, in the blending of Latino and Anglo culture in the Southwest. The further south you travel in the United States, the more these cultures blend and the more the border dissolves. Go to the border itself, in Nogales or elsewhere, and you see the constant flow of people across it.

Yet despite this flow and the fact that there is little psychological or social space between residents in communities that straddle the border, the idea of a border – a sharp division between the countries – is paramount in American politics. Much of the United States sees two groups, sharply defined by a border that is a convergence of cultural, ethnic, national, and geographic boundaries, when in fact, it is only the convergence of national and geographic boundaries. Part of the reason for the border's prominence as a political issue is probably that, while the fluidity of culture and identity is plain to see when you're near the border, it is less and less recognized the more distant one is from the border. For Anglo Americans away from the border, say in Ohio, the line between the United States and Mexico – Anglo and Latino, "us" and "them" – is clearly demarcated. (This is the process of construal abstraction that I discussed in Chapter 4.) The fuzziness of the actual border, which allows Latinos into the United States, in contrast to the symbolic clarity of the barrier that so many Anglos imagine the border to be, is a source of group-based bias.

Over time, the fuzziness of the US-Mexico border – the continuity of culture and people – has extended further and further north. Immigrants keep coming across this border, joining the fluid communities in places further and further from it. This increases the local social-geographic impact and inspires backlash in the towns of the South and Midwest. Part of this backlash manifested in the election of Trump. This diffusion of the immigrant population is, of course, largely similar to America's previous experiences with immigration, but in this case, the border itself may amplify the social-geographic impact because the local outgroup of Latino immigrants in many communities is combined, in the minds of Anglos, with a large, segregated, and proximate population of Latinos in a neighboring country.

The Valley of the Sun: Intergroup Interactions in the Future of Urban Space

When Claude Brown drew on his own experience to write about Harlem of the 1940s, after the waves of Black migration from the South, he described it as "too many people...crowded into a dirty, stinky, uncared-for closet-size section of a great city."[24] Such descriptions of overcrowding, filled with Blacks or Italians or Irish, in the harsh cities of the Northeast remain the indelible image of immigration in the United States. When many of us think of immigrants, we see images of Ellis Island and inner-city tenements. But such conditions are no longer typical of the immigrant experience or the future of the urban environment in the United States. It is the sprawling cities of the Southwest – places like Houston, Dallas, San Antonio, and Phoenix, which have among the largest Latino populations in the United States – that are the demographic and urban future.

The immigrant city of the future is exemplified by Phoenix, which spreads in a clumpy mass through seemingly endless space. Cities like Scottsdale, Tempe, and Glendale contribute to the urban area in the Valley of the Sun, as do lesser-known places like Buckeye and Surprise. Maricopa County is the fourth-most populous county in the United States and a place of constant growth, absorbing most of the over 1.1 million people who have moved to Arizona from other states since 2010 – a tremendous number in a state of 6.5

million. This contributes to Phoenix's haphazard growth; even within its city limits, there are still farms in the places not covered by sprawl or desert.

Phoenix is defined by growth. It is the type of growth that other urban areas saw in the early and mid-twentieth century, with the constant shifting of population and development of new housing. However, the growth of the boom cities of the twentieth century was often constrained by natural geography, in the form of oceans, or by transportation and communication technology, so that new housing was packed into, next to, and on top of other housing. Phoenix, on the other hand, seems to be virtually unbounded. There is no ocean to stop development and the mountains are only to the north and not yet a problem; only the presence of Indian reservations slows development. As long as it remains possible to provide cheap energy and water (there are, of course, reasons to believe this might not always be possible), housing can continue to spring up amongst the pastures.

Take a freeway and travel through this sprawl in almost any direction from downtown and you will arrive at cul-de-sac developments, with houses baking in the desert sun with extensive yards, multi-car garages, and often pools. One of the few exceptions would be if you traveled south to where the old homes of crumbling wood or adobe are interlaced with empty lots. These neighborhoods have an aura of neglect. The residents are almost entirely Latino or Black – populations that are either new or lack the means for exit. Exit for many Anglos is such an easy option in the Phoenix area that even though the median home in Maricopa Country was built in 1987, some neighborhoods have already been abandoned by those with means. This creates segregation: in 2010, the level of Anglo/Latino dissimilarity was 0.49, higher than the national metropolitan area median of 0.36 and comparable to the levels of Black/Latino segregation in Los Angeles and Black/white segregation in Camden, New Jersey. Residents of Phoenix will tell you of the "maps in their heads," saying there is a "clear...dividing line," on one side of which the immigrants will settle.[25]

With respect to segregation then, cities like Phoenix are recreating the social geography of the gateways of immigrants of old, when natives took the option of exit to escape from the newcomers and patterns of segregation quickly formed, which affect our attitudes and behaviors to this day. But the urban landscape of these growing Sunbelt cities means that, while the social geography that creates segregation is present, the primary antidote to segregation – interpersonal contact – generally is not.

Political scientist J. Eric Oliver described in 2001 how the suburbanization of American life was undermining civic participation.[26] Part of the reason, he speculated, was the simple lack of contact between citizens. The residential architecture of single-family homes with large backyards, for example, means that social contact is less likely. Cities like Phoenix are suburbanization on a mass scale. This means not only that people within the same social group are not meeting on their front porches, but also that contact across social groups is diminished even as these cities are experiencing rapid diversification. We have here an unfortunate combination: high social-geographic impact and low interpersonal contact. This is exactly the spot on the plane of context where we don't want to be if we are looking for intergroup harmony.

The famous journalist of cities, Jane Jacobs writing about the consequences of the low-density suburban sprawl of Los Angeles in 1961 said:

Los Angeles is an extreme example of a metropolis with little public life, depending mainly instead on contacts of a more private social nature.

On one plane, for instance, an acquaintance there comments that although she has lived in the city for ten years and knows it contains Mexicans, she has never laid eyes on a Mexican or an item of Mexican culture, much less ever exchanged any words with a Mexican.[27]

In 2017, four of the five fastest-growing cities in the United States have population densities less than half that of Los Angeles. This has consequences for how people come together. The dynamic of sprawl and car-based transportation reduces the probability of interpersonal contact. In many cities, the central business district – where people come to work, shop, and visit cultural institutions – is the mixing bowl of groups, allowing for some face-to-face contact, even if the groups ultimately occupy largely separate worlds. Phoenix and similar cities, however, are what urban planners call *polycentric* cities,[28] with many centers of business rather than one. In Los Angeles, if you visit the Griffith Observatory, the famous location in the Hollywood Hills with sweeping views of the Los Angeles Basin, you can see the fruits of decisions made in the mid-twentieth century by city planners to purposefully decentralize the city, believing it would improve efficiency by relieving congestion. Look to the left and you will see downtown Los Angeles, with its skyscrapers rising out of the hills. Turn to the right and you will see Century City, a business district some 10 miles west of downtown with its own cluster of tall buildings. And if you could look behind you, over the hills into the San Fernando Valley, you would see yet more clusters of tall buildings.

Phoenix, when it comes to polycentrism, is Los Angeles on steroids. Of the 52 metropolitan areas in the United States with over one million residents, Phoenix is 51st in the percentage of employment concentrated in the center of the city; only Riverside, California, another fast-growing, desert metro area, is lower.[29] In Phoenix and similar cities, going "downtown" to work, rather than being the norm, is the rare exception.

But this number doesn't really capture the dynamic of dispersion in these cities – how much this dispersion changes the vibe of interpersonal contact. Go to a sprawling city and you can feel the lack of contact between people. Walk on a Phoenix street at rush hour and there will be no crush of people on the sidewalk or trying to board the bus. In many cities, people come together, if not for recreation or commerce, at least while getting from one place to another. But contact in transit is also limited in Phoenix. Residents seldom use public transportation and many seldom walk, either. In a sense, the experiment I conducted in Boston would be useless in Phoenix or, at least, would lack ecological validity, because so few people take public transportation.[30] Instead, a person can get in her car (in her garage, not in a driveway where she might happen to encounter a neighbor), quickly get onto a freeway, and drive to a parking garage that is immediately connected to her workplace. In such cities, a substantial part of the workforce also works from home,[31] making intergroup contact even less likely. Now take a different city – Washington, DC is a good example. It's not even the densest American city, but when you're in the city center or riding the public transportation, it certainly feels more active than Phoenix does. (Washington has the third-highest percent of employment in the center of the city, behind only New York and San Francisco.) This tends to give one the impression that Washington is more diverse than Phoenix because, in Phoenix, you are not exposed to outgroups in public places – such as sidewalks, train stations, and parks – the way you are in Washington. But this is just an illusion, a perception that reinforces the space between groups. Actually, these two cities are quite similar in terms of diversity (the Herfindahl Index was 0.37 for Washington and 0.38 for Phoenix in 2013).[32]

The urban environment of unbounded growth is also reflected in institutions. As Phoenix-like cities unfold into the plentifully available space, relatively cheap housing makes the construction of enclaves possible and segregation takes on a new form: groups not only segregate within the city, but often exit the city and form separate municipalities. This not only further prevents intergroup contact, but likely accentuates the impact of segregation, both psychologically and politically, as groups don't even share a common political arena in which their tax dollars are allocated.

We have seen how the space between groups make it difficult to share resources across social identity groups (see Chapter 7). When groups share a common political entity, such as a large-city government, or are anchored by a common resource, such as a regional transportation system, there is at least an impetus to share resources, even if the allocation turns out to be socially inefficient. But if groups are balkanized across political entities – for example, small but politically independent municipalities – there is no impetus to share resources. If one group never uses the same roads or parks or police as the other, why would they help pay for them?

If all municipalities could equally support themselves, this might be less of a problem. But, of course, this is not the case. In the Phoenix area, for example, median incomes diverge by more than \$100,000 between poor cities like Avondale in the west and the more affluent Paradise Valley to the northeast. Predictably, the Latino proportion is much higher in Avondale (over 50 percent in 2010) than in Paradise Valley (less than 3 percent in 2010).[33]

This division by municipal boundaries not only divides the tax base, making it more difficult to share resources, but also reinforces the psychological space between groups because municipalities can segregate not only on income, but also on race. Zoning ordinances are often designed to make housing unaffordable to low-status groups, thus homogenizing cities.[34] And moving between municipalities in a metropolitan area is relatively easy compared to, say, moving between states, so residents can "sort" into cities with tax rates and services they can afford,[35] further separating groups with different incomes. With such boundaries, not only are material incentives for sharing resources between communities reduced, but our psychology may also work against sharing. An entire city can become a "Black city" (such as Gary, Indiana, 82 percent Black) or a "Latino city" (Bell Gardens, California, 95 percent Latino) – a place that is psychologically distant for the non-Black or non-Latino people living in a different city which may actually be nearby. This is the convergence of boundaries – in this case, racial, economic, geographic, and political – and, as we have seen, the convergence of such boundaries greatly increases group-based bias (see Chapter 3).

On top of a balkanization of groups into municipalities which may lead to the convergence of boundaries and greater psychological space between groups, other barriers to interpersonal contact can be found in the lack of those institutions that encourage contact by bringing people from the balkanized suburbs into the central cities. In many Phoenix-like polycentric cities, not only is there no central business cluster to bring people together, but there are few cultural institutions that do so. There is no Central Park or Venice Beach in these cities to bring people together across groups. Moreover, there is no Yankee or Dodger Stadium; even if many racial minorities are probably priced out of actually attending games at these stadiums, their locations in New York's South Bronx and Los Angeles's Echo Park at least forces Anglos to pass through these Hispanic neighborhoods and have some awareness of the situation and maybe even an impetus to maintain services there, such as police. The same could be said for the anchoring of other cultural institutions, such as museums and theaters, in central cities even after the white flight of the 1970s.

This anchoring also means, of course, that social groups are forced to come together to share resources if these institutions – and the cities in which they are located – are to be supported. Even as white flight depopulated cities like Boston in the mid-twentieth century, those cities provided economic, social, and psychological anchors because of the institutions they still supported. Residents of Massachusetts still went to Red Sox games and benefited from the economic and cultural output of the universities in Cambridge, adjacent to Boston. This meant that there was a de-facto commitment on the part of state residents to support cities like Boston and Cambridge, contributing resources to maintain their roads, schools, and public safety.

Moreover, the fact that many people feel a psychological identification with the largest cities in their states probably also strengthens their commitment as taxpayers. For example, the shrinking of Detroit's population may be inevitable, even without white flight, because of changes in economic structure. Nevertheless, the state of Michigan has devoted resources to Detroit's infrastructure, financing projects such as the People Mover, the much-maligned and underused 2.94-mile downtown light rail, and thus subsidizing the city's largely Black population. Why does the state invest in such projects? I have a guess that Michigan supports Detroit not only because the "sunk costs" in theaters, museums, and stadiums that were built when the city was thriving create a "path dependence" of support,[36] but also simply because many – though certainly not all – Michiganders have a psychological connection to the city. They would find it hard to imagine Michigan without Detroit, just as many people would find it hard to imagine Massachusetts without Boston or Missouri without St. Louis. This psychological identification may motivate a state's citizens and lawmakers to spend money to try to preserve important cities.

This economic, cultural, and psychological anchoring of Anglo whites to central cities is less prominent in places like Phoenix where, despite its large population, such anchoring institutions either lack prominence or are located in suburbs. (Two of Phoenix's four major professional sports franchises play in Glendale, rather than Phoenix.) I also suspect, although I can't be sure, that because Phoenix does not have the same depth of history as a city like Boston and because many of its citizens are not native to the area, Phoenix does not seem as irreplaceable to Arizona as, say, Boston does to Massachusetts. I suspect, too, that many Texans can easily imagine Texas without Houston and that many Californians have little psychological connection to the similarly fast-growing, polycentric, and Latino plurality city of Fresno. Ask the white majority elsewhere in the state to contribute to support these poor minority communities and many will likely find little reason to do so.

In Chapter 2, I discussed the idea that we had experienced the death of both distance and community. Phoenix, in a certain respect, is the ultimate *post-distance* urban space. Residents have chosen to eschew the convenience of proximity in favor of other amenities. But, paradoxically, because it is post-distance in form, Phoenix shows us the supreme importance of distance. By living in a city with this sort of built environment, the residents of Phoenix have eschewed interpersonal contact across groups. Thus, we see – as we did in Chicago, where populations inside and outside the housing projects had no interpersonal contact – a situation in which social geography operates without any countervailing influence of contact. In these situations, we see the power of space to directly shape our behavior. It is in these places, where social geography has so much sway, that we will see the future incorporation – or not – of immigrants into the United States.

CONCLUSION: THE POWER AND PERMANENCE OF SPACE

I began this book by writing about our inability – as human beings – to cross the physical and psychological boundaries that separate groups, while machines – trains, for example – can "cross boundaries that people typically will not." A way to summarize the question lingering as I finish this book is: how can people become more like trains? How can we cross – by habit, incentive, or rule – the space between ourselves and other groups? Put another way, do we have to become less human to become more humane?

In unpacking the psychology of intergroup relations and space, I have recounted many biases and it became clear why we have trouble crossing boundaries and why our inclination toward these biases is not something we can easily escape. Our tendency toward group-based bias and the role that space plays in shaping it were formed during the long period of human evolution in a "state of nature." Modern society by no means created these psychological traits, but it gave them a new shape: making these traits all the more relevant because our booming and mobile population crowds heterogeneous people into the same places and our democratic institutions demand that we come together in political space to share resources and make decisions – the liberal dilemma. It is perhaps in this world of crowded democracies that geographic space has the most power to shape our behavior. We have seen how our tendencies to stereotype and use heuristics may have been individually efficient and rational in the past, but can have grave implications when acted on by millions in a mass society.

But even though the demons of our evolutionary past might be most powerful in the modern, crowded, and diverse world, modern society has also given us the tools to overcome those demons, because science has allowed us to recognize and understand them and because we have the ability to constrain them by means of laws, representative bodies, education, and other institutions.

Throughout this book, I have dealt with interventions that take place over a short period: a neighborhood changing over a few years, an experiment that lasts just a few days or even a few minutes. But, as the public housing in Chicago and the clash of Anglos and Latinos in the Valley of the Sun remind us, what I was trying to capture in those experiments were real-world trends that go on for much longer. A particular social-geographic context can shape generations of people.

This can seem pretty discouraging, given what we've seen in this book about how social geography encourages group-based bias. Of course, as we saw in this chapter, intergroup interactions can improve over time and seem to do so regularly. But it is not constructive to simply say that if we wait a few generations, contact and cultural mixing, of the type we saw in Tucson, will lead to the acceptance of immigrants and other outgroups. There are, unfortunately, reasons to believe that past immigration is not informative in thinking about the impact of current immigration. Perhaps more importantly, just waiting for things to improve with the passage of time is dissatisfying from the perspectives of both scholarship and policy. Of course, there is no easy policy solution for how to maintain harmony when groups occupy the same place, but given the evidence in this book, we can better understand what should be considered when shaping policy.

In discussing Phoenix, it is important to be clear that judging the relative worthiness of urban designs is not my intention. I recognize that people have very good reasons for wanting to live in communities that are spacious and convenient, like those of the Southwest. Many people choose to live in places with abundant land and more affordable housing out of economic necessity. I also believe that we should also be cautious in declaring that our current preferences are the best way to organize urban spaces. In the 1970s, in many large American cities, few people outside of certain intellectual circles were speaking of the virtues of dense urban living.

Speaking more constructively, the genie of urban sprawl is out of the bottle and the trend will not be reversed any time soon. But if we are convinced that such sprawl might be having a negative effect on intergroup relations, how can we manage that sprawl better? Rather than waiting for contact to happen with time, we can, of course, look for policies that promote it. As I have emphasized throughout this book, contact matters. I have tried to add a balance to scholars' almost exclusive focus on contact as the mechanism for determining what happens when groups occupy the same place, but none of this should be construed as an argument that contact does not matter. On the contrary, given that current trends in urban living may make residential contact even more difficult, promoting it through other means – schools, workplaces, and private organizations – becomes even more important than it already was.

But we must also understand that policy-induced contact can only do so much to solve our problems with group-based bias. A public policy, such as that in the United States that focuses on integrating public institutions, such as public schools, but otherwise largely leaves integration to private-sector institutions, such as businesses and private universities, only weakly addresses the forces that shape the elephant in the room: residential segregation.[37] Citizens are asked to interact across racial and ethnic groups for a few hours every weekday in the classroom or the workplace and then go home to their homogeneous households and neighborhoods. Such policies have limited effects on larger patterns of segregation.

It is understandable, then, that due to this lack of meaningful contact across groups and perhaps also due to the influence of Contact Theory, much of social science has focused on improving intergroup relations by changing the depth of contact but not its frequency. For example, non-governmental organizations, aided by social scientists, have tried interethnic contact experiments with relationships ranging from interethnic soccer teams to interethnic ballroom dancing. Few, if any, interventions have tried to change social geography. Other scholars have studied long-term – but very atypical – experiences such as having a college roommate of a different race.[38] Such studies, while valuable in their own right, don't teach us much about the effects of diversity in the larger world, where social geography is the dominant force shaping attitudes. Perhaps this focus has been due to the scientific intractability of studying geographic context rather than interpersonal relationships – a problem I have tried to overcome in this book. From a policy standpoint, too, there is something more tractable – more actionable – about interventions that build relationships, rather than interventions that change context. We can imagine policies encouraging deep interpersonal contact, such as shared sports teams or dance competitions, but a policy reshaping a city to encourage casual contact or a policy eliminating segregation is rather more complicated.

But the ease with which we can picture policies that encourage deep personal contact gives a misleading sense of their efficacy. Such relationship-based policy interventions are valuable, to be sure, and their contribution to intergroup harmony should not be overlooked. But their systematic value may be limited: it is hard to imagine ending systematic conflict through dance programs or sports teams.

The influence of space on our perception of groups suggests that, as long as we remain residentially segregated, our current policies for encouraging contact may not be enough, even for those people the policies actually reach. As long as people are segregated at home – a preeminent concern because, as Nancy Rosenblum puts it, it is a place from which "we have no exit"[39] – then it is hard to see how the power of spatial arrangements to shape our thinking can be overcome by policies that temporarily integrate us in other settings. This is not a mere academic argument about the particulars of statistical models. This has deep implications for public policy aimed at increasing intergroup harmony. If segregation affects our behavior, even in the presence of interpersonal contact, then segregation itself must be addressed.

If we believe my findings that social geography affects our interactions – that it shapes the space between us – then perhaps social geography is where we should be focusing our scientific, political, and policy energies. The policy prescriptions behind changing social geography are costly and complex, but they can have lasting effects and, in some cases, such as Chicago, can quickly change behavior. The evidence in this book shows us plainly that the built environment – the space on the Earth's surface – often guided by the hand of government, shapes the space between us in society and politics. In building a harmonious society, a central focus of policy should therefore be how to construct this space.

Notes

PREFACE

1. Jacobs (1961, front material).

ACKNOWLEDGMENTS

1. Enos (2010).

CHAPTER 1

1. Wirth (1938, p. 15).
2. The journalist Natalie Moore also talks about the "L" train as "an easy visual clue to Chicago's segregation" (Moore, 2016, p. 17).
3. Legewie and Schaeffer (2016).
4. See Chapter 5 for more about this.
5. Balcells et al. (2015).
6. Enos and Gidron (2016a).
7. Enos (2011).
8. See, for example, Alesina and Zhuravskaya (2008).
9. Godley (1969, p. 3).
10. Allport (1954).
11. Putnam (2007, p. 137).
12. This distortion of differences is important because it means that the effects of social geography are more than just a process of Bayesian updating, by which a person takes information from geography to update her prior beliefs about differences across groups. Rather, geography distorts these beliefs. I address this further in Chapter 3.
13. This was done by simply taking a spreadsheet of Block Groups and randomizing the ordering of the percent Black column.
14. Chicago does have some examples of racially integrated public housing, such as the Lanthrop homes, built on the near North Side by the Works Projects Administration in 1938 and still standing today.

15. This is, by no means, a unique insight. Geographers often treat geographic space – space on the Earth's surface – as but one manifestation of the general concept of space, which can be used to measure closeness across any physical or social dimension (see, for example, Gatrell (1983)). Measuring degrees of separation in social networks has a long history, going back at least to Milgram's famous experiment (Travers and Milgram, 1969). Scaling members of Congress and other legislators were first formalized by Poole and Rosenthal (1985). Downs (1957) famously introduced scaling voters and parties on a single dimension of space.

16. Jacobs (1961, p. 51).

17. Huckfeldt and Sprague (1987) make a similar distinction between "geographic" and "social context." Those terms, when used in a discussion of my terminology, can be confusing, given my use of the term "social geography," but their "geographic context" is my "social geography" and their "social context" is my "interpersonal contact." The two together are what I simply call "context."

18. This book is also not about what is often called "threat" – the idea that the presence of an outgroup is instrumentally costly and thereby changes behavior; for example, the idea that the propensity for white people to vote increases with the nearby presence of Blacks because white people feel that Blacks are a threat to their political power.

19. Despite much excellent research, the causes of segregation are still poorly understood. It certainly is driven in part by individual-level behavior; even behavior that is not in itself discriminatory may cause sorting by groups, as the economist Thomas Schelling powerfully demonstrated (Schelling, 1971, 2006). It also clearly results from intentional and unintentional actions by governments and business interests (Massey and Denton, 1993). I also do not address the philosophical debate around moral agency and segregation, such as that addressed by Shelby (2016).

20. Scacco and Warren (2016).

21. The Herfindahl Index, which measures the diversity of a market – in this case a city – in 2010 was 0.41 in Merced's CBSA, making it a little higher (less diverse) than Washington, DC's. Merced's Herfindahl has actually increased recently due to the rising share of the population that is Hispanic.
The Herfindahl index is:

$$H = \sum_{i=1}^{N} s_i,$$

where s is the proportion of the population represented by group i. This index ranges from 1, which is complete homogeneity, to $1/N$, where N is the number of groups. In this case, there are five racial/ethnic groups, so the minimum is 0.2.

CBSAs are Core Based Metropolitan Statistical Areas and include both Micropolitan Statistical Areas and Metropolitan Statistical Areas. CBSAs will appear frequently in this book. The Census Bureau defines a CBSA as:

A metro area contains a core urban area of 50,000 or more population, and a micro area contains an urban core of at least 10,000 (but less than 50,000) population. Each metro or micro area consists of one or more counties and includes the counties containing the core urban area, as well as any adjacent counties that have a high degree of social and economic integration (as measured by commuting to work) with the urban core.

22. See Wong et al. (2012) for an empirical example of this. Wong et al. (2012) also have an excellent discussion of the general problem of defining environments. My

definition parallels theirs. They define a person's context as the "situation of action," quoting from Parsons et al. (1951) to define it as:

> That part of the external world which means something to the actor whose behavior is being analyzed. It is only part of the whole realm of objects that might be seen. Specifically, it is that part to which the actor is oriented and in which the actor acts.

The local environment could also be called a "situation of action."

Wong (2010), drawing in her book on the work of Anderson (1983), demonstrates that the definition of a community varies across individuals.

23. It might also be useful to think of this as the unit that *minimizes error*. Naturally, measuring the latent concept without bias is important, too.
24. Reardon and O'Sullivan (2004, p. 122).
25. Reardon and O'Sullivan (2004) point to two primary dimensions of segregation: clustering and isolation or exposure (see Figure N1.1). Both may reflect segregation

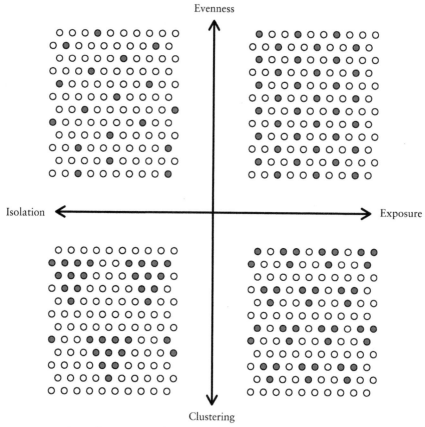

FIGURE N1.1. Two dimensions of segregation: clustering and isolation.
Adapted from Reardon and O'Sullivan (2004).

as it relates to the cohesiveness of groups, but isolation is a dimension of how often individuals are exposed to interactions across groups and, therefore does more to capture the experiential, rather than the perceptual, processes related to context.

26. The Dissimilarity Index can be interpreted as the percentage of one of the two groups (usually the minority) that would have to move to different geographic areas in order to produce a distribution in each smaller area that matches that of the larger area. Using Census Tracts as the smaller area and CBSA as the larger area, it is measured by:

$$\frac{1}{2} \sum_{i=1}^{N} \left| \frac{b_i}{B} - \frac{w_i}{W} \right|,$$

where b_i = the population of the minority group in a Census Tract.
B = the total minority population in the CBSA.
w_i = the population of the majority group in a Census Tract.
W = the total majority population in the CBSA. See Massey and Denton (1988).

Unless otherwise noted, segregation in this book is measured using Census Tracts and CBSAs. There are other ways to measure segregation, some of which also approximate the psychologically relevant clustering of groups in a local environment, and the results I present in this book are generally insensitive to which measure I use.

27. The general idea of people using benchmarks to understand size comes from the seminal work of Kahneman and Tversky (Kahneman and Frederick, 2002; Kahneman, 2003).

28. It is important to note that, for my purposes, group size does not mean the proportion of the entire population and it does not mean ethnic fragmentation; rather, I am concerned with size as it relates to pairs of groups. However, most of the original empirical results in this book are unchanged using these or other measures of group size.

29. Bertrand and Mullainathan (2004).

30. Tilcsik (2011).

31. Ahmed and Hammarstedt (2008).

32. Grossman et al. (2015).

33. White et al. (2015).

34. At least that is the common interpretation of the results of the resumé experiments of Bertrand and Mullainathan (2004), in which both applicants are equally qualified based on their identical resumés. However, a plausible alternative explanation is that the discriminating employers are not acting out of ingroup bias, but because they are rationally assuming, even though the applicants are identical on paper, that the white one has hidden endowments that make her more qualified. Economists call this "statistical discrimination," in contrast to "taste-based discrimination." Researchers have tried to correct for statistical discrimination in order to isolate taste-based discrimination.

On the other hand, given that it is the job of the clerk to facilitate voting and that equal access to voting, regardless of race or ethnicity, is a deeply held democratic value in the United States, it is hard not to call the actions of the county election clerks documented in White et al. (2015) discriminatory.

35. Yanagizawa-Drott (2014).

36. For such an argument, see Posner (2004).

37. Key (1949).

38. Acharya et al. (2016).

39. Almond (2009).
40. Nirenberg (1996).
41. To the best of my knowledge, there is no available measure of interpersonal contact that would allow me to systematically place these cities on this dimension.
42. Figure 1.7 is also not intended to represent the complete scope of context. There are certainly places with higher levels of social-geographic impact than the cities displayed here; in fact, most places in the United States would be to the left of Boston, with lower social-geographic impact. Nevertheless, most large cities – that is, where most Americans live – are included in the range presented here.
43. For example, Oliver (2010).
44. For example, Welch et al. (2001).

CHAPTER 2

1. Allport (1954, p. 269).
2. These are aggregate returns, not individual votes. There are obvious ecological inference problems here, which I address later in the chapter. In this specific case, Floyd County is 98 percent white, so the ecological issue is minimal.
3. See Tesler and Sears (2010).
4. See Enos (2011). The relationship between segregation and vote is robust to multivariate regression and to using spatial econometric techniques to account for spatial correlations in the error structure. Notably, the multivariate regressions also control for the percent Black in the counties. Black voters voted for Obama at such high rates that once this variable is taken into account, we can be fairly certain that the remaining relationship between segregation and Obama voting is driven by non-Blacks.
5. This number is taken from the 2008 *New York Times* exit poll, which puts 56 percent of women and 49 percent of men voting for Obama.
6. Cairncross (2001).
7. Friedman (2005).
8. Putnam (2001).
9. That politics is increasingly nationalized is a line of argument in Hopkins (2013a,b).
10. This is from Stephens-Davidowitz (2014), from where I also get the data for this analysis. Stephens-Davidowitz attempts to remove searches performed by Blacks by removing instances of "nigga(s)," the Black colloquial spelling of the word. Due to the extreme number of searches that are conducted on Google, every single term will necessarily comprise a small portion of the searches. As a benchmark, Stephens-Davidowitz (2014) reports that leading up to the 2008 election, "nigger" appeared in sea searches around as often, but slightly less than "Lakers," "Daily Show," and "Sweater" and appeared considerably more often than "Economist," "Migraine," and "Republicans."
11. See Appendix.
12. Notably, the effect size from the preferred specification on segregation is equal to more than three standard deviations of the distribution of derogatory search.
13. There is a long literature on addressing this problem. For the method I will use when I discuss Presidential voting and segregation shortly, see King (1997).
14. These are the core measures in the "Ethnocentrism" scale used by Kinder and Kam (2009).
15. See Appendix.
16. In the sample I use for this analysis, the standard deviation of this survey question, when asked about whites, is 1.16. So, the difference between whites and Blacks is

more than .5 standard deviations of the baseline. A T-test of this difference yields $t = 50.52, df = 30,233, p < .001$.

17. The least segregated CBSA is different than the least segregated DMA, although the Milwaukee area is both the most segregated DMA and CBSA and Detroit and Milwaukee CBSA's are virtually indistinguishable on the Dissimilarity Index using 2010 data.
18. See Talaska et al. (2008).
19. Soltas and Stephens-Davidowitz (2015).
20. This is the Chicago-Aurora-Joliet Metropolitan Division. The Chicago CBSA includes 14 counties in Illinois, Indiana, and Wisconsin.
21. See Appendix.
22. See Appendix.
23. "Partisanship so powerfully determines for whom we vote," see Enos (2016a). That the results are limited to independents, also suggests that the aggregate results were driven by movement of non-partisans.
24. Key (1949).
25. See Ansolabehere and Hersh (2012).
26. See Appendix.
27. See, for example, Sampson (2008) for a statement of this.
28. See Angrist and Pischke (2009).
29. Ananat (2011).
30. Cutler and Glaeser (1997); Trounstine (2016).
31. Ananat's data is measured at the city level, so it is an imperfect measure for any of the tests I perform, which all use segregation at the DMA or CBSA level and it is only practical to use it as an instrument for my tests that use CBSA level segregation (Ananat (2011) uses this as an instrument for MSA level segregation). Ananat's data also only includes 117 cities, so it significantly limits the sample. Nevertheless, I can attempt to instrument for the effect of segregation on anti-Black stereotypes and Obama vote, both of which I measure at the CBSA level. With Obama vote measured at the precinct level, segregation remains statistically significant and becomes larger in the IV regression. With individual-level voting, the Wu-Hausman test indicates that the OLS and IV estimates are similar. With stereotypes as the dependent variable, segregation loses statistical significance in the IV regression. See Appendix.
32. See, for example, Gay (2006).
33. Moreover, the instruments used by scholars, such as Ananat (2011) and Trounstine (2016) are measured in individual cities or even particular areas of cities, while segregation is usually measured on the level of a municipal area, which includes clusters of cities. See Massey and Denton (1993). This creates a potential mismatch between the instrument and the variable for which it is instrumenting.
34. Like all academic literatures, there is controversy around this area of research because some scholars find no relationship between space and group bias and some scholars even find the opposite: that increasing the size and segregation of the outgroup improves intergroup relations. For a good review of the inconsistencies in studies of the United States, see Oliver (2010). My current purpose is not to resolve that controversy. Much of the inconsistency, I believe, comes from the problems I will discuss below about a lack of connection between data and theory; problems with causal identification, which means that some findings may be spurious; problems with choice of aggregate units; and confusion about mechanisms.
35. Fossett and Kiecolt (1989); Fitzpatrick and Hwang (1992); Sigelman and Welch (1993); Glaser (1994); Quillian (1995); Bobo and Hutchings (1996); Forbes (1997); Taylor (1998); Oliver and Mendelberg (2000); Welch et al. (2001); Oliver and Wong (2003); Alesina and Glaeser (2004); Gay (2006); Putnam (2007); Tam et al. (2009);

Hopkins (2010); Oliver (2010); Dinesen and Sønderskov (2015); Velez and Lavine (2016).

36. Key (1949); Wright (1977); Giles and Buckner (1993); Carsey (1995); Campbell (2006); Oliver (2010); Hersh and Nall (2015); Charnysh (2015).

37. Key (1949); Matthews and Prothro (1963); Hill and Leighley (1999); Leighley and Vedlitz (1999); Spence and McClerking (2010).

38. Horowitz (1985); Nirenberg (1996); Olzak et al. (1996); Green et al. (1998); Balcells et al. (2015).

39. Nirenberg (1996).

40. Legewie and Schaeffer (2016).

41. Tam et al. (2009).

42. Some of it uses aggregate data, but makes ecological claims about individual behavior changing.

43. Easterly and Levine (1997).

44. Collier (2000).

45. Alesina et al. (1999); Miguel and Gugerty (2005); Habyarimana et al. (2007, 2009); Rugh and Trounstine (2011); Lieberman and McClendon (2013); Trounstine (2016).

46. Couzin et al. (2011).

47. Vanhanen (1999); Lim et al. (2007); Esteban and Ray (2008); Montalvo and Reynal-Querol (2010).

48. Enos and Gidron (2016a).

49. All four of these countries are listed as "Full" or "Flawed" democracies in *Economists* 2015 Democracy Index.

50. To borrow a phrase from Putnam et al. (1993).

51. See, for example, Page (2008).

52. Allport (1954); Baybeck (2006); Alesina and Zhuravskaya (2008); Oliver (2010); Rothwell (2012); Uslaner (2012); Zingher and Steen Thomas (2014); Dill and Jirjahn (2014).

53. Ananat and Washington (2009); Kasara (2013).

54. Massey and Denton (1993); Alesina et al. (1999); Gerometta et al. (2005); Alesina and Zhuravskaya (2008); De Kadt and Sands (2014); Quillian (2014).

55. Li et al. (2013).

56. Corvalan and Vargas (2015).

57. Also, segregation and the proportion of an outgroup are often positively correlated (see, for example, Massey and Denton (1993) for an argument that outgroup proportion causes segregation). As such, it may be that scholars were often making a mistake by attributing the effects of segregation to outgroup proportion because findings that outgroup proportion are related to group bias could suffer from omitted variable bias when segregation is not included.

58. Allport (1954, p. 263).

59. Ibid., p. 227.

60. Ibid., p. 227.

61. Ibid., p. 226.

62. Putnam (2007, p. 141).

63. This is represented by the significant quadratic term in most, but not all, of the regressions.

64. See Blalock (1967); Taylor (1998); Huffman and Cohen (2004); Stephens-Davidowitz (2014); Enos and Gidron (2016a).

65. This may also be one reason why in diverse societies (and in the analysis in this chapter), it is easier to find group-based bias from a majority group toward a minority group than a minority toward the majority group (see Sidanius and Pratto

(2001)). In the absence of complete segregation, minority group members will, all else equal, have more contact more with majority group members than majority group members with minority group members. This can be seen in survey data I explore in Chapter 7.

CHAPTER 3

1. Fiske (2000, p. 303).
2. I obviously don't know anything about this woman: she could have been Muslim or any other religion with or without the headscarf. I also don't know if she was accompanied by her husband, that was simply my impression. Here I am simply making an illustrative point. I use the word "American" in quotation marks to represent its common, but exclusionary, usage to refer to an American of European descent.
3. Blanz (1999).
4. Psychologists may say that these stereotypes are represented in the mind as "schema" or "prototypes" or "exemplars," but the distinctions are unimportant for our purposes (Stangor and Schaller, 2000).
5. For example, Henry and Sears (2002).
6. Zaller (1992); Gilens (1999).
7. Hardin (1968).
8. These images were created by taking photos of self-identified white and Black Americans and morphing them together to create a racially ambiguous face. They appear in the research described in Chapter 4.
9. See Turner et al. (1994). In psychology terminology, accessibility is a function of "perceiver readiness." "Comparative fit" is part of a larger necessary condition for categorization known as "category-stimulus fit," which includes comparative fit and normative fit. Normative fit is the degree to which individuals conform to expectations that are based on common knowledge, such as received cultural stereotypes (Oakes et al., 1994).
10. Sidanius and Pratto (2001) call non-age and non-sex based hierarchies "arbitrary-set" hierarchies to indicate such group-based distinctions vary from society to society.
11. Turner et al. (1987, 1994).
12. A closely related concept is *entitativity* (Campbell, 1958).
13. Zimbardo (2007) argued that there is a dark side to uniforms because they facilitate the abdication of individual responsibility and allow for the dehumanization of outgroups. This relies on psychological mechanisms similar to those I am describing.
14. Turner et al. (1987) called these necessary conditions of "psychological group formation." See also, Turner et al. (1994); Blanz (1999).
15. Turner and Oakes (1986).
16. McCrea et al. (2012).
17. E.g., Kinder and Kam (2009).
18. Wilder (1986); Wakslak et al. (2006).
19. Tajfel and Wilkes (1963); Tajfel (1969); Taylor et al. (1978); Allen and Stephenson (1983); Brewer and Miller (1984); Capozza and Nanni (1986); McGarty and Penny (1988); Oakes and Turner (1990); Guinote and Fiske (2003).
20. Tajfel and Wilkes (1963).
21. Gaertner and Schopler (1998); Castano et al. (2002); Spencer-Rodgers et al. (2007); Newheiser et al. (2009); Pettigrew et al. (2010).
22. See, for example, Fiske (2000).

23. Brewer (1999) argues that prejudice more often consists of pro-ingroup bias, rather than anti-outgroup bias and that the latter comes into play under certain conditions. This, of course, is consistent with my generalization that, on average, negative attitudes and behaviors are more likely toward outgroup members.

24. In an era when replicability is an important watchword in psychology, as far as I can tell, there is little doubt about the ability to replicate the minimal groups paradigm. For examples, see Tajfel et al. (1971); Chen and Li (2009); Dunham et al. (2011); Goette et al. (2012). I have replicated such results myself in the studies described in Chapter 4.

25. Other demonstrations have reversed the process: by emphasizing a common identity, bias can be reduced (Gaertner et al., 1993).

26. Sidanius et al. (1994).

27. Moy and Ng (1996); Harvey and Bourhis (2013).

28. Tajfel et al. (1971).

29. Kundra and Sinclair (1999).

30. Sherif et al. (1961).

31. Zimbardo (2007).

32. Reicher et al. (2016).

33. Levine et al. (2005).

34. Hurwitz and Peffley (2005).

35. Sidanius and Pratto (2001).

36. Tesler and Sears (2010); Tesler (2012, 2016).

37. And Lakoff and Johnson (1980) described our reliance on spatial metaphors in non-geographic speech.

38. See Muller (1996), Burgess et al. (2002), Ekstrom et al. (2003), Maguire (2006), and New et al. (2007).

39. Burgess et al. (2002).

40. See Foer (2011).

41. See Camerer et al. (1989).

42. Maddox et al. (2008).

43. Tavares et al. (2015).

44. Crawford and Cacioppo (2002).

45. See, for example, Fiske et al. (2002).

46. Banaji et al. (1993). Some readers may be aware that the interpretation of the tests of automatic association, known as Implicit Association Tests, is controversial (see, for example, Arkes and Tetlock (2004)). However, it is important to keep in mind that these debates are most often about whether such associations can actually show prejudice, such as racism, as it is commonly understood. There is no controversy, as far as I know, about whether these tests show automatic association.

47. Quillian and Pager (2001).

48. Latané (1981). It was Latané's phrase that I adopted to create the term "Spatial Impact," the title of my PhD dissertation (Enos, 2010) and what I modified to social-geographic impact.

49. Latané (1981); Latané and Wolf (1981); Lewenstein et al. (1992); Latané et al. (1995); Latané and L'Herrou (1996).

50. Carroll (2006).

51. Campbell (1958) proposed closed boundaries as specifically important for entitativity.

52. Brewer and Miller (1984).

53. The separateness of segregation may also mean that, because social and physical distance coincide, segregation causes us to turn to higher levels construals and thus

represent segregated people as more abstract (Henderson et al., 2006; Fujita et al., 2006).

54. This is similar to Latané (1981), who argued that social impact was a multiplicative function.

55. Of course, some empirical tests do not support this theoretical conjecture – for example, that the coefficient on the interaction variable will fail to achieve some level of statistical significance. This could be because of the distribution of the variables at some geographic levels. For example, when looking at the relationship between a proximate Black population and the attitudes of whites, large geographies, like DMA's, have a low percentage Black and the relationship between the percentage of blacks and the outcome variable will thus usually be weak and noisy and the coefficient on the interaction with segregation will also be weak.

56. This is how Reardon and O'Sullivan (2004) propose to construct measures of segregation in a local environment. It is also the case that, as a group becomes far enough away, they are represented as abstractions in our minds and attributes, such as spatial location, become unattached (Trope and Liberman, 2003).

57. Allport (1954, p. 269).

58. Tobler (1970).

59. For more on the relationship between social groups and the distortion of perceptions, see Xiao et al. (2016) and Enos (2016a).

60. See Petersen (2015).

61. See Kahneman (2003).

62. Partisanship is usually considered a social identity, behaving much like race or religion (Green et al., 2004).

63. Greene (2014).

64. Downs (1957).

65. For example, Berger et al. (2008).

66. Some of the effect of geography on voting behavior surely comes indirectly, through elite action rather than psychology. For example the clustering of people by social group facilitates targeted communications that can encourage voter turnout. And geographic concentration can also facilitate gerrymandering, which can also affect behavior. But, before any of this can occur, geography will also directly affect our cognition, and psychological and elite explanations are not mutually exclusive.

67. Ideological distance has also been argued to affect turnout in models by Palfrey and Poole (1987); Feddersen and Pesendorfer (1996); and Battaglini et al. (2010).

68. See Enos and Fowler (2014) on the calculus of voting.

69. Schattschneider (1942).

70. Key (1949, p. 646).

71. See Pettigrew and Tropp (2006) and Hewstone (2015). Although the strength of the evidence may be overstated (see Paluck et al. (2016)).

72. Massey and Denton (1993).

73. Pettigrew and Tropp (2006), in their meta-analysis, report that Allport's original conditions are not necessary for prejudice reduction, but rather the conditions make contact more efficacious in prejudice reduction. This does not undermine that perception may still be more important than experience because Allport's conditions still moderate the effect of contact and, without meeting the conditions, contact may not overcome perception.

74. Sidanius and Pratto (2001).

75. This is from the PRRI 2013 American Values Survey, a nationally representative sample of 2,317 adults collected via the Internet (Jones et al., 2013).

76. Allport (1954, p. 273).

77. For example Putnam (2007).
78. Uslaner (2012).
79. In his sophisticated response to Putnam (2007) and others, Hewstone (2015) makes a similar argument.
80. This was the argument of Voss (1996) and a parenthetical argument by Tesler and Sears (2010).
81. See Acharya et al. (2016).
82. Bobo (1983).
83. Spence and McClerking (2010).
84. Giles and Buckner (1993).
85. Key (1949).
86. Voss (1996).
87. King (1996).

CHAPTER 4

1. Some of the research in this chapter was funded by the Pershing Square Venture Fund for Research on the Foundations of Human Behavior at Harvard University.
2. Holland (1986).
3. Montello et al. (2004).
4. Guinote and Fiske (2003); Maddox et al. (2008).
5. Crawford and Cacioppo (2002).
6. This research was the project of Michael Gribben, Brenna Hilferty, and Ibrahim Ouf.
7. For example, Steele and Aronson (1995). Although, this work has been criticized because of suspicion that the results are driven by publication bias.
8. Fujita et al. (2006).
9. McCrea et al. (2012).
10. These findings were originally presented in a conference paper, coauthored with Tess Wise (Enos and Wise, 2012).
11. See Appendix.
12. See Appendix.
13. Nadeau et al. (1993); Sigelman and Niemi (2001); Gallagher (2003); Alba et al. (2005); Wong (2007); Martinez et al. (2008).
14. See, for example, Taleb (2007) on percentages. For proportions, there is a long literature in psychology and other fields documenting a tendency for overestimating small proportions and underestimating large proportions, even when dealing with inanimate objects (Folk, 1951; Kellogg and Dowdy, 1986; Varey et al., 1990; Fiedler and Armbruster, 1994; Cross, 2001).
15. Wong (2007) reports inaccuracies at the level of Primary Sampling Units (PSUs) from the 2000 General Social Survey (GSS). These units are primarily counties, but sometimes CBSA's or other units. Among GSS respondents, she finds that the mean deviation from the actual percent of each group in these PSUs are: White −15, Black +8, Asian +4, Hispanic +6. For my respondents, the mean deviation from the 2010 Census percent of each group in ZIP codes are: White −12, Black +8, Asian +5, Hispanic +13.
16. See Appendix.
17. Which is one reason why I operationalize group size in the studies in this book as the relative size between groups.
18. Chao et al. (2013) use the term *essentialism*, which they say "refers to the perceived inferential power of a given group membership," and Krosch et al. (2013) use these faces to measure individual tendencies for *hypodescent*, which is the tendency to categorize multiracial individuals in the most social subordinate racial category, e.g., the "one drop rule," in the United States.

19. These face stimuli were created by Krosch et al. (2013).
20. Chao et al. (2013); Krosch et al. (2013); Krosch and Amodio (2014).
21. Because in my test the mixtures were in 10 percentage point increments, a subject would actually have to jump 10 points to change categorization, so a PSE of 30 means that a face has to be 40 percent Black or above to categorized as Black and 80 percent white (20 percent Black) or above to categorized as white.
22. See Appendix.
23. The statistically significant coefficients are between −0.15 and −0.23 and the standard deviation of PSE is 0.14 (see Appendix). However, in my opinion, such measures of effect size are of limited value. I think that scholars overemphasize the use of standardized effect sizes for judging substantive significance. Cohen (1977) proposed that these standardized effect sizes (Cohen's d) could be used for ex ante judgments about whether a research design has sufficient statistical power. Scholars often misunderstand that the guidelines for effect size are not measure of substantive significance because, for example, a variable could have high variance, thus necessarily lowering the standardized effect, but still have an important substantive effect. See Enos (2014b).
24. This is moving from PSE of 0.553 to 0.446 and assuming, that all people encountered with an appearance above the PSE are classified as Black and everybody below as white (in reality, the curves may not look like this). This means that at $PSE = 0.55$ that 45 percent of people are classified as Black and this moves to 55 percent classified as white when $PSE = 0.45$. Conversely, this means that at $PSE = 0.55$ that 55 percent of people are classified as white and this moves to 45 percent classified as white when $PSE = 0.45$.
25. See Appendix. The dependent variable is the scale developed by Islam and Hewstone (1993). Of course, if this index is a "noisy" measure of contact, imperfectly capturing actual interpersonal contact, than this will be a poor test of the relative contribution of contact to these attitudes and perceptions. However, the index by Islam and Hewstone (1993) is well-accepted in the psychology literature and given that it is often used to show the importance of contact in shaping attitudes, it should not be easily discounted as a way to show that contact is relatively unimportant when it comes to attitudes. Reinforcing my claim that racial groups have little intergroup contact in the United States, when all three questions are turned into a simple average, the median amount of self-reported contact by whites is between "A little" and "A moderate amount" (2.67 on a five point scale). Given that social desirability may inflate these reports, this is a telling number.
26. Unkelbach et al. (2010); Weichselbaumer (2016).
27. Box et al. (1978).
28. See Rubin (2005).
29. In physics, this could be done in a Bubble Chamber or Cloud Chamber or other, more modern devices.
30. I sometimes believe that critics of observational work on contextual effects believe that selection bias is a special issue for contextual studies – which, of course, as a general statement, isn't true. In fact, selection might even be a less acute problem in the study of context than in proving other causal relationships – after all moving your residence is more costly than many other behaviors. However, I think it may be because of the readily available analogy of somebody physically selecting into a location by moving that this objection is raised for contextual studies more than it is for non-contextual studies.
31. Key (1949, p. 514).
32. See Gallego et al. (2016).
33. In political science in particular, see Wong et al. (2012).

34. The only other studies to manipulate the real-life spatial location of subjects, of which I am aware, are Guinote and Fiske (2003) and Takács (2007).
35. Sampson (2008, p. 191).
36. Tajfel and Wilkes (1963).
37. See Appendix.
38. As Kahneman (2003) puts it, the deliberate processing of System 2 is a "lazy controller," rarely intervening in the heuristic-based processing of System 1.
39. See Appendix.
40. In a single trial, each subject was exposed to each stimulus of interest (Integrated, Segregated White, and Segregated Black) in random order, with 24 distraction stimuli included, each for five seconds. The distraction stimuli were similar to the stimuli of interest, except with different faces marked. The test was done separately on men and women's faces. See Enos and Celaya (2015).
41. Turner et al. (1994).
42. See Hamilton (1981); Kunda (1999).
43. For example, Sears (1986) and Jones (2010).
44. For example, I teach the minimal groups paradigm in my undergraduate class. The bigger concern is that these students take part in so many experiments, for course credit and money, and it is impossible to tell what sort of biases they now bring to the way they react to treatments. I suspect an alarming portion of findings in psychology just reflect "demand effects" where subjects have figured out what experimenters want and, consciously or not, act in a way that meets those demands (Rosnow and Rosenthal, 1997). Talking to my undergraduate students, the anecdotal accounts of how many experiments these students participate in and how little they believe the manipulations is very worrying. Once I was in the hall of one of the psychology laboratories at Harvard and a young lady got of the elevator and was asked what study she was looking for, she replied, "I can't remember, this is like the sixth study I've done today." I shudder to think what effect this has on our inferences.
45. These were Scantron sheets, the common Optical Mark Recognition systems used for automatic marking of answers. This was important for us to claim we had marked their responses and assigned them to a "personality type" in the limited time available.
46. The subjects had been matched on pre-treatment covariates before being assigned to minimal groups in order to insure balance (see Enos and Celaya (2015)).
47. Individuals had also been assigned to the integrated or segregated conditions in matched pairs (see Enos and Celaya (2015)).
48. Some of these variables were also used in matching prior to random assignment.
49. Ultimately, we brought in 286 subjects and paid them each $30. We ended up with fewer subjects then anticipated because of unanticipated costs. For the experiment, we needed, at least, 22 rooms (1 lecture hall + 1 waiting room + 20 rooms for data collection) and 20 computers. Social science laboratories just aren't built to accommodate such experiments. Typically, the kind of laboratory you find at a university campus consists of rows of computers, but because we were assigning subjects to different spatial configurations, something almost never done before, we needed an atypical space. We finally settled on a classroom building, but being a classroom building, we couldn't just use it during any day of the week when classes were in session, so we had to run our experiments only on weekends – this means it took a long time to complete.
50. Physical perceptions were changed by .39 standard deviations and social perceptions by .23 standard deviations, both with $p < .05$. See Enos and Celaya (2015).
51. E.g., Bertrand and Mullainathan (2004).
52. Kahneman and Frederick (2002).

53. I offered this argument in Enos (2016a). There are, of course, many factors that explain the well-documented discrimination in hiring, including institutional forces and the culturally transmitted stereotypes – and this brief discussion is not intended to diminish those, rather I am offering another factor to consider in this complex process of intergroup bias.

54. This represented 0.41 standard deviations.

55. It is also important that I discuss something that didn't "work," in the sense that it didn't yield the result we expected. I am hoping that the reader will actually think this bolsters my overall case for the simple reason that you can see that I am forthcoming about all evidence. I say occasionally that you should never trust a scientist with no null results because it likely means he or she is not reporting everything. So here is one of mine. We asked subjects a third set of questions which was what we call their attribution of valence characteristics to the groups, which definitely represented group-based bias, following the Golden Rule of attitudes. We asked them to endorse statements about whether each group was "capable," "intelligent," "stupid," and "incompetent," using a seven-point Likert scale. These were drawn from minimal groups research by Sidanius et al. (1994). Although people showed ingroup bias in endorsing these statements, usually saying that the outgroup was more "stupid" than the ingroup, this did not differ by segregation or integration. In retrospect, people have suggested to me that such attitudes, while possible to record on a survey, are increasingly difficult to capture because social norms have made people less willing to say such things. It could therefore be that only a small number of people will do so and that something like segregation will not change this. To know if this true, we'd have to do more experiments.

56. Alesina and Spolaore (2003).

57. Enos and Celaya (2015).

CHAPTER 5

1. Interview with the author, April 8, 2014, South Shore, Chicago.

2. Research in this chapter benefited from support from the Malcolm Wiener Center at Harvard University.

3. To balance the covariates of my treatment and control groups, I paired arrival times that were as close together as possible, say 10:15 and 10:30, on the assumption that the waiting commuters would be similar. This turned out to be true because the treatment and control groups were well balanced on observable covariates. The times chosen also had one time in between them, say a train at 10:23, so that if a person missed a train and caught the next one, he or she would not be on the platform during the other experimental condition, thus avoiding contamination across conditions.

4. These were based on responses from Mechanical Turk, where they were asked to compare the faces of the confederates to other Latino and Anglo faces and to record how well particular adjectives described the face. See Enos (2014a).

5. The Census Tracts in which the experiment was targeted were 2.8 percent Hispanic in 2011. The mean percent Hispanic in a Census Tract in the US was 13.8 percent while the median was only 5.8 percent, showing the highly skewed distribution of Hispanics in the United States. These figures are from Enos (2014a).

6. Random assignment was actually done at the train level (see above), not at a geographic community level. Because different people rode different trains, the perception of change in the community varied across trains.

7. It also has an extensive commuter rail network, which was necessary for the design.

8. How do you get a person standing on a train platform to answer questions from a stranger? My research assistants handed out fliers, with two pre-paid gift cards attached. One had $5 on it and we told people that this $5 was theirs to keep. The other also had $5 on it, but the flier said that the card would only be activated if they visited a website on which they could take our anonymous survey.

9. We know they successfully completed these routes because they wore GPS units and I occasionally sent research assistants to check on them. We hired confederates in pairs, inviting people to submit applications with a friend or relative, because we assumed this would make them more comfortable with each other and, thus, more likely to speak.

10. This allows for a "within-subjects" design. This design is more statistically powerful than a "between-subjects" design, which would have involved surveying different subjects before and after the treatment.

11. Undergraduates who were sent to unobtrusively observe the confederates and who also did not know the purpose of the experiment were concerned about this boredom, thinking it might be bad for the experiment. But, for me, I took this as a good sign because it meant the confederates were executing their routes and not behaving unusually in a way that might undermine the validity of the experiment.

12. I know this repetition of exposure happened repeatedly because I asked subjects in the survey how often they had caught the same train in the previous period and nearly all of them had. If they missed the train, this will downward bias the effects. From Enos (2014a):

> Survey results confirmed that routinized behavior is common among the riders I surveyed. Pre-treatment, 88% said they took the train every weekday and 98% said they took it at least three times a week. Post-treatment, respondents indicated that over the 10 working days of the experiment, 78% had caught the train at the exact same time every day, while 96% indicated they had missed their usual train two or fewer times.

13. These results are reported in Enos (2014a). The English language question moved in an exclusionary direction but did not achieve conventional levels of statistical significance.

14. The largest effects were on liberals, not conservatives, see Enos (2014a). This is not surprising, given conservatives had higher baselines levels on most of these attitudes. Nevertheless, when I published an editorial about this in the *Washington Post* (Enos, 2013), pointing out that demographic shifts, such as immigration, may cause liberals to adopt conservative political attitudes, I received a lot of angry emails from liberals.

15. Borjas (1999); Scheve and Slaughter (2001); Kessler (2001); Hanson (2005); Mayda (2006); Hanson et al. (2007); Facchni and Mayda (2009).

16. Citrin et al. (1997); Citrin and Sides (2008); Hainmueller and Hiscox (2010); Newman et al. (2012).

17. Hainmueller and Hiscox (2010); Hainmueller and Hopkins (2014).

18. The treatment effect was also insensitive to the income level of the subject, see Enos (2014a).

19. e.g., Hainmueller and Hiscox (2010).

20. See Hopkins (2010); Newman (2012); Hainmueller and Hangartner (2013).

21. Hopkins (2015).

22. This was noted to me in at least four separate interviews: with Lori Oien, a former Republican candidate for the Tucson city council (November 4, 2013 in Tucson); Mike Polak, a Republican candidate for Tucson city council (November 5, 2013 in Tucson); Ralph Kayser, primary organizer of the Tucson Tea Party Coalition (November 5, 2013 in Tucson); and Kelly Townsend, Republican member of the

Arizona House of Representatives (November 6, 2013 in Phoenix). My guess is that some readers will doubt this claim; instead thinking that these people must harbor a dislike for Latino culture. Of course, they might; I have no way of knowing, but I also have no reason to doubt their sincerity. They may have also held negative stereotypes about Latinos on other dimensions, but still enjoyed the cultural influence. People opposing immigration in Arizona with whom I spoke universally raised two issues: a concern for undocumented immigrants breaking the law and, less often, the economic impact of undocumented immigration.

23. See, for example, Ignatiev (1995).
24. See Gamm (2009).
25. Steinbeck (1939, p. 296).
26. The history of the Hmong people in Merced is wonderfully captured by Anne Fadiman's book *The Spirit Catches You and You Fall Down* (Fadiman, 2012).
27. Sidanius and Pratto (2001).
28. American National Election Study data from 2012 reveal that, relative to other non-Hispanic Americans, those in Arizona have "colder" feelings toward Latinos on a feeling thermometer, which is intended to capture general intergroup affect. Additionally, non-Hispanic Arizonians are more likely to say that immigrants are "mostly a drain" on society, that immigrating to the United States should be made "much harder," and that they oppose a way for currently illegal immigrants to become citizens.
29. Such as SB107, which was largely invalidated by Federal Courts.
30. US Department of Justice Civil Rights Division findings letter on United States' Investigation of the Maricopa County Sheriff's Office, December 15, 2011.
31. Interview with Carlos Garcia, Lead Organizer, Puente Movement, by the author, November 7, 2013, Phoenix.
32. One could, of course, disagree with this assertion or find counter-evidence to say that Anglos in Arizona did not react negatively, but this is why Arizona is just an example. The important part is to realize there is variation in reaction to an immigrant population.
33. This is conclusion of Putnam (2007) about the effects of diversity on social capital.
34. See, for example, Nisbett and Cohen (1996) on the "culture of honor" and violence in the American South or, more generally, Sears and Henry (2003) on the intergenerational "conditioning" of sociopolitical attitudes, especially race. For a recent formulation of this idea, see Acharya et al. (2016).
35. Kinder and Kam (2009).
36. Zaller (1992); Lenz (2013).
37. Posner (2004).
38. For example, Welch et al. (2001).
39. An elite explanation might also be considered contextual, but, I think, is usually not considered as such. This is, perhaps, because, unlike demographics, the independent variable can easily change within a context: for example, new politicians could come into office or existing politicians could find anti-Latino rhetoric to be no longer useful and move to using something else. Elite theories might also just be a secondary effect of contextual theories, in that elites need something, like an immigrant population, on which to demagogue before they can choose to demagogue. If this were the case, certain contexts would be a *necessary condition* for elite explanations.
40. These four explanations could also fit into the categories proposed by Stinchcombe (1987): Demographic, Functional, and Historicist.
41. See Sampson (2012); Sharkey (2013).
42. Sampson (2008, p. 191).

43. Among other considerations, changing the demographics of a neighborhood may affect property values, which could justifiably be considered unethical.
44. This question has been explored by Dinesen and Sønderskov (2015).
45. A way to overcome this problem would be assigning everybody to move; that is, moving both treatment and control subjects; say, some to locations with Latinos and some to locations without. But then we might worry that the general shock from moving would overwhelm the treatment in both cases; for example, if all the subjects' social networks were disrupted, levels of trust might fall to low levels for both groups. We might conclude then that the new context had no effect, when, in reality, it was just overwhelmed by the effect of the move on both groups.
46. Gay (2012).
47. As evidence for this claim, it is notable that scholars have recently found evidence of positive long-term effects of the Moving to Opportunity experiments (Chetty et al., 2016). Perhaps the effects of the new context took time to materialize, especially after the short-term effects of the disruption of the move dissipated.
48. Besides Allport, the importance of repeat interactions was central to the game-theoretic approach of Axelrod (2006). I examine this in Chapter 7.
49. Allport (1954); Hewstone (2015).
50. Sacerdote (2001); Levin et al. (2003); Boisjoly et al. (2006); Shook and Fazio (2009).
51. Sherif et al. (1961); Green and Wong (2009).
52. As mentioned in Endnote 12, my survey evidence indicated that my subjects were routinized because they tended to catch the same train every day.
53. However, only the change in responses to the question about children achieved conventional levels of statistical significance. See Enos (2014a).
54. In this study, I could also see other evidence that the effects of contact and social geography were working against each other before the experiment even started. The first round of the survey included a question about the number of Latino friends the subject had. Those with zero such friends – this was the bottom quartile – had the strongest reaction to the immigrants, becoming the most exclusionary. Those with more Latino friends didn't become more exclusionary at all. See Enos (2014a). Having friends definitely is the type of deep interpersonal contact that Allport thought would improve intergroup relations and we see evidence for that here. Of course, having Latino friends was not randomly assigned, so we don't know if these people are resistant to the effects of social geography because they have Latino friends or if they have Latino friends because they are resistant to the effects of social geography. This problem of selection is why an RCT is necessary.
55. See Enos (2014a).
56. Interview with Micky Roache conducted by the author, January 13, 2014, West End, Boston.
57. See Reynolds (2009).
58. Interview with Jim Jordon conducted by the author, January 13, 2014, West End, Boston. Massachusetts was the only state to vote for the decidedly liberal McGovern over Nixon that year.
59. Interview with Jim Jordan conducted by the author, January 13, 2014, West End, Boston.
60. Rieder (1985).
61. Massey and Denton (1993).
62. See Fischel (2004).
63. White/Hispanic segregation in the Boston Metropolitan Statistical Area in 2010, based on the Dissimilarity Index, was 0.60, compared to an unweighted national average of 0.37. Black/white segregation in Los Angeles was 0.65.
64. Taylor (1988).

65. I would be remiss not to note that Roache was the police commissioner during the infamous "Charles Stuart Case," in which Charles Stuart, a white man, shot and killed his pregnant wife, then wounded himself to make it look like a robbery. He blamed it on an unidentified Black man. The police wrongly arrested a suspect, Willie Bennett, matching the description given by Stuart. Bennett was freed when Stuart's brother admitted to his role in the crime. This incident markedly increased racial tension in the city. Roache and his associate, Jim Jordan, considered the racial flames fanned by this case to even be related to the segregation of Boston between Black and white. Roache also reported that the arrest of Bennett was at the direction of the Suffolk District Attorney.

66. Interview with Mickey Roache conducted by the author, January 13, 2014, West End, Boston. Roache's assessment was that the level of racial violence in Boston was the worst in the United States at the time.

67. Interview with Jim Jordan conducted by the author, January 13, 2014, West End, Boston.

68. For an excellent political history of the racial change in these neighborhoods, see Gamm (2009).

69. Interview with Jim Jordan conducted by the author, January 13, 2014, West End, Boston.

70. Matthews (2016).

71. See Appendix.

72. See Appendix.

73. These findings are consistent with the model offered by Hopkins (2010), in which salient news coverage will raise anti-immigrant sentiment where the local immigrant population has increased.

CHAPTER 6

1. Zorbaugh (1929, p. xix).

2. The properties in this corridor also included the Robert Taylor Homes, Dearborn Homes, Harold Ickes Homes, and Hillard Homes.

3. Moore (2016, p. 1).

4. This number is taken from residency counts provided by the Chicago Housing Authority and likely severely undercounts the actual population of the projects because it included a high proportion of illegal occupants, including squatters and people living with relatives, see Kotlowitz (1992).

5. Kaufmann (2004); Trounstine (2010); Hajnal and Trounstine (2014).

6. In the film, Byrne describes this strategy as "stupid" (Hampton, 1987).

7. Interview with Carl C. Bell, psychiatrist, conducted by the author, April 7, 2014, Hyde Park, Chicago.

8. See Moore (2016).

9. Eugene Sawyer, a Black alderman, was elected by the city council to replace Washington and was defeated for reelection by Richard M. Daley in 1989.

10. Moore (2016) attests to these rumors as well.

11. I am using the term systematic here intentionally because, of course, even with randomization, non-zero correlations between treatment and other variables will occur by chance.

12. This was confirmed by balance tests. See Enos (2016b).

13. There is a subtlety to why we should expect small or zero effects for Blacks when their Black neighbors are removed. While the social geography changed for Blacks, too, it either changed insignificantly for some Blacks or for other Blacks they were already surrounded by so much of the outgroup (whites) that their group-based bias

was already low (see discussion of the curvilinear nature of the effects of outgroup size in Chapter 2). The first case applies to Black voters on the south or west sides of the city, where the housing projects were only a small part of the local Black population. In this case, while the removal of that population may have been dramatic for whites living very close to these projects, in terms of social geography it was likely much less meaningful for local Blacks. For Blacks living on the North Side, the removal of the housing projects meant a significant reduction in the Black population, but they were already an extreme minority because most of the local population was white. When a group is a very small minority, they are usually insensitive to social geography, perhaps because of selection, or even have their attitudes improve as the outgroup grows in proportion, possibly because of the countervailing effects of interpersonal contact.

14. See Enos (2016b) for details on matching and parallel trends and for details on the results of vote choice below.
15. See, for example, Tesler and Sears (2010).
16. Sidanius and Pratto (2001); Kinder and Kam (2009).
17. Valentino and Sears (2005).
18. Prior to these elections, Obama had been the state senator for the district that included the school in which I taught. I used to assign my students to learn the names of their elected officials, from alderman all the way to President. This is where I first came across the name Barack Obama and I remember having to look up whether that name belonged to a man or woman. Five years later, he was the most powerful man in the world. I don't count Obama's state senate elections or his unsuccessful bid for Congress in 2000 because he didn't run citywide.
19. Interview by the author with anonymous documentary film maker about the Cabrini-Green demolition, Chicago, Edgewater neighborhood, April 8, 2014.
20. In the spring of 1981, Byrne and her husband moved into a Cabrini-Green apartment to draw attention to the problem. This move was largely criticized as a publicity stunt.
21. This was before voter lists were widely available or used in political science. In fact, to obtain the voter list for use in this project, I had to use connections who had personal contacts within the state because the files were only provided to political operatives.
22. Some measures of segregation attempt to capture this component of spatial proximity; see Massey and Denton (1988).
23. Distance was measured from the edge of the project, which is important given how large many of them were. I was able to measure edges because I obtained a GIS shapefile with the two-dimensional polygons of each project. This was thanks to a fortunate call with a woman named Anna Fan from the city government of Chicago. Years later, after this project had come to fruition, I called again looking for data for a different project and Anna happened to answer the phone, so I was able to personally thank her.
24. Balcells et al. (2015); Legewie and Schaeffer (2016).
25. Interview by the author with anonymous documentary film maker about the Cabrini-Green demolition, Chicago, Edgewater neighborhood, April 8, 2014.
26. This was demonstrated in a field experiment by Sands (2016). The immigration literature cited in the previous chapter also addresses this (Hainmueller and Hiscox, 2010).
27. Massey and Denton (1993), but also see Wilson (1987).
28. Sidanius and Pratto (2001).
29. This was essentially the demonstration by Openshaw (1983).
30. See Cho and Baer (2011).

31. Giles and Buckner (1993).
32. Voss (1996).
33. See Cho and Baer (2011).
34. I did not use this method in early drafts of the paper and, instead, relied on finding homogeneous Census units; for example, Census Blocks in which everyone was white or Black. In a segregated city like Chicago, these do exist. Eventually, I switched to a Bayesian algorithm, inspired by advice from Jeffery Lewis, which I first wrote down in a conference paper (Enos, 2009), my dissertation (Enos, 2010), and an unpublished manuscript (Enos, 2012) and which eventually made its way into the published article on the housing projects (Enos, 2016b).
35. Figure 6.1 represents aldermanic lines, but the same could be seen with Congressional district lines.
36. Enos et al. (2014); Fowler (2015).
37. Green et al. (2013).
38. Green et al. (2004).
39. Hillygus and Shields (2008).
40. This was a short-lived amalgamation of the departments of Anthropology, Psychology, and Sociology.
41. Kramer (1950).
42. This was the former Parker High School, which was turned into an elementary school when Robeson was opened as a high school.
43. Zorbaugh (1929, p. xviii).
44. Interview by the author with anonymous documentary film maker about the Cabrini-Green demolition, Chicago, Edgewater neighborhood, April 8, 2014.

CHAPTER 7

1. Axelrod (2006, p. 12).
2. Research in this chapter was funded by the Harvard Academy and the Harvard Center for Jewish Studies.
3. Known as "Eruv," Ultra-Orthodox sometimes put up a string around a neighborhood; for example, attached to poles. This creates the understanding that the entire area is a "house," which means that residents can do things outside their own houses, such as carrying water, which it would otherwise be forbidden by religious law to do "outside." Many secular people object strenuously to this practice and try to make it illegal or just take the strings down.
4. Hardin (1968).
5. E.g., Olson (1971).
6. Hobbes (1900).
7. Axelrod (2006).
8. Axelrod and Hamilton (1981).
9. Greene (2014, p. 67).
10. Tajfel et al. (1971).
11. The minority share of a public school has been linked to the willingness of whites in the United States to spend on that school (Hopkins, 2009).
12. Zorbaugh (1929).
13. See Forbes (1997); Alesina and Spolaore (2003); Habyarimana et al. (2009).
14. Henrich et al. (2006) played economic games across many countries, but they were looking for cultural influences on play, not variation in social geography.
15. See Enos and Gidron (2016a).
16. Hasson and Gonen (1997); Ben-Porat et al. (2008).
17. Efron (2003, p. 99).
18. See Rubin (2012).

19. It is important to recognize that saying a group intentionally segregates itself or chooses any lifestyle, for that matter, will necessarily be partially inaccurate, especially for some members of that group. Nobody freely chooses every aspect of his or her lifestyle; there are cultural and family loyalties and pressures and simple path-dependence. It is also the case that the ability to choose one's lifestyle may not be equally shared by men and women and certainly not by children.

20. See, for example, Massey and Denton (1993).

21. Communicated to the author during conversation after lab-in-the-field experiments, July 2015, Ashdod, Israel.

22. Livneh (2012).

23. Jerusalem is the traditional capital of Judaism; central to Christianity because it was the site of the crucifixion of Christ; and the third-most holy city in Islam, the location of the original Qiblah (the direction of prayer) and of the ascent of Muhammad to heaven. It is claimed as the national capital of both Israel and the Palestinian people.

24. Greek Orthodox, Armenian Apostolic, Roman Catholic, Coptic Orthodox, Ethiopian Orthodox, and Syriac Orthodox.

25. The Moroccan Quarter.

26. The larger Christian population in Israel and the occupied Palestinian territories has been reduced from about 11 percent in the early twentieth century to somewhere around 2 percent now.

27. Habyarimana et al. (2007); Whitt and Wilson (2007); Habyarimana et al. (2009); Alexander and Christia (2011).

28. Sears (1986); Jones (2010).

29. This was a "random walk" to choose a building or home, combined with a systematic choice of apartments within a building based on predetermined number.

30. The game also included a chance to play against an Arab. We didn't examine play against Arabs as a function of social geography because we designed our sampling for variation in the social geography of ultra-Orthodox and secular Jews. We did, however, find high levels of group-based bias against Arabs, independent of social geography. See Enos and Gidron (2016b).

31. This is similar to the design of Whitt and Wilson (2007). Players were eventually actually paid their winnings from the game. No deception was used.

32. See Enos and Gidron (2016a).

33. See Enos and Gidron (2016a) for details. These results are based on holding the ultra-Orthodox proportion at the Jerusalem level and simulating an increase in segregation from the Tel Aviv level to the Jerusalem level. Segregation and the ultra-Orthodox proportion are measured using Yeshiva (Orthodox religious school) enrollment, as is standard in studying Israeli demographic analysis. There are other ways to measure ultra-Orthodox population counts and we also tested our results using these and found them to be consistent. Outgroup proportion is measured differently here than elsewhere in the book to keep it consistent with the measure in the original article. It is measured as a simple proportion of the Jewish population, rather than as a ratio of the in group.

34. In Enos and Gidron (2016a), we did not control for interpersonal contact, so in the Appendix, I reprint all results with controls for interpersonal contact included.

35. In their impressive work, Habyarimana et al. (2007) actually measured the success of their subjects in doing a task together, but they also created a variable similar to ours by measuring with whom their subjects chose to solve the puzzle.

36. See Enos and Gidron (2016a).

37. See Appendix.

38. The options provided were: fairness, concern for the opponent, concern for oneself, trust, and "other." Interestingly, for secular players showing bias in cooperation, fairness was chosen as often as trust.
39. Bogardus (1926).
40. See Appendix.
41. See Enos and Gidron (2016a).
42. This test is similar to the one designed by Farley et al. (1978) to study white and Black housing preferences in the US.
43. Enos and Gidron (2016a, p. 863).
44. On suburbanization, see, for example, Nall (2015).

CHAPTER 8

1. Brown (1965, p. 8).
2. Focus group interviews conducted by the author, October 10, 2009, Crenshaw district, Los Angeles.
3. Some of the research described in this chapter was funded by the John Randolph Haynes and Dora Haynes Foundation.
4. Schelling (1969, 1971).
5. Avila (2004).
6. Gamm (2009).
7. Sidanius and Pratto (2001).
8. Bobo and Hutchings (1996).
9. Sears and Kinder (1985).
10. As a small minority population, we might expect Blacks to show decreasing hostility toward Latinos, as the size of the Latino population increases. This is the curvilinear nature of the effect of group size noted in Chapter 2. Indeed, this may be reflected in the occasional intergroup harmony I note in this chapter. However, part of the curvilinear effect of group size is likely also induced by selection, as those with very negative attitudes leave a local environment as the outgroup becomes too large. And as I discuss in this chapter, such exit is less available for Blacks than it is for high-status groups, such as whites.
11. Sears and McConahay (1973).
12. See, for example, Sides (2003, 2004).
13. Schelling (2006, p. 141).
14. See Massey and Denton (1993).
15. The tract is bounded by West 60th Street to the north, West 67th Street to the south, Long Street to the west, and 8th Avenue to the east.
16. Sides (2003).
17. The Court ruled that these covenants were unenforceable in the 1948 case of *Shelley v. Kraemer*, thereby making them worthless. Prior to this ruling, 80 percent of the properties in Los Angeles were estimated to be under a restrictive covenant (US Commission on Civil Rights, 1973).
18. Sides (2004).
19. The population numbers behind the percent changes in Anglo population from 1970 to 2010 were 1,260,210 to 1,349,803 in Orange County, 619,009 to 343,495 in Suffolk County, and 1,931,521 to 924,710 in Wayne County. During this period, the Black population rose from 105,218 to 156,110 in Suffolk County and from 721,108 to 763,504 in Wayne County.
20. This analysis involved taking the 1992 Los Angeles County voterfile and imputing race, see below and Endnote 34 in Chapter 6. Then taking voters where Black was the highest probability category and looking for those still living in the basin after

matching with a 2008 statewide voter file. This means that I would lose people who had died or moved out of state.

21. E.g., Blumer (1958).

22. Focus group interviews conducted by the author, October 17, 2009, Crenshaw district, Los Angeles.

23. Sides (2004).

24. One way to characterize such bias in schools is through various manifestations of resource competition. The idea is that, because Blacks and Latinos compete over resources, there is conflict in schools. Indeed, social scientists have made this argument using data specifically coming from Los Angeles (Bobo, 1983) and focusing on Blacks and Latinos in the city (Gay, 2006). Of course, explanations of material competition and geographic impact are not mutually exclusive. We must also recognize that attitudes and resource competition are endogenous; groups can choose not to compete over resources, but might instead choose to compete if negative attitudes make cooperation difficult. Moreover, in situations where the effects of material competition are well controlled – as in the extensive literature on immigration (Hainmueller and Hiscox, 2010) and in the situations discussed in this book, such as Blacks in Chicago housing projects and whites living very nearby but in essentially different economic worlds – material competition proves to be a poor predictor of group-based bias.

25. Focus group interviews conducted by the author, October 10, 2009, Crenshaw district, Los Angeles.

26. The previous Latino mayor was Cristóbal Aguilar, who left office in 1872, when Los Angeles had approximately 6,000 residents.

27. See Sonenshein (1993).

28. Sonenshein and Drayse (2006). Hahn may have also received support as result of the legacy of his father Kenneth Hahn, the longtime County Supervisor, who was popular in the African American community.

29. Sonenshein and Drayse (2006).

30. Zaller (1992).

31. The signs said: "BE PART OF A STUDY THAT WANTS TO LEARN MORE ABOUT WHAT YOU AND YOUR NEIGHBORS THINK ABOUT YOUR NEIGH-BORHOOD." Subjects were given a phone number to call and leave their contact details and their availability. When they called, I looked them up on the voter file to confirm that they were registered voters and to check their probability of being Black based on the surname analysis described in Enos (2016b). If they were registered and had a high probability of being Black, they were assigned to a focus group time with attention to age and gender balance. After the group, subjects were paid $100 for their time. One person participated who was not actually invited. The focus groups were audio-recorded while research assistants took written notes.

32. Scholarly examples of similar exercises include Lynch (1960) and Milgram (2010).

33. This was after a survey, which participants completed upon arrival, and before the focus group itself got under way. The instructions for the map were:

On the large blank piece of paper provided to you, please use the marker to draw a map of your neighborhood. You can draw it however you like. However, on your map, be sure to include whatever about the neighborhood is important to you – these can be people or places – buildings, streets, businesses – whatever you feel is important. By neighborhood, we mean whatever you think of as your neighborhood – you decide. Your map does not have to be neat or complete. Please take about 10 minutes to do this.

34. Focus group interviews conducted by the author, October 17, 2009, Crenshaw district, Los Angeles.
35. Focus group interviews conducted by the author, October 10, 2009, Crenshaw district, Los Angeles.
36. Focus group interviews conducted by the author, October 17, 2009, Crenshaw district, Los Angeles.
37. Rieder (1985, p. 17).
38. Dawson (1995).
39. Focus group interviews conducted by the author, October 10, 2009, Crenshaw district, Los Angeles.
40. These were Ogden International School and Jenner Academy of the Arts.
41. Focus group interviews conducted by the author, October 17, 2009, Crenshaw district, Los Angeles.
42. Focus group interviews conducted by the author, October 17, 2009, Crenshaw district, Los Angeles.
43. Focus group interviews conducted by the author, October 10, 2009, Crenshaw district, Los Angeles.
44. Focus group interviews conducted by the author, October 17, 2009, Crenshaw district, Los Angeles.
45. Hirschmann (1970).
46. See Sears and McConahay (1973).
47. That the riot was a form of "functional redress" is the theory of Sears and McConahay (1973).
48. Focus group interviews conducted by the author, October 17, 2009, Crenshaw district, Los Angeles. Solis became a Los Angeles County supervisor in 2014.
49. Focus group interviews conducted by the author, October 10, 2009, Crenshaw district, Los Angeles.
50. In recent years, dot-density maps have become popular. They display populations by laying out single dots to represent groups of people inside areal units. Such maps offer a false precision; they are often touted as showing the "exact location" of a group, but they do nothing of the sort. The dots are taken from averages, as in a choropleth map, and distributed randomly inside an areal unit.
51. See Appendix. *New York Times* exit polls found Latino men and women going 62 and 69 percent for Hillary Clinton, respectively.
52. But see Gerber et al. (2010).
53. For example, Burden and Klofstad (2005).
54. Priming experiments, as a paradigm, have justifiably received a good deal of criticism, but there is little doubt about the general role of cognitive accessibility in changing our attitudes and behaviors. This is the model, for example, underlying the theory of survey response in Zaller (1992): when something is brought to mind, you use it in formulating your response to something else.
55. I again found voters on the voter list using the name-imputation technique.
56. The election was on June 3, 2008. Only 20.17 percent of the registered voters in Los Angeles County voted in the June primary, slightly more than the statewide participation of 19.75 percent. Party primary contests were held for US Congress, the California State Assembly and Senate, and the county party central committees. There were also non-partisan primary contests for Los Angeles County Supervisor seats and for a host of judgeships and two statewide ballot initiatives to reform the state constitution in order to change powers of eminent domain. Among the contests that could be considered reasonably competitive – that is, in which the runner-up had at least 20 percent of the vote – none included both a Black and a Latino candidate. In the Democratic primaries for the US House and the California State

Senate and Assembly, only two were contested: in the 37th Congressional District, Laura Richardson, an African American, won reelection with over 75 percent of the vote and in the 25th California Senate District, Assemblyman Roderick Wright, also African American, won with 43.75 percent of the vote. Perhaps the most high-profile contest was the non-partisan primary for the open seat in the 2nd Los Angeles County Board of Supervisors District. The top two candidates were Black: State Senator Mark Ridley-Thomas won 45.63 percent and Bernard Parks finished second with 39.53 percent. The next-closest candidate, a Latino, had only 3.84 percent. About 80 percent of the subjects in my experiment live in the 2nd Supervisor District and were evenly balanced across treatment conditions.

57. See Appendix.
58. Rieder (1985).
59. Focus group interviews conducted by the author, October 10, 2009, Crenshaw district, Los Angeles.
60. Focus group interviews conducted by the author, October 10, 2009, Crenshaw district, Los Angeles.
61. Sides (2003, p. 205).
62. See Tiebout (1956) and Fischel (2004).
63. Florida (2002).

CHAPTER 9

1. The correlation between county logged proximity to the border and percent Latino in a county in 2014 is 0.71.
2. Research in this chapter benefited from support from the Malcolm Wiener Center at Harvard University.
3. There is some inaccuracy to this characterization because Nogales was a single community and part of Mexico before the Gadsden Purchase of 1854 split the community.
4. Interview with Karl Hoffman, filmmaker, Arivaca, Arizona, by the author, November 4, 2014.
5. Interview with Mary Rose Wilcox, Maricopa County Supervisor, District 5, conducted by the author, November 6, 2013, Phoenix.
6. Interview with Kelly Townsend, Arizona House of Representatives, District 16, Phoenix, by the author, November 6, 2014.
7. Acemoglu and Robinson (2012) point to the Gadsden Purchase as a natural experiment of a different sort because it provided cultural continuity across a political division at Nogales.
8. See Massey et al. (2002).
9. Interview with Karl Hoffman, filmmaker, Arivaca, Arizona, by the author, November 4, 2014.
10. Interview with Jonathan Rothschild, Mayor of Tucson, by the author, November 5, 2014.
11. Interview with John Leavitt, Assistant Chief of Police, Tucson, by the author, November 5, 2014.
12. For example, see Craig Crawford in *CQ Politics*, May 5, 2010.
13. Similar patterns can be found in the Rio Grande Valley in Texas, which has a history of cultural mixing similar to that of southern Arizona.
14. These estimates are from the data used in Tausanovitch and Warshaw (2013). Arizona is 0.10, the most left state is Vermont at −0.39, and the most right is Idaho at 0.33.
15. See, for example, Wilson (1987).

16. Logan and Stults (2011).
17. See, for example, Tatum (2003).
18. For example, Huntington (2004).
19. Census data show that Italian immigrants were never more than a little over one percent of the US population. The largest non-Latin American group were the Irish in 1860 at 5.1 percent of the population. Immigrants from Latin America in 2010 were 6.7 percent of the US population. As a proportion of the immigrant population, the Irish in 1850 were 43.8 percent, while Latin American immigrants were 51.8 percent in 2000 and 46.0 percent in 2010. Mexican immigrants made up 29.5 percent of all immigrants in 2000 and 25.8 percent in 2010. No other group in the twentieth century exceeded 20 percent. And bear in mind that the immigrant shares from Latin America are almost certainly undercounts due to difficulties in enumerating undocumented people.
20. Borjas (1999).
21. Knowles et al. (2014).
22. See Anderson (1983).
23. Simmons (2016).
24. Brown (1965, p. 8).
25. Interview with Javier Bravo, Assistant Principal, Borugade Catholic High School, Phoenix, by the author, November 7, 2013, Phoenix.
26. Oliver (2001), see also Putnam (2001).
27. Jacobs (1961, p. 72).
28. See, for example, Arribas-Bel and Sanz-Gracia (2014).
29. This is calculated by percent of employment in the Central Business District, as defined by the Census, in 2010.
30. Only 2.2 percent of the workforce in the Phoenix metro area uses public transportation. Of the fast-growing cities mentioned in this chapter, San Jose is the leader in public transportation use – at a mere 3.3 percent.
31. Cox (2013).
32. See Endnote 21 in Chapter 1.
33. See Oliver (2001) for further discussion of the balkanization of municipal governments.
34. Fischel (2004).
35. This was the model introduced by Tiebout (1956).
36. Pierson (2000).
37. Notably, some countries, such as Singapore, have focused more aggressively on housing integration (Vasoo and Lee, 2001).
38. For example Sacerdote (2001); Levin et al. (2003); Boisjoly et al. (2006); Shook and Fazio (2009).
39. Rosenblum (2016, p. 2).

Bibliography

Acemoglu, D. and J. Robinson (2012). *Why Nations Fail: The Origins of Power, Prosperity, and Poverty*. New York: Crown Business.

Acharya, A., M. Blackwell, and M. Sen (2016). The political legacy of American slavery. *Journal of Politics* 78(3): 621–641.

Ahmed, A. M. and M. Hammarstedt (2008). Discrimination in the rental housing market: A field experiment on the internet. *Journal of Urban Economics* 64(2), 362–372.

Alba, R., R. G. Rumbaut, and K. Marotz (2005). A distorted nation: Perceptions of racial/ethnic group sizes and attitudes toward immigrants and other minorities. *Social Forces* 84(2), 901–919.

Alesina, A., R. Baqir, and W. Easterly (1999). Public goods and ethnic divisions. *The Quarterly Journal of Economics* 114(4), 1243–1284.

Alesina, A. and E. L. Glaeser (2004). *Fighting Poverty in the US and Europe: A World of Difference*. Oxford: Oxford University Press.

Alesina, A. and E. Spolaore (2003). *The Size of Nations*. Cambridge, MA: MIT Press.

Alesina, A. and E. Zhuravskaya (2008). Segregation and the quality of government in a cross-section of countries. Technical report, National Bureau of Economic Research.

Alexander, M. and F. Christia (2011). Context modularity of human altruism. *Science* 334(6061), 1392–1394.

Allen, P. and G. Stephenson (1983). Inter-group understanding and size of organisation. *British Journal of Industrial Relations* 21(3), 312–329.

Allport, G. W. (1954). *The Nature of Prejudice*. Reading, MA: Addison-Wesley.

Almond, I. (2009). *Two Faiths, One Banner: When Muslims Marched with Christians Across Europe's Battlegrounds*. Cambridge, MA: Harvard University Press.

Ananat, E. O. (2011). The wrong side(s) of the tracks: The causal effects of racial segregation on urban poverty and inequality. *American Economic Journal: Applied Economics* 3(2), 34–66.

Ananat, E. O. and E. Washington (2009). Segregation and black political efficacy. *Journal of Public Economics* 93(5), 807–822.

Anderson, B. (1983). *Imagined Communities: Reflections on the Origin and Spread of Nationalism*. London: Verso Books.

Angrist, J. D. and J.-S. Pischke (2009). *Mostly Harmless Econometrics: An Empiricist's Companion*. Princeton: Princeton University Press.

Ansolabehere, S. and E. Hersh (2012). Validation: What big data reveal about survey misreporting and the real electorate. *Political Analysis* 20(4), 437–459.

Arkes, H. R. and P. E. Tetlock (2004). Attributions of implicit prejudice, or "would Jesse Jackson 'fail' the implicit association test?" *Psychological Inquiry* 15(4), 257–278.

Arribas-Bel, D. and F. Sanz-Gracia (2014). The validity of the monocentric city model in a polycentric age: US metropolitan areas in 1990, 2000 and 2010. *Urban Geography* 35(7), 980–997.

Avila, E. (2004). *Popular Culture in the Age of White Flight: Fear and Fantasy in Suburban Los Angeles*. Berkeley, CA: University of California Press.

Axelrod, R. M. (2006). *The Evolution of Cooperation*. New York: Basic Books.

Axelrod, R. M. and W. D. Hamilton (1981). The evolution of cooperation. *Science* 211(27), 1390–1396.

Balcells, L., L.-A. Daniels, and A. Escribà-Folch (2015). The determinants of low-intensity intergroup violence. The case of Northern Ireland. *Journal of Peace Research*. 53(1), 33–48.

Banaji, M. R., C. Hardin, and A. J. Rothman (1993). Implicit stereotyping in person judgment. *Journal of Personality and Social Psychology* 65(2), 272–281.

Battaglini, M., R. B. Morton, and T. R. Palfrey (2010). The swing voter's curse in the laboratory. *Review of Economic Studies* 77(1), 61–89.

Baybeck, B. (2006). Sorting out the competing effects of racial context. *Journal of Politics* 68(2), 386–396.

Ben-Porat, G., Y. Levy, S. Mizrahi, A. Naor, and E. Tzfadia (2008). *Israel since 1980*. Cambridge: Cambridge University Press.

Berger, J., M. Meredith, and S. C. Wheeler (2008). Contextual priming: Where people vote affects how they vote. *Proceedings of the National Academy of Sciences* 105(26), 8846–8849.

Bertrand, M. and S. Mullainathan (2004). Are Emily and Greg more employable than Lakisha and Jamal? A field experiment on labor market discrimination. *American Economic Review* 94(4), 991–1013.

Blalock, H. M. (1967). *Toward a Theory of Minority-Group Relations*. New York: Wiley.

Blanz, M. (1999). Accessibility and fit as determinants of the salience of social categorizations. *European Journal of Social Psychology* 29(1), 43–74.

Blumer, H. (1958). Race prejudice as a sense of group position. *Pacific Sociological Review* 1(1), 3–7.

Bobo, L. (1983). Whites' opposition to busing: Symbolic racism or realistic group conflict? *Journal of Personality and Social Psychology* 45(6), 1196–1210.

Bobo, L. and V. Hutchings (1996). Perceptions of racial group competition: Extending Blumer's theory of group position to a multiracial social context. *American Sociological Review* 61(6), 951–972.

Bogardus, E. S. (1926). Social distance in the city. *Proceedings and Publications of the American Sociological Society* 20, 40–46.

Boisjoly, J., G. J. Duncan, M. Kremer, D. M. Levy, and J. Eccles (2006). Empathy or antipathy? The impact of diversity. *The American Economic Review* 96(5), 1890–1905.

Borjas, G. J. (1999). *Heaven's Door: Immigration Policy and the American Economy.* Princeton, NJ: Princeton University Press.

Box, G. E., W. G. Hunter, and J. S. Hunter (1978). *Statistics for Experimenters.* New York: Wiley.

Brewer, M. B. (1999). The psychology of prejudice: Ingroup love and outgroup hate? *Journal of Social Issues* 55(3), 429–444.

Brewer, M. B. and N. Miller (1984). Beyond the contact hypothesis: Theoretical perspectives on desegregation. In M. Brewer and N. Miller (eds.), *Groups in Contact: The Psychology of Desegregation,* San Diego: Academic pp. 281–302.

Brown, C. (1965). *Manchild in the Promised Land.* New York: Macmillan.

Burden, B. C. and C. A. Klofstad (2005). Affect and cognition in party identification. *Political Psychology* 26(6), 869–886.

Burgess, N., E. A. Maguire, and J. O'Keefe (2002). The human hippocampus and spatial and episodic memory. *Neuron* 35, 625–641.

Cairncross, F. (2001). *The Death of Distance: How the Communications Revolution is Changing our Lives.* Boston: Harvard Business Press.

Camerer, C., G. Loewenstein, and M. Weber (1989). The curse of knowledge in economic settings: An experimental analysis. *The Journal of Political Economy,* 97(5), 1232–1254.

Campbell, D. E. (2006). *Why We Vote: How Schools and Communities Shape Our Civic Life.* Princeton, NJ: Princeton University Press.

Campbell, D. T. (1958). Common fate, similarity, and other indices of the status of aggregates of persons as social entities. *Behavioral Science* 3(1), 14–25.

Capozza, D. and R. Nanni (1986). Differentiation processes for social stimuli with different degrees of category representativeness. *European Journal of Social Psychology* 16(4), 399–412.

Carroll, J. (2006). *House of War: The Pentagon and the Disastrous Rise of American Power.* Boston: Houghton Mifflin.

Carsey, T. M. (1995). The contextual effects of race on white voter behavior: The 1989 New York City mayoral election. *Journal of Politics* 57(1), 221–228.

Castano, E., V. Yzerbyt, M.-P. Paladino, and S. Sacchi (2002). I belong, therefore, I exist: Ingroup identification, ingroup entitativity, and ingroup bias. *Personality and Social Psychology Bulletin* 28(2), 135–143.

Chao, M. M., Y.-Y. Hong, and C.-Y. Chiu (2013). Essentializing race: Its implications on racial categorization. *Journal of Personality and Social Psychology* 104(4), 619–639.

Charnysh, V. (2015). Historical legacies of interethnic competition anti-semitism and the EU Referendum in Poland. *Comparative Political Studies* 48(13), 1711–1745.

Chen, Y. and S. X. Li (2009). Group identity and social preferences. *American Economic Review* 99(1), 431–457.

Chetty, R., N. Hendren, and L. Katz (2016). The effects of exposure to better neighborhoods on children: New evidence from the moving to opportunity experiment. *American Economic Review* 106(4), 855–902.

Cho, W. K. T. and N. Baer (2011). Environmental determinants of racial attitudes redux: The critical decisions related to operationalizing context. *American Politics Research* 39(3), 414–436.

Citrin, J., D. P. Green, C. Muste, and C. Wong (1997). Public opinion toward immigration reform: The role of economic motivations. *Journal of Politics* 59(3), 858–881.

Citrin, J. and J. Sides (2008). Immigration and the imagined community in Europe and the United States. *Political Studies* 56(1), 33–56.

Cohen, J. (1977). *Statistical Power Analysis for the Behavioral Sciences*. New York: Academic Press.

Collier, P. (2000). Ethnicity, politics and economic performance. *Economics & Politics* 12(3), 225–245.

Corvalan, A. and M. Vargas (2015). Segregation and conflict: An empirical analysis. *Journal of Development Economics* 116, 212–222.

Couzin, I. D., C. C. Ioannou, G. Demirel, T. Gross, C. J. Torney, A. Hartnett, L. Conradt, S. A. Levin, and N. E. Leonard (2011). Uninformed individuals promote democratic consensus in animal groups. *Science* 334, 1578–1580.

Cox, W. (2013). Transit legacy cities. www.newgeography.com/content/003507-transit-legacy-cities (accessed May 31, 2017).

Crawford, L. E. and J. T. Cacioppo (2002). Learning where to look for danger: Integrating affective and spatial information. *Psychological Science* 13(5), 449–453.

Cross, S. (2001). Observer accuracy in estimating proportions in images: Implications for the semiquantitative assessment of staining reactions and a proposal for a new system. *Journal of Clinical Pathology* 54(5), 385–390.

Cutler, D. M. and E. L. Glaeser (1997). Are ghettos good or bad? *Quarterly Journal of Economics* 112(3) 829–872.

Dawson, M. C. (1995). *Behind the Mule: Race and Class in African-American Politics*. Princeton, NJ: Princeton University Press.

De Kadt, D. and M. Sands (2014). The natural limits of segregation and re-integration. *American Political Science Association, Annual Meeting*, Washington DC.

Dill, V. and U. Jirjahn (2014). Ethnic residential segregation and immigrants' perceptions of discrimination in West Germany. *Urban Studies* 51(16), 3330–3347.

Dinesen, P. T. and K. M. Sønderskov (2015). Ethnic diversity and social trust evidence from the micro-context. *American Sociological Review* 80(3), 550–573.

Downs, A. (1957). *An Economic Theory of Democracy*. New York: Harper.

Dunham, Y., A. S. Baron, and S. Carey (2011). Consequences of "minimal" group affiliations in children. *Child Development* 82(3), 793–811.

Easterly, W. and R. Levine (1997). Africa's growth tragedy: policies and ethnic divisions. *Quarterly Journal of Economics* 112(4), 1203–1250.

Efron, N. J. (2003). *Real Jews: Secular versus Ultra-Orthodox and the Struggle for Jewish Identity in Israel*. New York: Basic Books.

Ekstrom, A. D., M. J. Kahana, J. B. Caplan, T. A. Fields, E. A. Isham, E. L. Newman, and I. Fried (2003). Cellular networks underlying human spatial navigation. *Nature* 425, 184–188.

Enos, R. D. (2009). The effect of African American proximity on Latino vote choice in the 2008 Presidential Primary. *American Political Science Association, Annual Meeting*, Toronto.

Enos, R. D. (2010). *Spatial Impact: The Influence of Groups in Geographic Space on Individual Political Behavior*. Dissertation, University of California, Los Angeles, Los Angeles.

Enos, R. D. (2011). Obama, race and the 2008 elections. In S. D. Brunn, G. R. Webster and J. C. Archer (eds.), *Atlas of the 2008 Election*. Lanham, MD: Rowman and Littlefield.

Enos, R. D. (2012). Testing the elusive: A field experiment on racial threat. *Working Paper*, Harvard University.

Enos, R. D. (2013). How the Demographic shift could hurt democrats, too. *Washington Post* 8 March.

Enos, R. D. (2014a). The causal effect of intergroup contact on exclusionary attitudes. *Proceedings of the National Academy of Sciences of the United States of America 111*(10), 3699–3704.

Enos, R. D. (2014b). Reply to Van Hoorn: Pitfalls of narrow interpretations of significance. *Proceedings of the National Academy of Sciences 111*(19), E1939.

Enos, R. D. (2016a). Context, perception, and intergroup relations. *Psychological Inquiry 27*(4), 294–298.

Enos, R. D. (2016b). What the demolition of public housing teaches us about the impact of racial threat on political behavior. *American Journal of Political Science 60*(1), 123–142.

Enos, R. D. and C. Celaya (2015). Segregation directly affects human perception and intergroup bias. In *American Political Science Association, Annual Meeting*, San Francisco.

Enos, R. D. and A. Fowler (2014). Pivotality and turnout: Evidence from a field experiment in the aftermath of a tied election. *Political Science Research and Methods 2*(2), 309–319.

Enos, R. D., A. Fowler, and L. Vavreck (2014). Increasing inequality: The effect of GOTV mobilization on the composition of the electorate. *Journal of Politics 76*(1), 273–288.

Enos, R. D. and N. Gidron (2016a). Intergroup behavioral strategies as contextually determined: Experimental evidence from Israel. *Journal of Politics 78*(3), 851–867.

Enos, R. D. and N. Gidron (2016b). Social distance and cooperation in diverse societies: Experimental evidence from Israel. In *American Political Science Association, Annual Meeting*, Philadelphia.

Enos, R. D. and T. Wise (2012). Maps in our heads: Socio-political attitudes and demographic awareness. *American Political Science Association, Annual Meeting*, New Orleans.

Esteban, J. and D. Ray (2008). On the salience of ethnic conflict. *The American Economic Review 98*(5), 2185–2202.

Facchni, G. and A. M. Mayda (2009). Does the welfare state affect individual attitudes toward immigrants? Evidence across countries. *The Review of Economics and Statistics 91*(2), 295–314.

Fadiman, A. (2012). *The Spirit Catches You and You Fall Down: A Hmong Child, Her American Doctors, and the Collision of Two Cultures*. New York: Macmillan.

Farley, R., H. Schuman, S. Bianchi, D. Colasanto, and S. Hatchett (1978). "Chocolate city, vanilla suburbs:" Will the trend toward racially separate communities continue? *Social Science Research 7*(4), 319–344.

Feddersen, T. J. and W. Pesendorfer (1996). The swing voter's curse. *The American Economic Review, 88*(3) 408–424.

Fiedler, K. and T. Armbruster (1994). Two halfs may be more than one whole: Category-split effects on frequency illusions. *Journal of Personality and Social Psychology 66*(4), 633–645.

Fischel, W. A. (2004). An economic history of zoning and a cure for its exclusionary effects. *Urban Studies 41*(2), 317–340.

Fiske, S. T. (2000). Stereotyping, prejudice, and discrimination at the seam between the centuries: Evolution, culture, mind, and brain. *European Journal of Social Psychology* 30(3), 299–322.

Fiske, S. T., A. J. Cuddy, P. Glick, and J. Xu (2002). A model of (often mixed) stereotype content: Competence and warmth respectively follow from perceived status and competition. *Journal of Personality and Social Psychology* 82(6), 878.

Fitzpatrick, K. and S. S. Hwang (1992). The effects of community structure on opportunities for interracial contact: Extending Blaus macrostructural theory. *Sociological Quarterly* 33(1), 51–61.

Florida, R. (2002). Bohemia and economic geography. *Journal of Economic Geography* 2(1), 55–71.

Foer, J. (2011). *Moonwalking with Einstein*. New York: Penguin.

Folk, R. L. (1951). A comparison chart for visual percentage estimation. *Journal of Sedimentary Research* 21(1) 32–33.

Forbes, H. D. (1997). *Ethnic Conflict: Commerce, Culture, and the Contact Hypothesis.* New Haven: Yale University Press.

Fossett, M. A. and K. J. Kiecolt (1989). The relative size of minority populations and white racial attitudes. *Social Science Quarterly* 70(4), 820–835.

Fowler, A. (2015). Regular voters, marginal voters and the electoral effects of turnout. *Political Science Research and Methods* 3(2), 205–219.

Friedman, T. L. (2005). *The World is Flat: A Brief History of the Twenty-First Century.* New York: Macmillan.

Fujita, K., M. D. Henderson, J. Eng, Y. Trope, and N. Liberman (2006). Spatial distance and mental construal of social events. *Psychological Science* 17(4), 278–282.

Gaertner, L. and J. Schopler (1998). Perceived ingroup entitativity and intergroup bias: An interconnection of self and others. *European Journal of Social Psychology* 28(6), 963–980.

Gaertner, S. L., J. F. Dovidio, P. A. Anastasio, B. A. Bachman, and M. C. Rust (1993). The common ingroup identity model: Recategorization and the reduction of intergroup bias. *European Review of Social Psychology* 4(1), 1–26.

Gallagher, C. A. (2003). Miscounting race: Explaining whites' misperceptions of racial group size. *Sociological Perspectives* 46(3), 381–396.

Gallego, A., F. Buscha, P. Sturgis, and D. Oberski (2016). Places and preferences: A longitudinal analysis of self-selection and contextual effects. *British Journal of Political Science* 46(3), 529–550.

Gamm, G. (2009). *Urban Exodus: Why the Jews Left Boston and the Catholics Stayed.* Cambridge, MA: Harvard University Press.

Gatrell, A. C. (1983). *Distance and Space: a Geographical Perspective.* Contemporary Problems in Geography. New York: Oxford University Press.

Gay, C. (2006). Seeing difference: The effect of economic disparity on Black attitudes toward Latinos. *American Journal of Political Science* 50(4), 982–997.

Gay, C. (2012). Moving to opportunity: The political effects of a housing mobility experiment. *Urban Affairs Review* 48(2), 147–179.

Gerber, A. S., G. A. Huber, and E. Washington (2010). Party affiliation, partisanship, and political beliefs: A field experiment. *American Political Science Review* 104(4), 720–744.

Gerometta, J., H. Haussermann, and G. Longo (2005). Social innovation and civil society in urban governance: Strategies for an inclusive city. *Urban Studies* 42(11), 2007–2021.

Gilens, M. (1999). *Why Americans Hate Welfare: Race, Media, and the Politics of Antipoverty Policy*. Chicago: University of Chicago Press.

Giles, M. W. and M. A. Buckner (1993). David Duke and black threat: An old hypothesis revisited. *Journal of Politics* 55(3), 702–13.

Glaser, J. M. (1994). Back to the black belt: Racial environment and white racial attitudes in the south. *Journal of Politics* 56(1), 21–41.

Godley, A. D. (1969). *Herodotus*. Cambridge, MA: Harvard University Press.

Goette, L., D. Huffman, and S. Meier (2012). The impact of social ties on group interactions: Evidence from minimal groups and randomly assigned real groups. *American Economic Journal: Microeconomics* 4(1), 101–115.

Green, D. P., M. C. McGrath, and P. M. Aronow (2013). Field experiments and the study of voter turnout. *Journal of Elections, Public Opinion & Parties* 23(1), 27–48.

Green, D. P., B. Palmquist, and E. Schickler (2004). *Partisan Hearts and Minds*. New Haven, CT: Yale University Press.

Green, D. P., D. Z. Strolovitch, and J. S. Wong (1998). Defended neighborhoods, integration, and racially motivated crime. *American Journal of Sociology* 104(2), 372–403.

Green, D. P. and J. S. Wong (2009). Tolerance and the contact hypothesis: A field experiment. In E. Borgida (ed.), *The Political Psychology of Democratic Citizenship*, pp. 559–600. New York: Oxford University Press.

Greene, J. (2014). *Moral Tribes: Emotion, Reason and the Gap between Us and Them*. New York: Penguin.

Grossman, G., O. Gazal-Ayal, S. D. Pimentel, and J. M. Weinstein (2015). Descriptive representation and judicial outcomes in multiethnic societies. *American Journal of Political Science* 60(1), 44–69.

Guinote, A. and S. T. Fiske (2003). Being in the outgroup territory increases stereotypic perceptions of outgroups: Situational sources of category activation. *Group Processes & Intergroup Relations* 6(4), 323–331.

Habyarimana, J., M. Humphreys, D. N. Posner, and J. M. Weinstein (2007). Why does ethnic diversity undermine public goods provision? *American Political Science Review* 101(4), 709–725.

Habyarimana, J., M. Humphreys, D. N. Posner, and J. M. Weinstein (2009). *Coethnicity: Diversity and the Dilemmas of Collective Action*. New York: Russell Sage.

Hainmueller, J. and D. Hangartner (2013). Who gets a Swiss passport? A natural experiment in immigrant discrimination. *American Political Science Review* 107(1), 159–187.

Hainmueller, J. and M. Hiscox (2010). Attitudes towards highly skilled and low skilled immigration: Evidence from a survey experiment. *American Political Science Review* 104(1), 61–84.

Hainmueller, J. and D. J. Hopkins (2014). Public attitudes toward immigration. *Annual Review of Political Science* 17(1), 225–249.

Hajnal, Z. and J. Trounstine (2014). What underlies urban politics? Race, class, ideology, partisanship, and the urban vote. *Urban Affairs Review* 50(1), 63–99.

Hamilton, D. L. (1981). *Cognitive Processes in Stereotyping and Intergroup Behavior*. Mahwah, NJ: Lawrence Erlbaum.

Hampton, H. (1987). *Eyes on the Prize*. San Francisco: PBS.

Hanson, G. H. (2005). *Why Does Immigration Divide America? Public Finance and Opposition to Open Borders*. Washington, DC: Institute for International Economics.

Hanson, G. H., K. Scheve, and M. J. Slaughter (2007). Public finance and individual preferences over globalization strategies. *Economics & Politics* 19(1), 1–33.

Hardin, G. (1968). The tragedy of the commons. *Science* 162(3859), 1243–1248.

Harvey, S.-P. and R. Y. Bourhis (2013). Discrimination between the rich and the poor under contrasting conditions of wealth stratification. *Journal of Applied Social Psychology* 43(S2), E351–E366.

Hasson, S. and A. Gonen (1997). *The Cultural Tension within Jerusalems Jewish Population*. Jerusalem: The Floersheimer Institute for Policy Studies Publications on Religion, Society, and State in Israel.

Henderson, M. D., K. Fujita, Y. Trope, and N. Liberman (2006). Transcending the "here": The effect of spatial distance on social judgment. *Journal of Personality and Social Psychology* 91(5), 845–856.

Henrich, J., R. McElreath, A. Barr, J. Ensminger, C. Barrett, A. Bolyanatz, J. C. Cardenas, M. Gurven, E. Gwako, N. Henrich, et al. (2006). Costly punishment across human societies. *Science* 312(5781), 1767–1770.

Henry, P. J. and D. O. Sears (2002). The symbolic racism 2000 scale. *Political Psychology* 23(2), 253–283.

Hersh, E. D. and C. Nall (2015). The primacy of race in the geography of income-based voting: New evidence from public voting records. *American Journal of Political Science* 60(2), 289–303.

Hewstone, M. (2015). Consequences of diversity for social cohesion and prejudice: The missing dimension of intergroup contact. *Journal of Social Issues* 71(2), 417–438.

Hill, K. Q. and J. E. Leighley (1999). Racial diversity, voter turnout, and mobilizing institutions in the United States. *American Politics Research* 27(3), 275–295.

Hillygus, D. S. and T. Shields (2008). The Persuadable Voter. Princeton, NJ: *Princeton University Press.*

Hirschmann, A. O. (1970). *Exit, Voice and Loyalty: Responses to Decline in Firms, Organizations, and States.* Cambridge, MA: Harvard University Press.

Hobbes, T. (1900). *Leviathan: Or the Matter, Forme and Power of a Commonwealth, Ecclesiasticall and Civil.* New Haven, CT: Yale University Press.

Holland, P. W. (1986). Statistics and causal inference. *Journal of the American Statistical Association* 81(396), 945–960.

Hopkins, D. J. (2009). The diversity discount: When increasing ethnic and racial diversity prevents tax increases. *Journal of Politics* 71(1), 160–177.

Hopkins, D. J. (2010). Politicized places: Explaining where and when immigrants provoke local opposition. *American Political Science Review* 104(1), 40–60.

Hopkins, D. J. (2013a). All politics is national. Working Paper: Georgetown University.

Hopkins, D. J. (2013b). Misplaced: The limits of contextual influence on Americans' political attitudes. In *American Political Science Association, Annual Meeting*, Chicago.

Hopkins, D. J. (2015). The upside of accents: Language, inter-group difference, and attitudes toward immigration. *British Journal of Political Science* 45(03), 531–557.

Horowitz, D. L. (1985). *Ethnic Groups in Conflict.* Berkeley, CA: University of California Press.

Huckfeldt, R. and J. Sprague (1987). Networks in context: The social flow of political information. *American Political Science Review* 81(4), 1197–1216.

Huffman, M. L. and P. N. Cohen (2004). Racial wage inequality: Job segregation and devaluation across US labor markets. *American Journal of Sociology* 109(4), 902–936.

Huntington, S. P. (2004). *Who Are We?: The Challenges to America's National Identity.* New York: Simon & Schuster.

Hurwitz, J. and M. Peffley (2005). Playing the race card in the post Willie Horton era: The impact of racialized code words on support for punitive crime policy. *Public Opinion Quarterly* 69(1), 99–112.

Ignatiev, N. (1995). *How the Irish Became White.* New York: Routledge.

Islam, M. R. and M. Hewstone (1993). Dimensions of contact as predictors of intergroup anxiety, perceived out-group variability, and out-group attitude: An integrative model. *Personality and Social Psychology Bulletin* 19(6), 700–710.

Jacobs, J. (1961). *The Death and Life of Great American Cities.* New York: Random House.

Jones, D. (2010). A weird view of human nature skews psychologists' studies. *Science* 328(5986), 1627–1627.

Jones, R. P., D. Cox, and J. Navarro-Rivera (2013). 2013 American values survey. Technical report, Public Religion Research Institute, Washington, DC.

Kahneman, D. (2003). A perspective on judgement and choice: Mapping bounded rationality. *American Psychologist* 58(9), 697–720.

Kahneman, D. and S. Frederick (2002). Representativeness revisited: Attribute substitution in intuitive judgment. In T. Gilovich, D. Griffin, and D. Kahneman (eds.), *Heuristics and Biases: The Psychology of Intuitive Judgment*, pp. 49–81. New York: Cambridge University Press.

Kasara, K. (2013). Separate and suspicious: The social environment and inter-ethnic trust in Kenya. *Journal of Politics* 75(3), 921–936.

Kaufmann, K. M. (2004). *The Urban Voter: Group Conflict and Mayoral Voting Behavior in American Cities.* Ann Arbor, MI: University of Michigan Press.

Kellogg, R. T. and J. C. Dowdy (1986). Automatic learning of the frequencies of occurrence of stimulus features. *The American Journal of Psychology* 99(1), 111–126.

Kessler, A. (2001). Immigration, economic insecurity, and the "ambivalent" American public. *Center for Comparative Immigration Studies.* Working Paper 41, September, San Diego, CA.

Key, V. (1949). *Southern Politics in State and Nation.* New York: Knopf.

Kinder, D. R. and C. D. Kam (2009). *Us Against Them: Ethnocentric Foundations of American Opinion.* Chicago: University of Chicago Press.

King, G. (1996). Why context should not count. *Political Geography* 15(2), 159–164.

King, G. (1997). *A Solution to the Ecological Inference Problem: Reconstructing Individual Behavior from Aggregate Data.* Princeton, NJ: Princeton University Press.

Knowles, E. D., B. S. Lowery, R. M. Chow, and M. M. Unzueta (2014). Deny, distance, or dismantle? how white Americans manage a privileged identity. *Perspectives on Psychological Science* 9(6), 594–609.

Kotlowitz, A. (1992). *There Are No Children Here: The Story of Two Boys Growing Up in the Other America.* New York: Doubleday.

Kramer, B. M. (1950). *Residential Contact as a Determinant of Attitudes toward Negroes.* Ph.D. thesis, Harvard University, Cambridge, MA.

Krosch, A. R. and D. M. Amodio (2014). Economic scarcity alters the perception of race. *Proceedings of the National Academy of Sciences of the United States of America* 111(25), 9079–9084.

Krosch, A. R., L. Berntsen, D. M. Amodio, J. T. Jost, and J. J. Van Bavel (2013). On the ideology of hypodescent: Political conservatism predicts categorization of racially ambiguous faces as black. *Journal of Experimental Social Psychology* 49(6), 1196–1203.

Kunda, Z. (1999). *Social Cognition: Making Sense of People*. Cambridge, MA: MIT Press.

Kundra, Z. and L. Sinclair (1999). Motivated reasoning with stereotypes: Activation, application, and inhibition. *Psychological Inquiry* 10(1), 12–22.

Lakoff, G. and M. Johnson (1980). *Metaphors We Live By*. Chicago: University of Chicago Press.

Latané, B. (1981). The psychology of social impact. *American Psychologist* 36(4), 343–356.

Latané, B. and T. L'Herrou (1996). Spatial clustering in the conformity game: Dynamic social impact in electronic groups. *Journal of Personality and Social Psychology* 70(6), 1218–1230.

Latané, B., J. H. Liu, A. Nowak, M. Bonevento, and L. Zheng (1995). Distance matters: Physical space and social impact. *Personality and Social Psychology Bulletin* 21(8), 795–805.

Latané, B. and S. Wolf (1981). The social impact of majorities and minorities. *Psychological Review* 88(5), 438–453.

Legewie, J. and M. Schaeffer (2016). Contested boundaries: Explaining where ethnoracial diversity provokes neighborhood conflict. *American Journal of Sociology* 122(1), 125–161.

Leighley, J. E. and A. Vedlitz (1999). Race, ethnicity, and political participation: Competing models and contrasting explanations. *Journal of Politics* 61(4), 1092–1114.

Lenz, G. S. (2013). *Follow the Leader?: How Voters Respond to Politicians' Policies and Performance*. Chicago: University of Chicago Press.

Levin, S., C. Van Laar, and J. Sidanius (2003). The effects of ingroup and outgroup friendships on ethnic attitudes in college: A longitudinal study. *Group Processes & Intergroup Relations* 6(1), 76–92.

Levine, M., A. Prosser, D. Evans, and S. Reicher (2005). Identity and emergency intervention: How social group membership and inclusiveness of group boundaries shape helping behavior. *Personality and Social Psychology Bulletin* 31(4), 443–453.

Lewenstein, M., A. Nowak, and B. Latané (1992). Statistical mechanics of social impact. *Physical Review A* 45(2), 763–776.

Li, H., H. Campbell, and S. Fernandez (2013). Residential segregation, spatial mismatch and economic growth across us metropolitan areas. *Urban Studies* 50(13), 2642–2660.

Lieberman, E. S. and G. H. McClendon (2013). The ethnicity–policy preference link in sub-Saharan Africa. *Comparative Political Studies* 46(5), 574–602.

Lim, M., R. Metzler, and Y. Bar-Yam (2007). Global pattern formation and ethnic/cultural violence. *Science* 317(5844), 1540–1544.

Livneh, N. (2012). Feeling they are 'losing' Jerusalem, Orthodox and secular Jewish residents join forces. *Ha'aretz* March 1. (in Hebrew).

Logan, J. R. and B. Stults (2011). The persistence of segregation in the metropolis: New findings from the 2010 census. Technical report, Brown University: Project US2010.

Lynch, K. (1960). *The Image of the City*. Cambridge, MA: MIT Press.

Maddox, K. B., D. N. Rapp, S. Brion, and H. A. Taylor (2008). Social influences on spatial memory. *Memory & Cognition* 36(3), 479–494.

Maguire, E. A. (2006). Spatial navigation. In R. Parashrama and M. Rizzo eds., *Neuroergonomics: The Brain at Work*, New York: Oxford University Press pp. 131–135.

Martinez, M. D., K. D. Wald, and S. C. Craig (2008). Homophobic innumeracy?: Estimating the size of the gay and lesbian population. *Public Opinion Quarterly* 72(4), 753–767.

Massey, D. S. and N. A. Denton (1988). The dimensions of residential segregation. *Social Forces* 67(2), 281–315.

Massey, D. S. and N. A. Denton (1993). *American Apartheid: Segregation and the Making of the Underclass*. Cambridge, MA: Harvard University Press.

Massey, D. S., J. Durand, and N. J. Malone (2002). *Beyond Smoke and Mirrors: Mexican Immigration in an Era of Economic Integration*. New York: Russell Sage Foundation.

Matthews, D. (2016). America is not, it turns out, better than this. *Vox* 9 November.

Matthews, D. R. and J. W. Prothro (1963). Social and economic factors and negro voter registration in the South. *American Political Science Review* 57(1), 24–44.

Mayda, A. M. (2006). Who is against immigration? A cross-country investigation of individual attitudes toward immigrants. *Review of Economics and Statistics* 88(3), 510–530.

McCrea, S. M., F. Wieber, and A. L. Myers (2012). Construal level mind-sets moderate self-and social stereotyping. *Journal of Personality and Social Psychology* 102(1), 51.

McGarty, C. and R. Penny (1988). Categorization, accentuation and social judgement. *British Journal of Social Psychology* 27(2), 147–157.

Miguel, E. and M. K. Gugerty (2005). Ethnic diversity, social sanctions, and public goods in Kenya. *Journal of Public Economics* 89(11), 2325–2368.

Milgram, S. (2010). Psychological maps of Paris. In T. Blais, ed., *The Individual in the Social World*. London: Pinter and Martin pp. 77–100.

Montalvo, J. G. and M. Reynal-Querol (2010). Ethnic polarization and the duration of civil wars. *Economics of Governance* 11(2), 123–143.

Montello, D. R., M. Hegarty, A. E. Richardson, and D. Waller (2004). Spatial memory of real environments, virtual environments, and maps. In G. L. Allen ed., *Human Spatial Memory*. Mahwah, NJ: Lawrence Erlbaum.

Moore, N. Y. (2016). *The South Side: A Portrait of Chicago and American Segregation*. New York: St. Martin's Press.

Moy, J. and S. H. Ng (1996). Expectation of outgroup behaviour: Can you trust the outgroup? *European Journal of Social Psychology* 26(2), 333–340.

Muller, R. (1996). A quarter of a century of place cells. *Neuron* 17(5), 813–822.

Nadeau, R., R. G. Niemi, and J. Levine (1993). Innumeracy about minority populations. *Public Opinion Quarterly* 57(3), 332–347.

Nall, C. (2015). The political consequences of spatial policies: How interstate highways facilitated geographic polarization. *Journal of Politics* 77(2), 394–406.

New, J., M. M. Krasnow, D. Truxaw, and S. J. Gaulin (2007). Spatial adaptations for plant foraging: Women excel and calories count. *Proceedings of the Royal Society of London B: Biological Sciences* 274(1626), 2679–2684.

Newheiser, A.-K., N. Tausch, J. F. Dovidio, and M. Hewstone (2009). Entitativity and prejudice: Examining their relationship and the moderating effect of attitude certainty. *Journal of Experimental Social Psychology* 45(4), 920–926.

Newman, B. J. (2012). Acculturating contexts and Anglo opposition to immigration in the United States. *American Journal of Political Science* 57(2), 374–390.

Newman, B. J., T. K. Hartman, and C. S. Taber (2012). Foreign language exposure, cultural threat, and opposition to immigration. *Political Psychology* 33(4), 635–657.

Nirenberg, D. (1996). *Communities of Violence: Persecution of Minorities in the Middle Ages*. Princeton, NJ: Princeton University Press.

Nisbett, R. E. and D. Cohen (1996). *Culture of Honor: The Psychology of Violence in the South*. Boulder, CO: Westview Press.

Oakes, P. J., S. A. Haslam, and J. C. Turner (1994). *Stereotyping and Social Reality*. Oxford: Blackwell Publishing.

Oakes, P. J. and J. C. Turner (1990). Is limited information processing capacity the cause of social stereotyping? *European Review of Social Psychology* 1(1), 111–135.

Oliver, E. (2001). *Democracy in Suburbia*. Princeton, NJ: Princeton University Press.

Oliver, J. E. (2010). *The Paradoxes of Integration: Race, Neighborhood, and Civic Life in Multiethnic America*. Chicago: University of Chicago Press.

Oliver, J. E. and T. Mendelberg (2000). Reconsidering the environmental determinants of white racial attitudes. *American Journal of Political Science* 44(3), 574–589.

Oliver, J. E. and J. Wong (2003). Intergroup prejudice in multiethnic settings. *American Journal of Political Science* 47(4), 567–582.

Olson, M. (1971). *The Logic of Collective Action: Public Good and the Theory of Groups*. Cambridge, MA: Harvard University Press.

Olzak, S., S. Shanahan, and E. H. McEneaney (1996). Poverty, segregation, and race riots: 1960 to 1993. *American Sociological Review* 61(4), 590–613.

Openshaw, S. (1983). The modifiable areal unit problem. In *Concepts and Techniques in Modern Geography*, Norwich, UK: Geo Books.

Page, S. E. (2008). *The Difference: How the Power of Diversity Creates Better Groups, Firms, Schools, and Societies*. Princeton, NJ: Princeton University Press.

Palfrey, T. R. and K. T. Poole (1987). The relationship between information, ideology, and voting behavior. *American Journal of Political Science* 31(3), 511–530.

Paluck, E. L., S. A. Green, and D. P. Green (2016). The contact hypothesis revisited. *Working Paper, Princeton University*.

Parsons, T., E. A. Shils, and N. J. Smelser (1951). *Toward a General Theory of Action: Theoretical Foundations for the Social Sciences*. Cambridge, MA: Harvard University Press.

Petersen, M. B. (2015). Evolutionary political psychology: On the origin and structure of heuristics and biases in politics. *Political Psychology* 36(51): 45–78.

Pettigrew, T. F. and L. Tropp (2006). A meta-analytic test of intergroup contact theory. *Journal of Personality and Social Psychology* 90(5), 751–783.

Pettigrew, T. F., U. Wagner, and O. Christ (2010). Population ratios and prejudice: Modeling both contact and threat effects. *Journal of Ethnic and Migration Studies* 36(4), 635–650.

Pierson, P. (2000). Increasing returns, path dependence, and the study of politics. *American Political Science Review* 94(2), 251–267.

Poole, K. T. and H. Rosenthal (1985). A spatial model for legislative roll call analysis. *American Journal of Political Science* 29(2), 357–384.

Posner, D. N. (2004). The political salience of cultural difference: Why Chewas and Tumbukas are allies in Zambia and adversaries in Malawi. *American Political Science Review* 98(4), 529–545.

Putnam, R. D. (2001). *Bowling Alone: The Collapse and Revival of American Community*. New York: Simon & Schuster.

Putnam, R. D. (2007). E pluribus unum: Diversity and community in the twenty-first century: The 2006 Johan Skytte Prize Lecture. *Scandinavian Political Studies* 30(2), 137–174.

Putnam, R. D., R. Leonardi, and R. Y. Nanetti (1993). *Making Democracy Work: Civic Traditions in Modern Italy*. Princeton, NJ: Princeton University Press.

Quillian, L. (1995). Prejudice as a response to perceived group threat: Population composition and anti-immigrant and racial prejudice in Europe. *American Sociological Review* 60(4), 586–611.

Quillian, L. (2014). Does segregation create winners and losers? Residential segregation and inequality in educational attainment. *Social Problems* 61(3), 402–426.

Quillian, L. and D. Pager (2001). Black neighbors, higher crime? The role of racial stereotypes in evaluations of neighborhood crime. *American Journal of Sociology* 107(3), 717–767.

Reardon, S. F. and D. O'Sullivan (2004). Measures of spatial segregation. *Sociological Methodology* 34(1), 121–162.

Reicher, S. D., A. Templeton, F. Neville, L. Ferrari, and J. Drury (2016). Core disgust is attenuated by ingroup relations. *Proceedings of the National Academy of Sciences of the United States of America* 113(10), 2631–2635.

Reynolds, D. S. (2009). *John Brown, Abolitionist: the Man who Killed Slavery, Sparked the Civil War, and Seeded Civil Rights*. New York: Vintage.

Rieder, J. (1985). *Canarsie: The Jews and Italians of Brooklyn against Liberalism*. Cambridge, MA: Harvard University Press.

Rosenblum, N. L. (2016). *Good Neighbors: The Democracy of Everyday Life in America*. Princeton, NJ: Princeton University Press.

Rosnow, R. L. and R. Rosenthal (1997). *People Studying People*. New York: W.H. Freeman and Company.

Rothwell, J. T. (2012). The effects of racial segregation on trust and volunteering in US cities. *Urban Studies* 49(10), 2109–2136.

Rubin, B. (2012). *Israel: An Introduction*. New Haven: Yale University Press.

Rubin, D. B. (2005). Causal inference using potential outcomes: Design, modeling, decisions. *Journal of the American Statistical Association* 100(469) 322–331.

Rugh, J. S. and J. Trounstine (2011). The provision of local public goods in diverse communities: Analyzing municipal bond elections. *Journal of Politics* 73(4), 1038–1050.

Sacerdote, B. (2001). Peer effects with random assignment: Results for Dartmouth roommates. *Quarterly Journal of Economics* 116(2), 681–704.

Sampson, R. J. (2008). Moving to inequality: Neighborhood effects and experiments meet social structure. *American Journal of Sociology* 114(1), 189–231.

Sampson, R. J. (2012). *Great American City: Chicago and the Enduring Neighborhood Effect*. Chicago, IL: University of Chicago Press.

Sands, M. (2016). Who wants to tax a millionaire? Exposure to inequality reduces support for redistribution. In *American Political Science Association, Annual Meeting*, Philadelphia.

Scacco, A. and S. S. Warren (2016). Can social contact reduce prejudice and discrimination? Evidence from a field experiment in Nigeria. *Working Paper, New York University.*

Schattschneider, E. E. (1942). *Party Government.* Piscataway, NJ: Transaction Publishers.

Schelling, T. C. (1969). Models of segregation. *American Economic Review* 59(2), 488–493.

Schelling, T. C. (1971). Dynamic models of segregation. *Journal of Mathematical Sociology* 1(2), 143–186.

Schelling, T. C. (2006). *Micromotives and Macrobehavior.* New York: Norton.

Scheve, K. F. and M. J. Slaughter (2001). Labor market competition and individual preferences over immigration policy. *Review of Economics and Statistics* 83(1), 133–145.

Sears, D. O. (1986). College sophomores in the laboratory: Influences of a narrow data base on social psychology's view of human nature. *Journal of Personality and Social Psychology* 51(3), 515–530.

Sears, D. O. and P. Henry (2003). The origins of symbolic racism. *Journal of Personality and Social Psychology* 85(3), 259–275.

Sears, D. O. and D. R. Kinder (1985). Whites' opposition to busing: On conceptualizing and operationalizing group conflict. *Journal of Personality and Social Psychology* 48(5), 1141–1147.

Sears, D. O. and J. B. McConahay (1973). *The Politics of Violence; the New Urban Blacks and the Watts Riot.* Boston: Houghton Mifflin.

Sharkey, P. (2013). *Stuck in Place: Urban Neighborhoods and the End of Progress toward Racial Equality.* Chicago: University of Chicago Press.

Shelby, T. (2016). *Dark Ghettos: Injustice, Dissent, and Reform.* Cambridge, MA: Harvard University Press.

Sherif, M., O. Harvey, B. White, W. Hood, and C. Sherif (1961). *Intergroup Conflict and Cooperation: The Robbers Cave Experiment.* Norman, OK: University Book Exchange.

Shook, N. J. and R. H. Fazio (2009). Political ideology, exploration of novel stimuli, and attitude formation. *Journal of Experimental Social Psychology* 45(4), 995–998.

Sidanius, J. and F. Pratto (2001). *Social Dominance: An Intergroup Theory of Social Hierarchy and Oppression.* New York: Cambridge University Press.

Sidanius, J., F. Pratto, and M. Mitchell (1994). In-group identification, social dominance orientation, and differential intergroup social allocation. *Journal of Social Psychology* 134(2), 151–167.

Sides, J. (2003). *LA City Limits: African American Los Angeles from the Great Depression to the Present.* Berkeley, CA: University of California Press.

Sides, J. (2004). Straight into Compton: American dreams, urban nightmares, and the metamorphosis of a black suburb. *American Quarterly* 56(3), 583–605.

Sigelman, L. and R. G. Niemi (2001). Innumeracy about minority populations: African Americans and whites compared. *Public Opinion Quarterly* 65(1), 86–94.

Sigelman, L. and S. Welch (1993). The contact hypothesis revisited: Black–white interaction and positive social attitudes. *Social Forces* 71(3), 781–795.

Simmons, B. A. (2016). The built environment: State presence at border crossings in the modern world. In *American Political Science Association, Annual Meeting,* Philadelphia.

Soltas, E. and S. Stephens-Davidowitz (2015). The rise of hate search. *New York Times* 13 December.

Sonenshein, R. J. (1993). *Politics in Black and White: Race and Power in Los Angeles*. Princeton: Princeton University Press.

Sonenshein, R. J. and M. H. Drayse (2006). Urban electoral coalitions in an age of immigration: Time and place in the 2001 and 2005 Los Angeles mayoral primaries. *Political Geography* 25(5), 570–595.

Spence, L. K. and H. McClerking (2010). Context, black empowerment, and African American political participation. *American Politics Research* 38(5), 909–930.

Spencer-Rodgers, J., D. L. Hamilton, and S. J. Sherman (2007). The central role of entitativity in stereotypes of social categories and task groups. *Journal of Personality and Social Psychology* 92(3), 369.

Stangor, C. and M. Schaller (2000). Sterestypes as individual and collective representations. In C. Stangor (ed.), *Stereotypes and Prejudice: Essential Readings*, pp. 64–82. Ann Arbor, MI: Psychology Press.

Steele, C. M. and J. Aronson (1995). Stereotype threat and the intellectual test performance of African Americans. *Journal of Personality and Social Psychology* 69(5), 797–811.

Steinbeck, J. (1939). *The Grapes of Wrath*. New York: Viking Press.

Stephens-Davidowitz, S. (2014). The effects of racial animus on a black presidential candidate: Using Google search data to find what surveys miss. *Journal of Public Economics* 118, 26–40.

Stinchcombe, A. L. (1987). *Constructing Social Theories*. Chicago: University of Chicago Press.

Tajfel, H. (1969). Cognitive aspects of prejudice. *Journal of Social Issues* 25(4), 29–97.

Tajfel, H., M. G. Billig, R. P. Bundy, and C. Flament (1971). Social categorization and intergroup behavior. *European Journal of Social Psychology* 1(2), 149–178.

Tajfel, H. and A. Wilkes (1963). Classification and quantitative judgement. *British Journal of Psychology* 54(2), 101–114.

Takács, K. (2007). Effects of network segregation in intergroup conflict: An experimental analysis. *Connections* 27(2), 59–76.

Talaska, C. A., S. T. Fiske, and S. Chaiken (2008). Legitimating racial discrimination: Emotions, not beliefs, best predict discrimination in a meta-analysis. *Social Justice Research* 21(3), 263–296.

Taleb, N. N. (2007). *The Black Swan: The Impact of the Highly Improbable*. New York: Random House.

Tam, T., M. Hewstone, J. Kenworthy, and E. Cairns (2009). Intergroup trust in Northern Ireland. *Personality and Social Psychology Bulletin* 35(1), 45–59.

Tatum, B. D. (2003). *"Why Are All the Black Kids Sitting Together in the Cafeteria?": and Other Conversations about Race*. New York: Basic Books.

Tausanovitch, C. and C. Warshaw (2013). Measuring constituent policy preferences in Congress, state legislatures, and cities. *Journal of Politics* 75(2), 330–342.

Tavares, R. M., A. Mendelsohn, Y. Grossman, C. H. Williams, M. Shapiro, Y. Trope, and D. Schiller (2015). A map for social navigation in the human brain. *Neuron* 87(1), 231–243.

Taylor, M. (1998). How white attitudes vary with the racial composition of local populations: Numbers count. *American Sociological Review* 63(4), 512–535.

Taylor, R. B. (1988). *Human Territorial Functioning: An Empirical, Evolutionary Perspective on Individual and Small Group Territorial Cognitions, Behaviors, and Consequences.* New York: Cambridge University Press.

Taylor, S. E., S. T. Fiske, N. L. Etcoff, and A. J. Ruderman (1978). Categorical and contextual bases of person memory and stereotyping. *Journal of Personality and Social Psychology* 36(7), 778–793.

Tesler, M. (2012). The spillover of racialization into health care: How President Obama polarized public opinion by racial attitudes and race. *American Journal of Political Science* 56(3), 690–704.

Tesler, M. (2016). *Post-Racial or Most-Racial?* Chicago: University of Chicago Press.

Tesler, M. and D. O. Sears (2010). *Obama's Race.* Chicago: University of Chicago Press.

Tiebout, C. M. (1956). A pure theory of local expenditures. *Journal of Political Economy* 64(5), 416–424.

Tilcsik, A. (2011). Pride and prejudice: Employment discrimination against openly gay men in the United States. *American Journal of Sociology* 117(2), 586–626.

Tobler, W. R. (1970). A computer movie simulating urban growth in the Detroit region. *Economic Geography* 46, 234–240.

Travers, J. and S. Milgram (1969). An experimental study of the small world problem. *Sociometry* 32(4), 425–443.

Trope, Y. and N. Liberman (2003). Temporal construal. *Psychological Review* 110(3), 403–421.

Trounstine, J. (2010). Representation and accountability in cities. *Annual Review of Political Science* 13, 407–423.

Trounstine, J. (2016). Segregation and inequality in public goods. *American Journal of Political Science* 60(3) 709–725.

Turner, J. C., M. Hogg, P. J. Oakes, S. Reicher, and M. Wetherell (1987). *Rediscovering the Social Group: A Self-Categorization Theory.* Oxford, UK: Blackwell.

Turner, J. C. and P. J. Oakes (1986). The significance of the social identity concept for social psychology with reference to individualism, interactionism and social influence. *British Journal of Social Psychology* 25(3), 237–252.

Turner, J. C., P. J. Oakes, S. A. Haslam, and C. McGarty (1994). Self and collective: Cognition and social context. *Personality and Social Psychology Bulletin* 20(5), 454–463.

Unkelbach, C., H. Schneider, K. Gode, and M. Senft (2010). A turban effect, too: Selection biases against women wearing Muslim headscarves. *Social Psychological and Personality Science* 1(4), 378–383.

US Commission on Civil Rights (1973). *Understanding Fair Housing.* New York: Clearinghouse Publication.

Uslaner, E. M. (2012). *Segregation and Mistrust: Diversity, Isolation, and Social Cohesion.* New York: Cambridge University Press.

Valentino, N. A. and D. O. Sears (2005). Old times there are not forgotten: Race and partisan realignment in the contemporary South. *American Journal of Political Science* 49(3), 672–688.

Vanhanen, T. (1999). Domestic ethnic conflict and ethnic nepotism: A comparative analysis. *Journal of Peace Research* 36(1), 55–73.

Varey, C. A., B. A. Mellers, and M. H. Birnbaum (1990). Judgments of proportions. *Journal of Experimental Psychology: Human Perception and Performance* 16(3), 613–625.

Vasoo, S. and J. Lee (2001). Singapore: Social development, housing and the central provident fund. *International Journal of Social Welfare 10*, 276–283.

Velez, Y. R. and H. Lavine (2016). Racial diversity and the dynamics of authoritarianism. *Journal of Politics 79*(2), 519–533.

Voss, D. S. (1996). Beyond racial threat: Failure of an old hypothesis in the new South. *Journal of Politics 58*(4), 1156–1170.

Wakslak, C. J., Y. Trope, N. Liberman, and R. Alony (2006). Seeing the forest when entry is unlikely: Probability and the mental representation of events. *Journal of Experimental Psychology: General 135*(4), 641–653.

Weichselbaumer, D. (2016). Discrimination against female migrants wearing headscarves. *Working Paper, Institute for the Study of Labor.*

Welch, S., L. Sigelman, T. Bledsoe, and M. Combs (2001). *Race and Place: Race Relations in an American City.* New York: Cambridge University Press.

White, A. R., N. L. Nathan, and J. K. Faller (2015). What do I need to vote? Bureaucratic discretion and discrimination by local election officials. *American Political Science Review 109*(01), 129–142.

Whitt, S. and R. K. Wilson (2007). The dictator game, fairness and ethnicity in postwar Bosnia. *American Journal of Political Science 51*(3), 655–668.

Wilder, D. A. (1986). Social categorization: Implications for creation and reduction of intergroup bias. *Advances in Experimental Social Psychology 19*, 291–355.

Wilson, W. J. (1987). *The Truly Disadvantaged: The Inner City, the Underclass, and Public Policy.* Chicago: University of Chicago Press.

Wirth, L. (1938). Urbanism as a way of life. *American Journal of Sociology 44*(1), 1–24.

Wong, C. (2010). *Boundaries of Obligation in American Politics: Geographic, National, and Racial Communities.* New York: Cambridge University Press.

Wong, C., J. Bowers, T. Williams, and K. Drake (2012). Bringing the person back in: Boundaries, perceptions, and the measurement of racial context. *Journal of Politics 1*(1), 1–18.

Wong, C. J. (2007). "Little" and "big" pictures in our heads: Race, local context, and innumeracy about racial groups in the United States. *Public Opinion Quarterly 71*(3), 392–412.

Wright, G. (1977). Contextual models of electoral behavior: The Southern Wallace vote. *American Political Science Review 71*(2), 497–508.

Xiao, Y. J., G. Coppin, and J. J. Van Bavel (2016). Perceiving the world through group-colored glasses: A perceptual model of intergroup relations. *Psychological Inquiry 27*(4), 255–274.

Yanagizawa-Drott, D. (2014). Propaganda and conflict: Evidence from the Rwandan genocide. *Quarterly Journal of Economics 129*(4), 1947–1994.

Zaller, J. R. (1992). *The Nature and Origins of Mass Opinion.* New York: Cambridge University Press.

Zimbardo, P. (2007). *The Lucifer Effect: Understanding How Good People Turn Evil.* New York: Taylor & Francis.

Zingher, J. N. and M. Steen Thomas (2014). The spatial and demographic determinants of racial threat. *Social Science Quarterly 95*(4), 1137–1154.

Zorbaugh, H. W. (1929). *The Gold Coast and the Slum.* Chicago: University of Chicago Press.

Index